# Thomas' Sentencing Referencer

# THOMAS' SENTENCING REFERENCER

2025

LYNDON HARRIS
*Gray's Inn,*
*Barrister*

Sweet & Maxwell
Thomson Reuters™

Published in 2024 by Thomson Reuters, trading as Sweet & Maxwell.
Thomson Reuters is registered in England & Wales,
Company number 1679046.
Registered office: 5 Canada Square, Canary Wharf, London E14 5AQ.

For further information on our products and services, visit *http://www.sweetandmaxwell.co.uk*.

Computerset by Sweet & Maxwell.
Printed and bound in Great Britain by
CPI Group (UK) Ltd, Croydon, CR0 4YY.
A CIP catalogue record of this book is available from the British Library.

ISBN (print): 978-0-414-12308-3

ISBN (e-book): 978-0-414-12311-3

ISBN (print and e-book): 978-0-414-12309-0



FSC
www.fsc.org
MIX
Paper | Supporting responsible forestry
FSC® C013604

# FOREWORD TO THE 2021 EDITION

On 22 October 2020 the Sentencing Act 2020 received the Royal Assent, and it will come into force on 1 December 2020. When in force the Sentencing Act will mean that the myriad of sentencing powers and provisions are contained with a single Sentencing Code. This is a significant development for what otherwise is a morass of individual pieces of legislation covering sentencing and ancillary powers enacted over many years in numerous parliamentary sessions over several decades. For all practitioners and judges in the courts across England & Wales the enactment of a Sentencing Code will be a welcome development. The Sentencing Code is a consolidation and so for assistance with finding one's way through the complex web of available sentences and other orders that can be imposed at sentence, most of us will still turn to a text such as the *Referencer* to assist.

Lyndon Harris has an encyclopaedic knowledge of the topic of sentencing provisions. It might be said that what he doesn't know about the powers available on sentence in a particular situation, isn't worth knowing. He was extensively involved in the Sentencing Code project at the Law Commission and brings to this invaluable guide his wealth of expertise in that work and his understanding of what is, and what is not, permissible by way of sentence.

Lyndon took over responsibility for the *Referencer* after Dr. David Thomas' untimely death back in 2013. Lyndon has done much since then with successive editions to develop and enhance the format of this invaluable work. For the 2021 edition, work has been done to restructure the text to assist the reader through the whole sentencing process. Many of us take the Mark Twain approach to work: we like it and could sit watching it all day. I am sure there will be many of us who benefit greatly from all the great work Lyndon has put into this excellent volume.

HHJ Mark Lucraft QC
Recorder of London
November 2020.

# TABLE OF CONTENTS

# A: GENERAL PROVISIONS

# THE SENTENCING CODE

The Sentencing Act 2020, Parts 2 to 13 of which make up the Sentencing Code (SC). The Code is a consolidation of the existing law of sentencing procedure, drawing together provisions from various enactments. Additionally, it represents the effects of the Sentencing (Pre-consolidation Amendments) Act 2020 which effected what has been referred to as the "clean sweep". The clean sweep is a drafting device which removes the need to make reference to historic pieces of legislation which have been repealed but partially saved with complex transitional provisions. As a result, for offenders convicted on or after 1 December 2020, the powers of the sentencing court will be governed by the Sentencing Code regime, subject to any transitional provisions on the face of the Code (as new legislation post-dating the Code makes further changes to the law) such as the Police, Crime, Sentencing and Courts Act 2022.

There are a number of provisions which remain effective but which do not feature in the Sentencing Code. These include areas such as road traffic, confiscation, and some forfeiture powers.

As the Code is a consolidation, it does not effect a change in the law (save for that which is effected by the Sentencing (Pre-consolidation Amendments) Act 2020.) The effect of this is that decisions of the senior courts interpreting or otherwise providing guidance on legislative provisions now consolidated into the Sentencing Code continue to apply. Where any adjustment to a decision is necessary, consequent upon a pre-consolidation amendment, this is indicated in this work. Similarly, any secondary legislation made under an enactment consolidated by the Code remains effective and will continue to apply: SC Sch.27 para.2.

# DETERMINING THE SERIOUSNESS OF AN OFFENCE

## Sentencing Code s.63

*References: Current Sentencing Practice A1; Archbold 5A-4*

### Determining seriousness

In considering the seriousness of any offence, the court must consider the offender's culpability in committing the offence and any harm which the offence caused, was intended to cause or might foreseeably have caused: SC s.63. **1-001**

### Sentencing guidelines

For many offences, the Sentencing Council have issued offence-specific sentencing guidelines which will assist in the determination of the seriousness of an offence. For offences without an offence-specific guideline, the Sentencing Council has issued the General Guideline, which provides a structured approach to the determination of seriousness but without providing any starting points or category ranges. (See **SENTENCING GUIDELINES**, see s.4.) **1-002**

### Custody threshold

For details of the assessing whether or an offence crosses the "custody threshold", i.e. it is so serious that only a custodial sentence is proportionate to the seriousness of the offence. (See s.55.) **1-003**

### Release

The release regime is (generally) a matter for the executive, and the general rule is that it will be wrong for a sentencing court to have regard to the differing release arrangements for sentences when determining the length of the appropriate sentence: *Round; Dunn* [2009] EWCA Crim 2667; [2010] 2 Cr. App. R.(S.) 45; [2010] Crim. L.R. 329. There are a small number of exceptions, however: **1-004**

(a) where a court is considering whether to impose a determinate or extended sentence: *Bourke*; [2017] EWCA Crim 2150; [2018] 1 Cr. App. R. (S.) 42;

(b) by the same rationale, that must apply also to preventive ancillary orders, such as SHPOs or restraining orders;

(c) it was suggested, obiter, that release provisions can be considered in the context of objectional disparity between co-defendants: *R. (Stott) v Secretary of State for Justice* [2018] UKSC 59; [2018] 3 W.L.R. 1831; [2019] 1 Cr. App. R.(S.) 47;

(d) cases involving children and young offenders in which the offender has crossed a relevant age threshold, and where it is necessary to consider the effect of the sentence when applying the rule in *Ghafoor* [2002] EWCA Crim 1857; [2003] 1 Cr. App. R.(S.) 84; [2002] Crim. L.R. 73.

# PURPOSES OF SENTENCING—ADULTS

## Sentencing Code s.57

*References: Current Sentencing Practice A1; Archbold 5A-9*

### General

Where a court is dealing with an offender who was aged 18 or over when convicted, the court must have regard to the following purposes of sentencing: 2-001

(a) the punishment of offenders;
(b) the reduction of crime (including its reduction by deterrence);
(c) the reform and rehabilitation of offenders;
(d) the protection of the public; and
(e) the making of reparation by offenders to persons affected by their offences: SC s.57(1) and (2).

### Procedure

The court must impose a sentence which is proportionate to the offence(s): SC s.63. That exercise produces a range of sentences which are acceptable. Within that range, the court can make reference to the purposes of sentencing identified above to determine where in that range the sentence ought to fall. Therefore, where an offence is so serious that a custodial sentence must be imposed (see SC s.230), the purposes of sentencing provided in s.57 do not permit the court to impose a lesser sentence. 2-002

### Deterrence

Deterrence and prevalence overlap but they are not the same; a deterrent sentence might be imposed to suppress prevalent criminality and it may be proper even absent prevalence. A sentence reflecting, to some degree, a deterrent element as a warning to others may simply reflect the need to reduce crime, something to which the court would have regard under what is now SC s.57(2)(b): *Sidhu* [2019] EWCA Crim 1034; [2019] 2 Cr. App. R.(S.) 34. 2-003

### Rehabilitation

It is important to note that the interest in rehabilitation of the offender must be balanced against the public interest in the appropriate punishment of crime, and where serious crimes are committed there will need to be compelling reasons so as to justify a significant departure from the normal sentence for such an offence: *Attorney General's Reference (Lewis)* [2019] EWCA Crim 253; [2019] 2 Cr. App. R.(S.) 3; [2019] Crim. L.R. 643. 2-004

By way of example, in *Attorney General's Reference (Tame)* [2019] EWCA Crim 2013; [2020] 1 Cr. App. R.(S.) 62 although the defendant was addicted to drugs, there was a link between that addiction and their offending and they wished to break their addiction, the fact that they had been unable to in the past and there was no reason to believe they would be successful in the future tended towards the conclusion that in any event a suspended sentence order with a drug rehabilitation requirement was not appropriate.

**Exceptions**

**2-005** The provision does not apply to:

(a) an offender who is aged under 18 at the time of conviction;
(b) an offence for which the sentence is fixed by law;
(c) the court is obliged by one of the following provisions to pass a sentence of detention for life, custody for life or imprisonment for life;
(d) ss.258, 274 or 285 of the SC (life sentence for certain dangerous offenders):
    (i) ss.273 or 283 of the SC (life sentence for second listed offence); or
    (ii) a sentence is required by one of the following provisions and the court is not of the opinion mentioned in that provision;
    (iii) s.311(2) of the SC (minimum sentence for certain offences involving firearms that are prohibited weapons);
    (iv) s.312(2) of the SC (minimum sentence for offence of threatening with weapon or bladed article);
    (v) s.313(2) of the SC (minimum sentence of seven years for third class A drug trafficking offence);
    (vi) s.314(2) of the SC (minimum sentence of three years for third domestic burglary);
    (vii) s.315(2) of the SC (minimum sentence for repeat offence involving weapon or bladed article); or
(e) the imposition of the following under Pt 3 of the Mental Health Act 1983 (MHA 1983):
    (i) a hospital order (with or without a restriction order);
    (ii) an interim hospital order;
    (iii) a hospital direction; or
    (iv) a limitation direction.

# MAXIMUM SENTENCE

*References: Archbold 5A-648*

## General rule

The maximum sentence for an offence should normally be reserved for the most serious examples of that offence which are likely to be encountered in practice. Where there is a low maximum sentence, however, there will inevitably be a degree of "bunching": *Timmins* [2018] EWCA Crim 2579; [2019] 1 Cr. App. R.(S.) 39. **3-001**

## Particular circumstances

The maximum sentence for an offence should normally be reserved for the most serious examples of that offence which are likely to be encountered in practice. **3-002**

The maximum sentence should not normally be imposed for:

(a) an attempt to commit an offence: *Robson* unreported 6 May 1974;
(b) where there is substantial mitigation: *Thompson* (1980) 2 Cr. App. R.(S.) 244;
(c) an offence where there has been a guilty plea entered: *Carroll* (1995) 16 Cr. App. R.(S.) 488; [1995] Crim. L.R. 92; or
(d) where the judge considered the maximum sentence provided by parliament to be inadequate: *Sherif* [2008] EWCA Crim 2653; [2009] 2 Cr. App. R. (S.) 33.

## Consecutive sentences

Consecutive maximum sentences may be properly imposed provided that each individual offence is one of the most serious examples of the type of offence, and the sentences are properly made consecutive: *Hunter* (1979) 1 Cr. App. R.(S.) 7. (See **CONCURRENT AND CONSECUTIVE SENTENCES, para.17**) **3-003**

## Change in maximum sentence

Where the maximum sentence for an offence is increased, the new maximum sentence will apply only to offences committed after the increase has taken effect. Where an offender has been convicted of an offence committed on a date unknown between two dates, and the maximum sentence has been increased between those two dates, the lower maximum sentence applies: see *Penrith Justices Ex p. Hay* (1979) 1 Cr. App. R.(S.) 265; (1979) 123 S.J. 621. See also *Hobbs* [2002] EWCA Crim 387; [2002] 2 Cr. App. R.(S.) 93; [2002] Crim. L.R. 414 in relation to conspiracies. **3-004**

## Defendant could have been convicted of lesser offence on same facts

Where the offender has been convicted of an offence of a general nature, but the facts fall within the scope of a more narrowly defined offence for which a lower **3-005** maximum sentence has been provided, the court should have regard to the lower maximum sentence, but is not necessarily bound by it: *Bright* [2008] EWCA Crim 462; [2008] 2 Cr. App. R.(S.) 102; [2008] Crim. L.R. 482. *Bright* was endorsed in *Bridger* [2018] EWCA Crim 1678; [2018] 2 Cr. App. R.(S.) 44; [2018] Crim. L.R. 1016.

# SENTENCING GUIDELINES

## SENTENCING CODE ss.59–62

*References: Current Sentencing Practice A1; Archbold 5A-16*

### Duty to follow sentencing guidelines

**Duty to follow** Where the offender was convicted on or after the commencement of the Sentencing Code, the court must, in sentencing an offender or exercising any other function relating to the sentencing of offenders, follow any sentencing guidelines which are relevant to the offender's case, unless the court is satisfied that it would be contrary to the interests of justice to do so: SC s.59(1). **4-001**

**Applies to all guidelines** For this purpose, the term "guidelines" include definitive guidelines published by the Sentencing Guidelines Council which were in effect on 5 April 2010 and guidelines issued by the Sentencing Council under s.121 of the Coroners and Justice Act 2009 (CJA 2009), the Coroners and Justice Act 2009 (Commencement No. 4, Transitional and Saving Provisions) Order 2010 (SI 2010/816) art.7(1). **4-002**

**Extent of the duty** The duty to follow any sentencing guidelines which are relevant to the offender's case includes, in all cases: **4-003**

(a) a duty to impose on the offender, in accordance with the offence-specific guidelines, a sentence which is within the offence range: SC s.60(2); and
(b) where the offence-specific guidelines describe categories of case, a duty to decide which of the categories most resembles the offender's case in order to identify the sentencing starting point in the offence range: SC s.60(4)(a).

However, there is no duty to impose a sentence which is within the category range, where the guideline specifies a category range: SC s.60(4)(b). The duty to follow sentencing guidelines is subject to any power the court has to impose an extended determinate sentence: SC s.60(6). In determining the appropriate custodial term for the purposes of s.256(2), 268(2) or 281(2) (extended sentence for certain violent, sexual or terrorism offences), s.60 applies to the court as it applies to a court in determining the sentence for an offence: SC s.61(2).

The duty to identify the category and impose a sentence within the offence range does not apply if the court is of the opinion that, for the purpose of identifying the sentence within the offence range which is the appropriate starting point, none of the categories sufficiently resembles the offender's case: SC s.60(5).

**Reductions in sentence** The duty to pass a sentence within the offence range is subject to: **4-004**

(a) s.73 of the SC (guilty pleas);
(b) ss.74, 387 and 388 of the SC (reduction or review of sentence in respect of assistance by defendants); and
(c) any other rule of law by virtue of which an offender may receive a

discounted sentence in consequence of assistance given (or offered to be given) by the offender to the prosecutor or investigator of an offence; and

(d) any rule of law as to the totality of sentences: SC s.60(3).

4-005 **Other statutory duties** The duty to follow guidelines is subject to the following provisions of the Sentencing Code:

(a) s.125(1) (fine must reflect seriousness of offence);
(b) s.179(2) (restriction on youth rehabilitation order (YRO));
(c) s.186(3) and (6) (restrictions on choice of requirements of YRO);
(d) s.204(2) (restriction on community order);
(e) s.208(3) and (6) (restrictions on choice of requirements of community order);
(f) s.230 (threshold for imposing discretionary custodial sentence);
(g) s.231 (custodial sentence must be for shortest term commensurate with seriousness of offence);
(h) ss.273 and 283 (life sentence for second listed offence for certain dangerous offenders);
(i) s.321 and Sch.21 (determination of minimum term in relation to mandatory life sentence);
(j) the provisions mentioned in s.399(c) (mandatory minimum sentences); and
(k) ss.268B and 282B (requirement to impose serious terrorism sentence): SC s.59(2).

4-006 **Mentally disordered defendants** The duty to follow a guideline does not restrict any power which enables a court to deal with an offender suffering from a mental disorder in the manner it considers to be most appropriate in all the circumstances: SC s.59(3).

4-007 **Giving reasons** In giving reasons for the sentence imposed, the court must identify any definitive sentencing guidelines relevant to the offender's case and explain how the court discharged any duty imposed on it and where the court did not follow any such guidelines because it was of the opinion that it would be contrary to the interests of justice to do so, state why it was of that opinion: SC s.52(6).

**Guidance on the use of guidelines**

4-008 **Draft Guidelines** A court should not have regard to draft guidelines issued by the Council as a preliminary stage in the process of consultation: *Abbas* [2008] EWCA Crim 1897; [2009] R.T.R. 3. Such draft guidance is of interest as part of the background which judges may wish to bear in mind, but the proposals do not constitute guidance and do not provide any justifiable basis for interfering with a sentencing decision in which the judge had applied the existing guidance of the court: *Valentas* [2010] EWCA Crim 200; [2010] 2 Cr. App. R. (S.) 73; [2010] Crim. L.R. 435. This point was re-stated in *Connelly* [2017] EWCA Crim 1569; [2018] 1 Cr. App. R.(S.) 19.

4-009 **Guidelines not in force at date of sentence** Where guidelines are expressly stated to apply from a certain date, they could not be said to affect sentencing practice prior to that date: *Boakye* [2012] EWCA Crim 838; [2013] 1 Cr. App. R. (S.) 2; [2012] Crim. L.R. 626. In *Hodgkins* [2016] EWCA Crim 360; [2016] 2 Cr.

App. R.(S.) 13, the court applied *Boakye* and stated that it was unhelpful to refer to the Theft guideline which was not in force at the date of the offender's sentencing hearing.

**Guideline in force after date of offence** Where the offence is committed pre-publication, but the guideline is in force by the time of the sentencing hearing, the guideline is to be applied: *Bao* [2007] EWCA Crim 2781; [2008] 2 Cr. App. R.(S.) 10; [2008] Crim. L.R. 234. **4-010**

It is submitted that where a definitive guideline is published after an offence is committed, but before the offender is sentenced, there is no breach of art.7 of the European Convention on Human Rights if the sentencing judge takes the guideline into account. Support for this proposition comes from the decision in *R. (Uttley) v SSHD* [2004] UKHL 38; [2004] 1 W.L.R. 2278; [2005] 1 Cr. App. R. 15.

**No guideline for specific offence** When a case concerns an offence for which there is no guideline, the judge may well consider an analogous guideline: *Lewis* [2012] EWCA Crim 1071; [2013] 1 Cr. App. R.(S.) 23. Attention should also be drawn to the Sentencing Council's General Guideline. **4-011**

**Applying current guidelines to historic offences** As a general rule, sentencing for historic offences is governed by current sentencing practice: *Bell* [2015] EWCA Crim 1426; [2016] 1 W.L.R. 1; [2016] 1 Cr. App. R.(S.) 16. However, caution should be exercised in applying current guidelines for modern equivalent offences to historic offences: *Attorney General's Reference (No.75 of 2015) (L)* [2015] EWCA Crim 2116; [2016] 1 Cr. App. R. (S.) 61. **4-012**

Reference should also be made to the decision in *Ahmed* [2023] EWCA Crim 281 in which the LCJ gave guidance as to the sentencing of historic offences.

**Making findings of fact** When assessing roles (particularly under the drug offences guidelines) judges are encouraged to focus on the factors set out in detail in the guidelines and to make factual findings which clearly indicate how those factors apply in the particular case before them: *Martin* [2018] EWCA Crim 1569. **4-013**

**Citation of authorities** In relation to an offence to which a sentencing guideline applies, the citation of authorities which provide examples of the court's approach rather than laying down principles are of no assistance: *Hudson* [2018] EWCA Crim 1933; [2019] 1 Cr. App. R.(S.) 5. **4-014**

**List of sentencing guidelines**

This table lists all sentencing guidelines currently in force, and the date on which they came into force. Guidelines are operative for all offences sentenced after the "in force" date unless otherwise stated. **4-015**

Unless otherwise stated, guidelines are issued by the Sentencing Council.

| **Overarching guidelines** | |
|---|---|
| **Guideline topic** | **In force** |
| Allocation, Offences Taken into Consideration and Totality | 1 March 2016 (Allocation)<br>11 June 2012 (Offences to be taken into Consideration (TICs)<br>1 July 2023 (Totality) |
| Domestic Abuse: Overarching Principles | 24 May 2018 |
| General Guideline | 1 October 2019 |
| Guilty Plea | 1 June 2017 (where the first hearing occurs on or after that date) |
| Imposition of Community and Custodial Sentences | 1 February 2017 |
| Sentencing Offenders with Mental Disorders, Developmental Disorders, or Neurological Impairments | 1 October 2020 |
| Youths | 1 June 2017 |

| **Offence specific guidelines** | |
|---|---|
| **Guideline topic** | **In force** |
| Animal Cruelty Offences | 1 July 2023 |
| Arson and Criminal Damage Offences | 1 October 2019 |
| Assault | 1 July 2021 |
| Attempted Murder | 1 July 2021 |
| Bladed Articles and Offensive Weapons | 1 June 2018 |
| Breach Offences | 1 October 2018 |
| Burglary (revised 2022) | 1 July 2022 |
| Child Cruelty Offences | 1 April 2023 |
| Dangerous Dogs | 1 July 2016 |
| Drug Offences | 1 April 2021 |
| Environmental Offences | 1 July 2014 |
| Firearms Offences (general) | 1 January 2021 |
| Firearms Offences (importation) | 1 January 2022 |
| Fraud, Bribery and Money Laundering | 1 October 2014 |
| Health and Safety Offences, Corporate Manslaughter, Food Safety and Hygiene Offences | 1 February 2016 |
| Intimidatory Offences | 1 October 2018 |
| Magistrates' Court (SGC) | 4 August 2008 |
| Manslaughter | 1 November 2018 |
| Modern Slavery Offences | 1 October 2021 |
| Motoring Offences | 1 July 2023 |
| Perverting the Course of Justice/Witness Intimidation | 1 October 2023 |
| Public Order Offences | 1 January 2020 |

| **Offence specific guidelines** | |
|---|---|
| **Guideline topic** | **In force** |
| Robbery | 1 April 2016 |
| Sexual Offences | 1 April 2014 |
| Terrorism Offences | 27 April 2018 |
| Terrorism Offences | 1 October 2022 |
| Theft | 1 February 2016 |
| Trade Marks Offences | 1 October 2021 |
| Underage sale of knives | 1 April 2023 |

# AGGRAVATING FACTORS—ASSAULTS ON EMERGENCY WORKERS OR PERSONS PROVIDING A PUBLIC SERVICE

## Sentencing Code ss.67–68A

*References: Current Sentencing Practice A1; Archbold 5A-60*

### Application

The aggravating factor applies to listed offences (see below) in which the offence was committed against an emergency worker acting in the exercise of their functions as such a worker: SC s.67(1) and (2). **5-001**

### Duty to treat as aggravating factor: emergency worker

Where a listed offence was committed against an emergency worker acting in the exercise of their functions as such a worker, the court must treat that fact as an aggravating factor (that is to say, a factor that increases the seriousness of the offence): SC s.67(2)(a). **5-002**

Where the court has determined that a listed offence was aggravated by the fact that it was committed against an emergency worker acting in exercise of their function as such, the court must state in open court that the offence is so aggravated: SC s.67(2)(b).

Nothing in s.67 prevents a court from treating the fact that the offence was committed against an emergency worker acting in the exercise of their functions as such a worker as an aggravating factor in relation to non-listed offences: SC s.67(6).

### Listed offences: emergency worker

The following offences are those to which the duty to treat as an aggravating factor the fact that the offence was committed against an emergency worker applies: **5-003**

(a) an offence under any of the following provisions of the Offences against the Person Act 1861 (OAPA 1861):
  - (i) s.16 (threats to kill);
  - (ii) s.18 (wounding with intent to cause grievous bodily harm);
  - (iii) s.20 (malicious wounding);
  - (iv) s.23 (administering poison, etc.);
  - (v) s.28 (causing bodily injury by gunpowder, etc.);
  - (vi) s.29 (using explosive substances etc. with intent to cause grievous bodily harm); or
  - (vii) s.47 (assault occasioning actual bodily harm);

(b) s.3 of the Sexual Offences Act 2003 (SOA 2003) (sexual assault);
(c) s.75A of the Serious Crime Act 2015 (strangulation or suffocation);
(d) manslaughter;
(e) kidnapping; or
(f) an inchoate offence in relation to any of the preceding offences: SC s.67(3).

**Duty to treat as aggravating factor: provision of public service etc.**

5-004 Where a listed offence was committed against a person providing a public service, performing a public duty or providing services to the public, the court must treat that fact as an aggravating factor (that is to say, a factor that increases the seriousness of the offence): SC s.68A(2)(a).

Where the court has determined that a listed offence was so aggravated, the court must state in open court that the offence is so aggravated: SC s.68A(2)(b).

Nothing in s.68A prevents a court from treating the fact that the offence was committed against a person providing a public service, performing a public duty or providing services to the public as an aggravating factor in relation to non-listed offences: SC s.68A(5).

This duty has effect in relation to a person convicted on or after 28 June 2022.

**Listed offences: provision of public service etc.**

5-005 The following offences are those to which the duty to treat as an aggravating factor the fact that the offence was committed against a person providing a public service, performing a public duty or providing services to the public applies:

(a) an offence under any of the following provisions of OAPA 1861:
  (i) s.16 (threats to kill);
  (ii) s.18 (wounding with intent to cause grievous bodily harm);
  (iii) s.20 (malicious wounding);
  (iv) s.47 (assault occasioning actual bodily harm);
(b) s.3 of SOA 2003 (sexual assault);
(c) an inchoate offence in relation to any of the preceding offences: SC s.68A(3).

**Definitions**

5-006 An "emergency worker" means (whether paid or unpaid):

(a) a constable;
(b) a person (other than a constable) who has the powers of a constable or is otherwise employed for police purposes or is engaged to provide services for police purposes;
(c) a National Crime Agency officer;
(d) a prison officer;
(e) a person (other than a prison officer) employed or engaged to carry out functions in a custodial institution of a corresponding kind to those carried out by a prison officer;
(f) a prisoner custody officer, so far as relating to the exercise of escort functions;
(g) a custody officer, so far as relating to the exercise of escort functions;
(h) a person employed for the purposes of providing, or engaged to provide, fire services or fire and rescue services;
(i) a person employed for the purposes of providing, or engaged to provide, search services or rescue services (or both);
(j) a person employed for the purposes of providing, or engaged to provide:

(i) NHS health services; or
(ii) services in the support of the provision of NHS health services, and whose general activities in doing so involve face to face interaction with individuals receiving the services or with other members of the public: SC s.68(1).

In relation to the above list:

"custodial institution" means any of the following:

(a) a prison;
(b) a young offender institution, secure training centre, secure college or remand centre;
(c) a removal centre, a short-term holding facility or pre-departure accommodation, as defined by s.147 of the Immigration and Asylum Act 1999 (IAA 1999); or
(d) services custody premises, as defined by s.300(7) of the Armed Forces Act 2006 (AFA 2006);

"custody officer" has the meaning given by s.12(3) of the Criminal Justice and Public Order Act 1994 (CJPOA 1994);

"escort functions":

(a) in the case of a prisoner custody officer, means the functions specified in s.80(1) of the Criminal Justice Act 1991 (CJA 1991); and
(b) in the case of a custody officer, means the functions specified in para.1 of Sch.1 to the CJPOA 1994.

"NHS health services" means any kind of health services provided as part of the health service continued under s.1(1) of the National Health Service Act 2006 (NHSA 2006) and under s.1(1) of the National Health Service (Wales) Act 2006 (NHS(W)A 2006); prisoner custody officer has the meaning given by s.89(1) of the CJA 1991: SC s.68(3).

"Acting in the exercise of functions of an emergency worker" includes circumstances where the offence takes place at a time when the person is not at work but is carrying out functions which, if done in work time, would have been in the exercise of functions as an emergency worker: SC 67(4). It is immaterial for the purposes of subs.(1) whether the employment or engagement is paid or unpaid: SC s.68(2). See also: *DPP v Ahmed* [2021] EWHC 2122 (Admin); [2022] 1 W.L.R. 314; [2022] 1 Cr. App. R. 1.

A reference to "providing services to the public" includes a reference to providing goods or facilities to the public; and

a reference to "the public" includes a reference to a section of the public: s.68A(4).

# AGGRAVATING FACTORS—DRUG/SUBSTANCE SUPPLY

## Sentencing Code ss.71–72

*References: Current Sentencing Practice A1; Archbold 5A-64*

### Controlled drugs

Where the court is sentencing an offender for an offence under s.4(3) of the Misuse of Drugs Act 1971 (MDA 1971) (supplying, offering to supply or being concerned in the supply or offering to supply of a controlled drug), the offender was aged 18+ at the time of the offence, and either: **6-001**

(a) the offence was committed on or in the vicinity of school premises at a relevant time; or
(b) in connection with the commission of the offence the offender used a courier who, at the time the offence was committed, was under the age of 18,

the court must treat the fact that either condition is met as an aggravating factor: SC s.71(1)-(3) and (5).

The court must state in open court that the offence is so aggravated: SC s.71(2)(b).

"School premises" means land used for the purposes of a school excluding any land occupied solely as a dwelling by a person employed at the school: SC s.71(4).

"Relevant time" means any time when the school premises are in use by persons under the age of 18 and one hour before and one hour after such time: SC s.71(4).

### Psychoactive substances

Where the court is considering the seriousness of an offence under the Psychoactive Substances Act 2016 (PSA 2016) s.5 and the offender was aged 18+ at the time of the offence; and one of the following conditions is met, the court must treat the fact that the condition is met as an aggravating factor increasing the seriousness of the offence, and must state in open court that the offence is so aggravated: SC s.72(1) and (2). **6-002**

Condition A: the offence was committed on or in the vicinity of school premises at a relevant time.

Condition B: in connection with the commission of the offence the offender used a courier who, at the time the offence was committed, was under the age of 18.

Condition C: the offence was committed in a custodial institution: SC s.72(3), (5) and (8).

"Relevant time" means any time when the school premises are in use by persons under the age of 18 and one hour before the start and one hour after the end of any such time: SC s.72(4).

"School premises" means land used for the purposes of a school, other than any land occupied solely as a dwelling by a person employed at the school. "School" has the same meaning as in s.4 of the Education Act 1996 (EA 1996): SC s.72(4).

"Custodial institution" means any of the following:

(a) a prison;
(b) a young offender institution, secure training centre, secure college, young offender institution, young offenders centre, juvenile justice centre or remand centre;
(c) a removal centre, a short-term holding facility or pre-departure accommodation; or
(d) service custody premises: SC s.72(9).

## AGGRAVATING FACTORS—RACE; RELIGION; SEXUAL ORIENTATION, DISABILITY OR TRANSGENDER IDENTITY

### Sentencing Code s.66

*References: Current Sentencing Practice A1; Archbold 5A-51*

**Protected characteristics**

Where a court is considering the seriousness of an offence and it determines that the offence was aggravated by: **7-001**

(a) racial hostility;
(b) religious hostility;
(c) hostility related to disability;
(d) hostility related to sexual orientation; or
(e) hostility related to transgender identity,

the duties in s.66(2) apply: SC s.66(1).

**Duty to treat as aggravating factor**

Where the court is satisfied that an offence was aggravated by one or more of the protected characteristics listed above, the court must treat the fact that the offence is aggravated by hostility of any of those types as an aggravating factor: SC s.66(2)(a). **7-002**

**Duty to state in open court**

In any such case, the court must state in open court that the offence was aggravated in this way: SC s.66(2)(b). **7-003**

**Racially/Religiously aggravated offences**

So far as it relates to racial and religious hostility, s.66 does not apply in relation to an offence under ss.29 to 32 of the Crime and Disorder Act 1998 (CDA 1998) (racially or religiously aggravated offences): SC s.66(3). **7-004**

If the offender is convicted of an offence which could have been charged as a racially or religiously aggravated offence under CDA 1998 ss.29 to 32 (such as unlawful wounding or assault occasioning actual bodily harm), but they had not been charged with the racially or religiously aggravated offence, or they had been acquitted of the racially or religiously aggravated offence, generally it is not permissible to treat the offence as racially or religiously aggravated for the purposes of s.145.

**Approach**

The decision in *Kelly* [2001] EWCA Crim 170; [2001] 2 Cr. App. R.(S.) 73; [2001] Crim. L.R. 411 supported a two-stage approach to sentencing racially ag- **7-005** gravated offences: first, a consideration of what the sentence should be absent the aggravation; and, secondly, a consideration of what, and by how much, the sentence should be increased to reflect this. That approach is more readily applicable in cases where there was a distinct offence, such as an assault, even without the racial element. That is to be contrasted with the situation where the very essence of the offence was the racial nature of the remark: *Gargan* [2017] EWCA Crim 780; [2018] 1 Cr. App. R.(S.) 6.

**Procedure**

**7-006** Section 66 does not prescribe the procedure by which a court is to determine whether or not an offence was so aggravated.

Where evidence has been adduced during the trial as to the aggravation of the offence, the judge may make a finding to the criminal standard that the offence was so aggravated.

Where evidence has not been adduced during the trial as to the aggravation (because it was not admissible or not relevant to the elements of the offence), the prosecution should seek a *Newton* hearing to determine the issue. This can occur after a guilty verdict by a jury: *Finch* (1993) 14 Cr. App. R.(S.) 226; [1992] Crim. L.R. 901. In *DPP v Giles* [2019] EWHC 2015 (Admin); [2020] 1 Cr. App. R.(S.) 20, DC; [2019] Crim. L.R. 993 the court had declined to hold a *Newton* hearing in circumstances where hostility as to sexual orientation was contested, being of the opinion that even if the factor was present it would not materially increase the sentence. The Divisional Court held that it was difficult to conceive of circumstances where aggravation by homophobic abuse would be immaterial and a *Newton* hearing to find the facts would not be required.

**7-007** For the purposes of making that determination, an offence is aggravated by hostility of one of the kinds listed above if:

- (a) at the time of committing the offence, or immediately before or after doing so, the offender demonstrated towards the victim of the offence hostility based on:
  - (i) the victim's membership (or presumed membership) of a racial group;
  - (ii) the victim's membership (or presumed membership) of a religious group;
  - (iii) a disability (or presumed disability) of the victim;
  - (iv) the sexual orientation (or presumed sexual orientation) of the victim, or (as the case may be);
  - (v) the victim being (or being presumed to be) transgender, or;
- (b) the offence was motivated (wholly or partly) by:
  - (i) hostility towards members of a racial group based on their membership of that group;
  - (ii) hostility towards members of a religious group based on their membership of that group;
  - (iii) hostility towards persons who have a disability or a particular disability;
  - (iv) hostility towards persons who are of a particular sexual orientation, or (as the case may be); or

(v) hostility towards persons who are transgender: SC s.66(4).

It is immaterial whether or not the offender's hostility is also based, to any extent, on any other factor not mentioned in the list in the preceding paragraph: SC s.66(5).

## Interpretation

For the purposes of s.66: **7-008**

(a) references to a racial group are to a group of persons defined by reference to race, colour, nationality (including citizenship) or ethnic or national origins;
(b) references to a religious group are to a group of persons defined by reference to religious belief or lack of religious belief;
(c) the term "membership" in relation to a racial or religious group, includes association with members of that group;
(d) the word "disability" means any physical or mental impairment;
(e) references to being transgender include references to being transsexual, or undergoing, proposing to undergo or having undergone a process or part of a process of gender reassignment; and
(f) the word "presumed" means presumed by the offender: SC s.66(6).

# AGGRAVATING FACTORS—TERRORIST CONNECTION/FOREIGN POWER CONNECTION

## Sentencing Code s.69, s.69A

*References: Current Sentencing Practice A1; Archbold 5A-62 and 62a, and 25-213*

### Terrorist Connection

### Determination that an offence has a terrorist connection

**Applicability** Section 69 applies where: **8-001**

(a) a person is convicted of an offence listed in s.69(4) or (5); and
(b) the court is considering the seriousness of the offence for the purposes of sentencing: SC s.69(1).

Section 69(4) or (5) offences are:

(a) offences committed on or after 29 June 2021, punishable on indictment with imprisonment for more than two years, and not specified in Sch.A1; and
(b) offences committed before 29 June 2021, and specified in Sch.1.

### Duty to treat as an aggravating factor

Where the court considers that the offence has a terrorist connection, the court must treat that fact as an aggravating factor: SC s.69(1) and (2). **8-002**

Where the court has determined that the offence has a terrorist connection and has treated that fact as an aggravating factor, and must state in open court that the offence was so aggravated: SC s.69(2).

**Determining the issue** The court may hear evidence for the purpose of determining whether the offence has a terrorist connection, and must take account of any representations made by the prosecution and defence, and any other matter relevant for the purposes of sentence. This was formerly s.30(3) of the Counter-Terrorism Act 2008 (CTA 2008), however it has been repealed by the Sentencing Code and not re-enacted as the view was taken that the words were unnecessary. The position, however, remains the same. **8-003**

**Definition: terrorist connection** An offence has a terrorist connection if the offence: **8-004**

(a) is, or takes place in the course of, an act of terrorism; or
(b) is committed for the purposes of terrorism: SC s.69(3).

**Definition: terrorism** "Terrorism" means the use or threat of: **8-005**

(1) action where the action:
    (a) involves serious violence against a person;

(b) involves serious damage to property;
(c) endangers a person's life, other than that of the person who is committing the action;
(d) creates a serious risk to the health or safety of the public or a section of the public; or
(e) is designed seriously to interfere with or seriously to disrupt an electronic system; and

(2) the use or threat is designed to influence the government or to intimidate the public or a section of the public; and
(3) the use or threat is made for the purpose of advancing a political, religious, racial or ideological cause: CTA 2008 s.92 and Terrorism Act 2000 (TA 2000) s.1(1).

The use or threat of action falling within (1) above which involves the use of firearms or explosives is terrorism whether or not the requirement at (2) is satisfied: TA 2000 s.1(3) and CTA 2008 s.92.

"Action" includes action outside the UK, a reference to any person or to "property" is a reference to any person, or to property, wherever situated, a reference to the "public" includes a reference to the public of a country other than the UK, and "the government" means the government of the UK, of a part of the UK or of a country other than the UK. A reference to "action taken for the purposes of terrorism" includes a reference to action taken for the benefit of a proscribed organisation: CTA 2008 s.92 and TA 2000 s.1(4).

**Foreign Power Connection**

8-006 **Applicability** Section 69A applies where:

This section applies where a court is considering the seriousness of an offence that—

(a) the offence was committed on or after 20 December 2023; and
(b) the offence is not an offence under the National Security Act 2023 or an inchoate offence, or a relevant electoral offence within the meaning given by s.16 of that Act (foreign interference in elections): s.69A(1) and (2).

8-007 **Duty to treat as an aggravating factor** Where the foreign power condition is met, the court must treat that fact as an aggravating factor: SC s.69A(3).

Where the court has determined that the foreign power condition is met and has treated that fact as an aggravating factor and must state in open court that the offence was so aggravated: SC s.69A(3).

8-008 **Determining the issue** The court may hear evidence for the purpose of determining whether the offence has a terrorist connection and must take account of any representations made by the prosecution and defence, and any other matter relevant for the purposes of sentence. Note above that in relation to the terrorist connection provision, this was previously expressly stated in s.30(3) of the Counter-Terrorism Act 2008 (CTA 2008), however that was repealed by the Sentencing Code and not re-enacted as the view was taken that the words were unnecessary. It is therefore the position that the court can hear evidence in relation to the foreign power condition.

**Definition: foreign power condition** The foreign power condition is met in relation to a person's conduct if: **8-009**

(a) the conduct in question, or a course of conduct of which it forms part, is carried out for or on behalf of a foreign power; and
(b) the person knows, or having regard to other matters known to them ought reasonably to know, that to be the case: s.31(1) NSA 2023.

The conduct in question, or a course of conduct of which it forms part, is in particular to be treated as carried out for or on behalf of a foreign power if: **8-010**

(a) it is instigated by a foreign power;
(b) it is under the direction or control of a foreign power;
(c) it is carried out with financial or other assistance provided by a foreign power for that purpose; or
(d) it is carried out in collaboration with, or with the agreement of, a foreign power: s.31(2) NSA 2023.

See the remainder of s.31 for further provision regarding the foreign power condition, namely setting out how the court may determine whether the condition is met.

OFFENCES WHERE TERRORIST CONNECTION NOT REQUIRED TO BE CONSIDERED

## Terrorism Act 2000

1 An offence under any of the following provisions of the Terrorism Act 2000— **8-011**

(a) section 11 (membership of a proscribed organisation);
(b) section 11 (inviting or expressing support for a proscribed organisation);
(c) section 15 (fund-raising);
(d) section 16 (use of money or property for terrorist purposes);
(e) section 17 (involvement in terrorist funding arrangements);
(f) section 17A (insuring payments made in response to terrorist threats);
(g) section 18 (laundering of terrorist property);
(h) section 19 (failure to disclose professional belief or suspicion about terrorist offences);
(i) section 21A (failure in regulated sectors to disclose knowledge or suspicion about terrorist offences);
(j) section 38B (failure to disclose information about acts of terrorism);
(l) section 54 (weapons training);
(m) section 56 (directing a terrorist organisation);
(n) section 57 (possession of article for terrorist purposes);
(o) section 58 (collection of information likely to be of use to a terrorist);
(p) section 58A (publishing information about members of the armed forces etc.);
(q) section 58B (entering or remaining in a designated area);
(r) section 59 (inciting terrorism overseas).

## Anti-terrorism, Crime and Security Act 2001

2 An offence under section 113 of the Anti-terrorism, Crime and Security Act 2001 (use of noxious substance or thing to cause harm or intimidate).

## Terrorism Act 2006

3 An offence under any of the following provisions of the Terrorism Act 2006—

(a) section 1 (encouragement of terrorism);
(b) section 2 (dissemination of terrorist publications);
(c) section 5 (preparation of terrorist acts);
(d) section 6 (training for terrorism);
(e) section 8 (attendance at a place used for terrorist training);
(f) section 9 (making or possession of radioactive device or material);
(g) section 10 (misuse of radioactive device or material for terrorist purposes etc.);
(h) section 11 (terrorist threats relating to radioactive devices etc.).

**Counter-Terrorism Act 2008**

**8-012** 4 An offence under s.54 of the Counter-Terrorism Act 2008 (breach of police notification requirements etc.).

**Terrorism Prevention and Investigation Measures 2011**

**8-013** 5 An offence under s.23 of the Terrorism Prevention and Investigation Measures Act 2011 (breach of notices imposing terrorism prevention and investigation measures).

**Counter-Terrorism and Security Act 2015**

**8-014** 6 An offence under s.10 of the Counter-Terrorism and Security Act 2015 (breach of temporary exclusion order).

**Inchoate offences**

**8-015** 7 An inchoate offence (see s.398) in relation to an offence specified in any of the preceding paragraphs of this Schedule.

# AGGRAVATING FACTORS—USING A MINOR TO MIND A WEAPON

## SENTENCING CODE s.70

*References: Current Sentencing Practice A1; Archbold 5A-63*

### Applicability

Section 70 applies where: **9-001**

(a) a court is considering the seriousness of an offence under s.28 of the Violent Crime Reduction Act 2006 (VCRA 2006) (using someone to mind a weapon); and
(b) when the offence was committed:
  (i) the offender was aged 18 or over; and
  (ii) the person used to look after, hide or transport the weapon in question ("the person used") was not: SC s.70(1).

### Duty to treat as an aggravating factor

Where the conditions in subs.(1) are met, the court: **9-002**

(a) must treat the fact that the person used was under the age of 18 when the offence was committed as an aggravating factor; and
(b) must state in open court that the offence is so aggravated: SC s.70(2).

### Offences spanning two or more days

Where the offence is found to have involved the person used as having possession of a weapon, or being able to make it available: **9-003**

(a) over a period of two or more days; or
(b) at some time during a period of two or more days; and

if, on a day during that period, the offender was aged 18 or over, and the person used to look after, hide or transport the weapon in question ("the person used") was not, they are to be treated as both being satisfied when the offence was committed: SC s.70(3) and (4).

## AGGRAVATING FACTORS—PREVIOUS CONVICTIONS

SENTENCING CODE s.65

*References: Current Sentencing Practice A1; Archbold 5A-44*

### Duty to treat as aggravating factor

Where a court is considering the seriousness of an offence ("the current offence") committed by an offender who has one or more relevant previous convictions, the court must treat as an aggravating factor each relevant previous conviction that it considers can reasonably be so treated, having regard in particular to: **10-001**

(a) the nature of the offence to which the relevant previous conviction relates and its relevance to the current offence; and
(b) the time that has elapsed since the relevant previous conviction: SC s.65(1) and (2).

### Must state that seriousness of offence is aggravated by previous conviction(s)

Where the court treats a relevant previous conviction as an aggravating factor under subs.(2) it must state in open court that the offence is so aggravated: SC s.65(3). **10-002**

### What is a previous conviction?

Previous convictions are those for which the conviction was obtained prior to the commission of the offence for which the offender now falls to be sentenced: *Darrigan* [2017] EWCA Crim 169; [2017] 1 Cr. App. R.(S.) 50; [2017] Crim. L.R. 565. However, offending post-dating that offence may be relevant if, for example, it rebuts a claim of desistance or remorse. **10-003**

"Previous conviction" does not include convictions which are deemed not to be convictions by provisions dealing with discharges. A conviction which results in a discharge is deemed not to be a conviction, (save for the purposes of:

(a) the proceedings in which the order is made; and
(b) in the case of an order for conditional discharge, any subsequent proceedings which may be taken against the offender under Sch.2: SC s.82(1) and (2)).

"Previous conviction" includes convictions by a court in the UK and a previous conviction for a service offence.

A court is not required to treat convictions by a court outside the UK as aggravating factors, but may take them into account and treat them as aggravating factors if it considers it appropriate to do so: SC s.76.

**Previous convictions are different from being on licence**

**10-004** Previous convictions and an offence being committed while on licence are "conceptually different" and there is no impermissible double counting where both factors are reflected in the sentence: *May* [2022] EWCA Crim 622.

# AGGRAVATING FACTORS—OFFENCE COMMITTED ON BAIL

## Sentencing Code s.64

*References: Current Sentencing Practice A1; Archbold 5A-42*

### Duty to treat as aggravating factor

In considering the seriousness of an offence committed while the offender was on bail, the court must: **11-001**

(a) treat the fact that it was committed in those circumstances as an aggravating factor; and
(b) state in open court that the offence is so aggravated: SC s.64.

### Guidance

The duty applies even if the offender is acquitted of the offence for which the offender was on bail: *Thackwray* [2003] EWCA Crim 3362. **11-002**

In *Attorney General's Reference (Shaw)* [2021] EWCA Crim 685; [2022] 1 Cr. App. R.(S.) 5 the court suggested that there was no reason why offending while awaiting a first appearance following the receipt of a postal requisition should be treated any differently from offending while on bail. **11-003**

# ANTECEDENT STATEMENTS

## Criminal Practice Directions 2023, 5.3 Defendant's record

*References: See Archbold 5A-6*

5.3.1 The prosecution must provide up to date and accurate information about the defendant's record of previous convictions, cautions, reprimands, etc. in the Initial Details of the Prosecution Case. The record must be supplied to the court, the defence and (if applicable) Probation Service. **12-001**

5.32 The record should usually be provided as a Police National Computer (PNC) printout, supplemented by Forms MG16/17 if the police hold convictions/ cautions not shown on PNC.

5.3.3 If the defence object to the accuracy of the record, they should inform the prosecutor immediately.

# MITIGATING FACTORS

*References: Current Sentencing Practice A1; Archbold 5A-70*

## General

Unlike the position with aggravating factors, mitigating factors are not generally set out in statute (save, for example, factors such as guilty plea or assistance to the prosecution). **13-001**

## Mitigating in private

A sentencing court has jurisdiction to remove the public from the court in order to allow matters in mitigation to be advanced in private, but this is an exceptional step which should be avoided if there is any other way of serving the interests of justice: *R. (Weefer) v Ealing Justices* (1981) 3 Cr. App. R.(S.) 296, DC; [1982] Crim. L.R. 182. **13-002**

## Categories of mitigation

Core categories of mitigation revolve around the offence or the offender. In relation to the offence, these will be fact specific features of the offending where the offender acted in a such a way as to reduce the harm involved, or to demonstrate reduced culpability. For the most part, these are set out in the offence-specific sentencing guidelines (at Step Two) or the General Guideline. **13-003**

In relation to offender-related mitigation, the following categories are most common:

(a) age (youth or advanced age);
(b) ill-health;
(c) remorse;
(d) traumatic/abusive childhood (where linked to offending);
(e) employment or educational prospects;
(f) improvement in behaviour/steps to address offending;
(g) substance addiction;
(h) efforts at reparation; and
(i) good character.

It is suggested that it will be necessary to demonstrate the relevance of the factor to the offence or the imposition of punishment such that a reduction in sentence is required. Further, it is necessary to recall that the absence of aggravation is not mitigation.

In March 2023, the Court of Appeal (Criminal Division) gave guidance as to the approach, to prison over-crowding as a mitigating circumstance: *Ali* [2023] EWCA Crim 232. In October 2023, the Senior Presiding Judge asked courts to delay sentencing in cases where the defendant was on bail due to prison over-crowding.

# OFFENCES TAKEN INTO CONSIDERATION

## TICS GUIDELINE, SENTENCING COUNCIL

*References: Current Sentencing Practice A1; Archbold 5A-93*

### General

Where an offender admits an offence with which they have not been charged and asks the court to take it into consideration, the court may take account of that offence when passing sentence for the offence of which the offender has been convicted. **14-001**

When sentencing an offender who requests offences to be taken into consideration (TICs), courts should pass a total sentence which reflects all the offending behaviour. The sentence must be just and proportionate and must not exceed the statutory maximum for the conviction offence.

### Discretion

The court has discretion as to whether or not to take TICs into account. In exercising its discretion the court should take into account that TICs are capable of reflecting the offender's overall criminality. The court is likely to consider that the fact that the offender has assisted the police (particularly if the offences would not otherwise have been detected) and avoided the need for further proceedings demonstrates a genuine determination by the offender to "wipe the slate clean". **14-002**

Where the offender has been sentenced on an earlier occasion and, having expressed a desire to have a "clean slate", had failed to ask for an offence to be taken into consideration for which the offender later fell to be sentenced, no reduction will follow. It is incumbent on defendants to volunteer this information at the relevant time and to ensure that the police listed it as one of the TICs; otherwise, the defendant ran a risk: *Murray* [2018] EWCA Crim 1252; [2018] 2 Cr. App. R.(S.) 41.

### Circumstances in which TICs are generally undesirable

- where the TIC is likely to attract a greater sentence than the conviction offence; **14-003**
- where it is in the public interest that the TIC should be the subject of a separate charge;
- where the offender would avoid a prohibition, ancillary order or similar consequence which it would have been desirable to impose on conviction. For example where the TIC attracts mandatory disqualification or endorsement and the offence(s) for which the defendant is to be sentenced do not;
- where the TIC constitutes a breach of an earlier sentence;
- where the TIC is a specified offence for the purposes of Schs 18 or 19 to the Sentencing Code, but the conviction offence is non-specified; or
- where the TIC is not founded on the same facts or evidence or part of a series of offences of the same or similar character (unless the court is satisfied that it is in the interests of justice to do so): *TICs Guideline*, p.3.

Additionally, an offence should not normally be taken into consideration if the court would not have power to deal with the offender for the offence, or if the offence would result in a mandatory sentence.

**Effect of TICs**

**14-004** An offence which has been taken into consideration is an "associated offence": SC s.400(b).

A TIC does not amount to a conviction: *Howard* (1991) 92 Cr. App. R. 223; (1990-91) 12 Cr. App. R.(S.) 426.

**Procedure**

**14-005** A court should generally only take offences into consideration if the following procedural provisions have been satisfied:

- the police or prosecuting authorities have prepared a schedule of offences (TIC schedule) that they consider suitable to be taken into consideration. The TIC schedule should set out the nature of each offence, the date of the offence(s), relevant detail about the offence(s) (including, for example, monetary values of items) and any other brief details that the court should be aware of;
- a copy of the TIC schedule must be provided to the defendant and their representative (if they have one) before the sentence hearing. The defendant should sign the TIC schedule to provisionally admit the offences;
- at the sentence hearing, the court should ask the defendant in open court whether they admit each of the offences on the TIC schedule and whether they wish to have them taken into consideration;
- if there is any doubt about the admission of a particular offence, it should not be accepted as a TIC. Special care should be taken with vulnerable and/or unrepresented defendants;
- if the defendant is committed to the Crown Court for sentence, this procedure must take place again at the Crown Court even if the defendant has agreed to the schedule in the magistrates' court: *TICs Guideline*, p.3.

The exercise of asking the defendant whether they admit the offences on the TIC schedule does not need to take long, even where there are a significant number of additional offences. A judge can quite properly ask whether, for example, a defendant admits the 25 dwelling-house burglaries set out on the schedule and whether they wish the judge to take those offences into consideration when passing sentence, without reading out the individual dates and addresses of each offence, or the details of the property stolen on each occasion: *Gamble* [2019] EWCA Crim 600; [2019] 2 Cr. App. R.(S.) 30.

**14-006** **Specimen counts** Where an offender admits that the offences to which they have pleaded guilty are specimen offences representing a larger number of offences which are not separately identified, those other offences are not "offences taken into consideration".

## Determining sentence

The sentence imposed on an offender should, in most circumstances, be increased to reflect the fact that other offences have been taken into consideration. The court should: **14-007**

(a) determine the sentencing starting point for the conviction offence, referring to the relevant definitive sentencing guidelines. No regard should be had to the presence of TICs at this stage;
(b) consider whether there are any aggravating or mitigating factors that justify an upward or downward adjustment from the starting point. The presence of TICs should generally be treated as an aggravating feature that justifies an upward adjustment from the starting point. Where there are a large number of TICs, it may be appropriate to move outside the category range, although this must be considered in the context of the case and subject to the principle of totality. The court is limited to the statutory maximum for the conviction offence;
(c) continue through the sentencing process including:
    - consider whether the frank admission of a number of offences is an indication of a defendant's remorse or determination and/or demonstration of steps taken to address addiction or offending behaviour;
    - any reduction for a guilty plea should be applied to the overall sentence;
    - the principle of totality;
    - when considering ancillary orders these can be considered in relation to any or all of the TICs, specifically: compensation orders — in the magistrates' court the total compensation cannot exceed the limit for the conviction offence; and
    - restitution orders: *TICs Guideline*, p.4.

# ASSISTING THE PROSECUTION

## Sentencing Code ss.74, 75

*References: Current Sentencing Practice A1; Archbold 5A-107*

### General

A sentencing court may make a reduction in sentence to reflect assistance provided or offered in relation to their offence or other offences. **15-001**

The practice of reducing the sentence which would otherwise have been imposed on an offender to reflect the fact that they had provided information and assistance to the police has a purely pragmatic justification. The public interest in rewarding assistance to the authorities and protecting sources has long been recognized: *Royle* [2023] EWCA Crim 1311; [2024] 1 W.L.R. 2853.

In *Z* [2015] EWCA Crim 1427; [2016] 1 Cr. App. R.(S.) 15; [2016] Crim. L.R. 143, the court declined to alter the common law principle that an offender's sentence could not be discounted for assistance given to the police to enable a reduction to be made for assistance given post-sentence.

Material assistance to the prosecution leading to the apprehension and conviction of an offender in circumstances where the conviction concerned an offence where the defendant was a victim might merit a reduction in sentence: *Campbell* [2018] EWCA Crim 802; [2018] 2 Cr. App. R.(S.) 24.

### Written agreements (the statutory scheme)

**Availability** Where a defendant who has pleaded guilty in proceedings in the Crown Court, or who has been committed to the Crown Court for sentence following a plea of guilty, has entered a written agreement with a specified prosecutor, to assist or offered to assist the investigator or prosecutor in relation to the offence to which they have pleaded guilty or any other offence, the provisions of s.74 apply: SC s.74(1). **15-002**

**Procedure** The discount for assistance provided should be calculated first, against all other relevant considerations, and the notional sentence so achieved should be further discounted by the guilty plea: *P* [2007] EWCA Crim 2290; [2008] 2 Cr. App. R.(S.) 5. **15-003**

**The level of the reduction** The court may take into account the extent and nature of the assistance given or offered in determining what sentence to pass: SC s.74(2). **15-004**

Nothing in s.268C(2) or 282C(2) (minimum appropriate custodial term for serious terrorism sentences) affects the court's power under subs.(2) so far it relates to determining the appropriate custodial term: s.74(2A).

The court in *Royle* identified a number of factors relevant to identifying the appropriate reduction in a particular case:

- i) the quality and quantity of the information provided, including whether it related to trivial or to serious offences (the risk to the informer generally being greater when the criminality concerned is more serious);
- ii) the period of time over which the information was provided;
- iii) whether it assisted the authorities to bring to justice persons who would not otherwise have been brought to justice, or to prevent or disrupt the commission of serious crime, or to recover property (the value of the assistance being a crucial factor);
- iv) the degree of assistance which was provided, including whether the informer gave, or was willing to give, evidence confirming the information he had provided;
- v) the degree of risk to which the informer has exposed himself and his family by providing the information or assistance;
- vi) the nature and extent of the crime in which the informer has himself been involved, and the extent to which he has been prepared to admit the full extent of his criminality;
- vii) whether the informer has relied on the same provision of information and assistance when being sentenced on a previous occasion, or when making an application to the Parole Board (an informer can generally only expect to receive credit once for past information or assistance);
- viii) whether the informer has been paid for the assistance provided and, if so, how much; but it was important to note that in *T* [2021] EWCA Crim 1474; [2022] 1 Cr. App. R. (S.) 55, the court emphasised that a financial reward and a reduction in sentence are complementary means of showing offenders that it was worth their while to disclose the criminal activities of others: a financial reward, unless exceptionally generous, should therefore play only a small, if any, part in the sentencer's decision; and
- ix) in the case of assistance under s.388 (or the text regime), the fact that an offender has contested his trial may be one of the factors relevant to the extent of the reduction made.

**15-005** **General principles** The Court of Appeal has set down some general principles relating to the reduction:

- (a) no hard and fast rules can be laid down as to what, as in so many other aspects of sentencing, is a fact-specific decision;
- (b) the first factor is the criminality of the defendant, thereafter, the quality and quantity of the material provided by the defendant will be considered;
- (c) a mathematical approach is liable to produce an inappropriate answer; the totality principle is fundamental;
- (d) only in the most exceptional case will the discount exceed three-quarters of the total sentence; and
- (e) the normal level continues to be between half and two-thirds: *P* [2007] EWCA Crim 2290; [2008] 2 All E.R. 684; [2008] 2 Cr. App. R.(S.) 5.

The extent to which the assistance given or offered may affect the sentence is a matter within the discretion of the sentencing court.

**15-006** **Judge must state reduction given** If the court passes a sentence which is less than it would otherwise have passed, the court must state in open court that it has passed a lesser sentence than it would otherwise have passed, and what the greater sentence would have been: SC s.74(3).

This obligation does not apply if the court thinks that it would not be in the public interest to disclose that the sentence has been discounted: SC s.74(4)(a).

Where no statement is made in open court, the court must give written notice of the fact that it has passed a lesser sentence, and what the greater sentence would have been, to the prosecutor and to the offender: SC s.74(4)(b).

Where the duty under subs.(3) does not apply, the duty under ss.52(2) and 322(4) of the Sentencing Code (requirement to explain reasons for sentence) do not apply to the extent that the explanation will disclose that a discount has been given pursuant to a formal agreement: SC s.74(4)(c).

**Minimum sentences** Nothing in any enactment which requires that a "minimum sentence" is passed in respect of any offence or an offence of any description or by reference to the circumstances of any offender affects the power of a court to take into account the extent and nature of the assistance given or offered: SC s.74(5). **15-007**

**Murder** In a case of murder, nothing in any enactment which requires the court to take into account "certain matters" for the purposes of making an order which determines or has the effect of determining the minimum period of imprisonment which the offender must serve affects the power of the court to take into account the extent and nature of the assistance given or offered: SC s.74(5). **15-008**

**Additional mitigation** Taking account of the assistance given by a defendant does not prevent the court from also taking account of any other matter which it is entitled by virtue of any other enactment to take account of for the purposes of determining the sentence or in the case of a sentence which is fixed by law, any minimum period of imprisonment which an offender must serve: SC s.76. **15-009**

**Review of sentence**

**General** The review of sentence procedure applies where a defendant has been sentenced in the Crown Court, and: **15-010**

(a) has received a discounted sentence after having made a written agreement to give assistance to the prosecutor or investigator of an offence, but has knowingly failed "to any extent" to give assistance in accordance with the agreement;
(b) has received a discounted sentence as a consequence of having made a written agreement, and having given the assistance in accordance with the agreement, in pursuance of another written agreement gives or offers to give further assistance; or
(c) has received a sentence which was not discounted but in pursuance of a written agreement they subsequently give or offer to give assistance, a specified prosecutor may refer the case back to the court if the person concerned is still serving their sentence, and the prosecutor thinks that it is in the interest of justice to do so: SC s.387(1).

A case is not eligible for review if— **15-011**

(a) the sentence was discounted and the offender has not given the assistance offered in accordance with the written agreement by virtue of which it was discounted; or
(b) the offence was one for which the sentence was fixed by law and the offender did not plead guilty to it: SC s.388(2).

The case so referred must, if possible, be heard by the judge who passed the original sentence: SC s.387(3).

15-012 **Test** If the court is "satisfied" that a person whose sentence has been discounted has "knowingly failed to give the assistance", it may substitute for the sentence which has been referred "such greater sentence" as it thinks appropriate, provided that the new sentence does not exceed the sentence which it would have passed if the agreement had not been made: SC s.387(4).

On such a reference, the court may take into account the extent and nature of the assistance given or offered (under (b) or (c) above), and substitute for the original sentence such lesser sentence as it thinks appropriate: SC s.388(5).

15-013 **Explaining the sentence** The court must state in open court:

(a) the fact that the substitute sentence is a discounted sentence; and

(b) the original maximum: SC s.388(8).

Section 52(2) or, as the case may be, s.322(4) (requirement to explain reasons for sentence or other order) applies: SC s.388(9).

However, where the court considers that it would not be in the public interest to disclose that the substitute sentence is a discounted sentence—

the requirements do not apply. Instead, the court must give a written statement of the matters specified in s.388(8) to:

(i) the prosecutor, and
(ii) the offender.

In such circumstances, s.52(2) or, as the case may be, s.322(4) does not apply to the extent that the explanation would disclose that the substitute sentence is a discounted sentence: SC s.388(10).

Consideration of the interests of justice in that context involved an open-ended deliberation. Section 387(2) imposes no explicit constraint on how the specified prosecutor should approach the question and there was no warrant for implying a fetter on the exercise of the unrestricted discretion for which the statute clearly provided. It was not difficult to envisage a wide range of factors beyond the question of whether or not circumstances had changed that might be pivotal in deciding if the original sentence should be referred back to the court that imposed it: see *Re Loughlin* [2017] UKSC 63; [2017] 1 W.L.R. 3963; [2018] 1 Cr. App. R.(S.) 21.

15-014 **Appealing a review** A person in respect of whom a reference is made under s.74 and the specified prosecutor may, with the leave of the Court of Appeal, appeal to the Court of Appeal against the decision of the Crown Court: SC s.389(1).

The procedure and powers of the Court of Appeal are governed by The Serious Organised Crime and Police Act 2005 (Appeals under s.74) Order 2006 (SI 2006/2135).

**Excluding the public/publicity restrictions** On the hearing of a reference, or any other proceedings arising in consequence of a reference, the court may exclude from the proceedings anyone other than an officer of the court, a party to the proceedings or legal representatives of the parties, and may give such directions as it thinks appropriate prohibiting the publication of any matter relating to the proceedings, including the fact that the reference has been made: SC s.390. **15-015**

Such an order may be made only to the extent that it is necessary to do so to protect the safety of any person, and is in the interests of justice: SC s.390.

**The "text" regime**

**Assistance provided outside the statutory scheme** The statutory provisions do not replace the conventional practice by which a defendant who is unable or unwilling to enter onto a written agreement may ask the prosecuting or investigating body to produce a "text" setting out the details of the assistance or information provided by the defendant. In such cases, the court may discount the sentence imposed upon the defendant. For details of the "text" procedure: see *X* [1999] 2 Cr. App. R.(S.) 294; [1999] Crim. L.R. 678. **15-016**

**Contents** A text will set out: **15-017**

- (i) the offender's status and whether they are a Covert Human Intelligence Source (CHIS)[1] under the Regulation of Investigatory Powers Act 2000 (RIPA 2000);
- (ii) the details of the assistance provided, the information or intelligence provided and whether they are willing to be a witness;
- (iii) the effort to which the offender had gone to obtain the information;
- (iv) any risk to the offender or their family;
- (v) an assessment of the benefit derived by the police, including any arrests or convictions or any property recovered;
- (vi) any financial reward the offender has already received for the assistance provided; and
- (vii) a statement as to whether the offender will be of future use to the police: *AXN and ZAR* [2016] EWCA Crim 590; [2016] 1 W.L.R. 4006; [2016] 2 Cr. App. R.(S.) 33.

**General principles** As summarised in *X* [1999] 2 Cr. App. R.(S.) 294; [1999] Crim. L.R. 678: **15-018**

---

1 Under RIPA s.26(8), a person is a "CHIS" if:
- (a) they establish or maintain a personal or other relationship with a person for the covert purpose of facilitating the doing of anything falling within para.(b) or (c);
- (b) they covertly use such a relationship to obtain information or to provide access to any information to another person; or
- (c) they covertly disclose information obtained by the use of such a relationship or as a consequence of the existence of such a relationship. See CHIS Revised Code of Practice 2018.

(i) the text is supplied by the police at the request of the offender;
(ii) without confirmation by the police, an offender's statement that they have provided assistance is unlikely to be of assistance;
(iii) as the courts rely so heavily on police confirmation, the greatest care has to be exercised by the police in the provision of the information;
(iv) absent issues of Public Interest Immunity, the text should be shown to counsel for the defence who can discuss it with the offender; and
(v) there should normally be no question of evidence being given or an issue tried about it. If the offender disagreed, then questioning of the police officer would almost inevitably be contrary to the public interest.

15-019 **Procedure** The general position as regards the procedure is as follows (see *Royle and N* [2016] EWCA Crim 590; [2016] 2 Cr. App. R. (S.) 33):

1) An offender who wishes to achieve a reduction in sentence by providing information or assistance to the police must do so before being sentenced in the Crown Court. On an appeal, the function of the Court of Appeal is to review the sentence which was passed in the court below, not to conduct a fresh sentencing process.
2) There was a partial exception to that rule: if a reduction in sentence was made in the Crown Court, and the assistance provided exceeded that which the sentencer expected, the Court of Appeal may review the sentence to reflect the true value of the assistance given, and to be given, by the offender.
3) Except to the extent that the defendant's contention of having given assistance is supported by the police, it will not generally be likely that the sentencing judge will be able to make any adjustment in sentence.
4) If the defendant wishes to disagree with the contents of such a document, it is not appropriate for there to be cross-examination of the police, whether in court or in chambers. However, in an appropriate case, a defendant may wish to ask for an adjournment to allow any opportunity for further consideration to be given to the preparation of the document. Otherwise, if the defendant does not accept what the document says, their remedy is not to rely on it. A judge should ordinarily disregard such a document if asked by the defendant to do so.
5) If the judge does take the document into consideration, they should say only that they have taken into consideration all the information about the defendant, with which they have been provided.
6) Where an offender wishes to rely on assistance given to the police, that should be made clear at the earliest opportunity. A court should not readily contemplate granting an adjournment, unless the request to the police has been made in a timely manner and the delay has arisen because the police have been unable to provide the information despite every effort on their behalf.

15-020 **Extent of discount** The court in *Royle* identified a number of factors relevant to identifying the appropriate reduction in a particular case:

i) the quality and quantity of the information provided, including whether it related to trivial or to serious offences (the risk to the informer generally being greater when the criminality concerned is more serious);

ii) the period of time over which the information was provided;
iii) whether it assisted the authorities to bring to justice persons who would not otherwise have been brought to justice, or to prevent or disrupt the commission of serious crime, or to recover property (the value of the assistance being a crucial factor);
iv) the degree of assistance which was provided, including whether the informer gave, or was willing to give, evidence confirming the information he had provided;
v) the degree of risk to which the informer has exposed himself and his family by providing the information or assistance;
vi) the nature and extent of the crime in which the informer has himself been involved, and the extent to which he has been prepared to admit the full extent of his criminality;
vii) whether the informer has relied on the same provision of information and assistance when being sentenced on a previous occasion, or when making an application to the Parole Board (an informer can generally only expect to receive credit once for past information or assistance);
viii) whether the informer has been paid for the assistance provided and, if so, how much; but it was important to note that in *T* [2021] EWCA Crim 1474; [2022] 1 Cr. App. R. (S.) 55, the court emphasised that a financial reward and a reduction in sentence are complementary means of showing offenders that it was worth their while to disclose the criminal activities of others: a financial reward, unless exceptionally generous, should therefore play only a small, if any, part in the sentencer's decision; and
ix) in the case of assistance under s.388 (or the text regime), the fact that an offender has contested his trial may be one of the factors relevant to the extent of the reduction made.

**Information given post-sentence** Since the Court of Appeal is a court of review, however, assistance given to the police or the Crown post-sentence would normally be too late, subject to certain exceptions: *Emsden* [2015] EWCA Crim 2092; [2016] 1 Cr. App. R.(S.) 62; [2016] Crim. L.R. 668. **15-021**

**Taking account of information on appeal** Where assistance has been given by an offender but, by some oversight or misadventure, the judge was unaware of this, the Court of Appeal would consider mitigation which should have been before the Crown Court: *H* [2009] EWCA Crim 2485; [2010] 2 Cr. App. R.(S.) 18; [2010] Crim. L.R. 246. **15-022**

For further details of the "text" procedure, see *X* [1999] 2 Cr. App. R.(S.) 294; [1999] Crim. L.R. 678 and *R* [2002] EWCA Crim 267.

As to the obligation of the authorities to provide a text, and the safeguards in place where an offender believes the context of a text is incorrect: see *AXN and ZAR* [2016] EWCA Crim 590; [2016] 1 W.L.R. 4006; [2016] 2 Cr. App. R.(S.) 33.

### Otherwise than in accordance with the Sentencing Code/Text regimes

Credit can and should be given to the extent that the defendant has given material assistance, even where that assistance falls outside of the Sentencing Code or Text regimes, but reductions would be confined to cases of very serious crime and **15-023** that the degree of assistance would be determinative of the existence and extent of a reduction in sentence: *Campbell* [2018] EWCA Crim 802; [2018] 2 Cr. App. R.(S.) 24.

# GUILTY PLEA, DISCOUNT FOR

## Sentencing Council Reduction in Sentence for Guilty Plea Definitive Guideline (2017) and Sentencing Code s.73

*References: Current Sentencing Practice A1; Archbold 5A-147*

### General

The court must take into account: **16-001**

(a) the stage in the proceedings for the offence at which the offender indicated the intention to plead guilty; and
(b) the circumstances in which the indication was given: SC S.73(2).

The extent of the reduction is a matter of discretion, informed by the application of the Sentencing Council's guideline.

A court which passes a custodial sentence following a plea of guilty should always indicate that it has taken the plea into account: SC s.52(7).

Where, exceptionally, the court considers it would be in the interests of justice to not follow the guideline for guilty pleas the judge needs to explain why they have reached that conclusion, having first identified the sentence from which a reduction would otherwise fall to be made: *Defalco* [2021] EWCA Crim 725; [2021] 2 Cr. App. R.(S.) 50 | [2021] Crim. L.R. 1093.

### Application

The guideline applies to cases in which the first appearance was on or after 1 June 2017: *Guideline* p.4. **16-002**

### General approach

Stage 1 determines the appropriate sentence for the offence(s) in accordance with any offence specific sentencing guideline; **16-003**
Stage 2 determines the level of reduction for a guilty plea in accordance with this guideline;
Stage 3 states the amount of that reduction;
Stage 4 applies the reduction to the appropriate sentence;
Stage 5 follows any further steps in the offence specific guideline to determine the final sentence: *Guideline* p.5.

### Indications

An indication of the type envisaged by the guideline must make a clear acceptance of guilt; an indication of a consideration of pleading guilty will be insufficient: *Reid* [2017] EWCA Crim 1523; [2018] 1 Cr. App. R.(S.) 8. **16-004**

The words "likely to be guilty pleas on a basis" written on the Better Case

Management form filled in at the magistrates' court in respect of a first appearance is insufficient to attract full credit for a plea entered at the first reasonable opportunity: *Davids* [2019] EWCA Crim 553; [2019] 2 Cr. App. R.(S.) 33.

Even where at the magistrates' court it is not procedurally possible for a defendant to enter a guilty plea, there must be an unequivocal indication of the defendant's intention to plead guilty, an indication only that he is likely to plead guilty will not suffice: *Hodgin* [2020] EWCA Crim 1388; [2020] 4 W.L.R. 147; [2021] 1 Cr. App. R.(S.) 50.

**16-005** Informal discussions between advocates as to willingness to indicate pleas that are not indicated in open court to the judge are insufficient to attract full credit: *West* [2019] EWCA Crim 497; [2019] 2 Cr. App. R.(S.) 27.

Admissions in police interview do not constitute an indication and are to be taken account of separately to the indication of a plea at court: *Price* [2018] EWCA Crim 1784; [2019] 1 Cr. App. R.(S.) 24; [2019] Crim. L.R. 249.

In the magistrates' courts in relation to the BCM Form, it is the responsibility of the parties, and not the court, to raise the issue of plea and deal with it at that stage: *Yasin* [2019] EWCA Crim 1729.

**Giving lying evidence in aid of co-defendant**

**16-006** As a general rule, credit for a guilty plea should not be reduced on account of the offender having given lying evidence in support of a co-defendant at their trial: *Wilson* [2018] EWCA Crim 449; [2018] 2 Cr. App. R.(S.) 7; [2018] Crim. L.R. 680.

**Determining the reduction**

**16-007** The maximum level of discount is one-third. However, in a multi-handed case, the first defendant to "break ranks" may be entitled to an additional discount, assessed as mitigation and not part of the guilty plea discount: *Hoddinott* [2019] EWCA Crim 1462; [2020] 1 Cr. App. R.(S.) 26.

**16-008** **Plea indicated at first stage of proceedings** Plea indicated at first stage of proceedings Where a guilty plea is indicated at the first stage of proceedings, a reduction of one-third should be made (subject to the exceptions in section F of the guideline). The first stage will normally be the first hearing at which a plea or indication of plea is sought and recorded by the court.

Admissions in a police interview is not to be considered as part of the plea discount, but rather as personal mitigation: *Price* [2018] EWCA Crim 1784; [2019] 1 Cr. App. R.(S.) 24; [2019] Crim. L.R. 249.

**16-009** **Plea indicated after first stage of proceedings** After the first stage of the proceedings the maximum level of reduction is one-quarter (subject to the exceptions in section F of the guideline). The reduction should be decreased from one-quarter to a maximum of one-tenth on the first day of trial having regard to the time when the guilty plea is first indicated to the court relative to the progress of the case and the trial date (subject to the exceptions in section F of the guideline).

The reduction should normally be decreased further, even to zero, if the guilty plea is entered during the course of the trial.

For the purposes of the guideline, a trial will be deemed to have started when pre-recorded cross-examination has begun: *Guideline* p.5.

Page 6 of the guideline deals with the application of the reduction, in particular in relation to imposing another type of sentence or keeping a case in the magistrates' court rather than committing for sentence. **16-010**

Page 7 of the guideline deals with exceptions to the general approach, including where further advice may have been necessary or where there has been a *Newton* hearing.

Where a defendant does not indicate a guilty plea at the first stage of the proceedings but communicates an intention to plead guilty before they next appear in court, they should not, generally, receive a reduction of more than 25%; there may be exceptional circumstances which justify departing from this, but such circumstances will be rare; if there has been no indication of plea at the first appearance even if arraignment is postponed that will not preserve full credit; even if the judge allows the preservation of credit the maximum will be 25%: *Plaku* [2021] EWCA Crim 568; [2021] 4 W.L.R. 82; [2022] 1 Cr. App. R.(S.) 7.

Where a defendant pleads guilty prior to the start of an adjourned trial but after the original trial date, a defendant cannot expect more than approximately 10% credit as the trial date is fixed by the court would, if the system was functioning properly, have been the actual trial date: *Carter* [2021] EWCA Crim 667; [2022] 1 Cr. App. R.(S.) 2; [2022] Crim. L.R. 64.

### Young offenders

Discount for youth should be made before making a reduction for a guilty plea: *Payne* [2019] EWCA Crim 2219: *RB* [2020] EWCA Crim 643; [2021] 1 Cr. App. R.(S.) 1 | [2021] Crim. L.R. 64. **16-011**

### Dangerousness

While there are legitimate reasons for departing from the general approach of applying the stated reductions listed in the sentencing guidelines, doing so to keep the sentence within the four-year minimum so as to enable the imposition of an extended sentence is not one of them: *Nsumbu* [2017] EWCA Crim 1046; [2017] 2 Cr. App. R.(S.) 51. **16-012**

### Minimum sentences

In the case of an offender aged 18 or over convicted of an offence the sentence for which falls to be imposed under: **16-013**

(a) s.312 (minimum sentence for threatening with weapon or bladed article);
(b) s.313 (minimum of seven years for third class A drug trafficking offence);
(c) s.314 (minimum of three years for third domestic burglary); or
(d) s.315 (minimum sentence for repeat offence involving weapon or bladed article),

the discount for a guilty plea may only have the effect of reducing the period to not less than 80% of that specified: SC s.73(3) and (4).

If the court imposes a serious terrorism sentence, nothing in ss.268C(2) or 282C(2) prevents the court from imposing as the appropriate custodial term a term of any length which is not less than 80% of the term which would otherwise be required.

*The Offensive Weapons Act 2019 (OWA 2019) provisions relating to the offence of possession of corrosive liquid in a public place (and the associated minimum sentence provision) was not in force on 31 October 2024. Therefore the amendment to s.73 to insert into the list contained in s.73(4) the minimum sentence required for an offence contrary to s.6 of the Act) is not yet in force.*

**16-014** Where a young offender aged 16 or 17 pleads guilty to an offence under the Prevention of Crime Act 1953 (PCA 1953) s.1(2B) or 1A(5), or the Criminal Justice Act 1988 (CJA 1988) ss.139(6B), 139A(5B) or 139AA(7), to which the minimum sentences under ss.312 or 315 of the Sentencing Code apply, the court may impose any sentence it considers appropriate and is not limited to the minimum four-month DTO specified in the legislation: SC s.73(5).

**16-015** **Absconding** Where an offender has absconded prior to sentencing, although the approach will depend on the circumstances of the case, the following illustrated the proper approach. There would be some cases where it is appropriate to allow credit for plea in accordance with the guideline in relation to the substantive offence, and to pass a consecutive sentence for the Bail Act 1976 offence. But in other cases, it will be appropriate to reduce the amount of credit for the guilty plea (and to make the sentence for the BA 1976 offence concurrent where there is one): *Williamson* [2020] EWCA Crim 1085; [2021] 1 Cr. App. R. (S.) 29.

**Table of standard percentage reductions in sentence for guilty plea**

**16-016**

| Sentence in Years | Sentence after stated percentage reduction | | | |
|---|---|---|---|---|
| | 33% | 25% | 10% | 5% |
| 1 | 8 months | 9 months | 10.8 months | 11.4 months |
| 2 | 16 months | 18 months | 21.6 months | 22.8 months |
| 3 | 2 years | 2 years 3 months | 2 years 8.4 months | 2 years 10.2 months |
| 4 | 2 years 8 months | 3 years | 3 years 7.2 months | 3 years 9.6 months |
| 5 | 3 years 4 months | 3 years 9 months | 4 years 6 months | 4 years 9 months |
| 6 | 4 years | 4 years 6 months | 5 years 4.8 months | 5 years 8.4 months |
| 7 | 4 years 8 months | 5 years 3 months | 6 years 3.6 months | 6 years 7.8 months |
| 8 | 5 years 4 months | 6 years | 7 years 2.4 months | 7 years 7.2 months |

| **Sentence in Years** | **Sentence after stated percentage reduction** | | | |
|---|---|---|---|---|
| | **33%** | **25%** | **10%** | **5%** |
| 9 | 6 years | 6 years 9 months | 8 years 1.2 months | 8 years 6.6 months |
| 10 | 6 years 8 months | 7 years 6 months | 9 years | 9 years 6 months |
| 11 | 7 years 4 months | 8 years 3 months | 9 years 10.8 months | 10 years 5.4 months |
| 12 | 8 years | 9 years | 10 years 9.6 months | 11 years 4.8 months |
| 13 | 8 years 8 months | 9 years 9 months | 11 years 8.4 months | 12 years 4.2 months |
| 14 | 9 years 4 months | 10 years 6 months | 12 years 7.2 months | 13 years 3.6 months |
| 15 | 10 years | 11 years 3 months | 13 years 6 months | 14 years 3 months |
| 16 | 10 years 8 months | 12 years | 14 years 4.8 months | 15 years 2.5 months |
| 17 | 11 years 4 months | 12 years 9 months | 15 years 3.6 months | 16 years 1.8 months |
| 18 | 12 years | 13 years 6 months | 16 years 2.4 months | 17 years 1.2 months |
| 19 | 12 years 8 months | 14 years 3 months | 17 years 1.2 months | 18 years 0.6 months |
| 20 | 13 years 4 months | 15 years | 18 years | 19 years |

Notes

*All figures in this table have been rounded mathematically to one decimal place. These figures represent the precise reductions and of course, it is a matter for the individual judge to decide whether to increase or decrease that figure to the nearest whole month.*

# CONCURRENT AND CONSECUTIVE SENTENCES

*References: Current Sentencing Practice A1; Archbold 5A-191*

## General

There is no inflexible rule governing whether sentences should be structured as concurrent or consecutive components. The overriding principle is that the overall sentence must be just and proportionate. **17-001**

The principle of totality comprises two elements:

(1) all courts, when sentencing for more than a single offence, should pass a total sentence which reflects all the offending behaviour before it and is just and proportionate. This is so whether the sentences are structured as concurrent or consecutive. Therefore, concurrent sentences will ordinarily be longer than a single sentence for a single offence.

(2) it is usually impossible to arrive at a just and proportionate sentence for multiple offending simply by adding together notional single sentences. It is necessary to address the offending behaviour, together with the factors personal to the offender as a whole: *Totality Guideline*.

As a matter of generality:

(a) whether a judge had applied totality was a question of substance and not form and therefore the fact that a judge made a single generalised statement towards the end of their sentencing remarks to the effect that they had considered totality was perfectly adequate;

(b) the *Totality Guideline* made clear that the purpose behind a judge taking totality into account was to ensure that the final sentence was just and proportionate but there is no need for a judge to expressly use the expression "just and proportionate";

(c) totality was designed to ensure that the sentencing exercise was not formulaic and thus assists a judge to arrive at the correct sentence;

(d) the stages or steps set out in the Guideline were intended to guide how the judge should "consider" the structuring of the sentence to arrive at a just and appropriate end result. The steps set out were not drafting instructions: *Bailey* [2020] EWCA Crim 1719; [2021] 4 W.L.R. 114; [2021] 2 Cr. App. R.(S.) 15.

## Consecutive sentences

Consecutive sentences of imprisonment should not normally be passed in respect of offences which arise out of the same transaction or incident, but may be passed in such cases in exceptional circumstances. **17-002**

Consecutive sentences should normally be passed in the following cases:

(a) where a burglar used violence towards an occupant of premises who interrupted them;

(b) where violence is used to resist arrest for the primary offence;

(c) where an offender is convicted of an offence under the Firearms Act 1968 committed by having a firearm with them at the time of another offence;
(d) where one offence is committed while the offender is on bail in connection with the other offence;
(e) where a community order is revoked following the offender's conviction of a further offence;
(f) where a suspended sentence is activated following the offender's conviction of a further offence;
(g) where an offender is convicted of doing an act tending to pervert the course of justice in relation to the other offence; and
(h) where offences are of the same or similar kind but where the overall criminality will not be reflected by concurrent sentences, e.g. where there are multiple victims or where domestic or sexual abuse is committed against the same victim. However, where, e.g., injuries are caused to multiple victims by a single piece of dangerous driving, a concurrent sentence would normally be appropriate: *Totality Guideline*.

**Concurrent sentences**

**17-003** Concurrent sentences will usually be appropriate where multiple offences arise out of the same incident or facts or there is a series of offences of the same or similar kind, especially when committed against the same person: *Totality Guideline*.

**Particular scenarios**

**17-004** **Multiple offences** In a serious, multiple-count case the sentencing judge should endeavour to impose one term of imprisonment which reflects the defendant's overall criminality as that produces clarity and simplicity: *C* [2007] EWCA Crim 680; [2007] 3 All E.R. 735; [2007] 2 Cr. App. R.(S.) 98; *Wilding* [2019] EWCA Crim 694; [2019] 2 Cr. App. R.(S.) 37.

**Sentencing for offences committed prior to other offences for which a defendant has been convicted and sentenced** The court should first reach the appropriate sentence for the instant offences, taking into account totality in respect of the instant offences alone. The court then has a discretion whether to make further allowance to take into account the earlier sentence (whether or not that sentence has been served in full). The court should consider all the circumstances in deciding what, if any, impact the earlier sentence should have on the new sentence. It is not simply a matter of considering the overall sentence as though the previous court had been able to sentence all the offences and then deducting the earlier sentence from that figure.

A non-exhaustive list of circumstances could include:

(a) How recently the earlier sentence had been imposed, taking account of the reason for the gap and the offender's conduct in the interim.
(b) The similarity of the offences sentenced earlier to the instant offences.
(c) Whether the offences sentenced earlier and instant offences overlapped in time.
(d) Whether on a previous occasion the offender could have "cleaned the slate" by bringing the instant offences to the police's attention.
(e) Whether taking the earlier sentences into account would give the offender

an undeserved bonus-this will particularly be the case where a technical rule of sentencing has been avoided or where, for example, the court has been denied the opportunity to consider totality in terms of dangerousness.

(f) Whether the instant offence qualifies for a mandatory minimum sentence.

(g) The offender's age and health, and whether their health had significantly deteriorated.

(h) Whether, if the earlier and instant sentences had been passed together as consecutive sentences, the overall sentence would have required downward adjustment to achieve a just and proportionate sentence.

If the offender is still subject to the previous sentence:

(1) Where the offender is currently serving a custodial sentence for the offences sentenced earlier, consider whether the new sentence should be concurrent with or consecutive to that sentence taking into account the circumstances set out above and the general principles in this guideline.

(2) Where the offender is serving an indeterminate sentence for the offences sentenced earlier, see also the guidance in the section "Indeterminate sentences" below.

(3) Where the offender has been released on licence or post sentence supervision from a custodial sentence for the offences sentenced earlier, a custodial sentence for the instant offences cannot run consecutively to that earlier sentence, including where the offender has been recalled to custody—see the relevant guidance in the section below "Existing determinate sentence, where determinate sentence to be passed": Totality Guideline.

See also *Green* [2019] EWCA Crim 196; [2019] 4 W.L.R. 37.

## Life sentences

The Sentencing Council's *Totality Guideline* states that it is generally undesirable to order an indeterminate sentence to be served consecutively to any other determinate period of imprisonment. The guideline recommends that the court should instead order the sentence to run concurrently but can adjust the minimum term for the new offence to reflect half of any period still remaining to be served under the existing sentence (to take account of the early release provisions for determinate sentences). **17-005**

For an offender serving an indeterminate sentence in circumstances where the court wishes to impose another indeterminate sentence, the guideline states that where necessary the court can order an indeterminate sentence to run consecutively to an indeterminate sentence passed on an earlier occasion. In such circumstances, the second sentence will commence on the expiration of the minimum term of the original sentence and the offender will become eligible for a parole review after serving both minimum terms. The court should consider the length of the aggregate minimum terms that must be served before the offender will be eligible for consideration by the Parole Board. If this is not just and proportionate, the court can adjust the minimum term.

Finally, in the case of an offender serving an indeterminate sentence in circumstances where the court wishes to impose a determinate sentence, the court can order the determinate sentence to run consecutively to the indeterminate sentence. The determinate sentence will commence on the expiry of the minimum term of the indeterminate sentence and the offender will become eligible for a parole review after serving half of the determinate sentence (see p.11 of the guideline and *Taylor* [2011] EWCA Crim 2236; [2012] 1 W.L.R. 2113; [2012] 1 Cr. App. R.(S.) 75).

**Extended determinate sentences**

**17-006** It is not lawful to make extended sentences partly concurrent and partly consecutive: see *Francis* [2014] EWCA Crim 631.

There is no objection to imposing an extended sentence consecutive to a determinate sentence (either on the same occasion, or in addition to an existing determinate sentence): *Brown* [2006] EWCA Crim 1996; [2007] 1 Cr. App. R.(S.) 77; [2006] Crim. L.R. 1082 and *Hibbert* [2015] EWCA Crim 507; [2015] 2 Cr. App. R.(S.) 15.

However, the Court of Appeal has repeatedly stated that it is undesirable to impose a determinate sentence consecutive to an extended sentence (see e.g. *Brown* and *Prior* [2014] EWCA Crim 1290).

**17-007** This issue was considered in *Ulhaqdad* [2017] EWCA Crim 1216; [2018] 4 W.L.R. 65; [2017] 2 Cr. App. R.(S.) 46, where the court established that the order in which a court imposed an extended sentence and a determinate sentence (where those sentences are made to run consecutively) created no practical difficulty for the prison service in relation to the calculation of sentences and release dates, etc. However, having identified no practical or principled reason for the guidance given in *Brown*, the court in *Ulhaqdad* maintained the status quo. Therefore, the position remains that where extended and determinate sentences are being imposed to run consecutively, the determinate sentence should be imposed first.

Two further points remain. First, that in *Prior*, the court suggested that an alternative approach was to increase the custodial term of the extended sentence and make the sentences run concurrently. Secondly, despite the guidance in *Brown*, there is nothing unlawful about imposing an extended sentence consecutive to a determinate sentence in an appropriate case: *Hibbert* [2015] EWCA Crim 507; [2015] 2 Cr. App. R.(S.) 15.

In *B* [2015] EWCA Crim 1295; [2015] 2 Cr. App. R.(S.) 78; [2015] Crim. L.R. 1009, the Court of Appeal imposed two consecutive extended sentences where the total extended licence period was 10 years, that being in excess of the statutory maximum of eight years, this being a sexual case.

A five-judge court in *Thompson* [2018] EWCA Crim 639; [2018] 1 W.L.R. 4429; [2018] 2 Cr. App. R.(S.) 19 confirmed that this was lawful though noted that the circumstances in which it would be appropriate would be "exceptional".

**Licence Revoked**

**17-008** A court cannot order a term of imprisonment to commence on the expiration of any other sentence of imprisonment from which the offender has already been released and in respect of which the offender's licence has been revoked: SC s.225 and *McStravick* [2018] EWCA Crim 1207; [2018] 2 Cr. App. R.(S.) 26.

# AGE OF OFFENDER

## SENTENCING CODE s.405

*References: Archbold 5A-367*

### General rule

For the purposes of the availability of custodial sentences and non-custodial sentences, the general rule is that the age of the offender is their age on the day of conviction: SC s.405. **18-001**

### Children and young offenders

As to the severity of the sentence, the starting point for those aged under 18 at the date of the commission of the offence is the sentence that would have been imposed at that date: *Ghafoor* [2002] EWCA Crim 1857; [2003] 1 Cr. App. R.(S.) 84; [2002] Crim. L.R. 739. **18-002**

Where proceedings in respect of a young person are begun prior to the defendant attaining the age of 18, and where they attain that age before sentencing, the court may deal with the case and make any order which it could have made if the defendant had not attained that age: Children and Young Persons Act 1963 (CYPA 1963) s.29(1).

### Committal for sentence

An offender committed to the Crown Court for sentence under ss.14-20 of the Sentencing Code will be sentenced on the basis of their age at the date of their conviction: SC ss.21-23. **18-003**

### Determining the offender's age

For the purposes of sentences of imprisonment, detention in a young offender institution, detention under s.250 of the Sentencing Code, or DTOs, the age of an offender is deemed to be what it appears to the court to be, after the court has considered any available evidence, but where it is apparent that the age of the offender is in doubt or dispute, the court should adjourn and obtain proper evidence of age before sentencing: Criminal Justice Act 1982 (CJA 1982) s.1(6) and *Steed* (1990-91) 12 Cr. App. R.(S.) 230; [1990] Crim. L.R. 816. For details of the proper procedure when making an age assessment finding, see *Mohammed* [2021] EWCA Crim 1375; [2022] Crim. L.R. 152. **18-004**

### Determining which custodial sentence applies by virtue of defendant's age

The following table sets out the availability of custodial sentences depending on the offender's age at conviction. The table contains the form of each custodial sentence which must be imposed on offenders in each age category. **18-005**

| **Sentencing Order** | **Age at conviction** | | |
|---|---|---|---|
| | 10–17 | 18–20 | 21+ |
| *Mandatory life (murder)* | Detention during HM's Pleasure | Custody for life* | Imprisonment for life* |
| *Automatic life* (ss.273 and 283) | Not available | Custody for life | Imprisonment for life |
| *Discretionary life* (ss.274, 285 and common law) | Detention for life | Custody for life | Imprisonment for life |
| *Serious terrorism sentence* | Not available | Serious terrorism sentence of detention in a young offender institution | Serious terrorism sentence of imprisonment |
| *Extended sentence (ss.266 and 279)* | Extended sentence of detention | Extended sentence of detention in a young offender institution | Extended sentence of imprisonment |
| *Special custodial sentence for offenders of particular concern (ss.265 and 278)* | Not available | Detention in a young offender institution | Imprisonment |
| *Determinate sentence of custody (common law, ss.250 and 262)* | Detention under s.250 / DTO | Detention in a young offender institution | Imprisonment |
| *Suspended sentence order (ss.265 and 277)* | Not available | Suspended sentence of detention in a young offender institution | Suspended sentence of imprisonment |
| *Special custodial sentence for young terrorist offenders of particular concern (s.252A)* | Detention under s.250 | Not available | Not available |

** Note that where an offence of murder is committed by an offender aged 10–17, the sentence will always be one of Detention during HM's Pleasure.*

# SENTENCING AFTER A RETRIAL

## Criminal Appeal Act 1968 Sch.2 para.2

*Note: These provisions do not appear to apply to a venire de novo ordered by the Court of Appeal.*

### General

Where a person is convicted after a retrial ordered by the Court of Appeal (Criminal Division) under the Criminal Appeal Act 1968 (CAA 1968) s.7, the court may pass in respect of the offence any sentence authorised by law, not being a sentence of greater severity than that passed on the original conviction: CAA 1968 Sch.2 para.2(1). **19-001**

The court may pass any sentence passed in respect of that offence on the original conviction notwithstanding that, on the date of the conviction on retrial, the offender has ceased to be of an age at which such a sentence could otherwise be passed: CAA 1968 Sch.2 para.2(2).

### Approach

When sentencing after a retrial, the correct approach is to assess the offender's culpability on the basis of the evidence in the retrial and in accordance with the sentencing guidelines. The earlier trial and sentence should not be considered at that stage. The only relevance of the previous sentence was that the sentence imposed on the retrial could not be more severe than the first: *Bett* [2017] EWCA Crim 1909; [2018] 1 Cr. App. R.(S.) 29; [2018] R.T.R. 20. **19-002**

As to what constitutes a more "severe" sentence, the position is somewhat unclear. While *Thompson* [2018] EWCA Crim 639; [2018] 1 W.L.R. 4429; [2018] 2 Cr. App. R.(S.) 19 suggested that a particularly important consideration would be entitlement to release under a custodial sentence (i.e. the date on which release is automatic), the later decision in *KPR* [2018] EWCA Crim 2357; [2019] 1 Cr. App. R.(S.) 36; [2019] Crim. L.R. 548 appeared to weaken the emphasis on the maximum period which may be spent in custody before first release in favour of an emphasis on the eligibility for release (i.e. the earliest time at which the offender may be released).

### Start date of sentence

If the offender is sentenced to imprisonment or other detention, the sentence begins to run from the time when a similar sentence passed at the original trial would have begun to run: CAA 1968 Sch.2 para.2(3). **19-003**

### Calculating time to be served

In computing the term of the sentence or the period for which the offender may be detained, any time before their conviction on retrial which would have been **19-004** disregarded in computing that term or period if the sentence had been passed at the original trial and the original conviction had not been quashed, and any time during which they were released on bail under s.8(2) of the CAA 1968, is disregarded: CAA 1968 Sch.2 para.2(3).

### Credit for time on remand

**19-005** The judge should make appropriate orders in respect of any time spent on bail subject to a qualifying curfew condition, in relation to any sentence imposed on conviction on retrial as if they had been imposed on the original conviction: CAA 1968 Sch.2 para.2(4).

# B: MATTERS ARISING PRE-SENTENCE

## *GOODYEAR* INDICATIONS (ADVANCE INDICATION OF SENTENCE)

### *Goodyear* [2005] EWCA Crim 888; [2005] 2 Cr. App. R. 20

*References: Current Sentencing Practice A2; Archbold 5A-126*

**Objective**

The objective of the *Goodyear* guidelines is to safeguard against the creation or appearance of judicial pressure on a defendant and allow the defendant to make a more informed decision whether or not to plead guilty: *Goodyear* at [53] and CPD 2023 Indications of Sentence § 9.4. **20-001**

**Availability**

Prior to pleading guilty, it is open to a defendant in the Crown Court to request from the judge an indication of the maximum sentence that would be imposed if a guilty plea were to be tendered at that stage in the proceedings: CPD 2023 Indications of Sentence § 9.4. **20-002**

An indication should not be sought while there is any uncertainty about an acceptable plea or the factual basis of sentencing. An indication should not be sought on a basis of hypothetical facts. Where appropriate, there must be an agreed, written basis of plea. Unless there is, the judge should refuse to give an indication: otherwise they may become inappropriately involved in negotiations about the acceptance of pleas, and any agreed basis of plea: *Goodyear* at [62].

A *Goodyear* indication is not available in the magistrates' courts and magistrates should confine themselves to the statutory arrangements in CJA 2003 Sch.3: *Goodyear* at [78].

The judge should only give a *Goodyear* indication if one is requested by the defendant, although the judge can, in an appropriate case, remind the defence advocate of the defendant's entitlement to seek an advance indication of sentence: *Goodyear* at [55]–[56] and CPD 2023 Indications of Sentence § 9.4. **20-003**

An informal discussion between counsel and the judge based on a hypothetical basis of plea is insufficient to amount to the *Goodyear* procedure and therefore could not bind the judge's hands when sentencing: *Hobbs* [2019] EWCA Crim 2137; [2020] 1 Cr. App. R.(S.) 57.

Whether or not the judge has given an appropriate reminder, the defendant's advocate should not seek an indication without written authority, signed by their client, that the client wishes to seek an indication: *Goodyear* at [64].

A judge should not give an indication of sentence in advance of a *Newton* hearing, not only because the judge will likely find it hard to predict what basis they would be sentencing upon, but because it will not be known to what extent the amount of credit for pleading guilty will need to be reduced: *Martin* [2013] EWCA Crim 2565; [2014] 2 Cr. App. R.(S) 21 at [11]. **20-004**

The court retains a limited jurisdiction to provide an indication of sentence not following an application by the defendant. The court may provide an indication that the sentence would or would not take a particular form (a fine, a community order etc.), however this is only available where the indication is whether the defendant pleads guilty or not guilty: *Turner* [1970] 2 Q.B. 321; *AG's Ref (AB)* [2021] EWCA Crim 1959; [2022] 2 Cr. App. R. (S.) 17; [2022] Crim. L.R. 516.

**Judge entitled to refuse or defer the application**

**20-005** In whatever circumstances an advance indication of sentence is sought, the judge retains an unfettered discretion to refuse to give one: *Goodyear* at [57]. Just as the judge may refuse to give an indication, they may reserve their position until such time as they feel able to give one, for example, until a pre-sentence report is available: *Goodyear* at [58].

The judge may or may not give reasons. In many cases involving an outright refusal, the judge would probably conclude that it would be inappropriate to give reasons. If the judge has in mind to defer an indication, the probability is that the reasons would be explained and further indicate the circumstances in which, and when, they would be prepared to respond to a request for a sentence indication: *Goodyear* at [59].

If at any stage the judge refuses to give an indication (as opposed to deferring it) it remains open to the defendant to seek a further indication at a later stage. However, once the judge has refused to give an indication, they should not normally initiate the process, except, where it arises, to indicate that the circumstances had changed sufficiently for them to be prepared to consider a renewed application for an indication: *Goodyear* at [60].

**Giving the indication**

**20-006** Any advance indication of sentence to be given by the judge should normally be confined to the maximum sentence if a plea of guilty were tendered at the stage at which the indication is sought: *Goodyear* at [54].

The hearing should normally take place in open court, with a full recording of the entire proceedings, and both sides represented, in the defendant's presence: *Goodyear* at [75]. Reporting restrictions should normally be imposed: CPD 2023 Indications of Sentence § 9.4.9.

**Effect of the indication**

**20-007** Once an indication has been given, it is binding and remains binding on the judge who has given it, and it also binds any other judge who becomes responsible for the case. In principle, the judge who has given an indication should, where possible, deal with the case immediately, and if that is not possible, any subsequent hearings should be listed before that judge: *Goodyear* at [61].

The indication is binding save in exceptional circumstances, such as arose in *Newman* [2010] EWCA Crim 1566; [2011] 1 Cr. App. R.(S.) 68; [2010] Crim. L.R. 781 in which the judge gave an indicated but subsequently stated he had been wrong to do so and that the indication was wholly inadequate.

Revisions to *Goodyear* indications should be very much the exception, and can only be made in a manner which is fair to the defendant: in other words, where the matter can be revised without the defendant sustaining any prejudice other than mere disappointment: *Newman* at [18].

The right of the Attorney General to refer a sentence to the Court of Appeal on the ground that it is unduly lenient is not affected by the giving of an advance indication of sentence. The defendant's entitlement to apply for leave to appeal against sentence if, for example, insufficient allowance has been made for matters of genuine mitigation, is similarly unaffected: *Goodyear* at [71]–[72]. **20-008**

If the defendant does not plead guilty, the indication will not thereafter bind the court.

In *Davies* [2015] EWCA Crim 930; [2015] 2 Cr. App. R.(S.) 57, where a *Goodyear* indication had been given after which the defendant had pleaded guilty, but where the defendant had subsequently absconded, the court held that the judge was not entitled to depart from the indication.

**Advocates' duties**

The defendant's advocate is responsible for ensuring that the defendant fully appreciates that: **20-009**

(a) they should not plead guilty unless they are guilty;
(b) any sentence indication given by the judge remains subject to the entitlement of the Attorney General (where it arises) to refer an unduly lenient sentence to the Court of Appeal;
(c) any indication given by the judge reflects the situation at the time when it is given, and that if a "guilty plea" is not tendered in the light of that indication the indication ceases to have effect; and
(d) any indication which may be given relates only to the matters about which an indication is sought: *Goodyear* at [65].

The prosecution advocate is responsible for the following:

(a) if there is no final agreement about the plea to the indictment, or the basis of plea, and the defence nevertheless proceeds to seek an indication, which the judge appears minded to give, prosecuting counsel should remind the judge of the guidance given in *Goodyear*, that normally speaking an indication of sentence should not be given until the basis of the plea has been agreed, or the judge has concluded that they can properly deal with the case without the need for a *Newton* hearing;
(b) if an indication is sought, the prosecution should normally enquire whether the judge is in possession of, or has had access to, all the evidence relied on by the prosecution, including any impact statement from the victim of the crime, as well as any information of relevant previous convictions recorded against the defendant;
(c) if the process has been properly followed, it should not normally be necessary for counsel for the prosecution, before the judge gives any indication, to do more than, first, draw the judge's attention to any minimum or mandatory statutory sentencing requirements, and where they would be expected

to offer the judge assistance with relevant guideline cases, or the views of the Sentencing Council, to invite the judge to allow them to do so, and second, where it applies, to remind the judge that the position of the Attorney General to refer any eventual sentencing decision as unduly lenient is not affected;

in any event, counsel should not say anything which may create the impression that the sentence indication has the support or approval of the Crown: *Goodyear* at [70].

**Complex cases**

**20-010** Judges are most unlikely to be able to give an indication of sentence in complicated or difficult cases unless issues between the prosecution and defence have been addressed and resolved. In such cases, no less than seven days' notice of an intention to seek an indication should be given to the prosecution and to the court. If an application is made without notice when it should have been given, the judge may conclude that any inevitable adjournment should have been avoided and that the discount for pleading guilty should be reduced accordingly: *Goodyear* at [74].

**Dangerousness**

**20-011** If the offence is a specified offence such that the defendant might be liable to an assessment of "dangerousness" in accordance with the Sentencing Code it is unlikely that the necessary material for such an assessment will be available. The court can still proceed to give an indication of sentence, but should state clearly the limitations of the indication that can be given.

There is scope, additionally, for a judge to give what might be termed a qualified *Goodyear* indication, depending on the ultimate conclusion as to dangerousness, and applicable only if a determinate sentence was ultimately imposed, see *Newman* at [16].

**Subsequent trials**

**20-012** The fact that notice has been given, and any reference to a request for a sentence indication, or the circumstances in which it was sought, would be inadmissible in any subsequent trial: *Goodyear* at [76].

# DEFERMENT ORDER

## Sentencing Code ss.3-13

*References: Current Sentencing Practice A2; Archbold 5A-224*

### Making the order

**What is a deferment order?** A "deferment order" is an order deferring passing sentence on an offender in respect of one or more offences until the date specified in the order, to enable a court, in dealing with the offender, to have regard to: 21-001

(a) the offender's conduct after conviction (including, where appropriate, the offender's making reparation for the offence); or
(b) any change in the offender's circumstances: SC s.3(1).

**Availability** A deferment order is available to the Crown Court or a magistrates' court in where: 21-002

(a) the offender is before the court to be dealt with for the offence; and
(b) no previous deferment order has been made in respect of the offence.

But a deferment order is not available to a magistrates' court dealing with an offender in respect of an offence for which s.85(1)(a) (compulsory referral conditions) requires the court to make a referral order: SC s.4(1) and (2).

If a custodial sentence of two years or less could never be justified for the offending, and the sentence therefore could not be suspended, a decision to impose a deferred sentence will always be improper: *AG's Ref (Blackadder)* [2024] EWCA Crim 318; [2024] 2 Cr. App. R. (S.) 16.

**Making the order** A court may make a deferment order in respect of an offence only if: 21-003

(a) the offender consents;
(b) the offender undertakes to comply with any deferment requirements the court proposes to impose;
(c) if those requirements include a restorative justice requirement, s.7(2) (consent of participants in restorative justice activity) is satisfied; and
(d) the court is satisfied, having regard to the nature of the offence and the character and circumstances of the offender, that it would be in the interests of justice to make the order: SC s.5(1).

**Maximum period** Sentence may be deferred for a period of not more than six months: SC s.5(2). 21-004

**Bail** Where sentence is deferred, the defendant cannot be bailed and thus cannot be subject to bail conditions: *Mizan* [2020] EWCA Crim 1553; [2021] 1 Cr. App. R.(S.) 51. It is accordingly important that deferment requirements address any concerns the court would otherwise address with bail conditions. 21-005

**21-006** **Adding requirements** A deferment order may impose requirements ("deferment requirements") as to the offender's conduct during the period of deferment. The requirements may include:

(a) requirements as to the residence of the offender during all or part of the period of deferment;
(b) restorative justice requirements: SC s.3(2) and (3).

**21-007** **Requirements** The requirements which the court may require the offender to comply with during the period of deferment are not specified, but include restorative justice requirements (see below). The court may appoint an officer of probation services or other person to act as a supervisor: SC s.8(1).

The statutory power is not limited to the requirements which may be imposed in connection with a community order.

**21-008** **Restorative justice requirements** A restorative justice requirement is a requirement to participate in an activity:

(a) where the participants consist of, or include, the offender and one or more of the victims;
(b) which aims to maximise the offender's awareness of the impact of the offending concerned on the victims; and
(c) which gives an opportunity to a victim or victims to talk about, or by other means express experience of, the offending and its impact: SC s.7(1).

A restorative justice requirement may not be imposed as a deferment requirement without the consent of every person who would be a participant in the activity: SC s.7(2). A supervisor and the offender, however, do not count as proposed participants for these purposes: SC s.7(3).

**After period of deferment**

**21-009** **Attorney General's reference** An order deferring the passing of sentence is a sentence for the purposes of the CJA 1988 s.36 and therefore can be referred: *Attorney General's Reference (No.22 of 1992)* [1994] 1 All E.R. 105; (1993) 14 Cr. App. R.(S.) 435; [1993] Crim. L.R. 227.

**21-010** **Sentencing after deferment order** Where an offender who is subject to a deferment order is being dealt with for any offence in respect of which the order was made:

(a) by the court which made the order ("the original court"):
   (i) at the end of the period of deferment, in accordance with the deferment order;
   (ii) under s.9(3) (failure to comply with deferment requirement); or
   (iii) under s.10(2) (original court dealing with offender following conviction during period of deferment); or
(b) by any court under s.10(5) (conviction during period of deferment: convicting court dealing with offender),

the court may deal with the offender for the offence in any way in which the original court could have dealt with the offender for the offence if it had not made a deferment order: SC s.11(1) and (2).

Where a magistrates' court is dealing with the offender, its power under that subsection includes, in particular, the power in s.14 to commit the offender to the Crown Court for sentence: SC s.11(3).

Where a deferment order has been made in respect of an offence, the court which deals with the offender for the offence may have regard to:

(a) the offender's conduct after conviction; or
(b) any change in the offender's circumstances: SC s.6(1).

The matters to which the court may have regard in dealing with the offender include, in particular:

(a) where appropriate, the making by the offender of reparation for the offence; and
(b) the extent to which the offender has complied with any deferment requirements: SC s.6(2).

**Failure to attend** Where: 21-011

(a) the court which made a deferment order proposes to deal with the offender on the date specified in the order; or
(b) the offender does not appear on that date, the court may:
    (i) issue a summons requiring the offender to appear before the court at the time and place specified in the summons; or
    (ii) issue a warrant for the offender's arrest which requires the offender to be brought before the court at the time and place specified in the warrant: SC s.6(3) and (4).

**Failure to comply with requirement** If the offender fails to comply with the requirements imposed during the period of deferment, they may be brought before the court and dealt with before the end of the period of deferment: SC s.9. 21-012

**Convicted of an offence during period of deferment** A court which has deferred sentence may deal with the offender before the end of the period of deferment if they are convicted in Great Britain of an offence during the deferment period: SC s.10(2). 21-013

The court which passes sentence on the offender for the later offence may also deal with the offender for the offence or offences in respect of which the deferment order was made (if this has not already been done), except where:

(a) the deferment order was made by the Crown Court; and
(b) the court which passes sentence on the offender for the later offence is a magistrates' court: SC s.10(5) and (6).

# COMMITTAL FOR SENTENCE

## Sentencing Code ss.14–24

*References: Current Sentencing Practice A2; Archbold 5A-245*

### Adult and corporate offenders (s.14)

Where an offender aged 18 or over or a corporation is convicted on summary trial of an offence triable either way, they may be committed to the Crown Court for sentence, either in custody or on bail, if the court by which they are convicted is of the opinion that the offence or the combination of the offence and one or more offences associated with it was so serious that the Crown Court should, in the court's opinion, have the power to deal with the offender in any way in which it could deal with them if they had been convicted on indictment. **22-001**

*(This provision does not apply to offences where the section is excluded by reference to the value of the property involved.)*

A person committed for sentence under this provision may be dealt with by the Crown Court in any way in which the Crown Court could deal with them had they been convicted of the offence on the indictment. Thus, the sentencing powers are those of the Crown Court at the date of the conviction, and the offender's age for these purposes is that at conviction.

### "Dangerous" adult offenders (s.15)

Where an offender aged 18 or over is convicted on a summary trial of: **22-002**

(a) an either-way offence which is a specified offence for the purposes of s.306 of the Sentencing Code and it appears to the court that the criteria for the imposition of an extended sentence under ss.266 or 279 of the Sentencing Code are met; or
(b) to an offence specified in Sch.17A to the Sentencing Code, and the court is of the view that a serious terrorism sentence may have to be imposed, the court must commit the offender either in custody or on bail to the Crown Court for sentence.

In reaching any decision or their taking any steps under this section, the court is not to be bound by any indication of sentence given in respect of the offence under the Magistrates' Courts Act 1980 (MCA 1980) s.20, and nothing the court does under this section may be challenged or be the subject of any appeal in any court on the ground that it is not consistent with an indication of sentence.

A person committed for sentence under this provision may be dealt with by the Crown Court in any way in which the Crown Court could deal with them had they been convicted of the offence on the indictment. Thus, the sentencing powers are those of the Crown Court at the date of the conviction, and the offender's age for these purposes is that at conviction.

### Adult offenders: related offences (s.18)

22-003 Where a magistrates' court has convicted an offender aged 18 or over of an offence triable either way following an indication of a guilty plea, and has sent the offender to the Crown Court for trial for one or more related offences, it may commit the offender in custody or on bail to the Crown Court to be dealt with in respect of the offence.

The offender may be committed for sentence even though the court is not satisfied that greater punishment should be inflicted for those offences than the magistrates' court has power to inflict.

If the offender has indicated an intention to plead guilty to certain offences, but the magistrates' court has not yet determined whether to send the offender to the Crown Court for trial in respect of related offences, the magistrates' court must adjourn the proceedings in relation to the offences in respect of which the offender has indicated an intention to plead guilty, and if it sends the offender to the Crown Court for trial for the related offence or offences, it may then commit the offender for sentence.

22-004 If the magistrates' court commits an offender under this provision, it should state whether it has power also to commit the offender under s.14.

A person committed for sentence under this provision may be dealt with by the Crown Court in any way in which the Crown Court could deal with them had they been convicted of the offence on the indictment. Thus, the sentencing powers are those of the Crown Court at the date of the conviction, and the offender's age for these purposes is that at conviction.

If the defendant is not convicted of those offences for which they were sent for trial, and the magistrates' court has not stated that it had power to commit the offender under s.14, the Crown Court must deal with the offender for those offences in a manner in which the magistrates' court could have.

This procedure should not be used unless the defendant has been sent for trial for related offences. A defendant who has been convicted by a magistrates' court after indicating an intention to plead guilty in other circumstances should be committed under s.14.

### Young offenders: summary trial of certain serious offences (s.16)

22-005 Where on the summary trial of an offence listed in s.249(1) of the Sentencing Code, a person aged under 18 is convicted of the offence and the court is of the opinion that the offence or the combination of the offence and one or more offences associated with it was such that the Crown Court should in the court's opinion have power to deal with the offender by imposing a sentence of detention under s.250 of the Sentencing Code, the court may commit them in custody or on bail to the Crown Court for sentence.

Under s.16, the youth court was not making a once and for all decision at the point of allocation and, accordingly, taking the prosecution case at its highest was no longer necessary and whether there was a "*real prospect*" of a sentence in excess of the youth court powers required a different emphasis. In most cases, it would generally be after conviction when the assessment could and should be made. The observations in *Southampton Youth Court* [2004] EWHC 2912 (Admin); [2005] 2 Cr. App. R.(S.) 30; [2005] Crim. L.R. 395 that a Crown Court trial for a youth "*should be reserved for the most serious cases*" remained entirely apposite: *South Tyneside Youth Court and B* [2015] EWHC 1455 (Admin); [2015] 2 Cr. App. R.(S.) 59; [2015] Crim. L.R. 746.

A person committed for sentence under this provision may be dealt with by the Crown Court in any way in which the Crown Court could deal with them had they been convicted of the offence on the indictment. Thus, the sentencing powers are those of the Crown Court at the date of the conviction, and the offender's age for these purposes is that at conviction.

**Young offenders: certain terrorist offences (s.16A)**

Where on summary trial of an offence within s.252A(1)(a) (terrorism offences attracting special sentence for offenders of particular concern), a person is convicted of the offence, the person is aged under 18 at the time of conviction, and the court is of the opinion that **22-006**

(i) the offence; or

(ii) the combination of the offence and one or more offences associated with it, was such that the Crown Court should have power to deal with the offender by imposing a sentence of detention under s.252A for a term of more than two years, the court may commit the offender in custody or on bail to the Crown Court for sentence in accordance with s.22(2).

The court may also commit to the Crown Court in respect of other offences (see s.20).

The Crown Court is not bound to deal with the offender in accordance with s.252A.

Where a young defendant is committed for sentence under this provision the Crown Court may deal with the offender in any way in which it could deal with them if they had been convicted of the offence on indictment. Thus, the sentencing powers are those of the Crown Court at the date of the conviction, and the offender's age for these purposes is that at conviction. **22-007**

Nothing in s.17 prevents the court from committing a person convicted of a specified offence to the Crown Court for sentence under s.16 or 19 if the provisions of that section are satisfied.

Additionally, in the case of an offender who has attained the age of 18 during the course of proceedings, the court may deal with the offender and make any order it could have made if the offender had not attained that age: s.29 CYPA 1963.

**Young offenders: dangerousness provisions (s.17)**

A defendant under 18 who has been convicted by a magistrates' court of a specified offence must be committed to the Crown Court if the court considers that the **22-008** criteria for the imposition of an extended sentence the imposition of an extended sentence of detention would be met.

Nothing in s.17 prevents the court from committing a person convicted of a specified offence to the Crown Court for sentence under s.16, 16A, or 19 if the provisions of that section are satisfied.

Where a young defendant is committed for sentence under this provision the Crown Court may deal with the offender in any way in which it could deal with them if they had been convicted of the offence on indictment. Thus, the sentencing powers are those of the Crown Court at the date of the conviction, and the offender's age for these purposes is that at conviction.

**22-009** The Crown Court is not bound to deal with the defendant under s.254 of the Sentencing Code. If it considers that there is a significant risk of serious harm to the public caused by further specified offences committed by the defendant, it may impose an extended sentence. If it does not so consider, the Crown Court may impose any other sentence which is open to the court for an offender of the defendant's age.

Additionally, in the case of an offender who has attained the age of 18 during the course of proceedings, the court may deal with the offender and make any order it could have made if the offender had not attained that age, s.29 CYPA 1963.

**Young offenders: related offences (s.19)**

**22-010** If a magistrates' court has sent an offender aged under 18 for trial for some offences, but has to deal with the offender for other related offences in respect of which falls within s.249(1) or s.252A(1)(a) of the Sentencing Code, in respect of which they have indicated that they would plead guilty if the offence were to proceed to trial, the court may commit them in custody or on bail to the Crown Court for sentence.

The offender may be committed for sentence even though the court is not satisfied that greater punishment should be inflicted for those offences than the magistrates' court has power to inflict.

If the offender has indicated an intention to plead guilty to certain offences, but the magistrates' court has not yet determined whether to send the offender to the Crown Court for trial in respect of related offences, the magistrates' court must adjourn the proceedings in relation to the offences in respect of which the offender has indicated an intention to plead guilty, and if it sends the offender to the Crown Court for trial for the related offence or offences, it may then commit them for sentence.

**22-011** If the magistrates' court commits an offender under this provision, it should state whether it has power also to commit the offender under s.16, s.16A or s.17.

A person committed for sentence under this provision may be dealt with by the Crown Court in any way in which the Crown Court could deal with them had they been convicted of the offence on the indictment. Thus, the sentencing powers are those of the Crown Court at the date of the conviction, and the offender's age for these purposes is that at conviction.

If the defendant is not convicted of those offences for which they were sent for trial, and the magistrates' court has not stated that it had power to commit the offender under s.14, the Crown Court must deal with the offender for those offences in a manner in which the magistrates' court could have.

**Committal where offender committed in respect of another offence (s.20)**

There is an additional committal power in s.25. It applies where a magistrates' court has committed an offender to the Crown Court under: **22-012**

(a) ss.14 to 19 (committal for sentence for indictable offences);
(b) para.5(4) of Sch.2 (further offence committed by offender given conditional discharge order);
(c) para.24(2) of Sch.10 committal to Crown Court where offender convicted of further offence while community order is in force;
(d) para.11(2) of Sch.16 (committal to Crown Court where offender commits further offence during operational period of suspended sentence order);
(e) s.43 of the Mental Health Act 1980 (power of magistrates' courts to commit for restriction order);
(f) s.6(6) or 9(3) of the BA 1976 (committal to Crown Court for offences of absconding by person released on bail or agreeing to indemnify sureties in criminal proceedings); or
(g) the Vagrancy Act 1824 (incorrigible rogues), to be sentenced or otherwise dealt with in respect of an offence ("*the relevant offence*"), to be sentenced or otherwise dealt with in respect of an offence ("*the relevant offence*").

Where:

(1) the relevant offence is an indictable offence;
(2) the committing court has the power to deal with the offender in respect of the other offence,

the court may also commit the offender in respect of the relevant offence.

It is immaterial whether the court which convicted the offender of the other offence was the committing court or another court.

Where the relevant offence is a summary offence, the committing court may commit the offender to the Crown Court to be dealt with, in accordance with s.23, in respect of:

(a) any other offence of which the committing court has convicted the offender which is punishable with:
    (i) imprisonment; or
    (ii) driving disqualification; or
(b) any suspended sentence in respect of which it falls to the committing court to deal with the offender by virtue of para.11(1) of Sch.16.

For these purposes, an offence is punishable with driving disqualification if the committing court has a power or duty to order the offender to be disqualified under ss.34, 35 or 36 of the Road Traffic Offenders Act 1988 (RTOA 1988) (disqualification for certain motoring offences) in respect of it. **22-013**

Where an offender is committed under s.20, the Crown Court must observe all limits which would apply to a magistrates' court passing sentence for those offences, both in relation to the maximum term of imprisonment which the magistrates' court may pass for the individual offences, and the limitations on the aggregate maximum term of imprisonment which the magistrates' court may impose for all the offences.

Where under s.20(4)(b) a magistrates' court commits a person to be dealt with by the Crown Court in respect of a suspended sentence, the powers under paras 13 and 14 of Sch.16 (power of court to deal with suspended sentence) are exercisable by the Crown Court.

**Defective committals**

**22-014** Where an offender is committed to the Crown Court for sentence, and it is alleged that the committal is unlawful for want of jurisdiction or otherwise, the normal remedy is by way of judicial review. The Crown Court may decline to pass sentence only if the committal is obviously bad on its face.

In *Butt and Jenkin* [2023] EWCA Crim 1131, the court gave guidance as to the proper approach:

1) *What power was exercised*—That was a question of fact. The sending sheet was, presumptively, an accurate record of the power that the magistrates' court purported to exercise, but it was not conclusive. What mattered was the power that the magistrates' court exercised, not how it was recorded.
2) *Was the power exercised erroneously?* That depended on whether what occurred in the magistrates' court complied with the statutory requirements.
3) *Consequences of that error*—It was a matter of statutory construction to determine whether the legislature intended that the procedural error in question should nullify further steps in the proceedings or, if not, when the error could be remedied. The following examples illustrated the principle in operation. Where the procedure required by s.17A was not followed, that invalidated the subsequent proceedings. Where a defendant was sent to the Crown Court for offences that included at least one indictable only offence, but was then tried on an indictment alleging only either way offences where no mode of trial procedure had taken place, the proceedings were not thereby invalidated. The failure to follow the required mode of trial procedure requirements of para.7 and para.9 of Sch.3 to the 1998 Act in the Crown Court in that situation was not as fundamental as the failure to follow the s.17A process in the magistrates' court.
4) *Steps to be taken to correct error*—If the consequence of the error was that the Crown Court had no jurisdiction, then the matter could be remedied by the magistrates' court using the power under s.142 of the 1980 Act. Alternatively, a Crown Court judge could use s.66 of the 2003 Act to exercise the power of a district judge (magistrates' court) (DJ (MC)) under s.142. That power should be exercised with restraint, as the Crown Court judge and their staff would often have little experience of magistrates' court procedure.

A circuit judge and a High Court judge may reconstitute the court in order to exercise the powers of a district judge. There is the same power at the Court of Appeal: *Buisson* [2011] EWCA Crim 1841.

The Crown Court has no power to remit the case to the magistrates' courts where it appears that the defendant is not guilty of the offence for which they have been committed, but it may allow them to withdraw or change their plea and then remit the case to the magistrates' court, see *Isleworth Crown Court Ex p. Buda* [2000] 1 Cr. App. R.(S.) 538; [2000] Crim. L.R. 111.

### Other committal powers (s.24)

For other powers of a magistrates' court to commit an offender to the Crown Court to be dealt with for an offence see: **22-015**

(a) para.22(2) and (4) of Sch.7 (offender subject to youth rehabilitation order made by Crown Court convicted of further offence by magistrates' court);
(b) s.70 of the Proceeds of Crime Act 2002 (POCA 2002) (request by prosecution with a view to consideration of confiscation order under s.6 of that Act);
(c) s.43(1) of the MHA 1983 (power of magistrates' courts to commit for restriction order);
(d) s.6(6) of the BA 1976 (offence of absconding by person released on bail);
(e) s.9(3) of that Act (offence of agreeing to indemnify sureties in criminal proceedings); and
(f) the Vagrancy Act 1824 (incorrigible rogues).

# REMITTING AN ADULT FOR SENTENCE

## SENTENCING CODE s.25A

*References: Current Sentencing Practice A2; Archbold 5A-270*

The Crown Court may remit a person aged 18 or over, or a person who is not an individual, to the magistrates' court for sentence, where that person— **22-016**

(a) has been convicted of an offence by a magistrates' court and committed to the Crown Court for sentence, or
(b) has been convicted of an offence (other than an offence triable only on indictment) by the Crown Court following a plea of guilty: s.25A(1) and (2).

In deciding whether to exercise the power in subs.(2), the Crown Court must—

(a) take into account any other offence before the Crown Court that appears to the court to be related to that offence (whether the same, or a different, person is accused or has been convicted of the other offence), and
(b) have regard to any allocation guidelines (or revised allocation guidelines) issued as definitive guidelines by the Sentencing Council: s.25A(3).

There is no right of appeal against an order under remitting an offender's case to the magistrates' courts: s.25A(4).

## REMITTING A JUVENILE FOR SENTENCE

SENTENCING CODE ss.25–29

*References: Current Sentencing Practice A6; Archbold 5A-270*

**Discretion to remit** The Crown Court may remit a young person to the youth court for sentencing where the convicting court was a magistrates' court and that court committed the offender to the Crown Court for sentencing: s.25(2A). **22-017**

Where a person who appears or is brought before a youth court charged with an offence subsequently reaches the age of 18, the youth court may, at any time after conviction and before sentence, remit the offender for sentence to a magistrates' court other than a youth court ("the adult court"): SC s.27(1) and (2). Where an offender is so remitted, the adult court may deal with the offender in any way in which it could deal with the offender if it had convicted the offender of the offence: SC s.27(3). In those circumstances, s.25(4) (duty of adult magistrates' courts to remit young offenders to youth court for sentence) does not apply to the adult court: SC s.27(4).

**Duty to remit** Where a person under the age of 18 is found guilty before the Crown Court of an offence other than homicide, the Crown Court must remit the offender to the youth court, unless it is satisfied that it would be undesirable to do so: SC s.25(1) and (2). **22-018**

It will be undesirable to remit if:

(a) the judge who presided over the trial will be better informed as to the facts and circumstances;
(b) if there would be a risk of disparity if defendants were sentenced by different courts; or
(c) if there would be delay, duplication of proceedings or unnecessary expense: *Lewis* (1984) 6 Cr. App. R.(S.) 44; (1984) 148 J.P. 329; [1984] Crim. L.R. 303 and *Dillon* [2017] EWCA Crim 2671; [2019] 1 Cr. App. R.(S.) 22; [2019] Crim. L.R. 247.

In *S* [2021] EWCA Crim 960; [2023] 1 Cr. App. R. (S.) 33, the court confirmed, that when considering the proper course where a child who fell to be sentenced in the Crown Court would, if in the youth court, have received a referral order, the court had the option to exercise the power to remit the case to the youth court, and exercise the power under s.66 of the Courts Act 2003 and impose a referral order.

Where a person under the age of 18 is found guilty before a magistrates' court which is not a youth court, the magistrates' court must remit the offender to a youth court unless it proposes to deal with the offender by means of a discharge, a fine, or an order binding over the person's parents or guardians to take proper care and exercise proper control, or where the mandatory referral conditions for a referral order apply (see **REFERRAL ORDERS**, **para.92**: SC s.25(4) and (5)).

# ADJOURNMENT—POST CONVICTION

*References: Current Sentencing Practice A2; Archbold 5A-273*

## General matters

A magistrates' court may adjourn after conviction to enable enquiries to be made or to determine the most suitable method of dealing with the case. The adjournment must not be for more than four weeks at a time, or three weeks if the offender is in custody: MCA 1980 s.10(3). **23-001**

The Crown Court may adjourn after conviction for similar purposes; the power is derived from the common law. There is no statutory time limit. The Crown Court may adjourn part of the sentence only, however it will be necessary to state so at the time, otherwise the 56-day limit specified in s.385 of the Sentencing Code will apply: *Dorian* [2001] 1 Cr. App. R.(S.) 135; [2001] Crim. L.R. 56. Where the court rescinds its original sentence pursuant to s.385, the court may then adjourn the sentencing beyond the 56 days: *Reynolds* [2007] EWCA Crim 538; [2008] 1 W.L.R. 1075; [2007] 2 Cr. App. R.(S.) 87.

## Offender's expectation

On adjourning, the court should avoid giving the offender any reason to expect that they will be dealt with by means of a sentence not involving custody. If the offender is given the impression that the court will deal with them without sending them to custody, it may not be open to the court which adjourns, or any other court dealing with the offender subsequently, to impose a custodial sentence: *Gillam* (1980) 2 Cr. App. R.(S.) 267; [1981] Crim. L.R. 55. **23-002**

This applies to circumstances where the magistrates' court adjourns proceedings and subsequently commits the offender to the Crown Court for sentence: *Rennes* (1985) 7 Cr. App. R.(S.) 343; [1986] Crim. L.R. 193.

The principle in *Gillam* does not apply where no one present at the adjournment could have had an expectation that there would be a non-custodial penalty: *Horton and Alexander* (1985) 7 Cr. App. R.(S.) 299; [1986] Crim. L.R. 411.

## Pre-sentence reports

In light of the statutory obligation to obtain a report in certain circumstances, an adjournment for that purpose (and silence from the court) should not be taken as an indication that a non-custodial sentence would be considered to be appropriate. It was, however, better practice, for the court to explicitly deal with the point: *Renan* (1994) 15 Cr. App. R.(S.) 722; (1994) 158 J.P. 621; [1994] Crim. L.R. 379. **23-003**

## Particular issues

A magistrates' court which adjourns after convicting a defendant of an either-way offence should avoid giving the defendant any reason to expect that they will **23-004** not be committed to the Crown Court for sentence, e.g. *Rennes* (1985) 7 Cr. App. R.(S.) 343; [1986] Crim. L.R. 193, however any argument based on the expectation requires that the expectation is legitimately held: *Southampton Magistrates' Court Ex p. Sansome* [1999] 1 Cr. App. R.(S.) 112; [1998] Crim. L.R. 595; [1998] C.O.D. 264.

### Adjourning until offender attains a particular age

**23-005** It is not permissible to adjourn solely to allow the offender to attain a particular age so as to affect the availability of the court's sentencing powers: *Arthur v Stringer* (1987) 84 Cr. App. R. 361; (1987) 151 J.P. 97; [1987] Crim. L.R. 563. In any event, if a statute provides that a person of a particular age who is convicted of an offence is liable to a particular penalty, the date of conviction is generally to be taken to be the date of the finding of guilt or plea of guilty, not the date sentence is passed, if different: *Danga* [1992] Q.B. 476; [1992] 2 W.L.R. 277; (1992) 94 Cr. App. R. 252, CA.

**23-006** **Bail** The BA 1976 s.4 applies if the court adjourns for inquiries.

# C: SENTENCING HEARING: PROCEDURE

# PRE-SENTENCE REPORTS

## SENTENCING CODE SS.30–37

*References: Current Sentencing Practice A3; Archbold 5A-278*

### General

A "pre-sentence report" means a report which: **24-001**

(a) is made or submitted by an appropriate officer[1] with a view to assisting the court in determining the most suitable method of dealing with an offender; and
(b) contains information as to such matters, presented in such manner, as may be prescribed by rules made by the Secretary of State: SC s.31(1).

### Written reports

A pre-sentence report need not be in writing, unless it is required before a court passes a custodial sentence on an offender under the age of 18 or is required to be in writing by rules made by the Secretary of State: SC s.31(1)(b) and (4). **24-002**

### Pre-sentence report requirements

Where s.30 applies (pre-sentence report requirements), the following provisions apply. **24-003**

If the offender is aged 18 or over, the court must obtain and consider a pre-sentence report before forming the opinion unless, in the circumstances of the case, it considers that it is unnecessary to obtain a pre-sentence report: SC s.30(2).

If the offender is aged under 18, the court must obtain and consider a pre-sentence report before forming the opinion unless:

(a) there exists a previous pre-sentence report obtained in respect of the offender; and
(b) the court considers:
    (i) in the circumstances of the case; and
    (ii) having had regard to the information contained in that report or, if there is more than one, the most recent report,

    that it is unnecessary to obtain a pre-sentence report: SC s.30(3).

Where a court does not obtain and consider a pre-sentence report before forming an opinion in relation to which the pre-sentence report requirements apply, no **24-004**

[1] The words *"an appropriate officer"* means: (a) where the offender is aged 18 or over, an officer of a provider of probation services; (b) where the offender is aged under 18: (i) an officer of a provider of probation services; (ii) a social worker of a local authority; or (iii) a member of a youth offending team: SC s.31(2).

custodial sentence or community sentence is invalidated by the fact that it did not do so: SC s.30(4).

The pre-sentence report requirements apply as follows.

Aged 18 or over

- imposing a community order: s.204;
- imposing particular requirements as a part of a community order: s.208;
- considering whether the "custody threshold" has been crossed: s.230;
- determining the length of a discretionary custodial sentence: s.231;
- applying the "dangerousness" test for the purposes of an extended determinate sentence (aged 18–20): s.267;
- applying the "dangerousness" test for the purposes of a life sentence (aged 18–20): s.274. Applying the "dangerousness" test for the purposes of an extended determinate sentence (aged 21 or over): s.280.
- Applying the "dangerousness" test for the purposes of a life sentence (aged 21 or over): s.285.

Aged under 18

- imposing a YRO: s.179;
- imposing a YRO with intensive supervision and surveillance: s.180;
- imposing certain requirements as a part of a YRO: s.186;
- considering whether the "custody threshold" has been crossed: s.230;
- determining the length of a discretionary custodial sentence: s.231;
- applying the "dangerousness" test for the purposes of an extended determinate sentence: s.255;
- applying the "dangerousness" test for the purposes of a sentence of detention for life: s.258.

24-005 **General** It will usually be appropriate to order a report and in some of these cases a recent report may well be sufficient where:

(a) the defendant is aged 17 and under;
(b) the defendant is aged under 21 and is a first-time offender/has not served a prison sentence;
(c) the defendant falls to be assessed for "dangerousness";
(d) there is a realistic alternative to a custodial sentence (check the Sentencing Guidelines): Guidance, referred to in *Townsend* [2018] EWCA Crim 875; [2018] 2 Cr. App. R.(S.) 30; [2018] Crim. L.R. 870.

### Obtaining a pre-sentence report

24-006 Where the court is required to obtain a pre-sentence report, it may accept a pre-sentence report given orally in open court, save for where any rules prescribed by the Secretary of State prohibit this: SC s.31(4).

Additionally, and irrespective of s.31(4), a pre-sentence report must be in writing if it:

(a) relates to an offender aged under 18; and
(b) is required to be obtained and considered before the court forms an opinion mentioned in:

(i) s.230(2) (seriousness threshold for discretionary custodial sentence);
(ii) s.231(2) (determining term of custodial sentence);
(iii) s.255(1)(c) (determining risk of harm to public for purpose of extended sentence); or
(iv) s.258(1)(c) (determining risk of harm to public for purpose of required life sentence): SC s.31(5).

**Disclosure: pre-sentence reports**

Provisions relating to disclosure apply where the court obtains a pre-sentence report, other than a report given orally in open court: SC s.32(1). **24-007**

The court must give a copy of the report:

(a) to the offender or the offender's legal representative; and
(b) if the offender is aged under 18, to any parent or guardian of the offender who is present in court: SC s.32(2).

But if:

(a) the offender is aged under 18; and
(b) it appears to the court that the disclosure of any information contained in the report:
  (i) to the offender; or
  (ii) to a parent or guardian of the offender,
  would be likely to create a risk of significant harm to the offender, a complete copy of the report need not be given to the offender or, as the case may be, to that parent or guardian.

For this purpose, the word "harm" has the same meaning as in s.31 of the Children Act 1989: SC s.32(3). **24-008**

The court must give a copy of the report to the prosecutor, that is to say, the person having the conduct of the proceedings in respect of the offence: SC s.32(4).

But a copy of the report need not be given to the prosecutor if the court considers that it would be inappropriate for the prosecutor to be given it.

But this subsection does not apply if the prosecutor is of a description specified in regulations made by the Secretary of State: SC, s.32(5).

No information obtained by virtue of subs.(4) may be used or disclosed otherwise than for the purpose of:

(a) determining whether representations as to matters contained in the report need to be made to the court; or
(b) making such representations to the court: SC s.32(6).

**Disclosure: other reports**

Where: **24-009**

(a) a report by:
  (i) an officer of a provider of probation services; or

(ii) a member of a youth offending team,

is made to any court (other than a youth court) with a view to assisting the court in determining the most suitable method of dealing with any person in respect of an offence, and the report is not a pre-sentence report, the following provisions apply: SC s.34(1).

The court must give a copy of the report:

(a) to the offender or the offender's legal representative; and
(b) if the offender is aged under 18, to any parent or guardian of the offender who is present in court: SC s.34(2).

**24-010** But if:

(a) the offender is aged under 18; and
(b) it appears to the court that the disclosure of any information contained in the report:
  (i) to the offender; or
  (ii) to a parent or guardian of the offender,
  would be likely to create a risk of significant harm to the offender, a complete copy of the report need not be given to the offender or, as the case may be, to that parent or guardian.

For this purpose, the word "harm" has the same meaning as in s.31 of the Children Act 1989: SC s.34(3).

**Contents**

**24-011** It is important to remember that it was the role of the litigator and the advocate to put together the necessary mitigation by gathering all of the relevant information. It is not the role of the Probation Service to do that work. Statements of what a defendant said about their background carry no more weight because they are contained in a pre-sentence report than if they were put forward by an advocate: *Townsend* [2018] EWCA Crim 875 [2018] 2 Cr. App. R.(S.) 30.

# MEDICAL REPORTS/MEDICAL TREATMENT

## Sentencing Code s.232

*References: Current Sentencing Practice: A9; Archbold 5A-278*

### Reports on mentally disordered defendants prior to sentencing

**Duty to obtain report** In any case where the offender is or appears to be mentally disordered, the court must obtain and consider a medical report before passing a custodial sentence other than one fixed by law: SC s.232(1) and (3). **25-001**

Before passing the sentence, the court must consider:

(a) any information before it which relates to the offender's mental condition (whether given in a medical report, a pre-sentence report or otherwise); and
(b) the likely effect of such a sentence on that condition and on any treatment which may be available for it: SC s.232(3).

But the duty does not apply if, in the circumstances of the case, the court is of the opinion that it is unnecessary to obtain a medical report: SC s.232(2).

**Failure to comply with duty** No custodial sentence is invalid if it is imposed in breach of that duty: SC s.232(4). **25-002**

**Appeals** Any court on appeal against sentence must obtain a medical report if none was obtained by the court below, and must consider any such report obtained by it or by that court: SC s.232(5). **25-003**

**"Mental disorder"** "Mental disorder" in relation to any person, means suffering from a mental disorder within the meaning of the MHA 1983: SC s.232(6). **25-004**

**Procedure rules** Where, for sentencing purposes, the court requires a medical report or where the court is considering making a guardianship or hospital order, the court must: **25-005**

(a) identify each issue in respect of which the court requires expert medical opinion and the legislation applicable;
(b) specify the nature of the expertise likely to be required for giving such opinion;
(c) identify each party or participant by whom a commission for such opinion must be prepared, who may be:
    (i) a party (or party's representative) acting on that party's own behalf;
    (ii) a party (or party's representative) acting on behalf of the court; or
    (iii) the court officer acting on behalf of the court;
(d) where there are available to the court arrangements with the NHS under which an assessment of a defendant's mental health may be prepared, give such directions as are needed under those arrangements for obtaining the expert report or reports required;
(e) where no such arrangements are available to the court, or they will not be

used, give directions for the preparation of a commission or commissions for an expert report or expert reports, including:
   - (i) such directions as can be made about supplying the expert or experts with the defendant's medical records;
   - (ii) directions about the other information, about the defendant and about the offence or offences alleged to have been committed by the defendant, which is to be supplied to each expert; and
   - (iii) directions about the arrangements that will apply for the payment of each expert;
- (f) set a timetable providing for:
   - (i) the date by which a commission is to be delivered to each expert;
   - (ii) the date by which any failure to accept a commission is to be reported to the court;
   - (iii) the date or dates by which progress in the preparation of a report or reports is to be reviewed by the court officer; and
   - (iv) the date by which each report commissioned is to be received by the court; and
- (g) identify the person (each person, if more than one) to whom a copy of a report is to be supplied, and by whom: Criminal Procedure Rules 2020 (SI 2020/759) (CrimPR 2020) r.28.8.

**Timetable**

**25-006** The Criminal Procedure Rules 2020 r.28.8 requires the court to set a timetable appropriate to the case for the preparation and reception of a report. Subject, therefore, to contrary judicial direction it is suggested that the timetable should require:

- (a) the convening of a hearing to consider the report no more than six to eight weeks after the court makes its request;
- (b) the prompt identification of an appropriate medical practitioner or practitioners, if not already identified by the court, and the despatch of a commission or commissions accordingly, within two business days of the court's decision to request a report;
- (c) acknowledgement of a commission by its recipient, and acceptance or rejection of that commission, within five business days of its receipt;
- (d) enquiries by court staff to confirm that the commission has been received, and to ascertain the action being taken in response, in the event that no acknowledgement is received within 10 business days of its despatch;
- (e) delivery of the report within five weeks of the despatch of the commission; and
- (f) enquiries into progress by court staff in the event that no report is received within five weeks of the despatch of the commission.

**Power to adjourn for medical report**

**25-007** **Magistrates' Court** If, on the trial by a magistrates' court of an offence punishable on summary conviction with imprisonment, the court:

- (a) is satisfied that the accused did the act or made the omission charged; but
- (b) is of the opinion that an inquiry ought to be made into their physical or mental condition before the method of dealing with them is determined, the

court shall adjourn the case to enable a medical examination and report to be made, and shall remand the accused: Powers of Criminal Courts (Sentencing) Act 2000 (PCC(S)A 2000) s.11(1)).

The maximum period for adjourning a case under s.11(1) is three weeks if the accused is remanded in custody, or four weeks if the accused is remanded on bail: PCC(S)A 2000 s.11(2).

**Power to remand to hospital for medical report**

**Crown Court/Magistrates' Court** The Crown Court or a magistrates' court may remand an accused person (convicted of an offence in the Crown Court, or convicted of an imprisonable offence in the magistrates' court) to a hospital specified by the court for a report on their mental condition: MHA 1983 s.35(1) and (2). **25-008**

**Test to apply** The power to remand for a medical report is only exercisable if: **25-009**

(a) the court is satisfied, on the written or oral evidence of a registered medical practitioner, that there is reason to suspect that the accused person is suffering from mental disorder; and
(b) the court is of the opinion that it would be impracticable for a report on their mental condition to be made if they were remanded on bail; but those powers shall not be exercised by the Crown Court in respect of a person who has been convicted of murder: MHA 1983 s.35(3).

**Length of remand to hospital** An accused person shall not be remanded or further remanded under s.35 for more than 28 days at a time or for more than 12 weeks in all; and the court may at any time terminate the remand if it appears to the court that it is appropriate to do so: MHA 1983 s.35(7). **25-010**

**Power to remand to hospital for treatment**

**Availability** The power (see below) applies to someone who at any time before sentence is in custody in the course of a trial before that court for such an offence: MHA 1983 s.36(2). It is also exercisable pre-trial. **25-011**

**Power** The Crown Court may, instead of remanding an accused person in custody, remand them to a hospital specified by the court if satisfied, on the written or oral evidence of two registered medical practitioners, that: **25-012**

(a) they are suffering from mental disorder of a nature or degree which makes it appropriate for them to be detained in a hospital for medical treatment; and
(b) appropriate medical treatment is available for them: MHA 1983 s.36(1).

**Test to apply** The court shall not remand an accused person under s.36 to a hospital unless it is satisfied, on the written or oral evidence of the approved clinician who would have overall responsibility for their case or of some other person representing the managers of the hospital, that arrangements have been made for their admission to that hospital and for their admission to it within the period of seven days beginning with the date of the remand: MHA 1983 s.36(3). **25-013**

**Directions for conveyance to hospital** Where the court is satisfied that the test **25-014**

to apply is satisfied, it may, pending the accused's admission, give directions for their conveyance to and detention in a place of safety: MHA 1983 s.36(3).

25-015 **Length of remand to hospital** An accused person shall not be remanded or further remanded under s.35 for more than 28 days at a time or for more than 12 weeks in all; and the court may at any time terminate the remand if it appears to the court that it is appropriate to do so: MHA 1983 s.36(6).

# FINANCIAL CIRCUMSTANCES ORDERS

## Sentencing Code ss.35–36

*References: Current Sentencing Practice A2; Archbold 5A-291*

### What is a financial circumstances order?

A "financial circumstances order", in relation to an individual, means an order requiring the individual to give the court, before the end of the period specified in the order, such a statement of the individual's assets and other financial circumstances as the court may require: SC s.35(1). **26-001**

### Availability

Where an individual has been convicted of an offence, the court may, before sentencing, make a financial circumstances order: SC s.35(2). **26-002**

A court may make a financial circumstances order irrespective of the kind of sentence that it has in mind.

Where:

(a) an individual aged under 18 has been convicted of an offence; and
(b) the court is considering whether to make an order under s.380 in respect of the individual's parent or guardian (power to order parent or guardian to pay fine, costs, compensation or surcharge), the court may make a financial circumstances order with respect to the parent or (as the case may be) guardian: SC s.35(4).

A financial circumstances order may also be made by a magistrates' court which has been notified that an individual desires to plead guilty without appearing before the court, or by a court considering whether to make an order against the parent or guardian of a child or young person who has been convicted of an offence: SC s.35(3).

### Offences

Failure to comply with a financial circumstances order is a summary offence punishable by a fine of level 3: SC s.36(1) and (2). **26-003**

Making a false statement in response to a financial circumstances order, is a summary offence punishable by a fine of level 4: SC s.36(3) and (4).

# IMPACT STATEMENTS

*References: Current Sentencing Practice A3; Archbold 5A-351*

## General

Statements setting out the impact of an offence to be used for the purposes of sentencing are known as impact statements. They may be a victim impact statement, a family impact statement, a community impact statement or a business impact statement. **27-001**

The statement is evidence and must be in a formal witness statement, served on the defence in time for the defendant's instructions to be taken. This will enable any objection to its use to be prepared. As the statement is designed to inform the court of the consequences of the offence on the victim, responsibility for presenting admissible evidence remains with the prosecution. Therefore, the statement may be challenged, in cross-examination, and it may give rise to disclosure obligations: *Perkins* [2013] EWCA Crim 323; [2013] 2 Cr. App. R.(S.) 72; [2013] Crim. L.R. 533.

## Practice Directions

The Criminal Practice Directions set down principles in relation to each type of impact statement, see CPD 2023 § 9.5. **27-002**

The CPD provides:

9.5.1 Victims of crime are invited to make a Victim Personal Statement (VPS).[1] The court will take the statement into account when determining sentence. In some circumstances, it may be appropriate for relatives of a victim to make a VPS, for example where the victim has died as a result of the relevant criminal conduct.

9.5.2 The decision about whether or not to make a VPS is entirely a matter for the victim; no pressure should be brought to bear, and no conclusion should be drawn if no statement is made. A VPS, or a further VPS, may be made at any time prior to the disposal of the case. A VPS after disposal is an exceptional step, should be confined to presenting up to date factual material, such as medical information, and should be used sparingly, most usually in the event of an appeal.

9.5.3 Evidence of the effects of an offence on the victim contained in the VPS or other statement, must be:

1. in a witness statement made under s.9 Criminal Justice Act 1967 or an expert's report; and
2. served in good time upon the defendant's solicitor or the defendant, if they are not represented.

---

[1] The revised Code of Practice for Victims of Crime gives further information about victims' entitlements within the criminal justice system, and the duties placed on criminal justice agencies when dealing with victims of crime. [FN in source material]

9.5.4 Except where inferences can properly be drawn from the nature of or circumstances surrounding the offence, a sentencing court must not make assumptions unsupported by evidence about the effects of an offence on the victim.

9.5.5 The maker of a VPS may be cross-examined on its content.

9.5.6 At the discretion of the court, the VPS may also be read aloud or played in open court, in whole or in part, or it may be summarised. If the VPS is to be read aloud, the court should also determine who should do so. In making these decisions, the court should take account of the victim's preferences, and follow them unless there is good reason not to do so; examples include the inadmissibility of the content or the potentially harmful consequences for the victim or others.

9.5.7 Court hearings should not be adjourned solely to allow the victim to attend court to read the VPS. A VPS that is read aloud or played in open court in whole or in part ceases to be a confidential document. The VPS should be referred to in the course of the hearing.

9.5.8 The opinions of the victim or the victim's relatives as to what the sentence should be are not relevant, unlike the consequences of the offence on them, and should therefore not be included in the statement. If opinions as to sentence are included in the statement, then it is inappropriate for them to be referred to, and the court should have no regard to them.

There are additional sections in the CPD dealing with community and business impact statements.

### Statements and findings of fact

**27-003** In *Chall* [2019] EWCA Crim 865; [2019] 4 W.L.R. 102; [2019] 2 Cr. App. R.(S.) 44, the court provided additional guidance as to the use of victim personal statements (VPS):

(1) expert evidence was not an essential precondition of a finding that a victim had suffered severe psychological harm;

(2) a judge might assess that such harm had been suffered on the basis of evidence from the victim, including evidence contained in a VPS, and might rely on their observation of the victim whilst giving evidence;

(3) whether or not a VPS provided evidence that was sufficient for a finding of severe psychological harm depended on the circumstances of the particular case and the contents of the VPS; and

(4) VPS had to comply with the requirements of the Criminal Practice Direction and be served on the defence in sufficient time to enable them to consider its contents and decide how to address them. If late service gave rise to genuine problems for the defence, an application for an adjournment could be made.

In *Singh* [2024] EWCA Crim 259; [2024] 2 Cr. App. R. (S.) 17, the court stated where the victim personal statement was not signed until three days before the sentencing hearing and not served until the day before the hearing, that was too late as it deprived the defendant of a practical opportunity to object to the content of the statements in a meaningful way. Additionally, where there were new allegations in the statement, reliance on those was not proper and the content of the statement went beyond the proper purpose of informing the court of the effect of the defendant's offending on the victim.

# DEROGATORY ASSERTION ORDERS

## Sentencing Code ss.38–41

*References: Current Sentencing Practice A3; Archbold 5A-4-42*

### General

Where a speech in mitigation is made on behalf of an offender which includes a statement which is derogatory to a person's character, the court may make a derogatory assertion order which has the effect of prohibiting the reporting of the said assertion. **28-001**

### Effect

While a derogatory assertion order or interim derogatory assertion order has effect in relation to an assertion, the assertion must not: **28-002**

(a) be published in Great Britain in a written publication available to the public; or
(b) be included in a relevant programme for reception in Great Britain: SC s.38(1).

### Availability

The order is available where an assertion is made during a speech in mitigation on behalf of an offender: **28-003**

(a) before a court considering what sentence to impose on an offender;
(b) where a magistrates' court is considering whether to commit the offender for sentence to the Crown Court;
(c) a court reviewing any sentence (including an appeal); or
(d) a court deciding whether to give leave to appeal against a sentence: SC s.39(1).

### Test to apply

The court may make a derogatory assertion order in relation to an assertion to which this section applies where there are substantial grounds for believing: **28-004**

(a) that the assertion is derogatory to a person's character (for instance, because it suggests that the person's conduct is or has been criminal, immoral or improper); and
(b) that the assertion is false or that the facts asserted are irrelevant to the sentence: SC s.39(3).

### Interim orders

Where it appears to the court that there is a real possibility that a derogatory assertion order will be made in relation to an assertion, the court may make an interim derogatory assertion order in relation to it: SC s.39(4). **28-005**

An interim order ceases to have effect when the court makes a determination regarding a "full" order: SC s.39(8)(b).

### Length of the order

**28-006** A full order ceases to have effect at the end of a period of 12 months: SC s.39(7)(b).

# STATUTORY SURCHARGE

## Sentencing Code s.42

*References: Current Sentencing Practice A3; Archbold 5A-337*

### General

The court must impose a surcharge where the conditions are met: SC s.42. The court must impose the order; it is not an automatic consequence of conviction. Failure to do so results in the order not being imposed. **29-001**

The order is wrongly referred to as the "victim surcharge"; the legislation refers to a "surcharge" and the references to victims appears to stem from much of the monies raised funding victim support services (however the CPS also receive some of the funds raised).

**Applicability** There are in effect five parallel regimes, the application of which depend on the date of the commission of the offence(s). Where a court "deals with an offender" for an offence committed before the relevant date, or for multiple offences where two or more offences fall into different date bands, the earlier surcharge regime applies, Sentencing Act 2020 (Surcharge) (Amendment) Regulations 2022 (SI 2022/584) art.3; Criminal Justice Act 2003 (Surcharge) (Amendment) Order 2020 (SI 2020/310) art.3; Criminal Justice Act 2003 (Surcharge) (Amendment) Order 2019 (SI 2019/985) art.3; and the Criminal Justice Act 2003 (Surcharge) (Amendment) Order 2016 (SI 2016/389) art.3. **29-002**

The court does not "deal with an offender" for the purposes of the duty to impose a surcharge where it imposes an absolute discharge or an order under the MHA 1983: SC s.42(5).

Where an offender is convicted by a magistrates' court of a number of offences and is sentenced by the magistrates for some of those offences but committed to the Crown Court for sentence for others, s.42 of the Sentencing Code requires both the magistrates' court and the Crown Court to order them to pay a surcharge: *Cuthbertson* [2020] EWCA Crim 1883; [2021] 2 Cr. App. R.(S.) 14.

**Court imposes multiple sentences** The court must make a surcharge in the appropriate amount. If the court imposes more than one form of sentence, the highest surcharge order applies: The Criminal Justice Act 2003 (Surcharge) Order 2012 (SI 2012/1696) arts 3(2)(b), 4(2)(b), 5(2)(b) and 6(2): *Abbott* [2020] EWCA Crim 516; [2020] 1 W.L.R. 3739; [2020] 2 Cr. App. R.(S.) 39. **29-003**

Where the court imposes multiples sentences of the same type, it is the aggregate amount that applies. For example, three consecutive sentences of six months is a term of 18 months for the purposes of calculating the surcharge amount: *Abbott* [2020] EWCA Crim 516; [2020] 2 Cr. App. R.(S.) 39.

**Breaches of community orders and suspended sentence orders** Where the **29-004**

sentencing court is dealing with the activation of a suspended sentence, or breach of a community order, the further sentence does not attract another surcharge, and the surcharge must be calculated by reference to the sentence(s) imposed for the new offence(s) only: *Abbott* [2020] EWCA Crim 516; [2020] 2 Cr. App. R.(S.) 39.

This will likely involve the court dealing with offences committed at different times, such that different regimes apply:

(a) where the court deals with an offender for breach of a community order by making the order more onerous or by the imposition of a financial penalty and imposes a new sentence for the offence constituting the breach, the original offence (for which the community order was imposed) is relevant only for the purposes of determining which surcharge regime applies;
(b) where the court activates a suspended sentence order in whole or in part and imposes a new sentence for the new offence constituting the breach, the original offence for which the suspended sentence order was imposed is only relevant for determining which surcharge regime applies; and
(c) where the court does not deal with an offender for a breach of a community order (or other court order), and simply allows that order to continue, this would not constitute "dealing" with the offence and so the date of that offence will not matter: *Abbott* [2020] EWCA Crim 516; [2020] 2 Cr. App. R.(S.) 39.

29-005 **Crown Court and magistrates' courts** From 1 September 2014, the surcharge is applied to the magistrates' court as well as the Crown Court: The Criminal Justice Act 2003 (Surcharge) (Amendment) Order 2014 (SI 2014/2120) art.2.

29-006 **The amounts** The various statutory instruments have been compiled into three tables below:

(1) offences all committed by an offender aged under 18 (irrespective of date of conviction);
(2) offences all committed by an offender aged 18+; and
(3) offences committed by a person who is not an individual.

29-007 *Offences all committed by an offender aged under 18 (irrespective of age on date of conviction)*:

| Disposal | On/after 16 June 2022 | 14 April 2020-15 June 2022 | 28 June 2019–13 April 2020 | 8 April 2016–28 June 2019 | 1 October 2012–7 April 2016 | 1 April 2007–1 October 2012 |
|---|---|---|---|---|---|---|
| A conditional discharge | £20 | £17 | £16 | £15 | £10 | — |
| A fine | £26 | £22 | £21 | £20 | £15 | £15 |
| A YRO | £26 | £22 | £21 | £20 | £15 | — |
| A referral order | £26 | £22 | £21 | £20 | £15 | — |

| Disposal | On/after 16 June 2022 | 14 April 2020-15 June 2022 | 28 June 2019–13 April 2020 | 8 April 2016–28 June 2019 | 1 October 2012–7 April 2016 | 1 April 2007–1 October 2012 |
|---|---|---|---|---|---|---|
| A community order | £26 | £22 | £21 | £20 | £15 | — |
| A suspended sentence order | £41 | £34 | £32 | £30 | £20 | — |
| A custodial sentence | £41 | £34 | £32 | £30 | £20 | — |

*Offences all committed by an offender when aged 18 or over:* **29-008**

| Disposal | On/after 16 June 2022 | 14 April 2020-15 June 2022 | 28 June 2019–13 April 2020 | 8 April 2016–28 June 2019 | 1 October 2012–7 April 2016 | 1 April 2007–1 October 2012 |
|---|---|---|---|---|---|---|
| A conditional discharge | £26 | £22 | £21 | £20 | £15 | — |
| A fine | 40% of the value of the fine, rounded up or down to the nearest pound, subject to a maximum of £2,000 | 10% of the value of the fine, rounded up or down to the nearest pound. Subject to a minimum of £34 and a maximum of £190 | 10% of the value of the fine, rounded up or down to the nearest pound. Subject to a minimum of £32 and a maximum of £181 | 10% of the value of the fine, rounded up or down to the nearest pound. Subject to a minimum of £30 and a maximum of £170 | 10% of the value of the fine, rounded up or down to the nearest pound. Subject to a minimum of £20 and a maximum of £120 | £15 |
| A community order | £114 | £95 | £90 | £85 | £60 | — |
| A suspended sentence order (six months or less) | £154 | £125 | £122 | £115 | £80 | — |
| A suspended sentence order (more than six months) | £187 | £156 | £149 | £140 | £100 | — |
| A sentence of imprisonment or detention in a young offender insti- | £154 | £125 | £122 | £115 | £80 | — |

| Disposal | On/after 16 June 2022 | 14 April 2020-15 June 2022 | 28 June 2019–13 April 2020 | 8 April 2016–28 June 2019 | 1 October 2012–7 April 2016 | 1 April 2007–1 October 2012 |
|---|---|---|---|---|---|---|
| tution (six months or less) | | | | | | |
| A sentence of imprisonment or detention in a young offender institution (more than six months but not exceeding 24 months) | £187 | £156 | £149 | £140 | £100 | — |
| A sentence of imprisonment or detention in a young offender institution for more than 24 months | £228 | £190 | £181 | £170 | £120 | — |
| A sentence of imprisonment or custody for life | £228 | £190 | £181 | £170 | £120 | — |

**29-009** *Offences committed by a person who is not an individual*:

| Disposal | On/after 16 June 2022 | 14 April 2020-15 June 2022 | 28 June 2019–13 April 2020 | 8 April 2016–28 June 2019 | 1 October 2012–7 April 2016 | 1 April 2007–1 October 2012 |
|---|---|---|---|---|---|---|
| A conditional discharge | £26 | £22 | £21 | £20 | £15 | — |
| A fine | 40% of the value of the fine, rounded up or down to the nearest pound, subject to a maximum of £2,000 | 10% of the value of the fine, rounded up or down to pound. Subject to a minimum of £34 and a maximum of £190 | 10% of the value of the fine, rounded up or down to pound. Subject to a minimum of £32 and a maximum of £181 | 10% of the value of the fine, rounded up or down to pound. Subject to a minimum of £30 and a maximum of £170 | 10% of the value of the fine, rounded up or down to pound. Subject to a minimum of £15 and a maximum of £120 | — |

## Imposing other financial orders

**29-010** Where a court dealing with an offender considers:

(a) that it would be appropriate to make one or more of a compensation order, an unlawful profit order and a slavery and trafficking reparation order; but

(b) that the offender has insufficient means to pay both the surcharge and appropriate amounts under such of those orders as it would be appropriate to make, the court must reduce the surcharge accordingly (if necessary to nil): SC s.42(3).

This gives rise to three scenarios:

(a) the offender has sufficient means to pay both the surcharge and the compensatory order in full;
(b) the offender has limited means and cannot pay both orders in full; or
(c) the offender has no means to pay both orders.

In the first, the offender pays both. In the second, the court must reduce the surcharge (and may have to reduce the compensation order). In the third, the surcharge must be imposed in full. The illogicality of this is manifest, but that appears to be the effect. See [2018] EWCA Crim 2997; [2019] 1 Cr. App. R.(S.) 53 [2019] Crim. L.R. 552 for more detail.

**Enforcement**

Surcharge orders are enforced in accordance with the Administration of Justice Act 1970 Sch.9. The Crown Court does not fix a default term when making a surcharge order. **29-011**

# CRIMINAL COURTS CHARGE

## Sentencing Code ss.44-51

The criminal courts charge is a mandatory financial penalty to be imposed by courts upon sentencing offenders in certain circumstances. The sum to be paid was effectively reduced to zero and so in practice no obligation to impose the charge arises. **30-001**

# POSTPONEMENT—SENTENCING AND CONFISCATION

## Proceeds of Crime Act 2002 ss.13-15

*References: Current Sentencing Practice A3*

### General

In circumstances where an offender falls to be sentenced and there will in due course be confiscation proceedings under the POCA 2002, the court has two options: **31-001**

(1) proceed under s.6 of the POCA 2002 and conduct the confiscation proceedings prior to sentencing; or
(2) postpone the confiscation proceedings under s.14 of the POCA 2002 and proceed to sentence the defendant first.

If the court does postpone the confiscation proceedings to enable the imposition of sentence, it must not (by virtue of s.15 of the POCA 2002) impose certain financial or forfeiture orders.

### Surcharge

In *Bristowe* [2019] EWCA Crim 2005; [2020] 1 Cr. App. R.(S.) 58, the court held that what is now s.42 of the Code and s.15 of the POCA 2002 were seemingly contradictory provisions in that while a statutory surcharge "must be" imposed when dealing with a person for all offences such an order "must not be" imposed if confiscation proceedings are to take place which have been postponed by the sentencing judge. The proper interpretation was that if confiscation proceedings are to take place, which have been postponed by the sentencing judge, the statutory surcharge should not be imposed until after the decision has been made on the application for confiscation. **31-002**

### Effect of non-compliance

It is now well-established that non-compliance with s.15 does not invalidate any sentencing orders imposed. The court in *Bristowe* [2019] EWCA Crim 2005; [2020] 1 Cr. App. R.(S.) 58 therefore held that if an order was made during the postponement period or at the time when sentence was imposed, the order would not be quashed unless, exceptionally, the final outcome of the case meant that the circumstances and justice of the case made it necessary. The court also commented that there should be very few cases indeed in which an early order operates to the disadvantage of the offender. **31-003**

# FACTUAL BASIS FOR SENTENCING AND *NEWTON* HEARINGS

*References: Current Sentencing Practice A3; Archbold 5A-306*

## Summary

The court provided a summary of the authorities in *Marsh; Cato* [2018] EWCA Crim 986; [2018] 2 Cr. App. R.(S.) 28. **32-001**

## After a trial

**Interpreting the jury's verdict** The correct approach by the judge, after a trial, to the determination of the factual basis on which to pass sentence is clear: **32-002**

(a) if there is only one possible interpretation of a jury's verdict(s), the judge had to sentence on that basis;
(b) where there is more than one possible interpretation, the judge had to make up their own mind, to the criminal standard, as to the factual basis on which to pass sentence; and
(c) where there is more than one possible interpretation, and the judge is not sure of any of them, (in accordance with basic fairness) they are obliged to pass sentence on the basis of the interpretation (whether in whole or in relevant part) most favourable to the defendant: *King* [2017] EWCA Crim 128; [2017] 4 W.L.R. 95; [2017] 2 Cr. App. R.(S.) 6.

A *Newton* hearing may be held after a trial, for example in relation to the presence of racial aggravation: *Finch* (1993) 14 Cr. App. R.(S.) 226; [1992] Crim. L.R. 901. It is suggested that this, however, should be rare and that *King* represents the modern approach to such factual disputes.

## Guilty pleas

**Basis should be written** If the prosecution does accept the defendant's basis of plea, it must be reduced to writing: CPD 2023 9.4.2. **32-003**

**General** If the prosecution does accept the defendant's basis of plea, it must be reduced to writing, be signed by advocates for both sides, and made available to the judge prior to the prosecution's opening: CPD 2023 9.3.3. **32-004**

The purpose of a *Newton* hearing is to determine factual issues which are relevant to the sentence and which have not been resolved by the offender's plea of guilty to the charges in the indictment. It is not a substitute for a jury trial.

The same procedure applies in the magistrates' court as it does in the Crown Court: *Telford Justices Ex p. Darlington* (1988) 87 Cr. App. R. 194; (1988) 152 J.P. 215; [1988] Crim. L.R. 312.

**Defence duty to inform prosecution of dispute of facts** If the defendant intends to plead guilty to a charge on a basis of facts that differs significantly from that on which the prosecution will rely, the defendant's representatives must inform the **32-005**

prosecution and where the plea is entered, the judge must be informed of the basis of the plea: *Underwood* [2004] EWCA Crim 2256; [2005] 1 Cr. App. R.(S.) 90; (2004) 148 S.J.L.B. 974.

32-006 **Prosecution lack evidence to dispute basis of plea** Where the prosecution lack the evidence positively to dispute the defendant's account, for example, where the defendant asserts a matter outside the knowledge of the prosecution, the prosecution should not automatically agree to the basis of plea. In such a case, the prosecution should test the defendant's evidence and submissions by requesting a *Newton* hearing: *CPD 2015* [2015] EWCA Crim 1567 Sentencing B.8(e) (now revoked).

32-007 **Basis is subject to judicial approval** The judge is not bound to accept a plea offered by a defendant on a particular basis, even though the prosecution have agreed to accept the plea on that basis: CPD 2023 9.3.3.

**A *Newton* hearing may be appropriate where:**

32-008 (a) the defendant offers a plea on a basis which is not acceptable to the prosecution;
(b) the issue cannot be resolved by amending the indictment; or
(c) there is a substantial dispute of facts, the judge must either hear evidence and determine the issue of fact, or sentence on the basis put forward by the defendant: *Newton* (1982) 4 Cr. App. R.(S.) 388; [1983] Crim. L.R. 198.

Where a *Newton* hearing is ordered, the defendant is not entitled to withdraw their plea and counsel for the prosecution must present the evidence to the court: *Beswick* [1996] 1 Cr. App. R.(S.) 343; (1996) 160 J.P. 33; (1995) 159 J.P.N. 826.

32-009 **The hearing** Such a hearing is limited to the determination of matters which are consistent with the terms of the counts in the indictment to which the defendant has pleaded guilty. It is not open to the prosecution to allege that the defendant is guilty of more offences than are charged in the indictment or taken into consideration, or that the offence committed was more serious than the offence charged in the indictment: *Druce* (1993) 14 Cr. App. R.(S.) 691; [1993] Crim. L.R. 469.

The hearing is conducted in the form of a trial without a jury. Evidence is adduced and witnesses are examined in the normal way. The judge should not intervene in the examination of witnesses: *McGrath* (1983) 5 Cr. App. R.(S.) 460.

The judge should direct himself that the prosecution must establish their version of the facts to the criminal standard of proof: *Underwood* [2004] EWCA Crim 2256; [2005] 1 Cr. App. R.(S.) 90.

32-010 It is not necessary for the judge to hear evidence if the matter in issue is not relevant to sentence, or the defendant's story can be considered wholly false or manifestly implausible, or where the matters put forward by the defendant relate to personal mitigation only: CPD 2023 9.3.3.

In circumstances where an offender's version of events is rejected at a *Newton* hearing or special reasons hearing, the reduction which would have been available at the stage of proceedings the plea was indicated should normally be halved. Where witnesses are called during such a hearing, it may be appropriate further to decrease the reduction: *Reduction in Sentence for a Guilty Plea Guideline* (2017), para.F2.

## SENTENCING REMARKS

### Sentencing Code ss.52–56

*References: Current Sentencing Practice A3; Archbold 5A-394*

### General

**Explain sentence** The court must state in all cases, in open court, in ordinary language and in general terms, its reasons for deciding on the sentence imposed: SC s.52(2). 33-001

**Must be in open court** It is not permissible to impose sentence and decline to give reasons orally and open court on the basis that written reasons will be provided at a later date: *Billington* [2017] EWCA Crim 618; [2017] 4 W.L.R. 114; [2017] 2 Cr. App. R.(S.) 22. 33-002

**Must impose sentence on each count** A sentence must be imposed on each count and each sentence must be pronounced in open court: *Whitwell* [2018] EWCA Crim 2301; [2019] 1 Cr. App. R.(S.) 29. An order of "no separate penalty" is a sentence for these purposes. 33-003

**Must announce ancillary orders** Ancillary orders must be pronounced in open court — it is not sufficient to simply record matters such as the statutory surcharge on the court record: *Jones* [2018] EWCA Crim 2994; [2019] 1 Cr. App. R.(S.) 50. 33-004

### Length and content of sentencing remarks

**Sentencing remarks:**

33-005
- (a) should be framed "in ordinary language" and "in general terms";
- (b) should bear in mind that the offender was the first audience because they had to understand what sentence has been passed, why it has been passed, what it meant and what might happen in the event of non-compliance; this would also enable the victim, witnesses, public and the press to understand; and
- (c) should, in cases to which guidelines applied, identify the category in which a count sits by reference to harm and culpability, the consequent starting point and range, the fact that adjustments have been made to reflect aggravating and mitigating factors, where appropriate credit for plea (and amount of credit) and the conclusion. (It may be necessary briefly to set out what prompts the court to settle on culpability and harm, but only where the conclusion was not obvious or was in issue, and also to explain why the court moved from the starting point);

but sentencing remarks:

- (d) should not be crafted with an eye on the Court of Appeal (Criminal Division);
- (e) should not exhaustively rehearse the pre-sentence report, the Crown's open-

ing, any sentencing note and the mitigation should not be exhaustively rehearsed in sentencing remarks; on the contrary, if mentioned, they should be mentioned only briefly;

(f) should not — save in exceptional circumstances — cite authority;
(g) should not, in most cases, include a narrative which provided the foundations for the court's factual findings for sentence;
(h) should not in relation to a finding of dangerousness — save where essential to the understanding of the decision — include supporting facts; and
(i) should not make more than a brief reference to a victim personal statement, *Chin-Charles; Cullen* [2019] EWCA Crim 1140; [2019] 1 W.L.R. 5921; [2020] 1 Cr. App. R.(S.) 6.

It is submitted that this decision goes too far and that a literal application of the guidance given would result in the court acting contrary to the Criminal Practice Directions (in relation to impact statements) and several decisions of the Court of Appeal (Criminal Division) in relation to the need to state certain findings and the basis for them. It is further submitted that the appropriate approach is set out in the following paragraphs. See [2019] Crim. L.R. 893 for further commentary.

**All cases**

**33-006** **Sentencing guidelines** The court must identify any definitive sentencing guidelines relevant to the offender's case and:

(a) explain how the court discharged any duty to follow guidelines unless satisfied it would be contrary to the interests of justice to do so;
(b) where the court was satisfied it would be contrary to the interests of justice to follow the guidelines, state why: SC s.52(6).

**33-007** **Guilty plea** If the court has reduced the sentence as a result of taking into account the offender's guilty plea, state the fact that it has done so: SC s.52(7).

**33-008** **Effect of sentence** The court must explain to the offender in ordinary language:

(a) the effect of the sentence;
(b) the effects of non-compliance with any order that the offender is required to comply with and that forms part of the sentence;
(c) any power of the court to vary or review any order that forms part of the sentence; and
(d) the effects of failure to pay a fine, if the sentence consists of or includes a fine: SC s.52(3).

If the sentencing judge gives an inaccurate explanation of the effect of sentence, the inaccuracy of the explanation does not provide a ground of appeal against sentence.

In the case of a custodial sentence, s.52 appears to require an explanation of the relevant provisions governing release and licence, which will vary according to the nature of the sentence imposed (life imprisonment, extended sentence, fixed-term sentence etc.)

**33-009** In the case of a community order, the court must explain the requirements of the order, the effects of non-compliance, and the power of the court on application to vary the order.

In the case of a fine (but not a compensation order or confiscation order), the court must explain the effect of the order and the effect of failure to pay the fine.

**Statutory aggravating factors** In all cases, if an offence is aggravated by a statutory aggravating factor such as racial or religious hostility, or hostility based on presumed sexual orientation or transgender identity, the court must state that that has been treated as an aggravating factor: SC ss.66-72. **33-010**

**Those aged under 18**

**Custodial sentence** If the court passes a custodial sentence on an offender under 18, the court must in addition state that it is of the opinion that the offence or the combination of the offence and one or more offences associated with it was so serious that neither a fine nor a community sentence can be justified for the offence: SC s.52(9). **33-011**

**Enhanced YRO** If the court makes a youth rehabilitation order with intensive supervision and surveillance or fostering, state that the court is of the opinion that the offence, or the combination of the offence and one or more offences associated with it, was so serious that, but for the power to make a YRO with intensive supervision and surveillance or fostering, a custodial sentence would be appropriate, and if the offender was aged under 15 at the time of conviction, the court is of the opinion that the offender is a persistent offender; if the offender is under 12, the court must state that a custodial sentence would be appropriate if they had been aged 12: SC s.52(8). **33-012**

**Special cases**

Where the court decides: **33-013**

- (a) not to follow a relevant sentencing guideline;
- (b) not to make, where it could:
  - (i) a reparation order (unless it passes a custodial or community sentence) (see SC s.54);
  - (ii) a compensation order (see SC s.55); or
  - (iii) a travel restriction order (see SC s.56);
- (c) not to order, where it could:
  - (i) that a suspended sentence of imprisonment is to take effect;
  - (ii) the endorsement of the defendant's driving record; or
  - (iii) the defendant's disqualification from driving, for the usual minimum period or at all;
- (d) to pass a lesser sentence than it otherwise would have passed because the defendant has assisted, or has agreed to assist, an investigator or prosecutor in relation to an offence, the court must explain why it has so decided: Criminal Procedure Rules (Crim.P.R.) 2020 r.28.1.

Additionally, see s.56 of the Sentencing Code for similar duties in relation to unlawful profit orders, football banning orders, slavery and trafficking reparation orders, and deprivation or disqualification from owning an animal.

**Informants** Where the court decides to pass a lesser sentence than it otherwise would have passed because the defendant has assisted, or has agreed to assist, an **33-014**

investigator or prosecutor in relation to an offence, the court must arrange for such an explanation to be given to the defendant and to the prosecutor in writing, if the court thinks that it would not be in the public interest to explain in public: Crim.P.R. 2020 r.28.1(3).

33-015 **Non-compliance with sentencing orders** In the case of some orders (such as criminal behaviour orders (CBOs), football banning orders, sexual harm prevention orders (SHPOs), disqualification from driving, etc.), the court must explain the effect of the order, the effect of non-compliance with the order, and any power of the court to vary the order. See the individual legislation for details.

# D: PRIMARY DISPOSALS

# BINDING OVER

## Justices of the Peace Act 1968 s.1(7)

*References: Current Sentencing Practice A4; Archbold 5A-396*

### To come up for judgment

**General** Reference should be made to Crim PR rr.31.2, 31.10 and 31.11. **34-001**

**Availability** A person who has been convicted of an offence may be bound over to come up for judgment when called, on such conditions as the court may specify.

The order is not available in the magistrates' courts: *Ayu* [1958] 1 W.L.R. 1264; [1958] 3 All E.R. 636; (1959) 43 Cr. App. R. 31.

**Procedure** In addition to the procedure which applies to a bind over to keep the peace (as to which, see below), where the bind over is to come up for judgment, the court must also specify any date, place and time the person must attend court, or the means by which the court will give notice of such time, date and place: Crim PR r.31.10(7).

### To keep the peace

**General** Reference should be made to the Crim PR rr.31.2, 31.10 and 31.11.

**Availability** A person "who or whose case" is before the Crown Court or a magistrates' court may be bound over to keep the peace and to be of good behaviour, whether or not they have been charged with or convicted of an offence: Justices of the Peace Act 1968 (JPA 1968) s.1(7). **34-002**

A complainant may be bound over: *Sheldon v Bromfield Justices* [1964] 2 Q.B. 573; [1964] 2 W.L.R. 1066; [1964] 2 All E.R. 131.

A witness who has not given evidence is therefore not liable to be bound over: *Swindon Crown Court Ex p. Singh* [1984] 1 W.L.R. 449; [1984] 1 All E.R. 941; [1983] 5 Cr. App. R.(S.) 422.

An acquitted defendant may be bound over, however such orders should be rare: *Middlesex Crown Court Ex p. Khan* (1997) 161 J.P. 240; [1997] C.O.D. 186; (1997) 161 J.P.N. 212. **34-003**

A person who has not been charged with an offence should not be bound over without being given the opportunity to make representations before being bound over: *Sheldon v Bromfield Justices* [1964] 2 Q.B. 573; [1964] 2 W.L.R. 1066; [1964] 2 All E.R. 131.

An order can be made at any time during the proceedings: *Aubrey-Fletcher Ex p. Thompson* [1969] 1 W.L.R. 872; [1969] 2 All E.R. 84; [1969] 53 Cr. App. R. 380.

The power can be exercised by the magistrates' court and the Crown Court: JPA 1968 s.1(7) and *DPP v Speede* [1998] 2 Cr. App. R. 108.

34-004 **Procedure** Where the court can impose a bind over, the court must decide, in this sequence—

(i) whether or not to do so and if so in what terms, and then
(ii) the amount of the recognisance to require: Crim PR r.31.10(1).

Before imposing a bind over the court must—

(a) take into account, as well as any representations under rule 31.2 (Behaviour orders and bind overs: general rules)—
   (i) any evidence introduced, and
   (ii) any admission made; and
(b) satisfy itself so that it is sure that the criteria for the bind over are met: Crim PR r.31.10(2).

34-005 **Power** The court may exercise its powers—

(i) on application or on the court's own initiative, and
(ii) at a hearing in public, as a general rule, or, in exceptional circumstances, in private: Crim PR r.31.10(1).

34-006 **Test to apply** Before imposing a binding over order, the court must be satisfied so that it is sure that a breach of the peace involving violence, or an imminent threat of violence, has occurred or that there is a real risk of violence in the future. Such violence may be perpetrated by the individual who will be subject to the order or by a third party as a natural consequence of the individual's conduct: JPA 1361 s.1(7).

34-007 **Burden of proof** The court should be satisfied so that it is sure of the matters complained of before a binding over order may be imposed. Where the procedure has been commenced on complaint, the burden of proof rests on the complainant. In all other circumstances, the burden of proof rests upon the prosecution.

34-008 **Amount of recognisance** Before deciding the amount of any recognisance to require the court must take into account, as well as any representations under rule 31.2, such information as is readily available about the financial circumstances of the person to be bound over: Crim PR r.31.10(3).

34-009 **Length** As a general rule the court must not impose a bind over for more than 12 months: Crim PR r.31.10(4).

34-010 **Making the order** If the court decides to impose a bind over—

(a) the court must explain, in terms the person to be bound over can understand (with help if necessary)—
   (i) the effect of the court's decision,
   (ii) the consequences of refusing to enter into a recognisance,
   (iii) the consequences of breaching the bind over, and
   (iv) the possibility of appeal; and
(b) the court must announce its decision and reasons at a hearing in public: Crim PR r.31.10(5).

**The order** A bind over must be in writing and must— **34-011**

(a) describe in ordinary language the conduct from which the person to be bound over must refrain;
(b) specify the amount of the recognisance;
(c) specify the duration of the bind over; and
(d) identify any surety who is not the person to be bound over: Crim PR r.31.10(6).

**Refusal to be bound over** Where a person to be bound over refuses to enter into a recognisance, the court must— **34-012**

(a) consider such other steps as may be available, for example continuing or starting a prosecution; and
(b) treat committal to custody as a last resort: Crim PR r.31.11(1). See also r.48.8.

A person who refuses to be bound over may be committed to prison. A person aged under 18 may consent to be bound over, but may not be committed to custody if they refuse to be bound over: PCC(S)A 2000 ss.60(1)(b) and 108.

**Breach** Where a person bound over is alleged to have breached a requirement, before the court forfeits the recognisance it must satisfy itself on the balance of probabilities that a breach has occurred: Crim PR r.31.11(2). See also r.48.8. **34-013**

# ABSOLUTE AND CONDITIONAL DISCHARGE

Sentencing Code ss.79–82

*References: Current Sentencing Practice A4; Archbold 5A-417*

## Absolute discharge

**What is an absolute discharge?** An "order for absolute discharge" means an order discharging an offender absolutely in respect of an offence: SC s.79(1). **35-001**

**Availability** An order for absolute discharge is available to a court dealing with an offender for an offence where: **35-002**

(a) the offender is convicted by or before the court; and
(b) the offence is not one in relation to which a mandatory sentence requirement applies: SC s.79(2).

A mandatory sentence requirement applies in the following circumstances:

(a) the offence is one for which the sentence is fixed by law;
(b) the court is obliged by one of the following provisions to pass a sentence of detention for life, custody for life or imprisonment for life:
  (i) ss.258, 274 or 285 of the SC (life sentence for certain dangerous offenders);
  (ii) s.273 or 283 of the SC (life sentence for second listed offence), or
(ba) the court is obliged by s.268B or 282B to impose a serious terrorism sentence; or
(ba) the court is obliged by s.268B or 282B to impose a serious terrorism sentence; or
(ba) the court is obliged by s.268B or 282B to impose a serious terrorism sentence; or
(c) a sentence is required by one of the following provisions and the court is not of the opinion mentioned in that provision:
  (i) s.311(2) of the SC (minimum sentence for certain offences involving firearms that are prohibited weapons);
  (ii) s.312(2) of the SC (minimum sentence for offence of threatening with weapon or bladed article);
  (iii) s.313(2) of the SC (minimum sentence of seven years for third class A drug trafficking offence);
  (iv) s.314(2) of the SC (minimum sentence of three years for third domestic burglary);
  (v) s.315(2) of the SC (minimum sentence for repeat offence involving weapon or bladed article): SC s.399.

**Test** Where it is available, the court may make an order for absolute discharge if it is of the opinion that it is inexpedient to inflict punishment, having regard to the circumstances, including: **35-003**

(a) the nature of the offence; and

(b) the character of the offender: SC s.79(3).

35-004 **Effect on other orders** Imposing an absolute discharge does not prevent a court from:

(a) imposing any disqualification on the offender;
(b) making any of the following orders in respect of the offence:
  (i) a compensation order (see SC s.133);
  (ii) an order under SC s.152 (deprivation orders);
  (iii) a restitution order (see SC s.147);
  (iv) an unlawful profit order under s.4 of the Prevention of Social Housing Fraud Act 2013 (PSHFA 2013);
(c) making an order under SC s.46 (criminal courts charge); or
(d) making an order for costs against the offender: SC s.79(4).

35-005 **Effect of discharge** The conviction of that offence is to be deemed not to be a conviction for any purpose other than the purposes of:

(a) the proceedings in which the order is made; and
(b) in the case of an order for conditional discharge, any subsequent proceedings which may be taken against the offender under Sch.2 to the Sentencing Code: SC s.82(2).

**Conditional discharge**

35-006 **What is a conditional discharge?** An "order for absolute discharge" means an order discharging an offender for an offence subject to the condition that the offender commits no offence during the period specified in the order: SC s.80(1).

35-007 **Availability** An order for conditional discharge is available to a court dealing with an offender for an offence where:

(a) the offender is convicted by or before the court; and
(b) the offence is not one in relation to which a mandatory sentence requirement applies: SC s.80(2).

A mandatory sentence requirement applies in the following circumstances:

(a) the offence is one for which the sentence is fixed by law;
(b) the court is obliged by one of the following provisions to pass a sentence of detention for life, custody for life or imprisonment for life:
  (i) ss.258, 258A, 274, 274A, 285 or 285A (life sentence for certain dangerous offenders);
  (ii) ss.273 or 283 (life sentence for second listed offence);
(c) a sentence is required by one of the following provisions and the court is not of the opinion mentioned in that provision:
  (i) s.311(2) (minimum sentence for certain offences involving firearms that are prohibited weapons);
  (ii) s.312(2) (minimum sentence for offence of threatening with weapon or bladed article);
  (iii) s.313(2) (minimum sentence of seven years for third class A drug trafficking offence);

- (iv) s.314(2) (minimum sentence of three years for third domestic burglary);
- (v) s.315(2) (minimum sentence for repeat offence involving weapon or bladed article): SC s.399.

The following provisions prohibit the imposition of a conditional discharge:

- (a) s.66ZB(6) of the CDA 1998 (effect of youth cautions);
- (b) s.66F of that Act (youth conditional cautions);
- (c) s.103I(4) of the Sexual Offences Act 2003 (breach of stand alone SHPO and interim SHPO etc.);
- (d) s.339(3) (breach of CBO);
- (da) s.342G(4) (offences relating to a serious violence reduction order);
- (e) s.354(5) (breach of SHPO imposed on conviction): SC s.80(3).

**Test** Where it is available, the court may make an order for conditional discharge if it is of the opinion that it is inexpedient to inflict punishment, having regard to the circumstances, including: **35-008**

- (a) the nature of the offence; and
- (b) the character of the offender: SC s.80(4).

**Maximum period** The period of conditional discharge specified in an order for conditional discharge must be a period of not more than three years beginning with the day on which the order is made: SC s.80(5). There is no minimum period. **35-009**

**Security** On making an order for conditional discharge, the court may, if it thinks it expedient for the purpose of the offender's reformation, allow any person who consents to do so to give security for the good behaviour of the offender: SC s.80(6). **35-010**

**Effect on other orders** Making an order for conditional discharge in respect of an offence does not prevent the court from: **35-011**

- (a) imposing any disqualification on the offender;
- (b) making any of the following orders in respect of the offence:
  - (i) a compensation order (see s.133);
  - (ii) an order under s.152 (deprivation orders); or
  - (iii) a restitution order (see s.147); or
  - (iv) an unlawful profit order under s.4 of the PSHFA 2013;
- (c) making an order under s.46 (criminal courts charge); or
- (d) making an order for costs against the offender: SC s.80(7).

Additionally, the following orders may be made in conjunction with a conditional discharge:

- (a) a CBO, SC s.331(3);
- (b) a confiscation order, *Varma* [2012] UKSC 42; [2012] 3 W.L.R. 776; [2013] 1 Cr. App. R.(S.) 125; or
- (c) a football banning order, Football Spectators Act 1989 (FSA 1989) s.14A(4)(b).

When imposing a conditional discharge, the court may not also make a fine or a referral order: *Sanck* (1990-1991) 12 Cr. App. R.(S.) 155; [1990] Crim. L.R. 663 and SC s.89(3)(b)(iv).

**35-012 Effect of discharge** The conviction of that offence is to be deemed not to be a conviction for any purpose other than the purposes of:

(a) the proceedings in which the order is made; and
(b) in the case of an order for conditional discharge, any subsequent proceedings which may be taken against the offender under Sch.2 to the Sentencing Code: SC s.82(2).

If the offender is sentenced (under Sch.2) for an offence:

(a) the order ceases to have effect; and
(b) if the offender was aged 18 or over when convicted of the offence, the limitation in s.82(2) (above) ceases to apply to the conviction: SC s.82(3).

Without prejudice to subss.(2) and (3), the offender's conviction is in any event to be disregarded for the purposes of any enactment or instrument which:

(a) imposes any disqualification or disability upon convicted persons; or
(b) authorises or requires the imposition of any such disqualification or disability: SC s.82(4).

**Commission of further offence during conditional discharge period**

**Magistrates' courts**

**35-013 Issue of summons** Where:

(a) the order for conditional discharge was made by a magistrates' court , and
(b) it appears to a justice of the peace on information that the offender:
    (i) has been convicted by a court in Great Britain of an offence committed during the period of conditional discharge; and
    (ii) has been dealt with in respect of that offence

    the justice may:
    (a) issue a summons requiring the offender to appear at the place and time specified in it; or
    (b) if the information is in writing and on oath, issue a warrant for the offender's arrest.

The summons or warrant must direct the offender to appear or to be brought before the court which made the order for conditional discharge: SC Sch.2, para.3.

**35-014 Procedure** Where the offender is convicted by a magistrates' court ("the convicting court") of an offence committed during the period of conditional discharge:

(d) and the order for conditional discharge was made by the convicting court, that court may re-sentence the offender for the original offence;
(e) and the order for conditional discharge was made by another magistrates' court, the convicting court may, with the consent of the court which made the order, re-sentence the offender for the original offence;
(f) and the order for conditional discharge was made by the Crown Court, the convicting court may commit the offender in custody or on bail to the Crown Court,

and if it does so, must send the Crown Court a copy of the minute or memorandum of the conviction entered in the register, signed by the designated officer by whom the register is kept: SC Sch.2, para.5.

**Re-sentencing powers** Where the order for conditional discharge was made by a magistrates' court ("the original court") and it is proved to the satisfaction of the original court that the offender has been convicted by another court in Great Britain of an offence committed during the period of conditional discharge, the original court may re-sentence the offender for the original offence: SC Sch.2, para.6. **35-015**

### Crown Court

**Issue of summons** Where: **35-016**

- (a) the order for conditional discharge was made by the Crown Court; and
- (b) it appears to the Crown Court that the offender:
    - (i) has been convicted by a court in Great Britain of an offence committed during the period of conditional discharge; and
    - (ii) has been dealt with in respect of that offence.

The Crown Court may issue:

- (a) a summons requiring the offender to appear at the place and time specified in it; or
- (b) a warrant for the offender's arrest.

The summons or warrant must direct the offender to appear or to be brought before the Crown Court: SC Sch.2, para.4.

**Re-sentencing powers** Where: **35-017**

- (a) the offender:
    - (i) is convicted before the Crown Court of an offence committed during the period of conditional discharge; or
    - (ii) is brought or appears before the Crown Court having been committed by a magistrates' court for sentence in respect of any such offence; or
- (b) the order for conditional discharge was made by the Crown Court and it is proved to the satisfaction of the Crown Court that the offender has been convicted by a court in Great Britain of an offence committed during the period of conditional discharge, the Crown Court may re-sentence the offender for the original offence: SC Sch.2, para.7.

Any question whether the offender has been convicted of an offence committed during the period of conditional discharge is to be determined by the court and not by the verdict of a jury: SC Sch.2, para.7(3).

**Maximum served for the offence** Where the offender has already served the maximum sentence for the offence, it will be inappropriate to impose a conditional discharge: *Lynch* [2007] EWCA Crim 2624. **35-018**

## COMPENSATION ORDERS

### SENTENCING CODE ss.133–146

*References: Current Sentencing Practice A4; Archbold 5A-427*

### General

**What is a compensation order?** A "compensation order" is an order made in respect of an offender for an offence that requires the offender: **36-001**

(a) to pay compensation for any personal injury, loss or damage resulting from:
  (i) the offence; or
  (ii) any other offence which is taken into consideration by the court in determining the sentence for the offence; or
(b) to make payments for:
  (i) funeral expenses; or
  (ii) bereavement,

in respect of a death resulting from any such offence: SC s.133.

**Availability** A compensation order is available to a court by or before which an offender is convicted of an offence. **36-002**

This is subject to s.136 (road accidents): SC s.134(1).

Where a compensation order is available, the court may make such an order whether or not it also deals with the offender for the offence in any other way: SC s.134(2).

**No need for application** A court may make an order of its own volition. **36-003**

**Reduction in sentence** A compensation order does not allow a defendant to "buy" a shorter sentence: *Copley* (1979) 1 Cr. App. R.(S.) 55. **36-004**

**No profit from offence** The offender may be ordered to pay compensation even though they have not profited from the offence and their available assets are not themselves the proceeds of crime. **36-005**

### Making the order

**Determining the amount** A compensation order must specify the amount to be paid under it and that amount must be the amount that the court considers appropriate, having regard to any evidence and any representations that are made by or on behalf of the offender or the prosecution: SC s.135(1) and (2). **36-006**

A compensation order may if appropriate contain an element of interest: *Schofield* [1978] 1 W.L.R. 979; [1978] 2 All E.R. 705; [1978] 67 Cr. App. R. 282.

If the victim of an assault has provoked the assault by their own violent behaviour towards the offender, the amount of the compensation order may be reduced: *Flinton* [2007] EWCA Crim 2322; [2008] 1 Cr. App. R.(S.) 96.

36-007 **The loss/injury** The court must be satisfied that the injury, loss or damage which has occurred, is attributable to the offence in respect of which the compensation order is made: SC s.133 and *Boardman* (1987) 9 Cr. App. R.(S) 74; [1987] Crim. L.R. 430.

The amount of loss must be agreed or proved by evidence, not inference or guesswork: *Amey* [1983] 1 W.L.R. 345; [1983] 1 All E.R. 865; (1982) 4 Cr. App. R.(S). 410.

The process of making a compensation order should be a very simple one. A court should decline to make an order unless it is based on very simple propositions which have been agreed or are easy to resolve. Where the amount of loss or damage is disputed, the sentencer may hear evidence on the matter but should hesitate before undertaking any complicated investigation: *Kneeshaw* [1975] Q.B. 57; [1974] 2 W.L.R. 432; (1974) 58 Cr. App. R. 439 and *Hyde v Emery* (1984) 6 Cr. App. R.(S.) 206.

36-008 A compensation order may be made in respect of a loss which is not itself actionable: *Chappell* (1984) 6 Cr. App. R.(S.) 214; [1984] Crim. L.R. 574; (1984) 128 S.J. 629.

A compensation order can only be made for loss or injury, not general inconvenience: *Stapylton* [2012] EWCA Crim 728; [2013] 1 Cr. App. R.(S.) 12; [2012] Crim. L.R. 631.

36-009 **Offender's means** In determining:

(a) whether to make a compensation order against an offender; or
(b) the amount to be paid under such an order,

the court must have regard to the offender's means, so far as they appear or are known to the court: SC s.135(3).

Where the court considers:

(a) that it would be appropriate both to impose a fine and to make a compensation order; but
(b) that the offender has insufficient means to pay both an appropriate fine and appropriate compensation,

the court must give preference to compensation (though it may impose a fine as well): SC s.135(4).

The court does not need to have a precise calculation but rather must take a broad picture: *Howell* (1978) 66 Cr. App. R. 179; [1978] Crim. L.R. 567.

The court in *York* [2018] EWCA Crim 2754; [2019] 4 W.L.R. 13; [2019] 1 Cr. App. R.(S.) 41 summarised the principles:

(a) first, an offender had to give details of their means;
(b) secondly, before making a compensation order, a judge had to enquire about, and make clear findings about, an offender's means;

(c) thirdly, before making a compensation order, the court had to take into account an offender's means;
(d) fourthly, a compensation order should not be made unless it was realistic, in the sense that the court was satisfied that an offender had, or would have, the means to pay that order within a reasonable time. Although a compensation order based on a repayment period as long as 100 months has been upheld, it had been said that, while a repayment period of two or three years in an exceptional case would not be open to criticism, in general, excessively long repayment periods should be avoided;
(e) fifthly, a court should not make a compensation order against an offender without means on the assumption that the order would be paid by somebody else, for example, by a relative; and
(f) finally, it followed that it was wrong to fix an amount of compensation without regard to the instalments that were capable of being paid by an offender and the period over which those instalments should be paid but rather to leave those questions for the magistrate to resolve.

**No prospect of payment in reasonable time** It is wrong in principle to impose a compensation order when there is no realistic possibility that the compensation will be paid within a reasonable time: *Stapylton* [2012] EWCA Crim 728; [2013] 1 Cr. App. R.(S.) 12. **36-010**

**Immediate payment not possible** If the compensation cannot be paid out of resources immediately available to the offender the court should determine the amount that they can reasonably pay out of income and order payment by instalments. The period of payment by instalments may extend to three years in appropriate cases: *Magistrates' Court Sentencing Guidelines Introduction to compensation.* **36-011**

**Future income** A compensation order can be combined with a sentence of immediate custody where the offender is clearly able to pay or has good prospects of employment on release from custody: *Totality Guideline* 2023. **36-012**

**Selling assets to satisfy the order** If it is proposed to raise the necessary funds by selling assets, the court should satisfy itself that the assets do exist and should ensure that the assets have been valued by a competent person, before acting on the valuation, see *Chambers* [1981] 3 Cr. App. R.(S.) 318; [1982] Crim. L.R. 189. There is no principle that a compensation order should not be made where the order would force the sale of the matrimonial home, however the judge should take into account such a consequence of making an order, see *Parkinson* [2015] EWCA Crim 1448; [2016] 1 Cr. App. R.(S.) 6; [2015] Crim. L.R. 991. **36-013**

**Particular cases**

**Multiple offences** If the offender has been convicted of more than one offence, a separate order should be made in respect of each offence. If more than one offender has been convicted, a separate order should be made against each offender. If more than one offender has been convicted, but not all of them have the means to pay compensation, it is permissible to make an order against one offender for the whole amount of the loss, damage or injury: *Grundy and Moorehouse* [1974] 1 All. E.R. 292; [1974] 1 All E.R. 292; [1974] Crim. L.R. 128. **36-014**

36-015 **Road accidents** A "road accident" means an accident arising out of the presence of a motor vehicle on a road: SC s.136(5).

A compensation order may not be made in respect of funeral expenses or bereavement in respect of a death due to a road accident: SC s.136(1).

A compensation order may be made in respect of injury, loss or damage due to a road accident only if it is in respect of:

(a) loss suffered by a person's dependants in consequence of the person's death;
(b) damage which is treated by s.137 as resulting from an offence under the Theft Act 1968 or Fraud Act 2006; or
(c) uninsured harm:[1] SC s.136(2).

36-016 The amount to be paid may include an amount representing all or part of any loss of, or reduction in, preferential rates of insurance attributable to the accident: SC s.136(4).

In practice the effect of this appears to be that a compensation order may not be made in respect of loss, damage or injury, unless the claimant was driving a vehicle which was itself not insured for the purposes of the Road Traffic Acts, or the claimant was a person who at the relevant time knew or ought to have known that the vehicle in which they were travelling had been stolen or unlawfully taken, or was not covered by insurance. In these cases the claimant is not covered by the Motor Insurance Bureau Agreement and the court may make a compensation order for the full amount of the loss, damage or personal injury. The court may also make a compensation order in favour of a claimant claiming by virtue of a right of subrogation.

36-017 **Confiscation orders** If the court has made a confiscation order under CJA 1988 or the POCA 2002, the court should consider whether to make an order under CJA 1988 s.72(7) or the POCA 2002 s.13(6), which allows the court to direct that if the offender is unable to satisfy the compensation order because their means are inadequate, the deficiency shall then be made good from the proceeds of the confiscation order.

For the effect of proceedings in relation to confiscation orders on the court's powers in relation to compensation orders, see the following provisions of the POCA 2002:

(a) s.13(4) (where confiscation order has been made); and
(b) s.15 (where proceedings on a confiscation order have been postponed).

36-018 **Damage to property and clean-up costs: certain offences** In the case of an offence under the Theft Act 1968 or Fraud Act 2006, where the property in question is recovered, any damage to the property occurring while it was out of the owner's

---

[1] The term *"uninsured harm"* means injury, loss or damage as respects which: (a) the offender was uninsured in relation to the use of the vehicle in question; and (b) compensation is not payable under any arrangements to which the Secretary of State is a party. An offender is not uninsured in relation to the use of a vehicle for this purpose if that use of it is exempted from insurance by s.144 of the Road Traffic Act 1988: SC s.136(3).

possession is to be treated as having resulted from the offence. This applies regardless of how the damage was caused and who caused it: SC s.137(1) and (2).

Section 29 of the Ancient Monuments and Archaeological Areas Act 1979 makes provision about the person in whose favour a compensation order relating to certain offences involving damage to monuments is to be made.

Section 33B of the Environmental Protection Act 1990 (clean-up costs) provides for certain costs connected with certain offences relating to waste to be loss or damage resulting from those offences for the purposes of s.133.

**Funeral expenses and bereavement: other than road accidents** A compensation order in respect of funeral expenses may be made for the benefit of anyone who incurred the expenses: SC s.138(1). **36-019**

A compensation order in respect of bereavement may be made only for the benefit of a person for whose benefit a claim for damages for bereavement could be made under s.1A of the Fatal Accidents Act 1976: SC s.138(2). The sum specified in s.1A is currently £15,120.

The amount to be paid in respect of bereavement under a compensation order must not exceed the amount for the time being specified in s.1A(3) of that Act: SC s.138(3).

Section 138 is subject to s.136(1) (compensation order not available in respect of bereavement or funeral expenses in respect of a death due to a road accident): SC s.138(4).

**Young offenders: limits** Where: **36-020**

(a) a magistrates' court is dealing with an offender for one or more offences (each, a "main offence") of which the offender was convicted when aged under 18; and
(b) the court makes a compensation order in respect of:
  (i) a main offence; or
  (ii) any offence taken into consideration (TIC) by the court in determining sentence for a main offence (a "TIC offence"), the compensation in respect of a main offence must not exceed £5,000; and the total compensation in respect of main offences and TIC offences must not exceed £5,000 multiplied by the number of main offences: SC s.139(1)-(3).

This is subject to s.33B(5) of the Environmental Protection Act 1990 (clean-up costs relating to certain offences relating to waste): SC s.139(4).

**Young offenders: payment by parent/guardian** Where: **36-021**

(a) a court makes or is proposing to make a compensation order in respect of an offence; and
(b) the offender is aged under 18 when convicted, s.380 of the Sentencing Code (order for payment by parent or guardian) applies to the amount to be paid under any such compensation order: SC s.140(1) and (2).

For these purposes, the references in subss.(3) and (4) of s.135 (taking account of offender's means in determining amount of compensation) to the offender's means are to be read as references to the means of the offender's parent or guardian: SC s.140(3) and (4).

For the purposes of any order made under s.380 against a local authority, s.135(3) does not apply: SC s.140(5).

36-022 **Offences committed before 11 December 2003** See s.142 of the Sentencing Code.

**Appeals**

36-023 **Suspension of order** A person in whose favour a compensation order is made is not entitled to receive the amount due to the person until there is no further possibility of the order being varied or set aside on appeal (disregarding any power to grant leave to appeal out of time): SC s.141(1).

36-024 **Court of Appeal** The Court of Appeal may by order annul or vary any compensation order made by the Crown Court, even if the conviction is not quashed: SC s.141(3).

Where a compensation order is annulled or varied under subs.(3):

(a) the compensation order:
  (i) if annulled, is not to take effect;
  (ii) if varied, is to take effect as varied;
(b) the Court of Appeal must also vary any order previously made under s.42 (court's duty to order payment of surcharge) so as to secure that the offender's liability under that order is the same as it would have been if the offender were being dealt with by the Crown Court: SC s.141(4).

36-025 **Supreme Court** See s.141(5) and (6) of the Sentencing Code.

36-026 **TICs** Where, in any proceedings in which an offender is convicted of one or more offences (each, a "main offence"), a compensation order is made against the offender in respect of an offence taken into consideration in determining sentence:

(a) the order ceases to have effect if the offender successfully appeals against conviction of the main offence or, if more than one, all the main offences;
(b) the offender may appeal against the order as if it were part of the sentence imposed in respect of the main offence or, if more than one, any of the main offences: SC s.141(7).

**Enforcement**

36-027 **Attachment of earnings orders/application for benefit deductions** Unless it would be impracticable or inappropriate to do so, the court must make an attachment of earnings (AEO) or application for benefit deductions (ABD) whenever:

(a) compensation is imposed, Courts Act (CA) 2003 Sch.5 para.7A; or
(b) the court concludes that the offender is an existing defaulter and that the existing default(s) cannot be disregarded: CA 2003 Sch.5 para.8.

In other cases, the court may make an AEO or ABD with the offender's consent: CA 2003 Sch.5 para.9.

**Collection order** The court must make a collection order in every case in which a fine or compensation order is imposed unless this would be impracticable or inappropriate: CA 2003 Sch.5 para.12. The collection order must state: **36-028**

(a) the amount of the sum due, including the amount of any fine, compensation order or other sum;
(b) whether the court considers the offender to be an existing defaulter;
(c) whether an AEO or ABD has been made and information about the effect of the order;
(d) if the court has not made an AEO or ABD, the payment terms; and
(e) if an AEO or ABD has been made, the reserve terms (in other words, the payment terms that will apply if the AEO or ABD fails).

As to (e), it will often be appropriate to set a reserve term of payment in full within 14 days.

**Prison in default** The court does not fix any term of imprisonment in default, but may allow time for payment or fix payment by instalments. As enforcement is carried out by the magistrates' courts, the figures listed in Sch.4 to the MCA 1980 will apply. The maximum is 12 months. **36-029**

If the amount of the compensation order exceeds £20,000 and the Crown Court considers the magistrates' courts terms inadequate, the Crown Court may make an order that the maximum term of imprisonment in default should be a figure taken from the table below (which is a partial reproduction of the table applicable to fines), see SC s.129.

| **Amount:** | | **Maximum term:** |
|---|---|---|
| **More than** | **Not more than** | |
| £20,000 | £50,000 | 18 months |
| £50,000 | £100,000 | 24 months |
| £100,000 | £250,000 | 36 months |
| £250,000 | £1,000,000 | 60 months |
| £1 million | | 120 months |

# FINES

## SENTENCING CODE ss.118–121

*References: Current Sentencing Practice A4; Archbold 5A-465*

### Crown Court

**Availability** A fine is available to the Crown Court where it is dealing with an offender who is convicted on indictment for an offence: 37-001

(a) instead of; or
(b) in addition to,

dealing with the offender in any other way which is available to the court: SC s.120(1).

This is subject to s.120(2) of the SC which disapplies s.120(1) of the SC in the following cases:

(a) the offence is one for which the sentence is fixed by law;
(b) the court is obliged by one of the following provisions to pass a sentence of detention for life, custody for life or imprisonment for life:
    (i) s.258, 274 or 285 of the SC (life sentence for certain dangerous offenders);
    (ii) ss.273 or 283 of the SC (life sentence for second listed offence), or
(c) a sentence is required by s.314(2) of the SC (minimum sentence of three years for third domestic burglary); a serious terrorism sentence is required to be imposed.

For circumstances in which a fine is not available see:

(a) s.37(8) of the MHA 1983 (hospital order or guardianship order in case where person convicted of offence punishable with imprisonment); or
(b) s.89 (making of referral order: effect on court's other sentencing powers).

Section 120(1) is also is subject to any other enactment requiring the offender to be dealt with in a particular way; and does not apply if the court is precluded from sentencing the offender by its exercise of some other power: SC s.120(2).

**Amount of fine** There is no maximum level of fine in the Crown Court, Criminal Law Act 1977 (CLA 1977) s.32(1). The fine is fixed by reference to the seriousness of the offence: SC s.63. 37-002

**Offender's financial circumstances** Before fixing the amount, the court must inquire into the offender's financial circumstances: SC s.124(1). In fixing the amount of any fine to be imposed on an offender (whether an individual or other person), a court must take into account the circumstances of the case including, in particular, the financial circumstances of the offender so far as they are known, or appear, to the court: SC s.125(2). 37-003

The court may make a financial circumstances order. (See **FINANCIAL CIRCUMSTANCES ORDERS, para.26**.)

When taking into account the financial circumstances of the offender, this may have the effect of increasing or reducing the amount of the fine. But a court must not reduce the amount of a fine on account of any surcharge it orders the offender to pay under s.42, except to the extent that the offender has insufficient means to pay both: SC s.125(3) and (4).

For circumstances where the offender has failed to appear, see SC s.126 which makes provision as to when, in those circumstances, a court can continue to make an assessment of the offender's means.

**37-004** **Corporate offenders** In the case of a corporation, the court is not obliged to inquire into the means of the offender but must take them into account as far as they are known. See *Thames Water Ltd.* [2015] EWCA Crim 960; [2015] 1 W.L.R. 4411; [2015] 2 Cr. App. R.(S.) 63 and, for example, the Sentencing Council's *Environmental Offences Definitive Guideline* for guidance.

**37-005** **Remission of fines** If on subsequently inquiring into the offender's financial circumstances the court is satisfied that, had it had the results of that inquiry when sentencing the offender, it:

(a) would have fixed a smaller amount; or
(b) would not have fined the offender;

it may remit the whole or part of the fine: SC s.127(2).

**37-006** **Combined with suspended sentence order** It is permissible to impose a fine alongside a suspended sentence order: *Butt* [2018] EWCA Crim 1617; [2018] 1 W.L.R. 5391; [2019] 1 Cr. App. R.(S.) 4.

**37-007** **Time for payment/payment by instalments** Where the Crown Court imposes a fine it may allow time for payment and direct payment by instalments. Time for payment must be allowed unless the offender appears to have sufficient means to pay the fine immediately, or is unlikely to remain long enough at a fixed address to allow the fine to be enforced, or is simultaneously sentenced to, or is already serving, a custodial sentence: SC s.130.

**37-008** **Prison in default** The court must fix a term of imprisonment to be served in default of payment. (See **DEFAULT TERMS (CROWN COURT)—FINES, para.38**.) The default term is fixed in relation to the whole amount of the fine, not to individual instalments.

**Magistrates' courts**

**37-009** **Availability: power to fine specified** A fine is available to a magistrates' court dealing with an offender for an offence if under the relevant offence provision a person who is convicted of that offence is liable to a fine: SC s.118(1).

If under the relevant offence provision the offender is liable to:

(a) a fine of a specified amount,

(b) a fine of not more than a specified amount,
the amount of the fine:
(i) must not be more than that amount; but
(ii) may be less than that amount (unless an Act passed after 31 December 1879 expressly provides to the contrary): SC s.118(2).

This is subject to ss. 121 and 123 which place limitations on the availability of fines.

**Availability: power to fine not specified** Where an enactment states that an offence is punishable by imprisonment but does not also state that it is punishable by the imposition of a fine, the court may impose a fine instead of imprisonment. For summary only offences, the maximum is level 3 on the standard scale; for triable either way offences the maximum is £5,000 (if offence committed before 12 March 2015) or unlimited (if offence committed after that date): SC s.119. **37-010**

**The standard scale** The standard scale of fines was amended, non-textually, on 12 March 2015. For offences committed on or after that date, the standard scale is to be read as follows:[1] **37-011**

| | |
|---|---|
| Level 1 | £200 |
| Level 2 | £500 |
| Level 3 | £1,000 |
| Level 4 | £2,500 |
| Level 5 | Unlimited |

For offences committed between 1 October 1992 and 12 March 2015, the scale is as above save for the fact that Level 5 carries a £5,000 maximum. For offences committed prior to 1 October 1992, see SC s.122.

**Exceptions** There are a number of offences for which the removal of the limit on a Level 5 fine is disapplied, see The Legal Aid, Sentencing and Punishment of Offenders Act 2012 (Fines on Summary Conviction) Regulations 2015 (SI 2015/664) rr.2 and 3 and Schs.1 and 3. **37-012**

**Young offenders** Where an offender: **37-013**

(a) was convicted by a magistrates' court;
(b) was under 18 when convicted; and
(c) is before that court to be sentenced,

the court may not impose a fine of more than:

(a) £250, if the offender was aged under 14 when convicted; or
(b) £1,000, if the offender was aged 14 or over when convicted: SC s.123.

Where a court:

(a) is dealing with an offender for an offence;
(b) the offender is aged under 18 when convicted; and

---

[1] SC s.122(1) and the Legal Aid, Sentencing and Punishment of Offenders Act 2012 (LASPOA 2012) s.85(1).

(c) but for this subsection, the court would impose a fine on the offender

in respect of the offence, s.380 (order for payment by parent or guardian) applies to the fine: SC s.128(1) and (2).

37-014 **Time for payment/payment by instalments** A magistrates' court may allow time for payment and direct payment by instalments. Time for payment must be allowed unless the offender appears to have sufficient means to pay the fine immediately, or is unlikely to remain long enough at a fixed address to allow the fine to be enforced, or is simultaneously sentenced to, or is already serving, a custodial sentence: MCA 1980 s.75(1).

**Attachment of earnings orders/application for benefit deductions**

37-015 Unless it would be impracticable or inappropriate to do so, the court must make an AEO or ABD whenever:

(a) compensation is imposed, Courts Act 2003 (CA 2003) Sch.5 para.7A; or
(b) the court concludes that the offender is an existing defaulter and that the existing default(s) cannot be disregarded: CA 2003 Sch.5 para.8.

In other cases, the court may make an AEO or ABD with the offender's consent: CA 2003 Sch.5 para.9.

37-016 **Collection order** The court must make a collection order in every case in which a fine or compensation order is imposed unless this would be impracticable or inappropriate: CA 2003 Sch.5 para.12. The collection order must state:

(a) the amount of the sum due, including the amount of any fine, compensation order or other sum;
(b) whether the court considers the offender to be an existing defaulter;
(c) whether an AEO or ABD has been made and information about the effect of the order;
(d) if the court has not made an AEO or ABD, the payment terms; and
(e) if an AEO or ABD has been made, the reserve terms (in other words, the payment terms that will apply if the AEO or ABD fails).

As to (e), it will often be appropriate to set a reserve term of payment in full within 14 days.

37-017 **Prison in default** A magistrates' court does not fix a term to be served in default on the occasion when a fine is imposed, unless the offender appears to have insufficient means to pay the fine immediately, or is unlikely to remain long enough at a fixed address to allow the fine to be enforced, or is simultaneously sentenced to, or is already serving, a custodial sentence.

The default terms for fines imposed by magistrates' courts are the same as for the Crown Court (see **DEFAULT TERMS (CROWN COURT)—FINES, para.38**) except that the maximum default term which may be fixed is 12 months.

# DEFAULT TERMS (CROWN COURT)—FINES

SENTENCING CODE s.129

*References: Current Sentencing Practice A4; Archbold 5A-475*

**General** If the Crown Court imposes a fine on an offender aged 18 or over at conviction, the court must fix a term of imprisonment in default of payment of the fine. This duty does not apply to a Crown Court imposing a fine on an appeal from the magistrates' courts: SC s.129(1) and (3). **38-001**

The default terms for fines imposed by magistrates' courts are the same as for the Crown Court except that the maximum default term which may be fixed is 12 months.

The following table shows the default terms applicable to fines: SC s.129(4).

| Fine | Term |
|---|---|
| Not exceeding £200 | 7 days |
| More than £200, not exceeding £500 | 14 days |
| More than £500, not exceeding £1,000 | 28 days |
| More than £1,000, not exceeding £2,500 | 45 days |
| More than £2,500, not exceeding £5,000 | 3 months |
| More than £5,000, not exceeding £10,000 | 6 months |
| More than £10,000, not exceeding £20,000 | 12 months |
| More than £20,000, not exceeding £50,000 | 18 months |
| More than £50,000, not exceeding £100,000 | 2 years |
| More than £100,000, not exceeding £250,000 | 3 years |
| More than £250,000, not exceeding £1 million | 5 years |
| Over £1 million | 10 years |

These terms are maximum terms for the sums in question; SC s.129(4). The court should exercise its discretion and fix an appropriate default term within the relevant maximum.

## Compensation or costs orders

The Crown Court does not fix a default term when it makes a compensation order or orders the offender to pay the costs of the prosecution, but may enlarge the powers of the magistrates' court, see *Bunce* (1978) 66 Cr. App. R. 109; [1978] Crim. L.R. 236. **38-002**

## Confiscation

See **Confiscation Order—Proceeds of Crime Act 2002** for the terms applicable to confiscation orders. **38-003**

# UNLAWFUL PROFIT ORDERS

## PREVENTION OF SOCIAL HOUSING FRAUD ACT 2013 s.4

*References: Archbold 5A-1044*

### Definition

An unlawful profit order is an order requiring the defendant to pay a landlord the profit from unlawfully sub-letting a tenancy: PSHFA 2013 s.4(3). **39-001**

### Types of order

There are two types, one following a conviction and one on an application to the magistrates' courts. This section only deals with post-conviction orders. **39-002**

### Availability

The order is available where the defendant had been convicted of an offence under PSHFA 2013 ss.1 or 2 (unlawfully sub-letting a secured tenancy or an assured tenancy): PSHFA 2013 s.4(1). **39-003**

### Duty to consider making an order

The court by or before which the offender is convicted must, on application or otherwise, decide whether to make an unlawful profit order: PSHFA 2013 s.4(2)(a). **39-004**

### Combining sentences

The court may, if it considers it appropriate to do so, make such an order, instead of or in addition to dealing with the offender in any other way: PSHFA 2013 s.4(2)(b). **39-005**

When the court proposes to impose a fine and an unlawful profit order, but considers that the defendant has insufficient means to pay an appropriate amount under both orders, the court must give preference to making an unlawful profit order (though it may impose a fine as well): PSHFA 2013 s.4(8) and (9).

### Must give reasons when not making an order

If the court decides not to make an unlawful profit order, it must give reasons for that decision on passing sentence on the offender: PSHFA 2013 s.4(4). **39-006**

### Determining the amount

The amount payable under an unlawful profit order must be such amount as the court considers appropriate, having regard to any evidence and to any representations that are made by or on behalf of the offender or the prosecutor: PSHFA 2013 s.4(5). **39-007**

**Maximum amount**

**39-008** The maximum amount payable under an unlawful profit order is calculated as follows:

*Step 1* — determine the total amount the defendant received as a result of the conduct constituting the offence (or the best estimate of that amount).
*Step 2* — deduct from the amount determined under step 1 the total amount, if any, paid by the defendant as rent to the landlord (including service charges) over the period during which the offence was committed: PSHFA 2013 s.4(6).

# RESTITUTION ORDER

## Sentencing Code ss.147–151

*References: Current Sentencing Practice A4; Archbold 5A-528*

### General

**What is a restitution order?** A "restitution order" means an order made in an offender's case with respect to particular goods (referred to in this section as "the stolen goods") that: 40-001

- (a) requires anyone who has possession or control of the stolen goods ("the holder") to restore them to any other person entitled to recover them from the holder,
- (b) requires any other goods representing the stolen goods to be transferred or delivered to any person entitled to recover those other goods from the offender,
- (c) requires payment of a sum out of any removed money to any person who would be entitled to recover the stolen goods from the offender if they were in the offender's possession, or
- (d) requires payment of a sum out of any removed money to:
  - (i) any person to whom the offender has sold the stolen goods, or
  - (ii) any person from whom the offender has borrowed money on the security of the stolen goods: SC s.147(1).[1]

There are thus four types of order; two requiring the return of property to the person entitled to recover property (ss.147(1)(a) and (b)); one requiring the payment of a sum of money to the person entitled to recover the property (s.147(c)); and one requiring the payment of a sum of money to consequential victims (s.148(1)(d)).

**Interpretation** References to goods which have been stolen include references to goods which have been obtained: 40-002

- (a) by blackmail, or
- (b) by fraud (within the meaning of the Fraud Act 2006);

and references to "stealing" and "theft" are to be read accordingly: SC s.151(2).

References to stealing are to be read in accordance with s.1(1) of the Theft Act 1968 (read with the provisions of that Act relating to the construction of s.1(1)): SC s.151(1)(a).

---

[1] Goods represent the stolen goods if they are the proceeds of disposal or realisation of all or part of the stolen goods, or of other goods which represent the stolen goods; "removed money" means money of the offender which was taken out of the offender's possession when the offender was apprehended: SC s.147(2).

A restitution order may be made in respect of money owed by the Crown: SC s.151(5).

**Availability**

**40-003** **The conviction offence** A restitution order with respect to particular goods is available to a court in an offender's case where:

(a) the goods have been stolen; and
(b) either:
  (i) the offender is convicted by or before the court of an offence with reference to the theft of the goods, whether or not the stealing was the gist of it (an "offence related to the theft"); or
  (ii) the court takes an offence related to the theft into consideration in determining sentence for any other offence of which the offender is convicted by or before the court: SC s.148(1).

**40-004** **Need for an application** A restitution order under s.147(1)(b) (see above) is available only on the application of the person in whose favour it is to be made: SC s.148(2).

**40-005** **Orders relating to consequential victims** A restitution order with respect to any goods under s.147(1)(d) (see above) is available only if the court has made a restitution order under s.147(1)(a) (see above) with respect to the goods: SC s.148(3).

A restitution order under s.147(1)(d) is available only where the court is satisfied that:

(a) the purchaser was acting in good faith when purchasing the goods; or
(b) the lender was acting in good faith when lending money on the security of the goods: SC s.149(6).

**40-006** **Deferment order** Making a deferment order, or otherwise deferring sentence, does not preclude a court from making a restitution order: SC s.148(4).

**Making the order**

**40-007** **Evidence** The court may make a restitution order only if in the opinion of the court the relevant facts sufficiently appear from any of the following:

(a) evidence given at the trial;
(b) any written statements or admissions which were made for use, and would have been admissible, as evidence at the trial;
(c) any documents served on the offender in pursuance of regulations made under para.1 of Sch.3 to the CDA 1998 (procedure where persons sent for trial); or
(d) admissions made by or on behalf of any person in connection with any proposed exercise of the powers to make a restitution order: SC s.149(2).

**40-008** **Limitations** If the court makes restitution orders under paras (b) and (c) of s.147(1) (see **40-001** above) in respect of the theft of the same goods, they must not result in the person in whose favour they are made recovering more than the value of those goods: SC s.149(3).

A restitution order under s.147(1)(c) may not require payment of more than the value of the stolen goods: SC s.149(4).

An order under s.147(1)(d) may not require payment of more than:

(a) the amount which the purchaser paid for the purchase; or
(b) the amount owed to the lender in respect of the loan: SC s.149(7).

## Post-sentencing

**Breach** Failure to comply with a restitution order is a contempt of court; the statute does not make any order provision dealing with failure to comply. **40-009**

## Appeals

A restitution order made by a magistrates' court does not take effect until there is no further possibility of the order being varied or set aside on appeal (disregarding any power to grant leave to appeal out of time). However, a magistrates' court may direct that subs.(5) is not to apply to a restitution order if: **40-010**

(a) the restitution order is made under s.147(1)(a) or (b); and
(b) the court is of the opinion that the title to the goods to be restored or, as the case may be, delivered or transferred under the order is not in dispute: SC s.150(5) and (6).

Where the restitution order was made in respect of an offence taken into consideration by the court in determining sentence for one or more other offences of which the offender was convicted (each, a "main offence") and where the offender successfully appeals against conviction of the main offence or, if more than one, all the main offences, the restitution order ceases to have effect: SC s.150(2) and (3).

A restitution order is to be treated as an order for the restitution of property for the purposes of s.30 of the CAA 1968 (effect of appeals on such orders): SC s.150(7).

# FORFEITURE/DEPRIVATION—GENERAL POWER

SENTENCING CODE ss.152–159

*References: Current Sentencing Practice A4; Archbold 5A-503*

## What is a deprivation order?

A "deprivation order" is an order which: **41-001**

(a) is made in respect of an offender for an offence; and
(b) deprives the offender of any rights in the property to which it relates: SC s.152.

## Purpose

The order can serve a dual purpose; the removal from public circulation of an article which has been used to commit an offence, and the punishment of the offender: *Highbury Magistrates' Court Ex p. Di Matteo* [1991] 1 W.L.R. 1374; [1992] 1 All E.R. 102; (1991) 92 Cr. App. R. 263. Accordingly, the absence of such an order when one might have been imposed can constitute "credit" in the form of a reduction in sentence: *Price* [2015] EWCA Crim 318; [2015] 2 Cr. App. R.(S.) 8; [2015] Crim. L.R. 549. **41-002**

Deprivation orders should be used in simple and uncomplicated circumstances; the order can only affect the rights of the defendant and where complicating features such as hire purchase or part-ownership are present, an order may be inappropriate: *Kearney* [2011] EWCA Crim 826; [2011] 2 Cr. App. R.(S.) 106; [2011] Crim. L.R. 567.

## Jurisdiction

The power may be used by the Crown Court or by a magistrates' court on conviction for any offence. **41-003**

## Availability

The court may make an order whether or not it deals with the offender in any other way for the offence: SC s.155(2). **41-004**

The property must either:

(a) have been lawfully seized from the offender; or
(b) have been in their possession or control at the time when they were apprehended for the offence; or
(c) have been in their possession or control at the time when a summons in respect of the offence was issued: SC s.153(2).

Additionally, the court must be satisfied that either:

(a) the property has been used for the purpose of committing or facilitating the commission of any offence; or

(b) the property was intended by the offender to be used for the purpose of committing or facilitating the commission of any offence; or
(c) that the offender has been convicted of and offence which consisted of unlawful possession of the property concerned; or
(d) that an offence consisting of unlawfully possessing the property concerned has been taken into consideration: SC s.153(2)-(5).[1]

It is not necessary that the offence in relation to which the property has been used or was intended to be used should be the offence of which the offender has been convicted: SC s.153(3)(a).

**41-005** **Limitations/exclusions** The availability of an order is subject to:

(a) any restriction on forfeiture in any enactment contained in an Act passed on or after 29 July 1988;
(b) s.33C(8) of the Environmental Protection Act 1990 (subs.(1) not to apply where s.33C of that Act provides for forfeiture of vehicles in connection with offence under that section); and
(c) para.7 of Sch.5 to the Wireless Telegraphy Act 2006 (subs.(1) not to apply where person convicted of offence under Pts 2, 3 or 5 of that Act): SC s.153(6).

Deprivation orders do not apply to land or buildings see, for example, *Khan* [1982] 1 W.L.R. 1405; [1982] 3 All E.R. 969; (1983) 76 Cr. App. R. 29.

**Making the order**

**41-006** **Proper investigation** A deprivation order should not be made without a proper investigation of the grounds for making an order: *Pemberton* (1982) 4 Cr. App. R.(S.) 328; [1983] Crim. L.R. 121. A court considering whether to make an order must normally have evidence of the value of the property concerned before making a deprivation order, see e.g. *Joyce* (1989) 11 Cr. App. R.(S.) 253; [1991] R.T.R. 241.

A deprivation order should be considered as part of the total sentence, and the court should bear in mind that the overall penalty, including the deprivation order, should be commensurate with the offence.

The need for a proper enquiry was restated in *Jones (Rowan)* [2017] EWCA Crim 2192; [2018] 1 Cr. App. R.(S.) 35.

**41-007** **Considerations** In considering whether to make an order under this section in respect of any property, a court shall have regard to the value of the property; and to the likely financial and other effects on the offender of the making of the order (taken together with any other order that the court contemplates making): SC s.155(1).

In *De Jesus* [2015] EWCA Crim 1118; [2015] 2 Cr. App. R.(S.) 44, the court

---

[1] Facilitating the commission of an offence includes taking any steps after it has been committed for the purpose of: (a) disposing of any property to which the offence relates; or (b) avoiding apprehension or detection: SC s.153(4).

quashed a deprivation order in circumstances where the sentencing judge had failed to consider the total effect of the custodial sentence and deprivation order imposed upon the offender.

**Disparity** Where a deprivation order is to be made against one of a number of offenders, who are all equally responsible, there may be unjustifiable disparity: *Burgess* [2001] 2 Cr. App. R.(S.) 2. **41-008**

**Confiscation order** Where a court has postponed confiscation proceedings and proceeds to sentence the offender before making the confiscation order, it must not make a deprivation order until the confiscation order has been made: POCA 2002 ss.13(3) and 15. **41-009**

**Vehicles**

If a person commits an offence: **41-010**

(a) under the Road Traffic Act 1988 (RTA 1988) punishable with imprisonment;
(b) of manslaughter; or
(c) of wanton and furious driving (OAPA 1861 s.35); by driving, attempting to drive or being in charge of a vehicle, failing to provide a specimen for analysis or laboratory test or to give permission for such a test, or failing to stop and give information or report an accident,

the vehicle shall be regarded as used for the purpose of committing the offence and any offence of aiding the commission of the offence: SC s.154.

**Property relating to immigration or asylum offence** Where the court makes a deprivation order and the court considers that the offence: **41-011**

(a) related to immigration or asylum; or
(b) was committed for a purpose in connection with immigration or asylum, it may order that the property is to be taken into the possession of the Secretary of State: SC s.156(1) and (2).

# FORFEITURE/DEPRIVATION—SPECIFIC POWERS

*References: Current Sentencing Practice A4; Archbold 5A-525*

This section includes orders in relation to: **42-001**

(1) drugs;
(2) terrorism offences;
(3) offensive weapons;
(4) crossbows;
(5) knives;
(6) forgery and counterfeiting;
(7) written material (racial hatred);
(8) immigration offences; and
(9) trafficking offences.

## (1) Misuse of Drugs Act 1971 s.27

**Availability** The offender must be convicted of a drug trafficking offence (as defined in the POCA 2002 Sch.2) or an offence under the MDA 1971 s.27(1). **42-002**

**Test** The court may order forfeiture of anything shown to the satisfaction of the court to relate to the offence, MDA 1971 s.27(1). The offender may give evidence to show that the property is not related to the offence: *Churcher* (1986) 8 Cr. App. R.(S.) 94. **42-003**

**Purpose** Orders can serve a dual function: (a) punishment; and (b) removal from public circulation of an item used to commit an offence: *Highbury Corner Magistrates' Court Ex p. Di Matteo* [1991] 1 W.L.R. 1374; [1992] 1 All E.R. 102; (1991) 92 Cr. App. R. 263. **42-004**

A deprivation order is to be considered as part of the overall penalty: *Buddo* (1982) 4 Cr. App. R.(S.) 268. It may be necessary to reduce other elements of the sentence that would otherwise be imposed in consequence of a deprivation order to ensure the punishment is not disproportionate: *De Jesus* [2015] EWCA Crim 1118; [2015] 2 Cr. App. R.(S.) 44.

**Property** The court may not order forfeiture of intangible property or land or buildings, see e.g. *Cuthbertson* (1980) 2 Cr. App. R.(S.) 214. Property may not be forfeited on the grounds that it is the proceeds of offences of which the offender has not been convicted, or is intended to be used to facilitate the commission of future offences: *Ribeyre* (1982) 4 Cr. App. R.(S.) 165; [1982] Crim. L.R. 538. **42-005**

**Others claiming to own the property** If anyone claims to be the owner of the property or otherwise interested in it, they must be given the chance to show cause why the forfeiture order should not be made: MDA 1971 s.27(2). **42-006**

As to property subject to hire-purchase agreements: *Kearney* [2011] EWCA Crim 826; [2011] 2 Cr. App. R.(S.) 106; [2011] Crim. L.R. 567.

Deprivation orders should not be made except in simple uncomplicated cases: *Troth* [1998] 1 Cr. App. R.(S.) 341; [1998] Crim. L.R. 73.

42-007 **Effect** The court may order the property concerned to be destroyed, or dealt with in such manner as the court may order: MDA 1971 s.27(1).

42-008 **Confiscation** Where a court has postponed confiscation proceedings and proceeds to sentence the offender before making the confiscation order, it must not make a forfeiture order until the confiscation order has been made: POCA 2002 s.15(2)(b).

42-009 **Direct money paid to charity** When ordering money to be forfeited under this section, the court may direct that the sum is to be paid to a specific charity. The charity must be registered with the Charity Commission and have indicated its willingness to receive the monies. The judge must have no substantive connection with the charity awarded the monies so as to avoid the appearance of a conflict of interest, Guidance on forfeiture of monies to specific charities: Senior Presiding Judge, 10 June 2015.

**(2) Terrorist offences**

**Powers**

42-010 **TA 2000 ss.15(1) or (2) or 16** The court may order the forfeiture of any money or other property which, at the time of the offence, the person had in their possession or under their control and which had been used for the purposes of terrorism, or they intended should be used, or had reasonable cause to suspect might be used, for those purposes: TA 2000 s.23(2).

42-011 **TA 2000 s.15(3)** The court may order the forfeiture of any money or other property which, at the time of the offence, the person had in their possession or under their control and which had been used for the purposes of terrorism, or which, at that time, they knew or had reasonable cause to suspect would or might be used for those purposes: TA 2000 s.23(3).

42-012 **TA 2000 ss.17 or 18** The court may order the forfeiture of any money or other property which, at the time of the offence, the person had in their possession or under their control and which had been used for the purposes of terrorism, or was, at that time, intended by them to be used for those purposes: TA 2000 s.23(4).

42-013 **TA 2000 s.17** The court may order the forfeiture of the money or other property to which the arrangement in question related, and which had been used for the purposes of terrorism, or at the time of the offence, the person knew or had reasonable cause to suspect would or might be used for those purposes: TA 2000 s.23(5).

42-014 **TA 2000 s.18** The court may order the forfeiture of the money or other property to which the arrangement in question related: TA 2000 s.23(6).

42-015 **TA 2000 ss.15 to 18** The court may order the forfeiture of any money or other property which wholly or partly, and directly or indirectly, is received by any person as a payment or other reward in connection with the commission of the offence: TA 2000 s.23(7).

**TA 2000, TA 2006 and other offences** Where a person is convicted of an offence under: 42-016

(a) TA 2000 ss.54, 57, 58 or 58A, 58B, 59, 60 or 61;
(b) TA 2006 ss.2, 5, 6, 9, 10, or 11;
(c) an offence that the court has determined in accordance with s.69 of the Sentencing Code;
(d) any ancillary offence related to these offences,

the court may order the forfeiture of any money or other property which was, at the time of the offence, in the possession or control of the person convicted and had been used for the purposes of terrorism, was intended by that person to be used for the purposes of terrorism, or the court believes that it will be used for the purposes of terrorism unless forfeited: TA 2000 s.23A.

**Others claiming to own the property** Before making a forfeiture order, the court must give an opportunity to be heard to any person, other than the convicted person, who claims to be the owner or otherwise interested in anything which can be forfeited. The court must have regard to the value of the property, and the likely financial and other effects on the convicted person of the making of the order (taken together with any other order that the court contemplates making): TA 2000 s.23B(1) and (2). 42-017

**Compensating for loss, etc.** Where a court makes a forfeiture order where the offender has been convicted of an offence that has resulted in a person suffering personal injury, loss or damage, or any such offence is taken into consideration by the court in determining sentence, the court may also order that an amount not exceeding a sum specified by the court is to be paid to that person out of the proceeds of the forfeiture. The court may make an order only if it is satisfied that but for the inadequacy of the offender's means it would have made a compensation under which the offender would have been required to pay compensation of an amount not less than the specified amount: TA 2000 Sch.4 para.4A. 42-018

**Additional powers** Before making an order under the following provisions, the court must give an opportunity to be heard to any person, other than the convicted person, who claims to be the owner or otherwise interested in anything which can be forfeited. The court may also make such other provision as appears to it to be necessary for giving effect to the forfeiture, including, in particular, provision relating to the retention, handling, disposal or destruction of what is forfeited: TA 2000 s.120A(2) and TA 2006 ss.7(2) and 11A(3). 42-019

**TA 2000 s.54** The court may order the forfeiture of anything that the court considers to have been in the possession of the person for purposes connected with the offence: TA 2000 s.120A(1). 42-020

**TA 2000 s.57** The court may order the forfeiture of any article that is the subject matter of the offence: TA 2000 s.120A(1). 42-021

**TA 2000 s.58** The court may order the forfeiture of any document or record containing information of the kind mentioned in subs.(1)(a) of that section: TA 2000 s.120A(1). 42-022

**TA 2000 s.58A** The court may order the forfeiture of any document or record 42-023 containing information of the kind mentioned in subs.(1)(a) of that section: TA 2000 s.120A(1).

42-024 **TA 2006 s.6** The court may order the forfeiture of anything the court considers to have been in the person's possession for purposes connected with the offence: TA 2006 s.7(1).

42-025 **TA 2006 s.9 or s.10** The court may order the forfeiture of any radioactive device or radioactive material, or any nuclear facility, made or used in committing the offence: TA 2006 s.11A(1).

42-026 **TA 2006 s.11** The court may order the forfeiture of any radioactive device or radioactive material, or any nuclear facility, which is the subject of a demand under subs.(1) of that section, or a threat falling within subs.(3) of that section: TA 2006 s.11A(2).

**(3) Offensive weapons**

42-027 **Power** Where a person is convicted of an offence under the Prevention of Crime Act 1953 (PCA 1953) s.1(1), the court may make an order for the forfeiture or disposal of any weapon in respect of which the offence was committed: PCA 1953 s.1(2).

**(4) Crossbows Act 1987**

42-028 **Power** The court by which a person is convicted of an offence under the Crossbows Act 1987 (CA 1987) may make such order as it thinks fit as to the forfeiture or disposal of any crossbow or part of a crossbow in respect of which the offence was committed: CA 1987 s.6(3).

**(5) Knives Act 1997**

42-029 **Knives** If a person is convicted of an offence under s.1 (unlawful marketing of knives) in relation to a knife of a particular description, the court may make an order for forfeiture in respect of any knives of that description:

(a) seized under a warrant issued under s.5; or
(b) in the offender's possession or under their control at the relevant time: Knives Act 1997 (KA 1997) s.6(1).

42-030 **Publications** If a person is convicted of an offence under s.2 (publications) in relation to particular material, the court may make an order for forfeiture in respect of any publications consisting of or containing that material which:

(a) have been seized under a warrant issued under s.5; or
(b) were in the offender's possession or under their control at the relevant time: KA 1997 s.6(2).

42-031 **Duty to consider value, etc.** The court must consider the value of the item/material and the effect it will have upon the offender: KA 1997 s.6(4).

**Recovery order** The court may make an order for the delivery of the forfeited item/material upon an application by an individual who claims to be the owner and is not the offender from whom it was forfeited: KA 1997 s.7(3). 42-032

**(6) Forgery and Counterfeiting Act 1981**

**Forgery, etc. offences** The court by or before which a person is convicted of an offence under the Forgery and Counterfeiting Act 1981 (FCA 1981) Pt 1 may order any object shown to the satisfaction of the court to relate to the offence to be forfeited and either destroyed or dealt with in such other manner as the court may order: FCA 1981 s.7(3). 42-033

The court shall not order any object to be forfeited under where a person claiming to be the owner of or otherwise interested in it applies to be heard by the court, unless an opportunity has been given to them to show cause why the order should not be made: FCA 1981 s.7(4).

**Counterfeiting, etc. offences** The court by or before which a person is convicted of an offence under the FCA 1981 Pt 2 may order any thing shown to the satisfaction of the court to relate to the offence to be forfeited and either destroyed or dealt with in such other manner as the court may order: FCA 1981 s.24(3). 42-034

The court shall not order any thing to be forfeited where a person claiming to be the owner of or otherwise interested in it applies to be heard by the court, unless an opportunity has been given to them to show cause why the order should not be made: FCA 1981 s.24(4).

The powers conferred on the court by s.24(3) and (4) include the power to direct that any object shall be passed to an authority with power to issue notes or coins or to any person authorised by such an authority to receive the object: FCA 1981 s.24(5).

**(7) Written material (racial hatred)**

**Powers** A court by or before which a person is convicted of: 42-035

(a) an offence under s.18 (use of words or behaviour or display of written material); or
(b) an offence under s.19 (publishing or distributing written material); s.21 (distributing, showing or playing a recording) or s.23 (possession of racially inflammatory material), shall order to be forfeited any written material or recording produced to the court and shown to its satisfaction to be written material or a recording to which the offence relates: Public Order Act 1986 (POA 1986) s.25(1).

A court by or before which a person is convicted of:

(a) an offence under s.29B (use of words or behaviour or display of written material) relating to the display of written material; or
(b) an offence under s.29C (publishing or distributing written material), s.29E (distributing, showing or playing a recording) or s.29G (possession of inflammatory material), shall order to be forfeited any written material or

recording produced to the court and shown to its satisfaction to be written material or a recording to which the offence relates: POA 1986 s.29I(1).

The order is suspended until the time limit for applying to appeal has expired: POA 1986 ss.25(2) and 29I(2).

**(8) Immigration offences**

42-036 **Power** The court may order the forfeiture of a vehicle, ship or aircraft used or intended to be used in connection with the offence if the convicted person:

(a) owned the vehicle, ship or aircraft at the time the offence was committed;
(b) was at that time a director, secretary or manager of a company which owned the vehicle, ship or aircraft;
(c) was at that time in possession of the vehicle, ship or aircraft under a hire-purchase agreement;
(d) was at that time a director, secretary or manager of a company which was in possession of the vehicle under a hire-purchase agreement;
(e) was at that time a charterer of the ship or aircraft;
(f) was driving the vehicle, ship or aircraft in the course of the commission of the offence; or
(g) committed the offence while acting as captain of the ship or aircraft: Immigration Act 1971 (IA 1971) s.25C(2) and (3).

42-037 **Limitations** There are certain limitations on forfeiture which arise depending on the link between the individual and the ship, vehicle or aircraft being forfeited: IA 1971 s.25C(4)-(6).

42-038 **Representations** Where a person who claims to have an interest in a vehicle, ship or aircraft applies to a court to make representations on the question of forfeiture, the court may not make an order under this section in respect of the ship, aircraft or vehicle unless the person has been given an opportunity to make representations: IA 1971 s.25C(8).

**(9) Trafficking offences**

42-039 **Power** Where an individual is convicted of an offence under the Modern Slavery Act 2015 (MSA 2015) s.2 trafficking), the court has the power to make a forfeiture order: MSA 2015 s.11(1).

42-040 **Land vehicles** The court may order the forfeiture of a land vehicle used or intended to be used in connection with the offence if the convicted person:

(a) owned the vehicle at the time the offence was committed;
(b) was at that time a director, secretary or manager of a company which owned the vehicle;
(c) was at that time in possession of the vehicle under a hire-purchase agreement;
(d) was at that time a director, secretary or manager of a company which was in possession of the vehicle under a hire-purchase agreement; or
(e) was driving the vehicle in the course of the commission of the offence: MSA 2015 s.11(2).

**Ships or aircraft** The court may order the forfeiture of a ship or aircraft used or intended to be used in connection with the offence if the convicted person: **42-041**

- (a) owned the ship or aircraft at the time the offence was committed;
- (b) was at that time a director, secretary or manager of a company which owned the ship or aircraft;
- (c) was at that time in possession of the ship or aircraft under a hire purchase agreement;
- (d) was at that time a director, secretary or manager of a company which was in possession of the ship or aircraft under a hire-purchase agreement;
- (e) was at that time a charterer of the ship or aircraft; or
- (f) committed the offence while acting as captain of the ship or aircraft: MSA 2015 s.11(3).

*Note: There are limited exceptions in the case of ships and aircraft. See MSA 2015 s.11(4) and (5).*

**Third party interest** Where a person who claims to have an interest in a land vehicle, ship or aircraft applies to a court to make representations about its forfeiture, the court may not order its forfeiture without giving the person an opportunity to make representations: MSA 2015 s.11(6). **42-042**

# DISQUALIFICATION FROM DRIVING—DISCRETIONARY (GENERAL POWER)

## SENTENCING CODE ss.162–169

*References: Current Sentencing Practice; A4; Archbold 5A-539*

### General

**What is a driving disqualification order?** In the Sentencing Code, "driving disqualification order" means an order made under Pt 8, Ch.1, in respect of an offender that the offender is disqualified, for the period specified in the order, for holding or obtaining a driving licence: SC s.162. **43-001**

### Two orders

There are two "general powers"; one which enables the court to disqualify an offender convicted of any offence (SC s.163), and one which requires the court to be of the opinion that a vehicle was used for the purposes of crime (SC s.164). See below for specific provision regarding those orders. **43-002**

### Determining the period

**Disqualification period** By virtue of ss.165 and 66, there are three parts to the disqualification period: the "discretionary period" (see s.165) the "extension period" (see s.166) and the "uplift" (see s.167). **43-003**

The discretionary period must be such period as the court considers appropriate: SC s.165.

There is a duty to impose an extension period where the court imposes a custodial sentence imposed in relation to the offence for which disqualification was ordered: SC s.166(3). This does not apply to a suspended sentence or a whole life order imposed as part of a life sentence: SC s.166(3).

Additionally where:

(a) the court imposes a custodial sentence (that is not a suspended sentence) in relation to another offence before the court for sentencing on the same occasion; or
(b) where another custodial sentence previously imposed has not expired, there is a duty to impose an uplift to the disqualification: SC s.167(1).

**Checklist** The court in *Needham* [2016] EWCA Crim 455; [2016] 1 W.L.R. 4449; [2016] 2 Cr. App. R. (S.) 26 suggested the following checklist be used in such cases. **43-004**

*Step 1* — does the court intend to impose a "discretionary" disqualification for any offence?

*Yes* — go to Step 2.

*Step 2* — does the court intend to impose a custodial term for that same offence?

*Yes* — s.166 applies and the court must impose an extension period for that same offence and consider Step 3).
*No* — does not apply to all — go on to consider s.166 does not apply at all — go on to consider s.167 and Step 4.

*Step 3* — does the court intend to impose a custodial term for another offence (which is longer or consecutive) or is the defendant already serving a custodial sentence?

Yes — then consider what increase ("uplift") in the period of "discretionary" disqualification is required to comply with s.167(2) and ignore any custodial term imposed for an offence involving disqualification under s.166.
*Discretionary period + extension period + uplift = total period of disqualification*
*No* — no need to consider s.167 at all.
*Discretionary period + extension period = total period of disqualification*

*Step 4* — does the court intend to impose a custodial term for another offence or is the defendant already serving a custodial sentence?

*Yes* — then consider what increase ("uplift") in the period of "discretionary disqualification" is required to comply with s.167(2).
*Discretionary period + uplift = total period of disqualification*

See *Needham* [2016] EWCA Crim 455; [2016] 2 Cr. App. R.(S.) 26 for further guidance.

It is open to a judge obliged by statute to impose disqualification, to reflect in the calculation of the period of disqualification, the fact that the offender has spent time remanded in custody: *Grant* [2023] EWCA Crim 1414; [2024] 1 Cr. App. R. (S.) 40.

43-005 **Extension periods** The extension does not apply to a suspended sentence order. The extension periods are as follows:

| **Sentence** | **Extension period** |
|---|---|
| A DTO (s.233) | Half the term of the DTO |
| A sentence of detention under s.252A (special sentence of detention for terrorist offenders of particular concern) | Two-thirds of the term imposed pursuant to s.252A(5) (the appropriate custodial term) |
| An extended sentence of detention (s.254) | Two-thirds of the appropriate custodial term |
| A sentence under s.265 (special custodial sentence for certain offenders of particular concern: adults aged 18 to 20) | Two-thirds of the term imposed pursuant to s.265(2)(a) (the appropriate custodial term) |
| An extended sentence of detention in a young offender institution | Two-thirds of the term imposed pursuant to s.266(a) (the appropriate custodial term) |

| Sentence | Extension period |
|---|---|
| A sentence under s.278 (special custodial sentence for certain offenders of particular concern: adults aged 21 and over) | Two-thirds of the term imposed pursuant to s.278(2)(a) (the appropriate custodial term) |
| A serious terrorism sentence | The term imposed under ss.268C(2) or 282C(2) (the appropriate custodial term) |
| An extended sentence of imprisonment | Two-thirds of the term imposed pursuant to s.279(a) (the appropriate custodial term) |
| A custodial sentence in respect of which s.244ZA of the Criminal Justice Act 2003 applies to the offender | Two-thirds of the sentence |
| A custodial sentence not within any of the preceding entries in respect of which s.247A of the Criminal Justice Act 2003 applies to the offender | Two-thirds of the sentence |
| A life sentence in relation to which a minimum term order is made under s.321(2) | The term specified in the minimum term order |
| Any other case | Half the custodial sentence imposed |

**Uplift** Additionally, where: **43-006**

(a) the court imposes a custodial sentence (that is not a suspended sentence) in relation to another offence before the court for sentencing on the same occasion; or
(b) where another custodial sentence previously imposed has not expired, there is a duty to impose an uplift to the disqualification: SC s.167(1).

**Two or more offences involving discretionary disqualification** As orders of disqualification take effect immediately, it is generally desirable for the court to impose a single disqualification order that reflects the overall criminality of the offending behaviour: *TICs and Totality Guideline* 2012, p.15. **43-007**

**Warn the defence**

If the court proposes to disqualify, the offender's advocate should be warned of the possibility of disqualification: *Doherty* [2011] EWCA Crim 1591; [2012] 1 Cr. App. R.(S.) 48. **43-008**

**"Any Offence" — s.163**

**Availability** The power to disqualify may be used by the Crown Court or a magistrates' court, where the offender is convicted of an offence committed on or after 1 January 1998 and the court has been notified by the Secretary of State that the power to make such orders is exercisable by the court (and the notice has not been withdrawn): SC s.163(1). **43-009**

43-010 **Power** Any court may disqualify an offender from driving on conviction for any offence, either in addition to any other sentence or instead of any other sentence: SC s.163(2).

It is not necessary that the offence should be connected in any way with the use of a motor vehicle.

43-011 **Public protection** Authorities regarding the public protection function of a driving disqualification were "probably not apt" to the power in s.163 as there is no requirement that the offences were connected with a motor vehicle: *Griffin* [2019] EWCA Crim 563; [2019] 2 Cr. App. R. (S.) 32.

**"Used for the Purposes of Crime"— s.164**

43-012 **Availability** There are two circumstances in which an order under s.164 are available.

The power is available where:

(a) an offender is convicted on indictment of an offence;
(b) the offence is punishable on indictment with imprisonment for a term of two years or more; and
(c) the Crown Court is satisfied that a motor vehicle was used (by the offender or by anyone else) for the purpose of committing, or facilitating the commission of, the offence: SC s.164(1).[1]

The power is also available to the court by or before which an offender is convicted of an offence also where:

(a) the offence is:
   (i) common assault; or
   (ii) any other offence involving an assault (including an offence under Pt 2 of the Serious Crime Act 2007 (SCA 2007) (encouraging or assisting) related to, or incitement to commit, an offence);
(b) the offence was committed on or after 1 July 1992; and
(c) the court is satisfied that the assault was committed by driving a motor vehicle: SC s.164(3).

The only type of conspiracy which a defendant can be disqualified under s.164 on conviction for is one in which the vehicle was used directly in the formation of the conspiracy itself. The mere fact that vehicles were used in acts performed in furtherance of a conspiracy is not sufficient to engage the powers in s.164 as was made clear in *Riley* (1983) 5 Cr. App. R.(S.) 335; [1984] R.T.R. 159; [1984] Crim. L.R. 48: *Gorry* [2018] EWCA Crim 1867; [2019] 1 Cr. App. R.(S.) 8; [2019] R.T.R. 23.

---

[1] Facilitating the commission of an offence includes taking any steps after it has been committed for the purpose of: (a) disposing of any property to which the offence relates; or (b) avoiding apprehension or detection: SC s.164(2).

# DISQUALIFICATION FROM DRIVING—DISCRETIONARY (ROAD TRAFFIC)

## Road Traffic Offenders Act 1988 s.34

*References: Current Sentencing Practice A4; Archbold 32-249*

### Availability

Where a person is convicted of an offence involving discretionary disqualification, and either: **44-001**

(a) the penalty points to be taken into account on that occasion number fewer than 12; or
(b) the offence is not one involving obligatory endorsement, the court may order that person to be disqualified for such period as the court thinks fit: RTOA 1988 s.34(2).

### Offences

See RTOA 1988 Sch.2 for the list of offences carrying discretionary disqualification. As a general rule, offences which are endorsable are also liable to discretionary disqualification. **44-002**

The following offences are subject to discretionary disqualification but not endorsement:

(a) stealing or attempting to steal a motor vehicle;
(b) taking a motor vehicle without consent, or being carried; and
(c) going equipped to steal a motor vehicle: RTOA 1988 Sch.2 Pt II para.1.

### Discretion

There is no obligation to disqualify. **44-003**

### Penalty points

If the court does disqualify, the court does not award penalty points: *Kent* [1983] 1 W.L.R. 794; [1983] 3 All E.R. 1; (1983) 5 Cr. App. R.(S.) 171 and *Usaceva* [2015] EWCA Crim 166; [2016] 4 W.L.R. 66; [2015] 2 Cr. App. R.(S.) 7. **44-004**

In some cases in which the court is considering discretionary disqualification, the offender may already have sufficient penalty points on their licence that they would be liable to a "totting up" disqualification if further points were imposed. In these circumstances, the court should impose penalty points rather than discretionary disqualification so that the minimum totting up disqualification period applies: *Magistrates' Court Sentencing Guidelines* 2008, p.185.

### Length

**44-005** If an offender is convicted of any of these offences, the court may order the offender to be disqualified for such period as it thinks fit. There is no maximum or minimum period: RTOA 1988 s.34(2).

It is open to a judge obliged by statute to impose disqualification, to reflect in the calculation of the period of disqualification, the fact that the offender has spent time remanded in custody: *Grant* [2023] EWCA Crim 1414; [2024] 1 Cr. App. R. (S.) 40.

### Extension of disqualification where custodial sentence also imposed

**44-006** Where the court imposes a custodial sentence and a driving disqualification, the order under s.34 or 35 must provide for the person to be disqualified for the appropriate extension period, in addition to the discretionary disqualification period: RTOA 1988 s.35A.

The extension does not apply to a suspended sentence order.

The extension periods are as follows:

| **Sentence** | **Extension period** |
|---|---|
| A DTO (s.233) | Half the term of the DTO |
| A sentence of detention under s.252A (special sentence of detention for terrorist offenders of particular concern) | Two-thirds of the term imposed pursuant to s.252A(5) (the appropriate custodial term) |
| An extended sentence of detention (s.254) | Two-thirds of the appropriate custodial term |
| A sentence under s.265 (special custodial sentence for certain offenders of particular concern: adults aged 18 to 20) | Two-thirds of the term imposed pursuant to s.265(2)(a) (the appropriate custodial term) |
| An extended sentence of detention in a young offender institution | Two-thirds of the term imposed pursuant to s.266(a) (the appropriate custodial term) |
| A sentence under s.278 (special custodial sentence for certain offenders of particular concern: adults aged 21 and over) | Two-thirds of the term imposed pursuant to s.278(2)(a) (the appropriate custodial term) |
| A serious terrorism sentence | The term imposed under ss.268C(2) or 282C(2) (the appropriate custodial term). |
| An extended sentence of imprisonment | Two-thirds of the term imposed pursuant to s.279(a) (the appropriate custodial term) |
| A custodial sentence in respect of which s.244ZA of the Criminal Justice Act 2003 applies to the offender | Two-thirds of the sentence |

| Sentence | Extension period |
|---|---|
| A custodial sentence not within any of the preceding entries in respect of which s.247A of the Criminal Justice Act 2003 applies to the offender | Two-thirds of the sentence |
| A life sentence in relation to which a minimum term order is made under s.321(2) | The term specified in the minimum term order |
| Any other case | Half the custodial sentence imposed |

## Checklist

The court in *Needham* [2016] EWCA Crim 455; [2016] 1 W.L.R. 4449; [2016] 2 Cr. App. R.(S.) 2 suggested the following checklist be used in such cases: **44-007**

*Step 1* — does the court intend to impose a "discretionary" disqualification under s.34 or s.35 for any offence?

*Yes* — go to Step 2.

*Step 2* — does the court intend to impose a custodial term for that same offence?

*Yes* — s.35A applies and the court must impose an extension period (see s.35A, s.35A(4)(h) for that same offence and consider Step 3).
*No* — does not apply to all — go on to consider s.35A does not apply at all — go on to consider s.35B and Step 4.

*Step 3* — does the court intend to impose a custodial term for another offence (which is longer or consecutive) or is the defendant already serving a custodial sentence?

*Yes* — then consider what increase ("uplift") in the period of "discretionary" disqualification is required to comply with s.35B(2) and (3) — in accordance with s.35B(4), ignore any custodial term imposed for an offence involving disqualification under s.35A.

*Discretionary period + extension period + uplift = total period of disqualification*

*No* — no need to consider s.35B at all.

*Discretionary period + extension period = total period of disqualification*

*Step 4* — does the court intend to impose a custodial term for another offence or is the defendant already serving a custodial sentence?

*Yes* — then consider what increase ("uplift") in the period of "discretionary disqualification" is required to comply with s.35B(2) and (3).

*Discretionary period + uplift = total period of disqualification*

See *Needham* [2016] EWCA Crim 455; [2016] 1 W.L.R. 4449; [2016] 2 Cr. App. R.(S.) 26 for further guidance.

**Two or more offences involving discretionary disqualification**

**44-008** As orders of disqualification take effect immediately, it is generally desirable for the court to impose a single disqualification order that reflects the overall criminality of the offending behaviour: *Totality Guideline* 2023.

**Warn the defence**

**44-009** If the court proposes to disqualify, the offender's advocate should be warned of the possibility of disqualification: *Doherty* [2011] EWCA Crim 1591; [2012] 1 Cr. App. R.(S.) 48.

**Expressing the disqualification period**

**44-010** The period of disqualification may be expressed in weeks, to avoid any difficulty with s.35 RTOA 1988: *Morrison* [2021] EWCA Crim 917; [2022] 1 Cr. App. R.(S.) 20.

# DISQUALIFICATION FROM DRIVING—OBLIGATORY

## Road Traffic Offenders Act 1988 s.34

*References: Current Sentencing Practice A4; Archbold 32-249*

### General

**Obligation to disqualify** Where a person is convicted of an offence involving obligatory disqualification, the court must order the person to be disqualified: Road Traffic Offenders Act (RTOA) 1988 s.34(1). **45-001**

**Special reasons exception** The obligation to disqualify exists unless the court for special reasons thinks fit to order the person to be disqualified for a shorter period or not to order them to be disqualified: RTOA 1988 s.34(1). See below for more details. **45-002**

**Length** The disqualification period must be for such period not less than 12 months as the court thinks fit: RTOA 1988 s.34(1). **45-003**

It is open to a judge obliged by statute to impose disqualification, to reflect in the calculation of the period of disqualification, the fact that the offender has spent time remanded in custody: *Grant* [2023] EWCA Crim 1414; [2024] 1 Cr. App. R. (S.) 40.

**Extension of disqualification where custodial sentence also imposed** The disqualification period must be for such period not less than 12 months as the court thinks fit: RTOA 1988 s.34(1). **45-004**

Where the court imposes a custodial sentence and a driving disqualification, the order under s.34 or 35 must provide for the person to be disqualified for the appropriate extension period, in addition to the discretionary disqualification period: RTOA 1988 s.35A.

The extension does not apply to a suspended sentence order. The period for a determinate custodial sentence is one half of the custodial term. There are other periods specified in s.35A for other sentencing orders.

In *Needham* [2016] EWCA Crim 455; [2016] 1 W.L.R. 4449; [2016] 2 Cr. App. R.(S.) 26 the court offered guidance on the effect and operation of ss.35A and B, including providing a checklist to follow in such cases. The checklist can be seen at **DISQUALIFICATION FROM DRIVING—DISCRETIONARY (ROAD TRAFFIC), para.44**.

**Penalty points** If the court disqualifies the defendant, it does not award penalty points: RTOA 1988 s.44(1). **45-005**

45-006 **Expressing the disqualification period** The period of disqualification may be expressed in weeks, to avoid any difficulty with s.35 RTOA 1988: *Morrison* [2021] EWCA Crim 917; [2022] 1 Cr. App. R.(S.) 20.

**Offences carrying obligatory disqualification**

45-007 The following offences are subject to obligatory disqualification:

**Six months**

45-008 (a) using vehicle in a dangerous condition within three years of a previous conviction for same offence;

**One year**

45-009 (b) causing death by careless or inconsiderate driving;
(c) causing death by driving while unlicensed or uninsured;
(d) dangerous driving;
(e) driving or attempting to drive while unfit (three years for repeat offenders);
(f) driving or attempting to drive with excess alcohol (three years for repeat offenders);
(g) driving with concentration of specified drug above limit;
(h) failing to provide a specimen for analysis (driving or attempting to drive) (three years for repeat offenders);
(i) failing to allow a specimen to be subject to a laboratory test (three years for repeat offenders);
(j) racing or speed trials;

**Two years**

45-010 (k) causing death by dangerous driving;
(l) causing death by careless driving while under the influence of drink or drugs (three years for repeat offenders);
(m) causing serious injury by dangerous driving;
(n) manslaughter;
(o) causing death by driving: disqualified drivers; and
(p) causing serious injury by driving: disqualified drivers:

RTOA 1988 s.34(4)(a) and Sch.2.

Where the defendant has been twice disqualified for 56 days or more in the three years before the commission of the present offence the minimum is two years: RTOA 1988 s.34(4)(b).

Where the defendant has been convicted of an excess alcohol or failure to provide a specimen offence and has been convicted of such an offence within the last 10 years the minimum is three years: RTOA 1988 s.34(3). Where mandatory minimum periods of disqualification apply those periods are not "starting points"—they are simply minimums: *Morrison* [2021] EWCA Crim 917; [2022] 1 Cr. App. R.(S.) 20. Courts should provide brief reasons for the length of the discretionary disqualification where it exceeds the minimum: *Playfair* [2021] EWCA Crim 644; [2022] 1 Cr. App. R.(S.) 4.

### Minimum periods

To refer to the minimum mandatory periods for disqualification as "starting points" is not an apt description; they are not starting points but simply the minimum periods of disqualification below which a court could not go: *Morrison* [2021] EWCA Crim 917; [2022] 1 Cr. App. R.(S.) 20. **45-011**

### Special reasons

**Burden and standard of proof** The existence of special reasons must be established by the defendant by calling evidence on the relevant matter, unless the prosecution are willing to admit the existence of the facts which are alleged to constitute special reasons. The defendant must establish the relevant facts on the balance of probabilities: *Pugsley v Hunter* [1973] 1 W.L.R. 578; [1973] 2 All E.R. 10; [1973] R.T.R. 28. **45-012**

**Test** A special reason must be a mitigating or extenuating circumstance: **45-013**

(a) not amounting in law to a defence to the charge; but
(b) directly connected with the commission of the offence; and
(c) one which the court ought properly to take into consideration when imposing punishment: *Whittall v Kirby* [1947] K.B. 194; [1946] 2 All E.R. 552; 62 T.L.R. 696.

Matters related to the effect of disqualification on the offender (e.g. personal hardship), or their employer or clients or patients, cannot constitute special reasons for this purpose, see e.g. *Steel* (1968) 52 Cr. App. R. 510; [1968] Crim L.R. 450.

### What amounts to a special reason?

The following matters have been held to be capable of amounting to special reasons in excess alcohol cases: **45-014**

(a) the fact that the defendant consumed alcohol in the expectation that they would not be required to drive again that day, but was required to drive as a result of a sudden emergency see, for example: *Jacobs v Reed* [1974] R.T.R. 81; [1973] Crim. L.R. 531;
(b) the fact that the defendant's consumption of excess alcohol was due to the act of another person who had laced their drink, or caused the defendant to drink stronger liquor than they thought they were drinking, see e.g. *DPP v O'Connor* (1992) 13 Cr. App. R.(S.) 188; [1992] R.T.R. 66; [1992] C.O.D. 81; or
(c) the fact that the defendant has driven an extremely short distance in circumstances where there was no risk to other road users, see e.g. *Reay v Young* [1949] 1 All E.R. 1102; 65 T.L.R. 315; (1949) 113 J.P. 33.

Each of these matters may amount to a special reason in narrowly defined circumstances.

The following matters have been held not to be capable of amounting to special reasons:

- (a) the fact that the defendant's alcohol level is only just over the relevant limit: *Delroy-Hall v Tadman* [1969] 2 Q.B. 208; [1969] 2 W.L.R. 92; [1969] 1 All E.R. 25;
- (b) the fact that the defendant's capacity to drive was not affected: *Brown v Dyerson* [1969] 1 Q.B. 45; [1968] 3 W.L.R. 615; [1968] 3 All E.R. 39;
- (c) the fact the defendant's peculiar metabolism caused them to retain the alcohol in their body for longer than the normal period: *Kinsella v DPP* [2002] EWCA Crim 545;
- (d) the fact that no other road user was endangered by the defendant's driving: *Reay v Young* [1949] 1 All E.R. 1102; 65 T.L.R. 315; (1949) 113 J.P. 336;
- (e) the fact that the defendant had lost or destroyed part of their sample, see *Harding v Oliver* [1973] R.T.R. 497; [1973] Crim. L.R. 764, but see *Anderson* [1972] R.T.R. 113; [1972] Crim. L.R. 245; (1972) 116 S.J. 103 for a contrary decision;
- (f) the fact that the defendant had taken a test earlier on the same day which proved negative: *DPP v White* (1988) 10 Cr. App. R.(S.) 66; [1988] R.T.R. 267; and
- (g) the fact that the defendant had consumed the alcohol the day before they were tested and assumed that they had slept it off overnight: *DPP v O'Meara* (1988) 10 Cr. App. R.(S.) 56; [1989] R.T.R. 24.

**45-015** **Discretion** If the court finds that special reasons exist, it is not obliged to disqualify the defendant, but may do so in the exercise of its discretion.

**45-016** **Warn defence counsel** Before disqualifying, where disqualification is discretionary, the court should inform counsel of its intention and invite submissions on the question of disqualification, see *Doherty* [2011] EWCA Crim 1591; [2012] 1 Cr. App. R.(S.) 48.

**45-017** **Special reasons and penalty points** If the court finds that special reasons exist and does not disqualify, the court must award penalty points (within the range of 3 to 11) and follow the penalty points procedure. (See **DISQUALIFICATION FROM DRIVING—PENALTY POINTS (ENDORSEMENTAND TOTTING UP), para.46**).

**Extended driving test**

**45-018** Where the offender is convicted of an offence of:

- (i) manslaughter (where the defendant caused the death by driving a vehicle);
- (ii) causing death by dangerous driving (s.1 Road Traffic Act (RTA) 1988);
- (iii) causing serious injury by dangerous driving (s.1A RTA 1988);
- (iv) dangerous driving (s.2 RTA 1988);
- (v) causing death by driving (disqualified drivers) (s.3ZC RTA 1988); or
- (vi) causing serious injury by driving: disqualified drivers) (s.3ZD RTA 1988),
- (vii) causing death by careless driving when under the influence of drink or drugs (s.3A RTA 1988).

and the court has disqualified the offender under s.34 RTOA 1988, the court must impose an order for an extended driving test: RTOA 1988 s.36(1) and (2).

Where a person is disqualified until they pass the extended driving test:

(a) any earlier order under this section shall cease to have effect; and
(b) a court shall not make a further order under this section while the person is so disqualified: RTOA 1988 s.36(7).

If the defendant is convicted of any other offence involving obligatory endorsement the court may impose an order for a re-test: RTOA 1988 s.36(4).

# DISQUALIFICATION FROM DRIVING—OBLIGATORY FLOWCHART

**45-019**

The court must disqualify unless there are SPECIAL REASONS for not disqualifying, or for disqualifying for a shorter period (s.34(1)).

↓

The obligation to establish special reasons lies on the defendant.

↓

Has the defendant established special reasons? → Yes → Go to Discretionary Disqualification

No ↓

The court must disqualify for at least 12 MONTHS (s.34(1))

*unless*:

the defendant is convicted of manslaughter, causing death by dangerous driving, causing serious injury by dangerous driving, causing death by driving: disqualified drivers, causing serious injury by driving: disqualified drivers, or causing death by careless driving while under the influence of drink or drugs—minimum TWO YEARS(s.34(4)(a);

*or*:

the defendant has been twice disqualified for 56 days or more in the three years before the commission of the present offence—minimum TWO YEARS (*N.B.* certain disqualifications do not count for this purpose: see s.34(4A);

*or*:

the defendant has been convicted of an offence under RTA 1933 ss.3A, 4(1), 5(1)(a), 5A(1)(a) and (2), 7(6) and 7A(6) and has a conviction for such an offence within the last 10 years.

↓

The court may disqualify the offender for any period longer than the minimum, but where imposing a custodial sentence, the court must also impose an extended disqualification under s.35A or B.

↓ ↓

If the defendant is convicted of manslaughter, causing death by dangerous driving, causing serious injury by dangerous driving, dangerous driving, causing death by driving: disqualified drivers or causing serious injury by driving: disqualified drivers, causing death by careless driving while under the influence of drink or drugs, the court must order him to take an extended driving test (s.36(1) and (2)). This power does not apply to cases of causing death by careless driving contrary to RTA 1988 s.2B.

If the defendant is convicted of any other offence involving obligatory endorsement, the court may order him to take a further driving test (s.36(4)).

# DISQUALIFICATION FROM DRIVING—PENALTY POINTS (ENDORSEMENT AND TOTTING UP)

## Road Traffic Offenders Act 1988 s.28

*References: Current Sentencing Practice A4; Archbold 32-236*

### Endorsement

**Applicability** If the offender is convicted of an offence subject to obligatory endorsement, the court must determine the number of penalty points which are to be attributed to the offence from the table below: RTOA 1988 s.28(1). **46-001**

If the table shows a range of points, the court must determine a number within that range: RTOA 1988 s.28(1).

(For offences not shown below: RTOA 1988 Sch.2.)

| Offence | Penalty points |
|---|---|
| Speeding | 3–6 |
| Careless driving | 3–9 |
| Being in charge of vehicle when unfit to drive | 10 |
| Being in charge of vehicle with excess alcohol level | 10 |
| Failing to provide breath specimen | 4 |
| Failing to provide specimen when disqualification not obligatory | 10 |
| Leaving vehicle in dangerous position | 3 |
| Failing to comply with directions or signs | 3 |
| Using vehicle in dangerous condition | 3 |
| Driving without licence | 3 |
| Driving with uncorrected eyesight | 3 |
| Driving while disqualified | 6 |
| Using vehicle without insurance | 6–8 |
| Failing to stop after accident | 5–10 |
| Failing to give information as to driver | 6 |
| Using a mobile telephone, etc. while driving | 6 |

**Multiple offences** If the offender has committed more than one offence on the same occasion, the court must normally determine points only for the offence carrying the highest number of points, unless the court decides to determine points for other offences: RTOA 1988 s.28(4) and (5). **46-002**

The court must add to these penalty points any other points on the offender's licence, except:

(a) points for offences committed more than three years before the date of the commission of the offences for which points have just been awarded; and
(b) points awarded before a disqualification imposed on the basis of penalty points: RTOA 1988 s.29(2).

**Disqualification as a "totter"**

46-003 If the total number of points is 12 or more, the defendant must be disqualified, unless there are grounds for mitigating the normal consequences of conviction: RTOA 1988 s.35(1) and (1A).

46-004 **Mitigating the normal consequences of conviction** The defendant must establish the mitigating grounds, normally by calling evidence: *Owen v Jones* (1987) 9 Cr. App. R.(S.) 34; [1988] R.T.R. 102.

The following matters "may not" constitute grounds for mitigating the normal consequences of conviction:

(a) circumstances alleged to make the offence or any of the offences not a serious one;
(b) hardship, other than exceptional hardship; or
(c) any circumstances which have been taken into account as mitigating grounds within the last three years: RTOA 1988 s.35(4).

The fact that the offender has been sentenced to custody on this occasion "may" constitute a mitigating ground in an appropriate case: *Thomas* [1983] 1 W.L.R. 1490; [1983] 3 All E.R. 756; (1983) 5 Cr. App. R.(S.) 354.

46-005 If the court finds that there are mitigating grounds, the court may either disqualify for a shorter period than would otherwise be required, or refrain from disqualifying at all: RTOA 1988 s.35(1).

If the court does not disqualify, it should order the licence to be endorsed with the appropriate penalty points unless there are special reasons for not doing so: RTOA 1988 s.44(1) and (2).

46-006 **No mitigating circumstances found** If the defendant does not establish mitigating grounds, the court must disqualify them for at least the relevant minimum period; there is no maximum period: RTOA 1988 s.35(2).

The normal minimum period is six months. If there are previous disqualifications to be taken into account, the minimum period of disqualification may be 12 months or two years. The court may order the offender to take an extended driving test: RTOA 1988 s.36(4).

**Extension of disqualification where custodial sentence also imposed**

46-007 Where the court imposes a custodial sentence and a driving disqualification, the order under s.34 or s.35 must provide for the person to be disqualified for the appropriate extension period, in addition to the discretionary disqualification period: RTOA 1988 s.35A.

The extension does not apply to a suspended sentence order. The period for a determinate custodial sentence is one half of the custodial term. There are other periods specified in s.35A for other sentencing orders.

In *Needham* [2016] EWCA Crim 455; [2016] 1 W.L.R. 4449; [2016] 2 Cr. App. R.(S.) 26 the court offered guidance on the effect and operation of ss.35A and B, including providing a checklist to follow in such cases. The checklist can be seen at **DISQUALIFICATION FROM DRIVING—DISCRETIONARY (ROAD TRAFFIC), para.44**.

**Extended driving test**

Where the offender is convicted of an offence of: **46-008**

(i) manslaughter (where the defendant caused the death by driving a vehicle);
(ii) causing death by dangerous driving (s.1 RTA 1988);
(iii) causing serious injury by dangerous driving (s.1A RTA 1988);
(iv) dangerous driving (s.2 RTA 1988);
(v) causing death by driving (disqualified drivers) (s.3ZC RTA 1988); or
(vi) causing serious injury by driving: (disqualified drivers) (s.3ZD RTA 1988),

and the court has disqualified the offender under s.34 RTOA 1988, the court must impose an order for an extended driving test: RTOA 1988 s.36(1) and (2).

If the defendant is convicted of any other offence involving obligatory endorsement the court may impose an order for an extended driving test: RTOA 1988 s.36(4).

Where a person is disqualified until they pass the extended driving test:

(a) any earlier order under this section shall cease to have effect; and
(b) a court shall not make a further order under this section while they are so disqualified: RTOA 1988 s.36(7).

# TOTTING UP AND ENDORSEMENT (PENALTY POINTS)—FLOWCHART

47-001

The court must determine the number of penalty points which are to be attributed to the offence (s.28(1)). Refer to the table on page 8: if the table shows a range of points, determine a number within that range (s.28(1)(b)).

↓

If the offender has committed more than one offence ON THE SAME OCCASION determine points only for the offence carrying the highest number of points (s.28(4)) unless s.28(5) applies.

↓

Add to these penalty points any other points on the offender's licence (s.29(1)) EXCEPT points for offences committed more than three years before the date of the commission of the offences for which points have just been awarded (s.29(2)) and points awarded before a disqualification *imposed on the basis of penalty points* (s.29(1)(b)).

↓

Is the total number of points 12 OR MORE? — No → Go to Discretionary Disqualification

↓ Yes

The defendant must be disqualified unless there are GROUNDS FOR MITIGATING THE NORMAL CONSEQUENCES OF CONVICTION (s.35(1)).

↓

The defendant must establish the mitigating grounds, normally by evidence.

↓

Are there grounds for mitigating the normal consequences of conviction?

↓

The court must disqualify for at least the relevant minimum period; there is no maximum period. Where imposing a custodial sentence, the court must also impose an extended disqualification under s.35A or B. — Yes → Go to Discretionary Disqualification

↓ No

The normal minimum period is SIX MONTHS (s.35(2)(a)). If there are previous disqualifications to be taken into account, the minimum period of disqualification may be 12 months or two years (s.35(2)(b)).

↓

The court may order the offender to take a further driving test (s.36(4)).

## OFFENCES TO WHICH ROAD TRAFFIC OFFENDERS ACT 1988 DISQUALIFICATION APPLIES

Begin by identifying the category to which the offence with which you are concerned belongs, and then follow the instructions. Repeat the process for each offence, but bear in mind the restrictions on imposing penalty points for offences committed on the same occasion and on imposing more than one disqualification in penalty point cases. **48-001**

All disqualifications run concurrently.

| **Offences Subject to Obligatory Disqualification:** | |
|---|---|
| Causing death by dangerous driving | 3-11 |
| Causing serious injury by dangerous driving | 3-11 |
| Dangerous driving | 3-11 |
| Causing death by driving: unlicensed or uninsured drivers | 3-11 |
| Causing death by driving: disqualified drivers | 3-11 |
| Causing serious injury by driving: disqualified drivers | 3-11 |
| Causing death by careless driving while under the influence of drink or drugs | 3-11 |
| Driving or attempting to drive while unfit | 3-11 |
| Driving or attempting to drive with excess alcohol | 3-11 |
| Failing to provide a specimen for analysis (driving or attempting to drive) | 3-11 |
| Racing or speed trials | 3-11 |
| Manslaughter | 3-11 |
| Aggravated vehicle taking | 3-11 |
| Go to "Obligatory Disqualification" | |

| **Offences Subject to Discretionary Disqualification but not Endorsement:** |
|---|
| Stealing or attempting to steal a motor vehicle |
| Taking a motor vehicle without consent, or being carried |
| Going equipped to steal a motor vehicle |
| Go to "Discretionary Disqualification" |

| **Offences Subject to Obligatory Endorsement (Selected; for Other Offences see RTOA 1988 Sch.2***):* | |
|---|---|
| Careless driving | 3-9 |
| Being in charge of a vehicle when unfit to drive | 10 |
| Being in charge of a vehicle with excess alcohol level | 10 |
| Failing to provide a breath specimen | 4 |
| Failing to provide a specimen when disqualification not obligatory | 10 |
| Leaving vehicle in dangerous position | 3 |
| Failing to comply with directions or signs | 3 |
| Using vehicle in dangerous condition | 3 |

| **Offences Subject to Obligatory Endorsement (Selected; for Other Offences see RTOA 1988 Sch.2)**: | |
|---|---|
| Driving without licence | 3-6 |
| Driving with uncorrected eyesight | 3 |
| Driving while disqualified | 6 |
| Using vehicle without insurance | 6-8 |
| Failing to stop after accident | 5-10 |
| Failing to give information as to driver | 3 |
| Go to "Penalty Points" | |

*Note: An offender convicted of any offence may be disqualified from driving under s.166 of the Sentencing Code. All references are to the RTOA 1988 as amended.*

# COMMUNITY ORDERS

## SENTENCING CODE SS.200–220 AND SCH.9

*References: Current Sentencing Practice A4; Archbold 5A-573*

### General

**What is a community order?** A "community order" means an order imposing one or more community order requirements: SC s.200(1). **49-001**

**Availability** A community order is available to a court by or before which an offender is convicted of an offence if: **49-002**

(a) the offender is aged 18 or over when convicted; and
(b) the offence is punishable with imprisonment by that court: SC s.202(1).

But, this is subject to:

(a) the fact that a community order is not available in respect of an offence to which a mandatory sentence requirement applies;
(b) s.203 (which states that a court may not make a community order in respect of an offence if it makes a suspended sentence order in respect of:
  (i) the offence;
  (ii) any other offence of which the offender is convicted by or before it; or
  (iii) any other offence for which it deals with the offender); and
(c) s.37(8) of the MHA 1983 (community order not to be made in combination with hospital order or guardianship order in respect of same offence): SC s.202(2).

A mandatory sentence requirement applies in the following circumstances:

(a) the offence is one for which the sentence is fixed by law;
(b) the court is obliged by one of the following provisions to pass a sentence of detention for life, custody for life or imprisonment for life:
  (i) ss.258, 258A, 274, 274A, 285 or 285A (life sentence for certain dangerous offenders);
  (ii) s.273 or 283 (life sentence for second listed offence), or
(ba) the court is obliged by s.268B or 282B to impose a serious terrorism sentence
(c) a sentence is required by one of the following provisions and the court is not of the opinion mentioned in that provision:
  (i) s.311(2) or (2A) (minimum sentence for certain offences involving firearms that are prohibited weapons);
  (ii) s.312(2) or (2A) (minimum sentence for offence of threatening with weapon or bladed article);
  (iii) s.313(2) or (2A) (minimum sentence of seven years for third class A drug trafficking offence);
  (iv) s.314(2) or (2A) (minimum sentence of three years for third domestic burglary); or

(v) s.315(2) or (2A) (minimum sentence for repeat offence involving weapon or bladed article or corrosive substance): SC s.399.

49-003 **Test to apply** The court must not make a community order unless it is of the opinion that:

(a) the offence; or
(b) the combination of the offence and one or more offences associated with it,

was serious enough to warrant the making of such an order: SC s.204(2).

In forming its opinion, the court must take into account all the information that is available to it about the circumstances of the offence, or of it and the associated offence or offences, including any aggravating or mitigating factors: SC s.204(3).

The pre-sentence report requirements (see s.30 of the Sentencing Code) apply to the court in relation to forming that opinion: SC s.204(4).

The fact that the offence is serious enough to warrant a community order or the proposed requirements are commensurate with the seriousness of the offence or the combination of offences for which the order would be imposed, does not mean that the court is required to make a community order or to impose those restrictions: SC s.204(5).

**Making the order**

49-004 **Punitive element** The order must include at least one requirement imposed for the purpose of punishment: SC s.208(10). That obligation does not apply where the court imposes a fine for the offence in respect of which the community order is made, or where the court is of the view that there are exceptional circumstances which relate to the offender which would make it unjust to impose a requirement for the purposes of punishment and/or a fine: SC s.208(11).

49-005 **Maximum length** A community order must specify a date, not more than three years after the date of the order, by which all the requirements must have been complied with: SC s.209.

Where the court imposes two or more requirements, it may specify a date by which each of those requirements must be completed, the last of which must be the end date of the order,: SC s.209(3).

A community order ceases to be in force:

(a) at the end of the end date;
(b) if later, when the offender has completed any unpaid work requirement imposed by the order; or
(c) when it is revoked: SC s.220(1) and (2).[1]

The order itself cannot exist other than as a vehicle through which a particular requirement was performed. Therefore, where a single requirement is time-

[1] An unpaid work requirement is completed when the offender has worked under it for the number of hours specified in the order: SC s.220(3).

limited, e.g. unpaid work, 12 months, the order cannot extend beyond 12 months in absence of another requirement with a longer permissible maximum period: *Khan* [2015] EWCA Crim 835; [2015] 2 Cr. App. R.(S.) 39.

**Discount for time on remand** Where a court makes a community order in respect of an offender who has previously been remanded in custody, it may have regard to any period during which the offender has been remanded in custody in connection with the offence for which the order is made, or any offence founded on the same facts or evidence, in determining the restrictions on liberty to be imposed on the offender: SC s.205. **49-006**

Thus, the court has a discretion; there is no obligation to make any allowance in the terms of the order for time spent in custody on remand.

See *Pereira-Lee* [2016] EWCA Crim 1705; [2017] 1 Cr. App. R.(S.) 17; [2017] Crim. L.R. 243 as an example of the issues that can arise.

**Local justice area** A community order must specify the local justice area in which the offender resides or will reside: SC s.210. **49-007**

**Copies of the order** The court must forthwith provide copies of the order: **49-008**

(a) to the offender;
(b) to the responsible officer;
(c) to an officer of a provider of probation services that is a public sector provider who is acting at the court; and
(d) if the court does not act in the offender's home local justice area, to a provider of probation services that is a public sector provider and is operating in that area: SC s.212(1) and (2).

Additionally, an exclusion requirement (for the purpose of protecting a person from being approached by an offender), a residence requirement involving residence in an institution, a mental health treatment requirement, a drug rehabilitation requirement, an alcohol treatment requirement and an electronic monitoring requirement involve further obligations in relation to the provision of copies of the order: SC s.212(2) and (3).

**Breach** The Crown Court may include in the order a direction that any breach of the order is to be dealt with by a magistrates' court. If no such direction is made, any breach will be dealt with by the Crown Court. **49-009**

### Requirements

**General** The requirements are listed in the table in s.201, with a corresponding entry indicating which part of Sch.9 contains further provision about the particular requirement. **49-010**

A court may only impose a requirement which is an available requirement: SC s.206. Requirements imposed must be, in the opinion of the court, the most suitable for the offender: SC s.208(3). The pre-sentence report requirements apply to a court in relation to the determination of the most suitable requirements for the particular offender: SC 208(4). In forming the opinion, the court may take account of any information before it: SC s.208(5).

The restrictions on liberty imposed by the order must be such as are in the opinion of the court commensurate with the seriousness of:

(a) the offence; or
(b) the combination of the offence and one or more offences associated with it: SC s.208(6).

**49-011** The pre-sentence report requirements apply to a court in relation to the determination of the most suitable requirements for the particular offender: SC s.208(7). In forming the opinion, the court may take account of any information before it: SC s.208(8).

There is no restriction on the requirements which may be combined in the same community order, but the court must consider whether the requirements are compatible with each other: SC s.208(12).

The requirements of a community order shall, as far as is practicable, avoid any conflict with the offender's religious beliefs or the requirements of any other community order to which they may be subject, and any interference with the times at which they normally work, or attend school or an educational establishment: SC s.208(13).

**49-012** **Alcohol abstinence and monitoring requirements (SC Sch.9 Pt 12)** An "alcohol abstinence and monitoring requirement", in relation to a relevant order, means a requirement that, during a particular period ("the abstinence and monitoring period"), the offender:

(a) must:
  (i) abstain from consuming alcohol; or
  (ii) not consume alcohol so that at any time during the abstinence and monitoring period there is more than a particular level of alcohol in the offender's body; and
(b) must submit to monitoring in accordance with particular arrangements for the purpose of ascertaining whether the offender is complying with provision under para.(a): SC Sch.9 para.25.

An alcohol abstinence and monitoring requirement is not an available requirement unless regulations are in force under para.25(7)(c) of Sch.9 (prescribed arrangements for monitoring): SC s.207(1).

An alcohol abstinence and monitoring requirement imposing a requirement within para.25(1)(a)(ii) of Sch.9 (alcohol level to be kept below specified level) is not an available requirement unless regulations are in force under s.25(7)(b) of that Schedule (prescribed alcohol level): SC s.207(2). At 31 October 2024, no such regulations were in force.

**49-013** A relevant order that includes an alcohol abstinence and monitoring requirement must specify:

(a) the abstinence and monitoring period;
(b) if the order imposes a requirement to not consume alcohol so that there is at any time in the offender's body more than a particular level of alcohol, the level of alcohol;

(c) the arrangements for monitoring: SC Sch.9 para.25(2).

A relevant order that includes an alcohol abstinence and monitoring requirement may specify exceptions from any requirement imposed to abstain from consuming alcohol: SC Sch.9 para.25(3).

The specified period must not exceed 120 days: SC Sch.9 para.25(4).

A relevant order may not include both: **49-014**

(a) an alcohol treatment requirement; and
(b) an alcohol abstinence and monitoring requirement: SC Sch.9 para.26(1).

A court may not include an alcohol abstinence and monitoring requirement in a relevant order unless the following conditions are met:

(a) the relevance of alcohol condition;
(b) the non-dependency condition; and
(c) the availability of arrangements condition: SC Sch.9 para.26(2).

The relevance of alcohol condition is that:

(a) the offender's consumption of alcohol is an element of the offence for which the order is to be imposed or of an associated offence; or
(b) the court is satisfied that the offender's consumption of alcohol was a factor that contributed to the commission of that offence or to an associated offence: SC Sch.9 para.26(3).

The non-dependency condition is that the court is satisfied that the offender is **49-015**
not dependent on alcohol: SC Sch.9 para.26(4).

The availability of arrangements condition is that the court has been notified by the Secretary of State that arrangements for monitoring of the kind to be specified in the relevant order are available in the offender's home local justice area (and the notice has not been withdrawn): SC Sch.9 para.(5).

**Alcohol treatment requirements (SC Sch.9 Pt 11)** An alcohol treatment require- **49-016**
ment is a requirement that the offender must submit during a period specified in the order to treatment with a view to the reduction or elimination of the offender's dependency on alcohol. That treatment may be:

(a) resident treatment;
(b) institution-based treatment; or
(c) practitioner-based treatment: SC Sch.9 para.23(1) and (2).

The order may specify separate periods comprising the period specified in the order: SC Sch.9 para.23(4).

For each treatment period, the order must specify:

(a) the treatment director;
(b) whether the alcohol dependency treatment is to be resident treatment, institution-based treatment or practitioner-based treatment;
(c) if it is to be resident treatment, the institution or place where it is to be provided;

(d) if it is to be institution-based treatment:
   (i) the institution or place where it is to be provided, and
   (ii) the intervals at which it is to be provided;

but must not otherwise specify the nature of the treatment: SC Sch.9 para.23(5).

**49-017** A court may not impose an alcohol treatment requirement unless the following conditions are met:

(a) the need for treatment condition;
(b) the arrangements condition; and
(c) the consent condition: SC Sch.9 para.24(1).

The need for treatment condition is that the court is satisfied:

(a) that the offender is dependent on alcohol; and
(b) that the offender's dependency:
   (i) requires treatment; and
   (ii) may be susceptible to treatment: SC Sch.9 para.24(2).

The arrangements condition is that the court is satisfied that arrangements:

(a) have been made; or
(b) can be made,

for the treatment intended to be specified in the order.

**49-018** Those arrangements include arrangements for the reception of the offender, where the offender is to be required to submit to treatment as a resident: SC Sch.9 para.24(3).

The consent condition is that the offender expresses willingness to comply with the requirement: SC Sch.9 para.24(4).

*Attendance centre requirements (SC Sch.9 Pt 13) (convictions before 28 June 2022—see 2023 edition).*

**49-019** **Curfew requirements (SC Sch.9 Pt 5)** A curfew requirement requires the offender to remain, for periods specified in the requirement, at a place specified in the order: SC Sch.9 para.9(1) and (2).

The periods specified must not exceed 20 hours per day and must not be for a total in excess of 112 hours in any seven day period: SC Sch.9 para.9(2) and (4).

The requirement may specify different places or different periods for different days: SC Sch.9 para.9(3).

**49-020** All the specified periods must fall within the period of 12 months beginning with the day on which the order takes effect: SC Sch.9 para.9(5).

Before making a curfew requirement, the court must obtain and consider information about the place to be specified in the order and the attitude of persons likely to be affected by the enforced presence there of the offender: SC Sch.9 para.10(1) and (2).

The responsible officer may vary the start time or location of any curfew requirement (convictions on/after 28 June 2022): SC Sch.9 para.10A.

The court must impose an electronic monitoring requirement unless a person whose cooperation is necessary does not consent, or the court has not been notified that arrangements for electronic monitoring are available, or in the particular circumstances of the case the court considers it inappropriate to do so: SC Sch.9 para.10(3). See *Electronic Monitoring Requirements*, below.

**Drug rehabilitation requirements (SC Sch.9 Pt 10)** A "drug rehabilitation requirement", in relation to a relevant order, means a requirement that during a period specified in the order ("the treatment and testing period") the offender: **49-021**

(a) must submit to drug rehabilitation treatment, which may be resident treatment or non-resident treatment; and
(b) for the purpose of ascertaining whether there is any drug in the offender's body during that period, must provide samples in accordance with directions given by:
    (i) the responsible officer; or
    (ii) the treatment director: SC Sch.9 para.19(1).[2]

The order may specify separate periods which together comprise the drug treatment and testing period: SC Sch.9 para.19(4).

The order must specify, for each treatment period:

(a) the treatment director;
(b) if the treatment is to be resident treatment, the institution or place where it is to be provided;
(c) if it is to be non-resident treatment:
    (i) the institution or place where it is to be provided; and
    (ii) the intervals at which it is to be provided;

but must not otherwise specify the nature of the treatment: SC Sch.9 para.19(5). See para.19 for further definitions of terms used in that paragraph.

A court may not impose a drug rehabilitation requirement unless the following conditions are met: **49-022**

(a) the need for treatment condition;
(b) the arrangements condition;
(c) the suitability condition; and
(d) the consent condition: SC Sch.9 para.20(1).

The need for treatment condition is that the court is satisfied:

(a) that the offender:
    (i) is dependent on drugs; or
    (ii) has a propensity to misuse drugs; and
(b) that the offender's dependency or propensity:
    (i) requires treatment; and

---

2 *"Drug rehabilitation treatment,"* in relation to an offender, means treatment which is: (a) by or under the direction of a person who has the necessary qualifications or experience; and (b) with a view to the reduction or elimination of the offender's dependency on or propensity to misuse drugs; *"resident treatment"* means treatment as a resident in an institution or place; *"non-resident treatment"* means treatment as a non-resident at an institution or place; *"the treatment director"* means the person by or under whose direction the treatment is to be provided: SC Sch.9 para.19(2).

(ii) may be susceptible to treatment: SC Sch.9 para.20(2).

The arrangements condition is that the court is satisfied that arrangements:

(a) have been made; or
(b) can be made,

for the treatment intended to be specified in the order.

**49-023** Those arrangements include arrangements for the reception of the offender, where the offender is to be required to submit to resident treatment (within the meaning given in para.19(2)): SC Sch.9 para.20(3).

The suitability condition is that the requirement has been recommended to the court as being suitable for the offender by an officer of a provider of probation services: SC Sch.9 para.20(4).

The consent condition is that the offender expresses willingness to comply with the requirement: SC Sch.9 para.20(5).

**49-024** A relevant order imposing a drug rehabilitation requirement:

(a) must include provision for review if the treatment and testing period is more than 12 months; and
(b) may do so in any other case: SC Sch.9 para.21(1).

For this purpose, "provision for review" means provision:

(a) for the requirement to be reviewed periodically at intervals of not less than one month;
(b) for each review of the requirement to be made at a hearing held for the purpose by the responsible court (a "review hearing");
(c) requiring the offender to attend each review hearing;
(d) requiring a written report on the offender's progress under the requirement to be made by an officer of a provider of probation services to the responsible court before each review hearing; and
(e) requiring each such report to include:
    (i) the test results communicated to the responsible officer under para.19(7) or otherwise; and
    (ii) the views of the treatment provider as to the treatment and testing of the offender: SC Sch.9 para.21(2).

At a review hearing the court may, after considering the officer's report referred to in para.21(2)(d) ("the review officer's report"), amend the relevant order, so far as it relates to the drug rehabilitation requirement: SC Sch.9 para.22(2).

**49-025** The court:

(a) may not amend the drug rehabilitation requirement unless the offender expresses willingness to comply with the requirement as amended; and
(b) except with the consent of the offender, may not amend any requirement or provision of the order while an appeal against the order is pending: SC Sch.9 para.22(3).

If the offender fails to express willingness to comply with the drug rehabilitation requirement as proposed to be amended by the court, the court may:

(a) revoke the community order, or the suspended sentence order and the suspended sentence to which it relates; and
(b) re-sentence the offender: SC Sch.9 para.22(4).

In dealing with the offender under sub-para.(4)(b), the court:

(a) must take into account the extent to which the offender has complied with the requirements of the order; and
(b) may impose a custodial sentence even if it is not of the opinion mentioned in s.230(2) (general restrictions on imposing discretionary custodial sentences): SC Sch.9 para.22(5).

Where at a review hearing the court: **49-026**

(a) has considered the review officer's report; and
(b) is of the opinion that the offender's progress under the requirement is satisfactory,

the court may amend the order so that it provides for each subsequent review to be made by the court without a hearing: SC Sch.9 para.22(6).

Where at a review without a hearing the court:

(a) has considered the review officer's report; and
(b) is of the opinion that the offender's progress under the requirement is no longer satisfactory,

the court may require the offender to attend a hearing of the court at a specified time and place: SC Sch.9 para.22(7).

**Drug testing requirement (convictions on/after 28 June 2022)** A "drug testing requirement" means a requirement that during a period specified in the order, the offender must, for the purpose of ascertaining whether there is any drug or psychoactive substance in the offender's body during that period, provide samples in accordance with directions given by the responsible officer: SC Sch.9 para.22A(1). **49-027**

A court may not impose a drug testing requirement unless the following conditions are met—

(a) the misuse condition, and
(b) the availability of arrangements condition: SC Sch.9 para.22B(1).

The misuse condition is that the court is satisfied that the offender's misuse of a drug or psychoactive substance—

(a) caused or contributed to the offence to which the order relates or an associated offence, or
(b) is likely to cause or contribute to the commission of further offences by the offender: SC Sch.9 para.22B(2).

The availability of arrangements condition is that the court has been notified by the Secretary of State that arrangements for implementing drug testing requirements are available in the offender's home local justice area (and the notice has not been withdrawn): SC Sch.9 para.22B(3).

49-028 The order—

(a) must provide that if the offender provides samples to a person other than the responsible officer, the results of the tests carried out on the samples are to be communicated to the responsible officer;
(b) may make provision about the provision of samples by virtue of subpara.(1): SC Sch.9 para.22A(2).

The responsible officer may give directions about the provision of samples. This power is:

(a) a power to give directions about:
    (i) the type of samples to be provided, and
    (ii) the times at which, or circumstances in which, they are to be provided,
(b) subject to any provision made by the order, and
(c) to be exercised in accordance with guidance issued by the Secretary of State: SC Sch.9 para.22A(3).

Definitions: "drug" means a controlled drug as defined by s.2 of the Misuse of Drugs Act 1971; "psychoactive substance" has the meaning given by s.2(1) of the Psychoactive Substances Act 2016.

49-029 **Electronic monitoring requirements: General (SC Sch.9 Pt 14)** There are two types of electronic monitoring requirement: whereabouts monitoring and compliance monitoring.

Where an order imposes an electronic monitoring requirement, the offender must (in particular):

(a) submit, as required from time to time by the responsible officer or the person responsible for the monitoring, to:
    (i) being fitted with, or installation of, any necessary apparatus; and
    (ii) inspection or repair of any apparatus fitted or installed for the purposes of the monitoring;
(b) not interfere with, or with the working of, any apparatus fitted or installed for the purposes of the monitoring; and
(c) take any steps required by the responsible officer, or the person responsible for the monitoring, for the purpose of keeping in working order any apparatus fitted or installed for the purposes of the monitoring: SC Sch.9 para.32.

Where:

(a) it is proposed to include in a relevant order an electronic monitoring requirement; but
(b) there is a person (other than the offender) without whose cooperation it will not be practicable to secure the monitoring,

the requirement may not be included in the order without that person's consent: SC Sch.9 para.33.

49-030 **Electronic compliance monitoring requirements (SC Sch.9 Pt 14)** An electronic monitoring requirement is not an available requirement unless the community order imposes at least one other requirement (excluding an alcohol abstinence monitoring requirement or an electronic whereabouts monitoring requirement): SC s.207(4).

An "electronic compliance monitoring requirement" means a requirement for securing the electronic monitoring of the offender's compliance with other requirements imposed by the order during a period ("the monitoring period"):

(a) specified in the order; or
(b) determined by the responsible officer in accordance with the relevant order: SC Sch.9 para.29(1).

An electronic compliance monitoring requirement may not be imposed for securing the electronic monitoring of the offender's compliance with an alcohol abstinence and monitoring requirement: SC Sch.9 para.29(4). But that does not prevent an order which imposes an alcohol abstinence and monitoring requirement from including an electronic compliance monitoring requirement for securing the electronic monitoring of the offender's compliance with any other requirement: SC Sch.9 para.29(5).

A court may not include an electronic compliance monitoring requirement in a relevant order in respect of an offender unless: **49-031**

(a) the court has been notified by the Secretary of State that electronic monitoring arrangements are available in the relevant area (and the notice has not been withdrawn); and
(b) the court is satisfied that the necessary provision can be made under those arrangements: SC Sch.9 para.34.

For further provision regarding the "relevant area": see SC Sch.9 para.34(2)–(4).

**Electronic whereabouts monitoring requirement (SC Sch.9 Pt 14)** An "electronic whereabouts monitoring requirement" means a requirement to submit to electronic monitoring of the offender's whereabouts (otherwise than for the purpose of monitoring the offender's compliance with any other requirement included in the order) during a period specified in the order: SC Sch.9 para.30. **49-032**

A court may not include an electronic whereabouts monitoring requirement in a relevant order in respect of an offender unless:

(a) the court has been notified by the Secretary of State that electronic monitoring arrangements are available in the local justice area proposed to be specified in the order (and the notice has not been withdrawn);
(b) the court is satisfied that:
    (i) the offender can be fitted with any necessary apparatus under the arrangements currently available; and
    (ii) any other necessary provision can be made under those arrangements; and
(c) the court is satisfied that arrangements are generally operational throughout England and Wales (even if not always operational everywhere there) under which the offender's whereabouts can be electronically monitored: SC Sch.9 para.35.

**Exclusion requirements (SC Sch.9 Pt 6)** An exclusion requirement prohibits the offender from entering any place specified in the order ("the prohibited place"): SC Sch.9 para.11(1). **49-033**

The order must specific the prohibited place and the exclusion period: SC Sch.9 para.11(2). A prohibited place may be an area: SC Sch.9 para.11(5).

The order may specify:

(a) more than one prohibited place;
(b) more than one exclusion period; or
(c) different prohibited places for different exclusion periods or different days: SC Sch.9 para.11(3).

The requirement cannot exceed two years (whatever the length of the community order): SC Sch.9 para.11(4).

The court must impose an electronic monitoring requirement unless a person whose cooperation is necessary does not consent, or the court has not been notified that arrangements for electronic monitoring are available, or in the particular circumstances of the case the court considers it inappropriate to do so: SC Sch.9 para.12.

49-034 **Foreign travel prohibition requirement (SC Sch.9 Pt 8)** A foreign travel prohibition requirement may prohibit the offender from travelling to any country (or countries) or territory (or territories) outside the British Islands specified in the order: SC Sch.9 para.15.

The requirement may apply to the day or days specified in the order, or for a period specified in the order: SC Sch.9 para.15(2).

The period specified may not exceed 12 months beginning with the day on which the order is made, and the day or days specified may not fall outside the period of 12 months beginning with the day on which the order is made: SC Sch.9 para.15(3) and (4).

49-035 **Mental health treatment requirements (SC Sch.9 Pt 9)** A mental health treatment requirement is a requirement that the offender must submit, during a period or periods specified in the order, to:

(a) in-patient treatment;
(b institution-based out-patient treatment; or
(c) practitioner-based treatment: Sch.9 para.16(1).

A relevant order which imposes a mental health treatment requirement must specify:

(a) the period or periods during which the offender is required to submit to mental health treatment; and
(b) for each of those periods:
    (i) if the mental health treatment is to be in-patient treatment, the care home or hospital at which it is to be provided;
    (ii) if it is to be institution-based out-patient treatment, the institution or place at which it is to be provided; or
    (iii) if it is to be practitioner-based treatment, the registered medical practitioner or registered psychologist (or both) by whom or under whose direction it is to be provided; but may not otherwise specify the nature of the treatment: SC Sch.9 para.16(3).

Different treatment may be specified for different periods: SC Sch.9 para.16(4).

A court may not include a mental health treatment requirement in a relevant order unless the following conditions are met: **49-036**

(a) the need for treatment condition;
(b) the arrangements condition; and
(c) the consent condition.

The need for treatment condition is that the court is satisfied that the mental condition of the offender:

(a) requires treatment;
(b) may be susceptible to treatment; and
(c) does not warrant the making of a hospital order or guardianship order within the meaning of the MHA 1983: SC Sch.9 para.17(2).

The arrangements condition is that the court is satisfied that arrangements:

(a) have been made; or
(b) can be made, for the treatment intended to be specified in the order: SC Sch.9 para.17(3).

The consent condition is that the offender has expressed willingness to comply with the requirement: SC Sch.9 para.17(4).

**Programme requirements (SC Sch.9 Pt 3)** A programme requirement requires the offender to participate in an accredited programme: SC Sch.9 para.6(1). **49-037**

"Programme" means a systematic set of activities: SC Sch.9 para.6(4).

Where a relevant order includes a programme requirement:

(a) the order must specify the number of days on which the offender is to be required to participate in an accredited programme under the requirement;
(b) it is for the responsible officer to specify:
    (i) the accredited programme in which the offender is to participate; and
    (ii) the place at which the offender is to do so: SC Sch.9 para.6(5).

**Prohibited activity requirements (SC Sch.9 Pt 4)** A prohibited activity requirement requires the offender to refrain from participating in activities specified in the requirement on a day or days specified in the order or during a period specified in the requirement: SC Sch.9 para.7(1) and (2). **49-038**

The primary purpose is not to punish but to prevent — or at least reduce — further offending: *J* [2008] EWCA Crim 2002; (2008) 172 J.P. 513; (2008) 172 J.P.N. 742.

The prohibited activity requirements may include requirements relating to possessing, carrying or using firearms: SC Sch.9 para.7(3).

**Rehabilitation activity requirements (SC Sch.9 Pt 2)** A "rehabilitation activity requirement" (RAR) is a requirement that, during the relevant period, the offender must comply with any instructions given by the responsible officer to attend appointments or participate in activities or both: SC Sch.9 para.4(1). **49-039**

The maximum number of days on which the offender may be instructed to participate in activities must be specified in the relevant order: SC Sch.9 para.4(2).

The activities in which offenders may be instructed to participate include activities forming an accredited programme and activities whose purpose is reparative, such as restorative justice activities: SC Sch.9 para.5(6).

The imposition of an RAR requirement only did not conform with the requirement that an order including a punitive element, on the facts of *AG's Ref (Singh)* [2021] EWCA Crim 1426; [2022] 1 Cr. App. R.(S.) 48.

**49-040** **Residence requirements (SC Sch.9 Pt 7)** A residence requirement is a requirement that, during a period specified in the relevant order, the offender must reside at a place specified in the order, or at another place with the prior approval of the responsible officer: SC Sch.9 para.13(1).

A relevant order imposing a residence requirement must specify:

(a) the required place;
(b) the required period; and
(c) if the offender is to be permitted to reside at some other place with the prior approval of the responsible officer, that fact: SC Sch.9 para.13(2).

A hostel or other institution may not be specified as the place of residence except on the recommendation of an officer of a local probation board: SC Sch.9 para.13(3).

Before making an order containing a residence requirement, the court must consider the home surroundings of the offender: SC Sch.9 para.14.

**49-041** **Unpaid work requirements (SC Sch.9 Pt 1)** An unpaid work requirement requires the offender to perform unpaid work for a number of hours, not less than 40 and not more than 300, specified in the order: SC Sch.9 para.2.

The unpaid work must be completed within a period of 12 months: SC Sch.9 para.1(1).

An unpaid work requirement may not be made unless the court is satisfied that the offender is a suitable person to perform work under such a requirement and that provision for the offender to work under such a requirement can be made under the arrangements for persons to perform work under such a requirement which exist in the offender's home local justice area: SC Sch.9 para.3.

Where an offender is convicted of more than one offence, an unpaid work requirement may be made in respect of each offence, and may direct that the hours of work specified in any of the requirements should be concurrent with or in addition to the hours of work required by the other requirement, but the total number of hours which are not concurrent must not exceed the permissible maximum of 300: SC Sch.9 paras 3 and 4.

**Offender's obligations**

**49-042** The offender must keep in touch with the responsible officer: SC s.215(2). This obligation is enforceable as if it were a requirement of the order: SC s.215(3). The offender must not change residence without permission given by the responsible officer, or a court: SC s.216.

# CUSTODIAL SENTENCES—GENERAL PRINCIPLES

## Sentencing Code s.222

*References: Archbold 5A-642*

### Meaning of custodial sentence

In the Sentencing Code "custodial sentence" means: **50-001**

(a) a DTO under s.233;
(b) a sentence of detention under Ch.2 of this Part;
(c) a sentence of detention in a young offender institution;
(d) a sentence of custody for life under s.272 or 275; or
(e) a sentence of imprisonment: SC s.222(1).

This:

(a) does not apply to "custodial sentence" in the following expressions:
    "appropriate custodial sentence";
    "current custodial sentence";
    "pre-Code custodial sentence";
    "relevant custodial sentence"; and
(b) is subject to express provision to the contrary: SC s.222(3).

A "sentence of imprisonment" does not include a committal for contempt of court or any kindred offence: SC s.222(2).

In the Sentencing Code, "pre-Code custodial sentence" means:

(a) a DTO imposed under s.100 of the PCC(S)A 2000;
(b) a sentence of detention imposed under any of the following (sentences of detention for children):
    (i) s.90 or 91 of the PCC(S)A 2000;
    (ii) s.53(1) or (3) of the Children and Young Persons Act 1933 (CYPA 1933); or
    (iii) s.226B or 228 of the CJA 2003;
(c) a sentence of detention for public protection imposed under s.226 of the CJA 2003; or
(d) a sentence of custody for life under:
    (i) s.93 or 94 of the PCC(S)A 2000; or
    (ii) s.8 of the CJA 1982: SC s.222(4).

## REQUIREMENT FOR LEGAL REPRESENTATION

### Sentencing Code s.226

*References: Current Sentencing Practice A4*

### General

This section applies where: **51-001**

(a) a magistrates' court is dealing with an offender on summary conviction; or
(b) the Crown Court is dealing with an offender:
  (i) on committal for sentence; or
  (ii) on conviction on indictment: SC s.226(1).

### Offenders aged under 21

The court may not: **51-002**

(a) make a DTO;
(b) pass a sentence of detention under s.250, s.254, s.252A or under s.259 (offenders under 18);
(c) pass a sentence of detention in a young offender institution; or
(d) pass a sentence of custody for life (see ss.272 and 275),

unless the offender is legally represented in that court, or has failed, or is ineligible on financial grounds, to benefit from relevant representation: SC s.226(2).

### Offenders aged 21 or over

The court may not pass a sentence of imprisonment unless: **51-003**

(a) the offender:
  (i) is legally represented in that court; or
  (ii) has failed, or is ineligible on financial grounds, to benefit from relevant representation (see subs.(7) and (8)); or
(b) the offender has previously been sentenced to imprisonment by a court in any part of the UK: SC s.226(3).

A previous sentence of imprisonment which has been suspended and which has not taken effect under:

(a) para.8 of Sch.16;
(b) para.8 of Sch.12 to the CJA 2003;
(c) s.119 of the PCC(S)A 2000; or
(d) s.19 of the Treatment of Offenders Act (Northern Ireland) 1968,

is to be disregarded for these purposes: SC s.226(4).

For these purposes, "sentence of imprisonment" does not include a committal for contempt of court or any kindred offence (and "sentenced to imprisonment" is to be read accordingly): SC s.226(5).

51-004 **When a person is legally represented** An offender is legally represented in a court if the offender has the assistance of counsel or a solicitor to represent them in the proceedings in that court at some time after being found guilty and before being sentenced: SC s.226(6).

51-005 **Relevant representation: failure or ineligibility to benefit** "Relevant representation", in relation to proceedings in a court, means representation under Pt 1 of the LASPOA 2012 (legal aid) for the purposes of the proceedings: SC s.226(7).

For those purposes, an offender has failed, or is ineligible on financial grounds, to benefit from relevant representation if:

(a) the offender has refused or failed to apply for relevant representation, having:
    (i) been informed of the right to apply for it; and
    (ii) had the opportunity to do so;
(b) the offender's application for relevant representation was refused on financial grounds; or
(c) relevant representation was made available to the offender but withdrawn:
    (i) because of the offender's conduct; or
    (ii) on financial grounds: SC s.226(8).

Relevant representation is refused or withdrawn on financial grounds if it appears that the offender's financial resources are such that the offender is not eligible for such representation: SC s.226(8).

**Effect of breach**

51-006 A sentence passed in breach of these requirements is unlawful, but the Court of Appeal on an appeal against such a sentence may substitute a lawful sentence: *McGinlay* (1976) 62 Cr. App. R. 156; [1976] Crim. L.R. 78. See also *Nguyen* [2022] EWCA Crim 1444.

**General restrictions on imposing custodial sentences**

51-007 **Custody threshold** A court must not pass a custodial sentence unless it is of the opinion that the offence or the combination of the offence and one or more offences associated with it was so serious that neither a fine alone nor a community sentence can be justified for the offence, save where the offence is subject to a mandatory sentence requirement: SC ss.230(1)-(3).

Section 399 of the Sentencing Code provides that a mandatory sentence requirement applies in the following cases:

(a) the offence is one for which the sentence is fixed by law;
(b) the court is obliged by one of the following provisions to pass a sentence of detention for life, custody for life or imprisonment for life:
    (i) ss.258, 258A, 274, 274A, 285 or 285A (life sentence for certain offenders);
    (ii) ss.273 or 283 (life sentence for second listed offence);
(ba) the court is obliged by s.268B or 282B to impose a serious terrorism sentence; or

(c) a sentence is required by one of the following provisions and the court is not of the opinion mentioned in that provision:
    (i) s.311(2) or (2A) (minimum sentence for certain offences involving firearms that are prohibited weapons);
    (ii) s.312(2) or (2A) (minimum sentence for offence of threatening with weapon or bladed article);
    (iii) s.313(2) or (2A) (minimum sentence of seven years for third class A drug trafficking offence);
    (iv) s.314(2) or (2A) (minimum sentence of three years for third domestic burglary);
    (v) s.315(2) or (2A) (minimum sentence for repeat offence involving weapon or bladed article or corrosive substance)

**Community order exception** A custodial sentence may be passed for an offence which is not "so serious that neither a fine alone nor a community sentence can be justified" if the offender refuses to express their willingness to comply with a proposed requirement of a community order which requires them to express their willingness to comply: SC s.230(4) and (5) (See **COMMUNITY ORDERS, para.49**). **51-008**

**Sentence of imprisonment** No court may pass a sentence of imprisonment on an offender for an offence if the offender is aged under 21 when convicted of the offence: SC s.227(1). **51-009**

### Committal to prison

No court may commit a person who is aged under 21 to prison for any reason, except of a person aged under 21 who is: **51-010**

(a) remanded in custody;
(b) committed in custody for sentence; or
(c) sent in custody for trial under ss.51 or 51A of the CDA 1998: SC s.227(2) and (3).

### Hospital order or guardianship order

Where an order is made under s.37 of the MHA 1983, the court shall not: **51-011**

(a) pass a sentence of imprisonment or impose a fine or make a community or a YRO in respect of the offence;
(b) if the order under this section is a hospital order, make a referral order in respect of the offence; or
(c) make in respect of the offender an order binding over a parent or guardian),

but the court may make any other order which it has power to make apart from s.37; and for the purposes of s.37(8) of the MHA 1983 "sentence of imprisonment" includes any sentence or order for detention: MHA 1983 s.37(8).

### Length of discretionary custodial sentences

Subject to an offence to which a minimum sentence requirement applies (see above) a custodial sentence must be for the shortest term (not exceeding the permitted maximum) that in the opinion of the court is commensurate with the serious- **51-012** ness of the offence, or the combination of the offence and one or more offences associated with it: SC s.231(2) and (5).

The court must take account of all available information about the circumstances of the offence when forming an opinion about the seriousness of the offence, for the purpose of deciding whether the offence is so serious that a custodial sentence is necessary and what is the shortest term which is commensurate with the seriousness of the offence: SC s.231(7).

# RESTRICTION ON IMPOSING CONSECUTIVE SENTENCES ON RELEASED PRISONERS

## Sentencing Code s.225

*Current Sentencing Practice A1; Archbold 5A-199*

### Limitation on court's powers

A court sentencing a person to a relevant custodial term may not order or direct that the term is to commence on the expiry of any current custodial sentence from which the offender has been released under: **52-001**

(a) Ch.6 of Pt 12 of the CJA 2003 (release, licences, supervision and recall); or
(b) Pt 2 of the CJA 1991 (early release of prisoners): SC s.225(1).

"*Relevant custodial term*" means a term of:

(a) detention under Ch.2 of Pt 10 of the Sentencing Code (Custodial sentences: Offenders aged under 18);
(b) detention in a young offender institution (under the Sentencing Code); or
(c) imprisonment: SC s.225(2).

"*Current custodial sentence*" means a sentence that has not yet expired which is:

(a) a sentence of imprisonment;
(b) a sentence of detention in a young offender institution; or
(c) a sentence of detention imposed under any of the following:
  (i)(i) s.250 of the Sentencing Code;
  (ii) s.254 of the Sentencing Code (including one passed as a result of s.221A of the AFA 2006);
  (iii) s.252A of the Sentencing Code;
  (iv) ss.226B or 228 of the CJA 2003 (including one passed as a result of s.221A or s.222 of the AFA 2006);
  (v) s.91 of the PCC(S)A 2000;
  (vi) s.53(3) of the Children and Young Persons Act 1933;
  (vii) s.209 of the AFA 2006; or
  (viii) s.71A(4) of the Army Act 1955 or the Air Force Act 1955 or s.43A(4) of the Naval Discipline Act 1957: SC s.225(3).

# CROWN COURT POWERS

## SENTENCING CODE S.223

### No maximum sentence specified

Where: **53-001**

(a) a person is convicted on indictment of an offence under any enactment which is punishable with imprisonment; and
(b) no enactment:
    (i) limits the sentence to a specified term; or
    (ii) expresses it to extend to imprisonment for life,

the person is liable to imprisonment for not more than two years: SC s.223.

### Applicability of magistrates' courts limits

**Crown Court** The restrictions must be observed by the Crown Court when dealing with an offender in respect of the following matters: **53-002**

(a) an offence for which they have been committed for sentence under s.20 of the Sentencing Code;
(b) an offence in respect of which the offender has been committed which a view to a restriction order under the MHA 1983 s.43 and in respect of whom the Crown Court does not make a hospital order;
(c) an offence in respect of which a magistrates' court has made a community order which the Crown Court has revoked;
(d) an offence for which the Crown Court has power to deal with the offender under the CJA 1988 s.40;
(e) an offence in respect of which the offender has appealed against their conviction or sentence; or
(f) an offence for which the offender is sentenced under s.21(4) of the Sentencing Code.

# MAGISTRATES' COURTS' POWERS

## Sentencing Code s.224; Magistrates' Courts Act 1980 s.132

*References: Current Sentencing Practice A4*

### Custodial sentence not indicated in indication of sentence

For restrictions on a custodial sentence where the case is dealt with under s.20(7) of the MCA 1980 (procedure where summary trial appears more suitable and indication of sentence is given), see s.20A(1) of that Act (restriction where indication of sentence does not indicate custodial sentence). **54-001**

**Applicability** The following limitations apply to sentences of imprisonment and detention in a young offender institution. They do not apply to DTOs. **54-002**

**Specified term** Where a magistrates' court has power to sentence an offender to imprisonment for a period specified by an enactment (whether passed or made before or after this Act), the court may sentence the offender to imprisonment for less than that period: SC s.229(1). This is subject to the minimum term specified in s.132 MCA 1980 and any express statutory provision passed after 31 December 1879. **54-003**

**Minimum term** A magistrates' court shall not impose imprisonment for fewer than five days: MCA 1980 s.132. **54-004**

### Summary offences

The maximum for any one offence is 12 months, or the maximum provided for the offence in question, if that is less: SC s.224(1). **54-005**

Unless expressly excluded, that limit applies even if the offence in question is one for which a person would otherwise be liable on summary conviction to imprisonment or detention in a young offender institution for more than the applicable limit: SC s.224(2).

The maximum aggregate term for more than one summary offence is six months: MCA 1980 s.133(1): SC s.224(3).

### Either-way offences

The maximum term for any one offence is 12 months: SC s.224(1), MCA 1980 s.32(1). **54-006**

Unless expressly excluded, that limit applies even if the offence in question is one for which a person would otherwise be liable on summary conviction to imprisonment or detention in a young offender institution for more than the applicable limit: SC s.224(2).

The maximum aggregate term for a case involving more than one either-way offence is 12 months: MCA 1980 s.133(2): SC s.224(3).

54-007 **Suspended sentence activation** The restrictions on aggregate terms do not include activation of suspended sentences: *Chamberlain* (1992) 13 Cr. App. R.(S.) 525; (1992) 156 J.P. 440; [1992] Crim. L.R. 380.

54-008 **Default terms** The restrictions do not apply to default terms fixed in respect of fines imposed on the same occasion as a custodial sentence is imposed, but they do apply where an offender is sentenced to a custodial sentence and committed in default on the same occasion: SC s.224(4).

# CUSTODY/COMMUNITY THRESHOLD AND DETERMINING THE LENGTH OF A DISCRETIONARY CUSTODIAL SENTENCE

Sentencing Code ss.230–232

*References: Current Sentencing Practice: A4; Archbold 5A-718*

## Custody threshold

The court must not pass a custodial sentence unless it is of the opinion that: **55-001**

(a) the offence; or
(b) the combination of the offence and one or more offences associated with it,

was so serious that neither a fine alone nor a community sentence can be justified for the offence: SC s.230(2).

## Threshold generally not applicable where mandatory sentence requirement applies

The custody threshold provision does not apply if the offence is one in relation to which a mandatory sentence requirement applies (see s.399), except as provided in ss.273(4) and 283(4) (pre-condition for life sentence for second listed offence): SC s.230(3). **55-002**

## Exceptions relating to community sentences

The custody threshold provision does not prevent the court from passing a custodial sentence on the offender if the offender fails to express willingness to comply with a requirement: **55-003**

(a) which the court proposes to include in a community order; but
(b) which may be included only if the offender expresses willingness to comply with it: SC s.230(4).

The custody threshold provision is also subject to:

(i) para.22(5)(b) of Sch.9 (power to deal with offender who does not express willingness to comply with amended drug rehabilitation requirement);
(ii) para.10(9) of Sch.10 (power of magistrates' court to impose custodial sentence following wilful and persistent breach of community order);
(iii) para.11(6) of that Schedule (corresponding power of Crown Court); and
(iv) para.18(9)(b) of that Schedule (power to deal with offender who does not express willingness to comply with amended treatment requirement): SC s.230(5)(b).

The custody threshold provision is also subject to para.11(3) of Sch.7 (power to impose custodial sentence in case involving wilful and persistent breach of YRO with intensive supervision and surveillance): SC s.230(5)(a).

**Forming opinions** In forming its opinion for the purposes of the custody **55-004**

threshold provision, the court must take into account all the information that is available to it about the circumstances of the offence, or of it and the associated offence or offences, including any aggravating or mitigating factors: SC s.230(6).

The pre-sentence report requirements (see s.30 of the Sentencing Code) apply to the court in relation to forming that opinion: SC s.230(7).

55-005 **Length of discretionary custodial sentences** Where a court passes a custodial sentence in respect of an offence, the custodial sentence must be for the shortest term (not exceeding the permitted maximum) that in the opinion of the court is commensurate with the seriousness of:

(a) the offence, or
(b) the combination of the offence and one or more offences associated with it: SC s.231(1) and (2).

However, that provision:

(a) does not apply where the sentence is:
  (i) fixed by law; or
  (ii) a required life sentence,
  except as provided in ss.273(4) and 283(4) (pre-condition for life sentence for second listed offence);
(b) does not apply where the custodial sentence is an extended sentence, except as provided in ss.256(2), 268(2) and 281(2) (determination of appropriate custodial term); and
(c) is subject to the provisions mentioned in s.399(c), namely:
  (i) s.311(2) or (2A) (minimum sentence for certain offences involving firearms that are prohibited weapons);
  (ii) s.312(2) or (2A) (minimum sentence for offence of threatening with weapon or bladed article);
  (iii) s.313(2) or (2A) (minimum sentence of seven years for third class A drug trafficking offence);
  (iv) s.314(2) or (2A) (minimum sentence of three years for third domestic burglary); and
  (v) s.315(2) or (2A) (minimum sentence for repeat offence involving weapon or bladed article or corrosive substance): SC s.231(3)-(6).

In forming its opinion for these purposes:

(a) the court must take into account all the information that is available to it about the circumstances of the offence, or of it and the associated offence or offences, including any aggravating or mitigating factors; and
(b) the pre-sentence report requirements (see s.30) apply, except where the sentence is an extended sentence: SC s.231(7) and (8).

# SUSPENDED SENTENCE ORDERS

## Sentencing Code ss.264, 286–305 and Sch.9

*References: Current Sentencing Practice A4; Archbold 5A-690*

### General

**What is a suspended sentence order?** A suspended sentence order is an order providing that a sentence of imprisonment or detention in a young offender institution in respect of an offence is not to take effect unless: 56-001

(a) an activation event occurs, and
(b) a court having power to do so subsequently orders under para.13 of Sch.16 that the sentence is to take effect: SC s.286(1).

A suspended sentence order may also specify one or more available community requirements with which the offender must comply during the supervision period: SC s.286(2).

**Operational period and supervision period** The operational period is the period for which the order lasts, i.e. the period for which the custodial sentence is suspended. 56-002

The supervision period is the period during which any requirements imposed by the order must be completed, and the period for which the offender is supervised.

A suspended sentence order must specify the operational period; the operational period must be a period, beginning with the day on which the order is made, of:

(a) at least six months; and
(b) not more than two years: SC s.288(1) and (2).

If a suspended sentence order imposes any community requirement or requirements, the order must specify the supervision period; the supervision period specified must be a period, beginning with the day on which the order is made, of: 56-003

(a) at least six months; and
(b) not more than:
(i) two years; or
(ii) if less, the operational period: SC s.288(3) and (4).

But if the suspended sentence order imposes an unpaid work requirement, the supervision period:

(a) continues until the offender has worked under the order for the number of hours specified in the order under para.2(1) of Sch.9; but
(b) does not continue beyond the end of the operational period: SC s.288(5).

**Suspended sentence to be treated as imprisonment** A suspended sentence which has not taken effect under para.13 of Sch.16 is to be treated as: 56-004

(a) a sentence of imprisonment; or
(b) as the case may be, a sentence of detention in a young offender institution,

for the purposes of all enactments and instruments made under enactments: SC s.289(1).

This is subject to any provision to the contrary contained in:

(a) the Criminal Justice Act 1967; or
(b) any enactment passed or instrument made under any enactment after 31 December 1967: SC s.289(2).

56-005 **Time on bail subject to qualifying curfew** For the purposes of SC s.325 (time on bail subject to qualifying curfew) the court passes a determinate sentence in respect of a suspended sentence order if that sentence is ordered to take effect under Sch.16 to the Sentencing Code: SC s.325(1) and (6). Thus, time spent on bail subject to a qualifying curfew is not to be deducted "manually" at the point at which the suspended sentence is imposed.

56-006 **Time on remand** For the purposes of CJA 2003 s.240ZA (time on remand to count as time served), a suspended sentence is to be treated as a sentence of imprisonment if it is ordered to take effect under Sch.16 to the Sentencing Code: CJA 2003 s.240ZA(1) and (7).

There is no power to order that time served prior to the imposition of a suspended sentence order will not count towards the custodial sentence if it is later activated: *Rushworth* [2018] EWCA Crim 2196.

Where time on remand would entirely "swallow up" the period of the suspended sentence (if activated), a suspended sentence order should not usually be imposed: *Rakib* [2011] EWCA Crim 870; [2012] 1 Cr. App. R.(S.) 1; [2011] Crim. L.R. 570. This was re-stated (without reference to *Rakib*) in *Dawes* [2019] EWCA Crim 848; [2020] 1 Cr. App. R.(S.) 1. In *Coates* [2022] EWCA Crim 1603; [2023] 2 Cr. App. R. (S.) 4 (a community order case), the court considered, the time the defendant had spent in custody, justified the quashing of an unpaid work requirement such that no punitive element of the sentence was required.

**Availability**

56-007 **Aged 18-20 at conviction** Where, in dealing with an offender for an offence, the court imposes a sentence of detention in a young offender institution, a suspended sentence is available in relation to that sentence if the term of the sentence of detention in a young offender institution is not more than two years: SC s.264(1) and (2).

But a suspended sentence order is not available in relation to that sentence if:

(a) the sentence of detention in a young offender institution is one of two or more sentences imposed on the same occasion which are to be served consecutively; and
(b) the terms of those sentences are in aggregate more than two years: SC s.264(3).

56-008 **Aged 21+ at conviction** Where, in dealing with an offender for an offence, a court passes a sentence of imprisonment, a suspended sentence order is available in relation to that sentence if the term of the sentence of imprisonment is:

(a) at least 14 days; but
(b) not more than two years: SC s.277(1) and (2).

But a suspended sentence order is not available in relation to that sentence if:

(a) the sentence of imprisonment is one of two or more sentences imposed on the same occasion which are to be served consecutively; and
(b) the terms of those sentences are in aggregate more than two years: SC s.277(3).

### Making the order

**Process** There are two stages to imposing a suspended sentence order. **56-009**

(1) The court must first decide to impose a sentence of immediate imprisonment (or detention) upon the offender. This must be in accordance with statutory obligations concerning custodial sentences, such as the requirement for custody to be of the shortest period commensurate with the seriousness of the offence: SC s.230.
(2) Once the court has determined the appropriate length of immediate imprisonment (or detention), where a suspended sentence is available, the court may impose such a sentence: SC ss.264 and 277.

Where a custodial sentence was on the cusp of that capable of being suspended, the court is under an obligation to ensure it has the fullest possible evidence before considering the appropriate sentence: *Montaut* [2019] EWCA Crim 2252; [2020] 2 Cr. App. R.(S.) 7.

**Whether to make an order** When considering whether or not to impose a suspended sentence order, the court should make reference to the Sentencing Council's Imposition of Community and Custodial Sentences Definitive Guideline which lists a number of factors which weigh in favour/against suspension. **56-010**

There is a balancing exercise to be performed when considering the decision as to whether or not a sentence may be suspended: *Tharmaratnam* [2017] EWCA Crim 887; [2017] 2 Cr. App. R.(S.) 36. It is possible that one factor tending against suspension can outweigh multiple factors tending towards suspension: *Middleton* [2019] EWCA Crim 663; [2019] 2 Cr. App. R.(S.) 28. Even if a judge takes the view that appropriate punishment would only be achievable by immediate custody, there remains a discretion to suspend if there are sufficient factors against such a course: *Hussain* [2019] EWCA Crim 1542; [2020] 1 Cr. App. R.(S.) 32; [2020] Crim. L.R. 467.

In particular, the absence of reassurance that a plea of guilty might have provided may entitle a judge to conclude that they could not be satisfied that there was a realistic prospect of rehabilitation as a factor supporting suspension: *Evans* [2019] EWCA Crim 606; [2019] 2 Cr. App. R.(S.) 35; [2019] Crim. L.R. 1071. However, in *Kumwenda* [2018] EWCA Crim 2856; [2019] 1 Cr. App. R.(S.) 44, it was held that the simple fact that an offender had failed to plead guilty to the offence was not a good reason for not suspending a sentence; rather, consideration needs to be given to all the circumstances of the offender and the offence.

The fact that the imposition of sentence was adjourned to enable the victim to be contacted to see if they would consent to participating in a restorative justice procedure could not possibly create a legitimate expectation on the part of the defendant that a suspended sentence would be imposed: *Blyth* [2019] EWCA Crim 2107; [2020] 1 Cr. App. R.(S.) 60.

**56-011** **Local justice area** A suspended sentence order which imposes any community requirement must specify the area which is the offender's home local justice area. That area must be the local justice area in which the offender resides or will reside: SC s.296.

**56-012** **Magistrates' courts supervision** Where the Crown Court makes a suspended sentence order which imposes any community requirement, it may make a direction that the order is to be subject to magistrates' court supervision: SC s.297. An order that qualifies for special procedures (see s.293A) may not be made the subject of magistrates' courts supervision: s.297.

For the effect of such a direction, see Pts 2 and 3 of Sch.16 (breach or amendment of a community requirement of a suspended sentence order).

**56-013** **Copies of the order** The court must forthwith provide copies of the order:

(a) to the offender;
(b) to the responsible officer;
(c) to an officer of a provider of probation services that is a public sector provider who is acting at the court; and
(d) if the court does not act in the offender's home local justice area, to a provider of probation services that is a public sector provider and is operating in that area: SC s.298(1) and (2).

Additionally, an exclusion requirement (for the purpose of protecting a person from being approached by an offender), a residence requirement involving residence in an institution, a mental health treatment requirement, a drug rehabilitation requirement, an alcohol treatment requirement, and an electronic monitoring requirement involve further obligations in relation to the provision of copies of the order. See SC s.298(2) and (3).

**56-014** **Combining sentences** A court may not make a community order in respect of an offence if it makes a suspended sentence order in respect of:

(a) the offence;
(b) any other offence of which the offender is convicted by or before it; or
(c) any other offence for which it deals with the offender: SC s.203.

A suspended sentence order is not available in relation to that sentence if:

(a) the sentence of imprisonment or detention in a young offender institution is one of two or more sentences imposed on the same occasion which are to be served consecutively; and
(b) the terms of those sentences are in aggregate more than two years: SC s.264(3) and s.277(3).

A suspended sentence order cannot be combined with immediate custody: *Sapiano* (1968) 52 Cr. App. R. 674; [1968] Crim. L.R. 497; (1968) 112 S.J. 799.

The court may impose a suspended sentence order and a fine in combination, in appropriate cases: *Butt* [2018] EWCA Crim 1617; [2018] 1 W.L.R. 5391; [2019] 1 Cr. App. R.(S.) 4.

**Requirements**

**General** A suspended sentence order may not impose a community requirement that is not an available requirement. A community requirement is an available requirement in relation to a suspended sentence order unless a provision provides otherwise: SC s.290. **56-015**

There is no obligation to impose a requirement or more than requirement as a part of a suspended sentence.

The requirements are listed in the table in s.287, with a corresponding entry indicating which part of Sch.9 contains further provision about the particular requirement.

There is no restriction on the requirements which may be combined in the same community order, but the court must consider whether the requirements are compatible with each other: SC s.292(3). **56-016**

The requirements of a community order shall, as far as is practicable, avoid any conflict with the offender's religious beliefs or the requirements of any other community order to which they may be subject, and any interference with the times at which they normally work, or attend school or an educational establishment: SC s.292(4).

**Alcohol abstinence and monitoring requirements (SC Sch.9 Pt 12)** An "alcohol abstinence and monitoring requirement", in relation to a relevant order, means a requirement that, during a particular period ("the abstinence and monitoring period"), the offender: **56-017**

(a) must:
  (i) abstain from consuming alcohol; or
  (ii) not consume alcohol so that at any time during the abstinence and monitoring period there is more than a particular level of alcohol in the offender's body; and
(b) must submit to monitoring in accordance with particular arrangements for the purpose of ascertaining whether the offender is complying with provision under para.(a): SC Sch.9 para.25.

An alcohol abstinence and monitoring requirement is not an available requirement unless regulations are in force under para.25(7)(c) of Sch.9 (prescribed arrangements for monitoring): SC s.291(1).

An alcohol abstinence and monitoring requirement imposing a requirement within para.25(1)(a)(ii) of Sch.9 (alcohol level to be kept below specified level) is not an available requirement unless regulations are in force under s.25(7)(b) of that Schedule (prescribed alcohol level): SC s.291(2). At 31 October 2024, no such regulations were in force.

A relevant order that includes an alcohol abstinence and monitoring require- **56-018** ment must specify:

(a) the abstinence and monitoring period;
(b) if the order imposes a requirement to not consume alcohol so that there is at any time in the offender's body more than a particular level of alcohol, the level of alcohol; and
(c) the arrangements for monitoring: SC Sch.9 para.25(2).

A relevant order that includes an alcohol abstinence and monitoring requirement may specify exceptions from any requirement imposed to abstain from consuming alcohol: SC Sch.9 para.25(3).

The specified period must not exceed 120 days: SC Sch.9 para.25(4).

A relevant order may not include both:

(a) an alcohol treatment requirement; and
(b) an alcohol abstinence and monitoring requirement: SC Sch.9 para.26(1).

**56-019** A court may not include an alcohol abstinence and monitoring requirement in a relevant order unless the following conditions are met:

(a) the relevance of alcohol condition;
(b) the non-dependency condition; and
(c) the availability of arrangements condition: SC Sch.9 para.26(2).

The relevance of alcohol condition is that:

(a) the offender's consumption of alcohol is an element of the offence for which the order is to be imposed or of an associated offence; or
(b) the court is satisfied that the offender's consumption of alcohol was a factor that contributed to the commission of that offence or to an associated offence: SC Sch.9 para.26(3).

The non-dependency condition is that the court is satisfied that the offender is not dependent on alcohol: SC Sch.9 para.26(4).

The availability of arrangements condition is that the court has been notified by the Secretary of State that arrangements for monitoring of the kind to be specified in the relevant order are available in the offender's home local justice area (and the notice has not been withdrawn): SC Sch.9 para.(5).

**56-020** **Alcohol treatment requirements (SC Sch.9 Pt 11)** An alcohol treatment requirement is a requirement that the offender must submit during a period specified in the order to treatment with a view to the reduction or elimination of the offender's dependency on alcohol. That treatment may be:

(a) resident treatment;
(b) institution-based treatment; or
(c) practitioner-based treatment: SC Sch.9 para.23(1) and (2).

The order may specify separate periods comprising the period specified in the order: SC Sch.9 para.23(4).

For each treatment period, the order must specify:

(a) the treatment director;
(b) whether the alcohol dependency treatment is to be resident treatment, institution-based treatment or practitioner-based treatment;
(c) if it is to be resident treatment, the institution or place where it is to be provided;
(d) if it is to be institution-based treatment:
    (i) the institution or place where it is to be provided; and
    (ii) the intervals at which it is to be provided,

but must not otherwise specify the nature of the treatment: SC Sch.9 para.23(5).

A court may not impose an alcohol treatment requirement unless the following conditions are met:

(a) the need for treatment condition;
(b) the arrangements condition; and
(c) the consent condition: SC Sch.9 para.24(1).

The need for treatment condition is that the court is satisfied:

(a) that the offender is dependent on alcohol; and
(b) that the offender's dependency:
    (i) requires treatment; and
    (ii) may be susceptible to treatment: SC Sch.9 para.24(2).

The arrangements condition is that the court is satisfied that arrangements: **56-021**

(a) have been made; or
(b) can be made,

for the treatment intended to be specified in the order.

Those arrangements include arrangements for the reception of the offender, where the offender is to be required to submit to treatment as a resident: SC Sch.9 para.24(3).

The consent condition is that the offender expresses willingness to comply with the requirement: SC Sch.9 para.24(4).

*Attendance centre requirements (SC Sch.9 Pt 13) (convictions before 28 June 2022—see 2023 edition).*

**Curfew requirements (SC Sch.9 Pt 5)** A curfew requirement requires the offender to remain, for periods specified in the requirement, at a place specified in the order: SC Sch.9 para.9(1) and (2). **56-022**

The periods specified must not exceed 20 hours per day and must not be for a total in excess of 112 hours in any seven day period: SC Sch.9 para.9(2) and (4).

The requirement may specify different places or different periods for different days: SC Sch.9 para.9(3).

All the specified periods must fall within the period of 12 months beginning with the day on which the order takes effect: SC Sch.9 para.9(5). **56-023**

Before making a curfew requirement, the court must obtain and consider information about the place to be specified in the order and the attitude of persons likely to be affected by the enforced presence there of the offender: SC Sch.9 para.10(1) and (2).

The responsible officer may vary the start time or location of any curfew requirement (convictions on/after 28 June 2022): SC Sch.9 para.10A.

The court must impose an electronic monitoring requirement unless a person whose cooperation is necessary does not consent, or the court has not been notified that arrangements for electronic monitoring are available, or in the particular circumstances of the case the court considers it inappropriate to do so: SC Sch.9 para.10(3). See *Electronic Monitoring Requirements*, **para.56-032**.

56-024 **Drug rehabilitation requirements (SC Sch.9 Pt 10)** A "drug rehabilitation requirement", in relation to a relevant order, means a requirement that during a period specified in the order ("the treatment and testing period") the offender:

(a) must submit to drug rehabilitation treatment, which may be resident treatment or non-resident treatment, and
(b) for the purpose of ascertaining whether there is any drug in the offender's body during that period, must provide samples in accordance with directions given by:
    (i) the responsible officer, or
    (ii) the treatment director: SC Sch.9 para.19(1).[1]

The order may specify separate periods which together comprise the drug treatment and testing period: SC Sch.9 para 19(4).

The order must specify, for each treatment period:

(a) the treatment director;
(b) if the treatment is to be resident treatment, the institution or place where it is to be provided;
(c) if it is to be non-resident treatment:
    (i) the institution or place where it is to be provided; and
    (ii) the intervals at which it is to be provided;

but must not otherwise specify the nature of the treatment: SC Sch.9 para.19(5).

See para.19 for further definitions of terms used in that paragraph.

56-025 A court may not impose a drug rehabilitation requirement unless the following conditions are met:

(a) the need for treatment condition;
(b) the arrangements condition;

---

[1] *"Drug rehabilitation treatment"*, in relation to an offender, means treatment which is: (a) by or under the direction of a person who has the necessary qualifications or experience; and (b) with a view to the reduction or elimination of the offender's dependency on or propensity to misuse drugs; *"resident treatment"* means treatment as a resident in an institution or place; *"non-resident treatment"* means treatment as a non-resident at an institution or place; and *"the treatment director"* means the person by or under whose direction the treatment is to be provided: SC Sch.9 para.19(2).

(c) the suitability condition; and
(d) the consent condition: SC Sch.9 para.20(1).

The need for treatment condition is that the court is satisfied:

(a) that the offender:
    (i) is dependent on drugs; or
    (ii) has a propensity to misuse drugs; and
(b) that the offender's dependency or propensity:
    (i) requires treatment; and
    (ii) may be susceptible to treatment: SC Sch.9 para.20(2).

The arrangements condition is that the court is satisfied that arrangements:

(a) have been made; or
(b) can be made,

for the treatment intended to be specified in the order.

Those arrangements include arrangements for the reception of the offender, where the offender is to be required to submit to resident treatment (within the meaning given in para.19(2)): SC Sch.9 para.20(3). **56-026**

The suitability condition is that the requirement has been recommended to the court as being suitable for the offender by an officer of a provider of probation services: SC Sch.9 para.20(4).

The consent condition is that the offender expresses willingness to comply with the requirement: SC Sch.9 para.20(5).

A relevant order imposing a drug rehabilitation requirement: **56-027**

(a) must include provision for review if the treatment and testing period is more than 12 months; and
(b) may do so in any other case: SC Sch.9 para.21(1).

For this purpose, "*provision for review*" means provision:

(a) for the requirement to be reviewed periodically at intervals of not less than one month;
(b) for each review of the requirement to be made at a hearing held for the purpose by the responsible court (a "review hearing");
(c) requiring the offender to attend each review hearing;
(d) requiring a written report on the offender's progress under the requirement to be made by an officer of a provider of probation services to the responsible court before each review hearing; and
(e) requiring each such report to include:
    (i) the test results communicated to the responsible officer under para.19(7) or otherwise; and
    (ii) the views of the treatment provider as to the treatment and testing of the offender: SC Sch.9 para.21(2).

At a review hearing the court may, after considering the officer's report referred to in para.21(2)(d) ("*the review officer's report*"), amend the relevant order, so far as it relates to the drug rehabilitation requirement: SC Sch.9 para.22(2).

56-028 The court:

(a) may not amend the drug rehabilitation requirement unless the offender expresses willingness to comply with the requirement as amended; and
(b) except with the consent of the offender, may not amend any requirement or provision of the order while an appeal against the order is pending: SC Sch.9 para.22(3).

If the offender fails to express willingness to comply with the drug rehabilitation requirement as proposed to be amended by the court, the court may:

(a) revoke the community order, or the suspended sentence order and the suspended sentence to which it relates; and
(b) re-sentence the offender: SC Sch.9 para.22(4).

In dealing with the offender under subpara.(4)(b), the court:

(a) must take into account the extent to which the offender has complied with the requirements of the order; and
(b) may impose a custodial sentence even if it is not of the opinion mentioned in s.230(2) (general restrictions on imposing discretionary custodial sentences): SC Sch.9 para.22(5).

56-029 Where at a review without a hearing the court:

(a) has considered the review officer's report; and
(b) is of the opinion that the offender's progress under the requirement is no longer satisfactory,

the court may require the offender to attend a hearing of the court at a specified time and place: SC Sch.9 para.22(7).

Where the court imposes an activity requirement, it may also impose an electronic monitoring requirement (see *Electronic Monitoring Requirements* below).

Where at a review hearing the court:

(a) has considered the review officer's report; and
(b) is of the opinion that the offender's progress under the requirement is satisfactory,

the court may amend the order so that it provides for each subsequent review to be made by the court without a hearing: SC Sch.9 para.22(6).

56-030 **Drug testing requirement (convictions on/after 28 June 2022)** A "*drug testing requirement*" means a requirement that during a period specified in the order, the offender must, for the purpose of ascertaining whether there is any drug or psychoactive substance in the offender's body during that period, provide samples in accordance with directions given by the responsible officer: SC Sch.9 para.22A(1).

A court may not impose a drug testing requirement unless the following conditions are met—

(a) the misuse condition, and
(b) the availability of arrangements condition: SC Sch.9 para.22B(1).

The misuse condition is that the court is satisfied that the offender's misuse of a drug or psychoactive substance—

(a) caused or contributed to the offence to which the order relates or an associated offence, or
(b) is likely to cause or contribute to the commission of further offences by the offender: SC Sch.9 para.22B(2).

The availability of arrangements condition is that the court has been notified by the Secretary of State that arrangements for implementing drug testing requirements are available in the offender's home local justice area (and the notice has not been withdrawn): SC Sch.9 para.22B(3).

The order— **56-031**

(a) must provide that if the offender provides samples to a person other than the responsible officer, the results of the tests carried out on the samples are to be communicated to the responsible officer;
(b) may make provision about the provision of samples by virtue of subpara.(1): SC Sch.9 para.22A(2).

The responsible officer may give directions about the provision of samples. This power is:

(a) a power to give directions about:
    (i) the type of samples to be provided, and
    (ii) the times at which, or circumstances in which, they are to be provided,
(b) subject to any provision made by the order, and
(c) to be exercised in accordance with guidance issued by the Secretary of State: SC Sch.9 para.22A(3).

Definitions: "*drug*" means a controlled drug as defined by s.2 of the Misuse of Drugs Act 1971; "*psychoactive substance*" has the meaning given by s.2(1) of the Psychoactive Substances Act 2016.

**Electronic monitoring requirements: general (SC Sch.9 Pt 14)** There are two types of electronic monitoring requirement: whereabouts monitoring and compliance monitoring. **56-032**

Where an order imposes an electronic monitoring requirement, the offender must (in particular):

(a) submit, as required from time to time by the responsible officer or the person responsible for the monitoring, to:
    (i) being fitted with, or installation of, any necessary apparatus; and
    (ii) inspection or repair of any apparatus fitted or installed for the purposes of the monitoring;
(b) not interfere with, or with the working of, any apparatus fitted or installed for the purposes of the monitoring; and
(c) take any steps required by the responsible officer, or the person responsible for the monitoring, for the purpose of keeping in working order any apparatus fitted or installed for the purposes of the monitoring: SC Sch.9 para.32.

Where:

(a) it is proposed to include in a relevant order an electronic monitoring requirement; but
(b) there is a person (other than the offender) without whose cooperation it will not be practicable to secure the monitoring,

the requirement may not be included in the order without that person's consent: SC Sch.9 para.33.

An electronic monitoring requirement is not an available requirement unless the community order imposes at least one other requirement (excluding an alcohol abstinence monitoring requirement or an electronic whereabouts monitoring requirement): SC s.291(4).

56-033 **Electronic compliance monitoring requirements (SC Sch.9 Pt 14)** An "electronic compliance monitoring requirement" means a requirement for securing the electronic monitoring of the offender's compliance with other requirements imposed by the order during a period ("*the monitoring period*"):

(a) specified in the order; or
(b) determined by the responsible officer in accordance with the relevant order: SC Sch.9 para.29(1).

An electronic compliance monitoring requirement may not be imposed for securing the electronic monitoring of the offender's compliance with an alcohol abstinence and monitoring requirement: SC Sch.9 para.29(4). But that does not prevent an order which imposes an alcohol abstinence and monitoring requirement from including an electronic compliance monitoring requirement for securing the electronic monitoring of the offender's compliance with any other requirement: SC Sch.9 para.29(5).

A court may not include an electronic compliance monitoring requirement in a relevant order in respect of an offender unless:

(a) the court has been notified by the Secretary of State that electronic monitoring arrangements are available in the relevant area (and the notice has not been withdrawn), and
(b) the court is satisfied that the necessary provision can be made under those arrangements: SC Sch.9 para.34.

For further provision regarding the "*relevant area*": see para.34(2)-(4).

56-034 **Electronic whereabouts monitoring requirement (SC Sch.9 Pt 14)** An "*electronic whereabouts monitoring requirement*" means a requirement to submit to electronic monitoring of the offender's whereabouts (otherwise than for the purpose of monitoring the offender's compliance with any other requirement included in the order) during a period specified in the order: SC Sch.9 para.30.

A court may not include an electronic whereabouts monitoring requirement in a relevant order in respect of an offender unless:

(a) the court has been notified by the Secretary of State that electronic monitoring arrangements are available in the local justice area proposed to be specified in the order (and the notice has not been withdrawn);

(b) the court is satisfied that:
 (i) the offender can be fitted with any necessary apparatus under the arrangements currently available; and
 (ii) any other necessary provision can be made under those arrangements; and
(c) the court is satisfied that arrangements are generally operational throughout England and Wales (even if not always operational everywhere there) under which the offender's whereabouts can be electronically monitored: SC Sch.9 para.35.

**Exclusion requirements (SC Sch.9 Pt 14)** An exclusion requirement prohibits the offender from entering any place specified in the order ("*the prohibited place*"): SC Sch.9 para.11(1). 56-035

The order must specific the prohibited place and the exclusion period: SC Sch.9 para.11(2). A prohibited place may be an area: SC Sch.9 para.11(5).

The order may specify:

(a) more than one prohibited place;
(b) more than one exclusion period; and
(c) different prohibited places for different exclusion periods or different days: SC Sch.9 para.11(3).

The requirement cannot exceed two years (whatever the length of the community order): SC Sch.9 para.11(4).

The court must impose an electronic monitoring requirement unless a person whose cooperation is necessary does not consent, or the court has not been notified that arrangements for electronic monitoring are available, or in the particular circumstances of the case the court considers it inappropriate to do so: SC Sch.9 para.12.

**Foreign travel prohibition requirement (SC Sch.9 Pt 8)** A foreign travel prohibition requirement may prohibit the offender from travelling to any country (or countries) or territory (or territories) outside the British Islands specified in the order: SC Sch.9 para.15. 56-036

The requirement may apply to the day or days specified in the order, or for a period specified in the order: SC Sch.9 para.15(2).

The period specified may not exceed 12 months beginning with the day on which the order is made, and the day or days specified may not fall outside the period of 12 months beginning with the day on which the order is made: SC Sch.9 para.15(3) and (4).

**Mental health treatment requirements (SC Sch.9 Pt 9)** A mental health treatment requirement is a requirement that the offender must submit, during a period or periods specified in the order, to: 56-037

(a) in-patient treatment;
(b institution-based out-patient treatment; or
(c) practitioner-based treatment: Sch.9 para.16(1).

A relevant order which imposes a mental health treatment requirement must specify:

(a) the period or periods during which the offender is required to submit to mental health treatment; and
(b) for each of those periods:
    (i) if the mental health treatment is to be in-patient treatment, the care home or hospital at which it is to be provided;
    (ii) if it is to be institution-based out-patient treatment, the institution or place at which it is to be provided; and
    (iii) if it is to be practitioner-based treatment, the registered medical practitioner or registered psychologist (or both) by whom or under whose direction it is to be provided;

but may not otherwise specify the nature of the treatment: SC Sch.9 para.16(3).

Different treatment may be specified for different periods: SC Sch.9 para.16(4).

**56-038** A court may not include a mental health treatment requirement in a relevant order unless the following conditions are met:

(a) the need for treatment condition;
(b) the arrangements condition; and
(c) the consent condition.

The need for treatment condition is that the court is satisfied that the mental condition of the offender:

(a) requires treatment;
(b) may be susceptible to treatment; and
(c) does not warrant the making of a hospital order or guardianship order within the meaning of the MHA 1983: SC Sch.9 para.17(2).

The arrangements condition is that the court is satisfied that arrangements:

(a) have been made; or
(b) can be made, for the treatment intended to be specified in the order: SC Sch.9 para.17(3).

The consent condition is that the offender has expressed willingness to comply with the requirement: SC Sch.9 para.17(4).

**56-039** **Programme requirements (SC Sch.9 Pt 3)** A programme requirement requires the offender to participate in an accredited programme specified in the order, at a place so specified, on a number of days specified in the order: SC Sch.9 para.6(1).

"*Programme*" means a systematic set of activities: SC Sch.9 para.6(4).

Where a relevant order includes a programme requirement:

(a) the order must specify the number of days on which the offender is to be required to participate in an accredited programme under the requirement;
(b) it is for the responsible officer to specify:
    (i) the accredited programme in which the offender is to participate, and

(ii) the place at which the offender is to do so: SC Sch.9 para.6(5).

**Prohibited activity requirements (SC Sch.9 Pt 4)** A prohibited activity requirement requires the offender to refrain from participating in activities specified in the requirement on a day or days specified in the order or during a period specified in the requirement: SC Sch.9 para.7(1) and (2). **56-040**

The primary purpose is not to punish but to prevent—or at least reduce—further offending: *J* [2008] EWCA Crim 2002; (2008) 172 J.P. 513; (2008) 172 J.P.N. 742.

The prohibited activity requirements may include requirements relating to possessing, carrying or using firearms: SC Sch.9 para.7(3).

**Rehabilitation activity requirements (SC Sch.9 Pt 2)** A "rehabilitation activity requirement", is a requirement that, during the relevant period, the offender must comply with any instructions given by the responsible officer to attend appointments or participate in activities or both: SC Sch.9 para.4(1). **56-041**

The maximum number of days on which the offender may be instructed to participate in activities must be specified in the relevant order: SC Sch.9 para.4(2).

The activities in which offenders may be instructed to participate include activities forming an accredited programme and activities whose purpose is reparative, such as restorative justice activities: SC Sch.9 para.5(6).

The imposition of an RAR requirement only did not conform with the requirement that an order include a punitive element, on the facts of *AG's Ref (Singh)* [2021] EWCA Crim 1426; [2022] 1 Cr. App. R.(S.) 48.

**Residence requirements (SC Sch.9 Pt 7)** A residence requirement is a requirement that, during a period specified in the relevant order, the offender must reside at a place specified in the order, or at another place with the prior approval of the responsible officer: SC Sch.9 para.13(1). **56-042**

A relevant order imposing a residence requirement must specify:

(a) the required place;
(b) the required period; and
(c) if the offender is to be permitted to reside at some other place with the prior approval of the responsible officer, that fact: SC Sch.9 para.13(2).

A hostel or other institution may not be specified as the place of residence except on the recommendation of an officer of a local probation board: SC Sch.9 para.13(3).

Before making an order containing a residence requirement, the court must consider the home surroundings of the offender: SC Sch.9 para.14.

**Unpaid work requirements (SC Sch.9 Pt 1)** An unpaid work requirement requires the offender to perform unpaid work for a number of hours, not less than 40 and not more than 300, specified in the order: SC Sch.9 para.2. **56-043**

The unpaid work must be completed within a period of 12 months: SC Sch.9 para.1(1).

An unpaid work requirement may not be made unless the court is satisfied that the offender is a suitable person to perform work under such a requirement and that provision for the offender to work under such a requirement can be made under the arrangements for persons to perform work under such a requirement which exist in the offender's home local justice area: SC Sch.9 para.3.

Where an offender is convicted of more than one offence, an unpaid work requirement may be made in respect of each offence, and may direct that the hours of work specified in any of the requirements should be concurrent with or in addition to the hours of work required by the other requirement, but the total number of hours which are not concurrent must not exceed the permissible maximum of 300: SC Sch.9 paras 3 and 4.

### Offender's obligations

**56-044** The offender must keep in touch with the responsible officer: SC s.301(2). This obligation is enforceable as if it were a requirement of the order: SC s.301(3). The offender must not change residence without permission given by the responsible officer, or a court: SC s.302.

### Power to provide for review

**56-045** **Provision for review** A suspended sentence order which imposes one or more community requirements may make provision for the order to be reviewed periodically ("*provision for review*"). But if the suspended sentence order:

(a) imposes a drug rehabilitation requirement; and
(b) contains provision for review under this section,

the provision for review must not include provision relating to that requirement (but see para.22 of Sch.9 for separate provision about review of such a requirement): SC s.293(1) and (3).

Where an order contains provision for review, it must:

(a) specify the intervals at which the order is to be reviewed;
(b) provide for each review to be made, subject to s.295, at a hearing held for the purpose by the responsible court (a "review hearing");
(c) require the offender to attend each review hearing; and
(d) provide for a report by an officer of a provider of probation services on the offender's progress in complying with the community requirements of the order ("*a progress report*") to be made to the responsible court before each review: SC s.293(2).

At a review hearing under s.293, the court may, after considering the progress report, amend:

(a) the community requirements of the suspended sentence order; or
(b) any provision of the order which relates to those requirements: SC s.294(2).

**56-046** The court:

(a) may not amend the community requirements of the order so as to impose a requirement of a different kind unless the offender expresses willingness to comply with that requirement;
(b) may not amend:
  (i) a mental health treatment requirement;
  (ii) a drug rehabilitation requirement; or
  (iii) an alcohol treatment requirement; unless the offender expresses willingness to comply with the requirement as amended;
(c) may amend the supervision period only if the period as amended complies with s.288(4);
(d) may not amend the operational period; and
(e) except with the consent of the offender, may not amend the order while an appeal against the order is pending: SC s.294(3).

See ss.292-295 for further provision about review arrangements.

**Special procedures** A suspended sentence order that— **56-047**

(a) imposes one or more community requirements, and
(b) qualifies for special procedures for the purposes of this section, may make provision for the order to be reviewed periodically ("*provision for review*"): s.293A(1).

Where a suspended sentence order contains provision for review, it must—

(a) specify the intervals at which the order is to be reviewed,
(b) provide for each review to be made (subject to exceptions) at a hearing held for the purpose by the responsible court (a "*review hearing*"),
(c) require the offender to attend each review hearing, and
(d) provide for a report by an officer of a provider of probation services on the offender's progress in complying with the community requirements of the order (a "*progress report*") to be made to the responsible court before each review: s.293A(2)

"*The responsible court*" means the court by which the order is made: s.293A(3).

On 26 June 2023, the Sentencing Act 2020 (Special Procedures for Community and Suspended Sentence Orders) Regulations 2023 (SI 2023/559) came into force, specifying the four conditions that must be met for a suspended sentence order or community order to be subject to a review under the 'special procedures'. The conditions are:

(1) the order is made within 18 months of 26 June 2023;
(2) the court making the order is Birmingham Magistrates' Court; the Crown Court sitting at Liverpool or the Crown Court sitting at Teeside Combined Court Centre;
(3) the offender is aged 18+ when the order is made, is not a relevant offender within the meaning of s.80 of the Sexual Offences Act (SOA) 2003 and in the case of Birmingham Magistrates' Court, is a female;
(4) the conviction offence is not listed within reg.6 of the Regulations.

# DETENTION IN A YOUNG OFFENDER INSTITUTION

## Sentencing Code s.262

*References: Current Sentencing Practice: A4; Archbold 5A-739*

### Availability

A sentence of detention in a young offender institution is available to a court dealing with an offender for an offence where: **57-001**

(a) the offender is aged at least 18 but under 21 when convicted;
(b) the offence is punishable by that court with imprisonment in the case of a person aged 21 or over; and
(c) the court is not required to pass a sentence of:
  (i) detention during His Majesty's pleasure (see s.259); or
  (ii) custody for life (see ss.272 and 275): SC s.262(1).

### Length

The minimum term of a sentence of detention in a young offender institution is 21 days: SC s.263(2). **57-002**

The maximum term is the maximum term of imprisonment available to the court for the offence: SC s.263(1).

Section 231 (length of discretionary custodial sentences: general provision), in particular, applies in determining the term of a sentence of detention in a young offender institution: SC s.263(3).

The sentence takes effect in the same way as a sentence of imprisonment, and the court has the power to impose consecutive sentences in the same manner.

**Particular sentences** Reference should be made to the following sections in appropriate circumstances: **57-003**

(a) s.399 (mandatory minimum sentences);
(b) s.265 (special custodial sentence for offenders of particular concern);
(c) s.268 (extended sentences); and
(d) s.262A (serious terrorism sentence).

*Note: The sentence of detention in a young offender institution is abolished by the Criminal Justice and Court Services Act 2000 s.61 with effect from a day to be appointed. The minimum age for imprisonment is reduced by the same Act to 18 (see Sch.7 para.180). That provision had not been brought into force on 31 October 2024. References to sentences of imprisonment are for the most part to be read as references to imprisonment or detention in a young offender institution.*

## OFFENDERS OF PARTICULAR CONCERN: AGED 18+

### SENTENCING CODE SS.265 AND 278 AND SCH.13

*References: Current Sentencing Practice A4; Archbold 5A-744*

### Making the order

**Applicability** Sections 265 and 278 apply where: **58-001**

(a) a person is convicted of an offence (whenever committed) listed in Sch.13 to the Sentencing Code (see **para.58-008**);
(b) the person was aged 18 or over at the date of conviction; and
(c) the court does not impose one of the following for the offence (and any offences associated with it):
   (i) a sentence of imprisonment for life or a sentence of custody for life under s.272; or
   (ii) a serious terrorism sentence; or
   (iii) an extended sentence under ss.266 or 279: SC s.265(1) and s.278(1).

Sections 265 and 279 do not apply where the offender was aged under 18 at the date of the offence and:

(a) the offence was committed before 29 June 2021; or
(b) the offence is listed in Pt II of Sch.13 to the SC: SC s.265(1A) and s.278(1A).

**The sentence** The length of the sentence must be equal to the aggregate of: **58-002**

(a) the appropriate custodial term; and
(b) a further period of one year for which the offender is to be subject to a licence: SC s.265(2) and s.278(2).

The total term must not exceed the term that, at the time the offence was committed, was the maximum term permitted for the offence. This includes the "further period of one year": SC s.265(2) and s.278(2).

The "appropriate custodial term" is the term that, in the opinion of the court, ensures that the sentence is appropriate: SC s.265(3) and s.278(3).

**Suspended sentences** Courts should not suspend a sentence under s.265. Ordinarily the court will be considering an immediate custodial sentence: in the unusual event that the court might have considered suspending the sentence, it should consider making a community order instead: *LF and DS* [2016] EWCA Crim 561; [2016] 1 W.L.R. 4432; [2016] 2 Cr. App. R.(S.) 30. **58-003**

**Consecutive sentences** There is, in principle, no reason why a court should not be permitted to impose consecutive sentences if it considers it appropriate: *LF and DS* [2016] EWCA Crim 561; [2016] 1 W.L.R. 4432; [2016] 2 Cr. App. R.(S.) 30. This is supported by the decision in *Thompson* [2018] EWCA Crim 639; [2018] 1 W.L.R. 4429; [2018] 2 Cr. App. R.(S.) 19. **58-004**

*Note: Licence periods are cumulative as it is not possible to impose a partly concurrent, partly consecutive sentence. Accordingly, judges imposing consecutive sentences for offenders of particular concern should think carefully about structuring the sentences so as to avoid disproportionately long licence periods.*

**58-005** **Drafting indictments** It would clearly be helpful if those settling indictments were able to assist by drafting counts which take account of threshold ages of alleged victims or defendants, or by identifying if a relevant penetration occurred: see *LF and DS* [2016] EWCA Crim 561; [2016] 1 W.L.R. 4432; [2016] 2 Cr. App. R.(S.) 30.

**Release**

**58-006** **Referral to the Parole Board** The Secretary of State must refer the offender to the Parole Board at the expiration of the relevant custodial period; for sentences of offenders of particular concern that occurs at two-thirds of the custodial term: CJA 2003 s.244A(2) and (6). This does not apply to a person to whom s.247A of the CJA 2003 applies.

Where there has been such a referral and the Parole Board has declined to release the offender, the Secretary of State need not refer the offender to the Parole Board again until the second anniversary of the previous referral: CJA 2003 s.244A(2)(b).

**58-007** **Test for release** The offender will be released by the Parole Board when it is satisfied that it is not necessary for the protection of the public that the offender should be confined: CJA 2003 s.244A(4)(b).

## PART 1 OFFENCES INVOLVING OR CONNECTED WITH TERRORISM

### Terrorism Act 2000

1 An offence under any of the following provisions of the Terrorism Act 2000— **58-008**
- (a) section 11 (membership of a proscribed organisation);
- (b) section 12 (inviting or expressing support for a proscribed organisation);
- (c) section 15 (fund-raising);
- (d) section 16 (use of money or property for terrorist purposes);
- (e) section 17 (involvement in terrorist funding arrangements);
- (f) section 17A (insuring payments made in response to terrorist threats);
- (g) section 18 (laundering of terrorist property);
- (h) section 19 (failure to disclose professional belief or suspicion about terrorist offences);
- (i) section 21A (failure in regulated sectors to disclose knowledge or suspicion about terrorist offences);
- (j) section 38B (failure to disclose information about acts of terrorism);
- (k) section 39 (disclosure of information prejudicial to a terrorist investigation etc);
- (l) section 54 (weapons training);
- (m) section 56 (directing terrorist organisation);
- (n) section 57 (possession of article for terrorist purposes);
- (o) section 58 (collection of information likely to be of use to a terrorist);
- (p) section 58A (publishing information about members of the armed forces etc);
- (q) section 58B (entering or remaining in a designated area);
- (r) section 59 (inciting terrorism overseas).

### Anti-terrorism, Crime and Security Act 2001

2 An offence under section 113 of the Anti-terrorism, Crime and Security Act 2001 (use of noxious substance or thing to cause harm or intimidate).

### Terrorism Act 2006

3 An offence under any of the following provisions of the Terrorism Act 2006—
- (a) section 1 (encouragement of terrorism);
- (b) section 2 (dissemination of terrorist publications);
- (c) section 5 (preparation of terrorist acts);
- (d) section 6 (training for terrorism);
- (e) section 8 (attendance at a place used for terrorist training);
- (f) section 9 (making or possession of radioactive device or material);
- (g) section 10 (misuse of radioactive device or material for terrorist purposes etc);

(h) section 11 (terrorist threats relating to radioactive devices etc).

**Counter-Terrorism Act 2008**

4 An offence under section 54 of the Counter-Terrorism Act 2008 (breach of police notification requirements etc).

**Terrorism Prevention and Investigation Measures 2011**

5 An offence under section 23 of the Terrorism Prevention and Investigation Measures Act 2011 (breach of notices imposing terrorism prevention and investigation measures).

**Counter-Terrorism and Security Act 2015**

6 An offence under section 10 of the Counter-Terrorism and Security Act 2015 (breach of temporary exclusion order).

**Inchoate offences**

7 An inchoate offence in relation to an offence specified in any of the preceding paragraphs of this Part of this Schedule.

**Abolished offences**

8(1) An abolished offence in relation to an offence specified in any of the preceding paragraphs of this Part of this Schedule.

(2) Abolished offence" , in relation to an offence ("the current offence"), means an offence that—

(a) was abolished before the relevant date, and

(b) was abolished before the relevant date, and

(c) paragraph 7 by virtue of any provision referred to in paragraph (a) or (b),

(3) The relevant date is 13 April 2015, unless sub-paragraph (4) or (5) applies.

(4) If the current offence is within— (a) sub-paragraph (a), (b), (o), (p) or (q) of paragraph 1, the relevant date is 12 April 2019.

(5) If the current offence is within—

(a) sub-paragraphs (c) to (k) of paragraph 1,

(b) paragraph 4, 5 or 6, or

(c) paragraph 7 by virtue of any provision referred to in paragraph (a) or (b),

the relevant date is the date on which section 21 of the Counter-Terrorism and Sentencing Act 2021 comes into force.

**Offences connection with terrorism**

9 An offence, other than one for which the sentence is fixed by law as life imprisonment, which is determined to have a terrorist connection under section 69.

## PART 2 SEXUAL OFFENCES

### Sexual Offences Act 2003

10 An offence under either of the following provisions of the Sexual Offences Act 2003—
(a) section 5 (rape of a child under 13);
(b) section 6 (assault of a child under 13 by penetration).

### Inchoate offences

11 An inchoate offence in relation to an offence specified paragraph 10.

### Abolished offences

12(1) An abolished offence in relation to an offence specified in either of the preceding paragraphs of this Part of this Schedule.
(2) "Abolished offence", in relation to an offence ("the current offence"), means an offence that—
(a) was abolished before 13 April 2015, and
(b) would, if committed on the day on which the offender is or was convicted, have constituted the current offence.

# MANDATORY MINIMUM CUSTODIAL SENTENCES

59-001

<table>
<tr><th>Order</th><th>Required length</th><th>Discount for guilty plea</th><th>Minimum sentence with any guilty plea reduction</th></tr>
<tr><td>Third drug trafficking offence: (SC s.313)</td><td>Seven years</td><td>Yes: but resultant sentence must not be less and 80% of the required minimum</td><td>2,045 days (five years 7.2 months)</td></tr>
<tr><td>Possession of prohibited firearms: (SC s.311)</td><td>Five years (aged 18+). Three years (aged 16-17)</td><td>None, below the prescribed minimum</td><td>Five years (aged 18+). Three years (aged 16-17)</td></tr>
<tr><td>Minding weapons: (SC s.311)</td><td>Five years (aged 18+). Three years (aged 16-17)</td><td>None, below the prescribed minimum</td><td>Five years (aged 18+). Three years (aged 16-17)</td></tr>
<tr><td>Third domestic burglary offence: (SC s.314)</td><td>Three years</td><td>Yes: But the resultant sentence must not be less than 80% of the required minimum</td><td>876 days (two years 4.8 months)</td></tr>
<tr><td>Article with blade or point/Offensive weapon in a public place: (PCA 1953 s.1; CJA 1988 s.139; OWA 2019 ss.6, 8; SC s.315)</td><td rowspan="4">Six months (aged 18+). Four-month DTO (aged 16–17)</td><td rowspan="4">Yes: But where the defendant was aged 18+ at conviction, the resultant sentence must not be less than 80% of the required minimum</td><td rowspan="4">Age at conviction:18+: 146 days (4.8 months). Age at conviction: 16–17: Any appropriate sentence: SC s.73(5).</td></tr>
<tr><td>Article with blade or point on school premises: (CJA 1988 s.139A; SC s.315)</td></tr>
<tr><td>Threatening with article with blade or point or offensive weapon: (CJA 1988 s.139AA; SC s.312)</td></tr>
<tr><td>Threatening with offensive weapon in public: (PCA 1953 s.1A; SC s.312)</td></tr>
</table>

# MANDATORY MINIMUM SENTENCE — BLADED ARTICLES/ OFFENSIVE WEAPONS/CORROSIVE SUBSTANCES

## Sentencing Code ss.312 and 315

*References: Current Sentencing Practice A4; Archbold 5A-751*

There are two circumstances in which a prescribed sentence falls to be imposed; these are: (1) for the commission of a single trigger offence; and (2) for the commission of a trigger offence where the offender has a previous relevant conviction. **60-001**

### (1) Prescribed sentence (offences involving threats)

**Offences to which it applies** The prescribed sentences apply to the following offences: **60-002**

(a) PCA 1953 s.1A (threatening with an offensive weapon in a public place); and
(b) CJA 1988 s.139AA (offence of threatening with article with blade or point or offensive weapon).

**Circumstances in which the prescribed sentence applies** Where an offender aged 16 or over is convicted of an offence listed above, the court must impose: **60-003**

(a) in the case of a person aged 18 or over at conviction, a custodial sentence of at least six months; or
(b) in the case of a person aged 16 or 17 at conviction, a DTO of at least four months: SC s.312(2) and (3). But this is subject to s.252A (special custodial sentence for certain terrorist offences).

**Exceptional circumstances: disapplying the minimum sentence** The prescribed sentence does not apply where the court is of the opinion that there are exceptional circumstances which relate to the offence or to the offender, which justify not imposing the minimum: SC s.312(2). **60-004**

**Guilty plea discount** If the defendant has pleaded guilty the court may pass a sentence which is not less than 80% of the prescribed sentence: SC s.73(3) and (4). **60-005**

The restriction on the guilty plea discount does not apply to those aged 16 or 17 when convicted: SC s.73(5).

If the court finds that there are particular circumstances which would make it unjust to impose the prescribed custodial sentence, the discount for the plea of guilty is not limited to 20% of the sentence which would have been appropriate following a contested trial.

**Suspended sentence orders** In *Whyte* [2018] EWCA Crim 2437; [2019] 1 Cr. App. R. (S.) 35; [2019] Crim. L.R. 451, the court held that there was no power to suspend a minimum sentence required to be imposed under s.139 of the CJA 1988 as the reference to "imprisonment" was to be interpreted as immediate **60-006**

imprisonment. In [2019] Crim. L.R. 451 it was suggested that as a matter of law the view taken in *Whyte* was incorrect. In *AG's Ref (Uddin)* [2022] EWCA Crim 751 the court endorsed that analysis, reversing the decision in *Whyte* and holding that the sentence could be suspended, if the requisite criteria were met.

60-007 **Interaction with sentencing guidelines** Reference should first be made to the sentencing guidelines in order to determine the appropriate sentence and only then should the minimum sentence provision be consulted to ensure that the sentence complies with the statute: *Silvera* [2013] EWCA Crim 1764. *Silvera* was decided in relation to the minimum sentence under s.111 of the PCC(S)A 2000. The court in *Attorney General's Reference (Marland)* [2018] EWCA Crim 1770; [2018] 2 Cr. App. R.(S.) 51; [2018] Crim. L.R. 935 suggested that the guidelines could be used to check whether or not the required minimum sentence would be disproportionate and unjust. However, a minimum sentence is not to be regarded as "unjust" simply because it would be manifestly excessive: *Lucas* [2011] EWCA Crim 2806; [2012] 2 Cr. App. R.(S.) 14; [2012] Crim. L.R. 227.

**(2) Prescribed sentence for repeat offenders (possession offences)**

60-008 *Note: The OWA 2019 provisions were not in force on 31 October 2024.*

60-009 **Offences to which it applies** The prescribed sentences apply to the following offences:

(a) PCA 1953 s.1 (possession of an offensive weapon);
(b) CJA 1988 s.139 (possession of bladed article);
(c) CJA 1988 s.139A (having bladed article or offensive weapon on school premises); and
(d) OWA 2019 s.6 (possession of corrosive substance in public) (not yet in force).

60-010 **Circumstances in which the prescribed sentence applies** Where the instant offence was committed on or after 17 July 2015, and when the offence was committed:

(a) on or after 17 July 2015; and
(b) when the offence was committed, the person was aged 16 or over and had a conviction for a "relevant offence", the court must impose:
    (i) in the case of a person aged 18 or over at conviction, a custodial sentence of at least six months; or
    (ii) in the case of a person aged 16 or 17 at conviction, a detention and training order of at least four months: SC s.315(2) and (3).

60-011 **Exceptional circumstances: disapplying the minimum sentence** The prescribed sentence does not apply where the court is of the opinion that there are exceptional circumstances which relate to the offence, to the previous offence or to the offender, which justify not imposing the minimum: SC s.315(2).

The minimum sentence provisions should not be "watered down" either by a liberal application of the "unjust" circumstances test or by reference to totality: *Chaplin* [2015] EWCA Crim 1491; [2016] 1 Cr. App. R.(S.) 10; [2016] Crim. L.R. 73.

**Interaction with sentencing guidelines** Reference should first be made to the sentencing guidelines in order to determine the appropriate sentence and only then should the minimum sentence provision be consulted to ensure that the sentence complies with the statute: *Silvera* [2013] EWCA Crim 1764. *Silvera* was decided in relation to the minimum sentence under s.111 of the PCC(S)A 2000. The court in *Attorney General's Reference (Marland)* [2018] EWCA Crim 1770; [2018] 2 Cr. App. R. (S.) 51; [2018] Crim. L.R. 935 suggested that the guidelines could be used to check whether or not the required minimum sentence would be disproportionate and unjust. However, a minimum sentence is not to be regarded as "unjust" simply because it would be manifestly excessive: *Lucas* [2011] EWCA Crim 2806; [2012] 2 Cr. App. R.(S.) 14; [2012] Crim. L.R. 227. **60-012**

**Relevant offence** A "*relevant offence*" is a conviction for an offence under: **60-013**

(i) PCA 1953 ss.1 or 1A;
(ii) CJA 1988 ss.139, 139A; or 139AA; or
(iii) OWA 2019 s.6 (not yet in force): SC s.315(4).

**Guilty plea discount** If the defendant has pleaded guilty the court may pass a sentence which is not less than 80% of the prescribed sentence: SC s.73(3) and (4). **60-014**

The restriction on the guilty plea discount does not apply to those aged 16 or 17 when convicted: SC s.73(5).

If the court finds that there are particular circumstances which would make it unjust to impose the prescribed custodial sentence, the discount for the plea of guilty is not limited to 20% of the sentence which would have been appropriate following a contested trial.

**Suspended sentence orders** See **para.60-006** above. **60-015**

# MANDATORY MINIMUM SENTENCES—PROHIBITED WEAPONS

## Sentencing Code s.311

*References: Current Sentencing Practice A4; Archbold 5A-751*

### Approach

The proper approach to sentencing in a minimum sentence firearms case is to determine the length of the sentence by reference to the relevant principles and authorities and then to consider whether that provisional sentence infringes the prescribed minimum: *Boyle* [2018] EWCA Crim 2035; [2019] 1 Cr. App. R.(S.) 9. 61-001

**Applicability** The duty to impose a minimum sentence applies where: 61-002

(a) a person is convicted of an offence listed in Sch.20 (certain offences involving firearms that are prohibited weapons); and
(b) the offender was aged 16 or over when the offence was committed: SC s.311(1).

See **para.61-006** for Sch.20.

**Duty to impose minimum sentence** Where the duty to impose a minimum sentence applies, the court must impose an appropriate custodial sentence of at least the required minimum term: SC s.311(2). 61-003

"*Appropriate custodial sentence*" means: in the case of a person who is aged under 18 when convicted, a sentence of detention under s.250, or where s.252A applies, a sentence under that section; in the case of a person who is aged 18 or over but under 21 when convicted, a sentence of detention in a young offender institution (and, includes, if the offence is an offence for which a person aged 21 or over would be liable to imprisonment for life, a sentence of custody for life); and in the case of a person who is aged 21 or over when convicted, a sentence of imprisonment: SC s.311(3).

"*Required minimum term*" means: in the case of an offender who was aged under 18 when the offence was committed, three years; and in the case of an offender who was aged 18 or over when the offence was committed, five years: SC s.311(4).

For offences within para.5 of Sch.20 to the Sentencing Code, the court must impose:

(a) in the case of an offender who was aged under 18 when convicted, three years; and
(b) in the case of an offender who was aged 18 or over when convicted, five years: SC s.311(5).

**Exceptional circumstances** The court must impose an appropriate custodial sentence for a term of at least the required minimum term unless the court is of the opinion that there are exceptional circumstances which: 61-004

(a) relate to the offence or to the offender; and
(b) justify not doing so: SC s.311(2).

Where a defendant submits that exceptional circumstances exist, the procedure should follow that of a *Newton* hearing: *Rogers* [2016] EWCA Crim 801; [2017] 1 W.L.R. 481; [2016] 2 Cr. App. R.(S.) 36.

In particular:

(a) the circumstances relied upon should be set out in writing and signed by the defendant's advocate;
(b) the court would then determine whether a hearing was necessary (this being dependent upon the prosecution and judge accepted the statement of exceptional circumstances);
(c) if a hearing took place, the judge had to determine the matters to the criminal standard of proof and the burden was on the Crown to disprove the defendant's account;
(d) if the Crown failed to do so, the judge had to proceed on the basis that the defendant's version of events was correct; and
(e) it does not follow that the judge, even if they accepted the defendant's version of events, would find that this amounted to exceptional circumstances: *Lashari* [2010] EWCA Crim 1504; [2011] 1 Cr. App. R.(S.) 72; [2010] Crim. L.R. 783.

The difficulty with an exceptionality test was that it did not provide any clear standard from which the exceptional case would differ. In this particular case, the judge had described the case as neither ordinary nor wholly remarkable but that was not a helpful way of looking at the test. Ultimately, the test would be whether the imposition of the minimum sentence would lead to a sentence that was arbitrary or disproportionate, but the answer to that question had to be considered in the light of the clear statutory intent that the offences to which the mandatory sentence applied had to be met with strong deterrent sentences: *Bartell* [2020] EWCA Crim 625; [2020] 4 W.L.R. 79; [2020] 2 Cr. App. R.(S.) 51.

61-005 **Guilty plea discount** The court may not allow a discount for a plea of guilty if the effect of doing so would be to reduce the length of the sentence below the required minimum term: SC s.73(3) and (4).

DETENTION UNDER SECTION 250 AND MINIMUM SENTENCES: FIREARMS OFFENCES

## Part 1
*Offences*

1 An offence under section 5(1)(a), (ab), (aba), (ac), (ad), (ae), (af) or (c) of the Firearms Act 1968 (offence of having in possession, purchasing or acquiring, weapon or ammunition) committed on or after 22 January 2004. **61-006**

1A An offence under section 5(1)(ag) or (ba) of the Firearms Act 1968 committed on or after 6 April 2022.

2 An offence under section 5(1A)(a) of the Firearms Act 1968 (offence of having in possession, purchasing or acquiring firearm disguised as another object) committed on or after 22 January 2004.

3 An offence under section 5(2A) of the Firearms Act 1968 (manufacture, sale or transfer of firearm or ammunition, or possession etc. for sale or transfer) committed in respect of a relevant firearm or relevant ammunition.

4 (1) An offence under any of the provisions of the Firearms Act 1968 listed in sub-paragraph (2) committed on or after 6 April 2007 in respect of a relevant firearm or relevant ammunition.

(2) Those provisions are—

section 16 (possession of firearm or ammunition with intent to injure);

section 16A (possession of firearm with intent to cause fear or violence);

section 17 (use of firearm to resist arrest);

section 18 (carrying firearm with criminal intent);

section 19 (carrying a firearm in a public place);

section 20(1) (trespassing in a building with firearm).

5 An offence under section 28 of the Violent Crime Reduction Act 2006 (using someone to mind a weapon), where the dangerous weapon in respect of which the offence was committed was a relevant firearm.

## Part 2
*Interpretation of Schedule*

6 In this Schedule—

*"relevant firearm"* means a firearm specified in any of the following provisions of section 5 of the Firearms Act 1968 (weapons subject to general prohibition)—

(a) subsection (1)(a), (ab), (aba), (ac), (ad), (ae) or (af);

(b) subsection (1A)(a);

*"relevant ammunition"* means ammunition specified in subsection (1)(c) of that section.

For this purpose, "*firearm and ammunition*" have the same meanings as in the Firearms Act 1968.

# MANDATORY MINIMUM SENTENCE—DRUG TRAFFICKING

SENTENCING CODE s.313

*References: Current Sentencing Practice A4; Archbold 5A-751*

## Applicability

The mandatory sentence applies where: **62-001**

(a) a person is convicted of a class A drug trafficking offence (*"the index offence"*) committed on or after 1 October 1997;
(b) when the index offence was committed, the offender:
 (i) was aged 18 or over; and
 (ii) had two other relevant drug convictions; and
(c) one of the offences to which those other relevant drug convictions related was committed after the offender had been convicted of the other: SC s.313(1).

## Duty to impose minimum sentence

Where the mandatory sentence applies, the court must impose an appropriate custodial sentence for a term of at least seven years: SC s.313(2). **62-002**

**Exceptional circumstances: Disapplying the minimum sentence** The prescribed sentence does not apply where the court is of the opinion that there are exceptional circumstances which relate to any of the offences or to the offender, which justify not imposing the minimum. **62-003**

The minimum sentence provisions should not be "watered down" either by a liberal application of the "unjust" circumstances test or by reference to totality: *Chaplin* [2015] EWCA Crim 1491; [2016] 1 Cr. App. R.(S.) 10; [2016] Crim. L.R. 73.

## Drug trafficking offences

A *"drug trafficking offence"* is one listed within para.1 of Sch.2 to the POCA 2002. The offences are as follows: **62-004**

(i) producing, supplying or possessing with intent to supply controlled drugs, MDA 1971 ss.4(2); 4(3) and 5(3). (N.B. simple possession is not included);
(ii) permitting certain activities relating to controlled drugs, MDA 1971 s.8;
(iii) assisting in or inducing the commission outside the UK of an offence punishable under a corresponding law, MDA 1971 s.20;
(iv) improper importation, exportation, or fraudulently evading the prohibition or restriction on importation or exportation of controlled substances whose importation or exportation is prohibited by MDA 1971, Customs and Excise Management Act 1979 (CEMA 1979) ss.50(2) or (3), 68(2) or 170;

(v) manufacturing or supplying a scheduled substance, knowing or suspecting that it is to be used in the production of a controlled drug, Criminal Justice (International Co-operation) Act 1990 (CJ(IC)A 1990) s.12;
(vi) having possession of a controlled drug on a ship, or being concerned in carrying or concealing a controlled drug on a ship, knowing it is intended to be unlawfully imported or has been exported, CJ(IC)A 1990 s.19; and
(vii) inciting, attempting or conspiring to commit any of these offences or aiding, abetting, counselling or procuring the commission of any of them: SC s.313(1), (3) and (5) and POCA 2002 Sch.2 para.1.

62-005 **Previous convictions** "*Relevant drug conviction*" means:

(a) a conviction in any part of the UK of a class A drug trafficking offence;
(b) a conviction in another Member State of an offence committed on or after 16 August 2010 which would, if committed in the UK at the time of the conviction, have constituted a class A drug trafficking offence;
(c) a conviction of an offence under s.42 of the AFA 2006 in respect of which the corresponding offence under the law of England and Wales (within the meaning of that section) is a class A drug trafficking offence;
(d) a conviction of an offence under s.70 of the Army Act 1955, s.70 of the Air Force Act 1955 or s.42 of the Naval Discipline Act 1957 in respect of which the corresponding civil offence (within the meaning of the Act in question) is a class A drug trafficking offence; or
(e) a conviction of a Member State service offence committed on or after 16 August 2010 which would have constituted a class A drug trafficking offence if committed in England and Wales at the time of conviction: SC s.313(3).

A conviction which has been followed by a conditional or absolute discharge does not count for these purposes. A conviction which has been followed by a probation order made before 1 October 1992 does not count.

**Interaction with sentencing guidelines**

62-006 Reference should first be made to the sentencing guidelines in order to determine the appropriate sentence and only then should the minimum sentence provision be consulted to ensure that the sentence complies with the statute: *Silvera* [2013] EWCA Crim 1764. The court in *Attorney General's Reference (Marland)* [2018] EWCA Crim 1770 suggested that the guidelines should be used to check whether or not the required minimum sentence would be disproportionate and unjust. However, a minimum sentence is not to be regarded as "unjust" simply because it would be manifestly excessive: *Lucas* [2011] EWCA Crim 2806; [2012] 2 Cr. App. R.(S.) 14; [2012] Crim. L.R. 227.

**Guilty plea discount**

62-007 If the defendant has pleaded guilty the court may pass a sentence which is not less than 80% of the seven years (2,045 days, slightly less than five years and eight months): SC s.73(3) and (4).

If the court finds that there are particular circumstances which would make it unjust to impose the prescribed custodial sentence, the discount for the plea of guilty is not limited to 20% of the sentence which would have been appropriate following a contested trial.

**Mentally disordered defendants** If the offender qualifies for a hospital order under the MHA 1983, the court may make a hospital order: SC s.77 and the MHA 1983 s.37(1A)(b). **62-008**

**Pre-sentence reports**

The authorities do not suggest that a report was mandatory in all cases. It may be arguable that there was a threshold requirement for a defendant to give at least some indication of the circumstances capable of amounting to the "particular circumstances" referred that might be disclosed or corroborated by such a report. Certainly, an application for a pre-sentence report would be stronger if the advocate could point to a particular circumstance in relation to which further information could be expected to be obtained by the National Probation Service: *Wooff* [2019] EWCA Crim 2249; [2020] 2 Cr. App. R.(S.) 6. **62-009**

**Mode of trial**

A drug trafficking offence committed in circumstances in which the obligation to pass a minimum sentence applies is triable only on indictment: SC s.313(4). **62-010**

# MANDATORY MINIMUM SENTENCE—DOMESTIC BURGLARY

## Sentencing Code s.314

*References: Current Sentencing Practice A4; Archbold 5A-751*

### Applicability

The duty to impose a minimum sentence applies where: **63-001**

(a) a person is convicted of a domestic burglary ("*the index offence*") committed on or after 1 December 1999;
(b) when the index offence was committed:
  (i) the offender was aged 18 or over;
  (ii) had two other relevant domestic burglary convictions; and
(c) one of the burglaries to which those other relevant domestic burglary convictions relate was committed after the person had been convicted of the other: SC s.314(1).

### Duty to impose minimum sentence

Where the duty to impose a minimum sentence applies, the court must impose an appropriate custodial sentence for a term of at least three years: SC s.314(2). **63-002**

### Exceptional circumstances: disapplying the minimum sentence

The prescribed sentence does not apply where the court is of the opinion that there are exceptional circumstances which relate to any of the offences or to the offender, which justify not imposing the minimum: s.314(2). **63-003**

Where the court does not impose the prescribed sentence, it must state in open court what the circumstances are.

The minimum sentence provisions should not be "watered down" either by a liberal application of the "unjust" circumstances test or by reference to totality: *Chaplin* [2015] EWCA Crim 1491; [2016] 1 Cr. App. R.(S.) 10; [2016] Crim. L.R. 73.

### Aged 18

The offender must have been 18 or over at the time of the third burglary, but it is not necessary that they should have been 18 at the time of either of the earlier burglaries: SC s.314(1)(b). **63-004**

### Domestic burglary

A domestic burglary is a burglary that is committed in respect of a building or part of a building which is a dwelling: SC s.314(5). A burglary may not be treated as a domestic burglary for this purpose unless the fact that it was committed in respect of a dwelling is alleged in the indictment or information. **63-005**

To trigger the minimum sentence, it is necessary for the indictment to specify that the offence was committed in relation to a dwelling: *Miller* [2010] EWCA Crim 809; [2011] 1 Cr. App. R.(S.) 2; [2010] Crim. L.R. 648.

A houseboat is a "*building or part of a building*" for the purposes of s.314, see *Coleman* [2013] EWCA Crim 544; [2013] 2 Cr. App. R.(S.) 79; [2013] Crim. L.R. 694.

As to whether an uninhabited domestic property is a "*dwelling*" for the purposes of the Theft Act 1968: see *Hudson v CPS* [2017] EWHC 841 (Admin); [2017] 4 W.L.R. 108; [2017] 2 Cr. App. R.(S.) 23.

**Attempts**

**63-006** Attempted burglaries do not fall within the minimum sentence provision: *McGuire* [2003] 2 Cr. App. R.(S.) 10.

**Previous convictions**

**63-007** "*Relevant domestic burglary*" conviction means:

(a) a conviction in England and Wales of a domestic burglary committed on or after 1 December 1999; or
(b) a conviction in another part of the UK or another Member State of an offence committed on or after 16 August 2010 which would have constituted an offence of domestic burglary, if committed in England and Wales at the time of the conviction;
(c) a conviction of an offence under s.42 of the AFA 2006 in respect of which the corresponding offence under the law of England and Wales (within the meaning of that section) is an offence of domestic burglary;
(d) a conviction of an offence under s.70 of the Army Act 1955, s.70 of the Air Force Act 1955 or s.42 of the Naval Discipline Act 1957 committed on or after 1 December 1999 in respect of which the corresponding civil offence (within the meaning of the Act in question) is an offence of domestic burglary; or
(e) a conviction of a Member State service offence committed on or after 16 August 2010 which would have constituted an offence of domestic burglary if committed in England and Wales at the time of conviction: SC s.314(3).

A conviction which has been followed by a conditional or absolute discharge does not count for these purposes.

**Interaction with sentencing guidelines**

**63-008** Reference should first be made to the sentencing guidelines in order to determine the appropriate sentence and only then should the minimum sentence provision be consulted to ensure that the sentence complies with the statute: *Silvera* [2013] EWCA Crim 1764. The court in *Attorney General's Reference (Marland)* [2018] EWCA Crim 1770; [2018] 2 Cr. App. R.(S.) 51; [2018] Crim. L.R. 935 suggested that the guidelines could be used to check whether or not the required minimum sentence would be disproportionate and unjust. However, a minimum sentence is not to be regarded as "unjust" simply because it would be manifestly excessive:

*Lucas* [2011] EWCA Crim 2806; [2012] 2 Cr. App. R.(S.) 14; [2012] Crim. L.R. 227.

### Guilty plea reduction

If the offender has pleaded guilty, the court may pass a sentence which is not less than 80% of three years (876 days, slightly less than two years and five months): SC s.73(3) and (4). **63-009**

If the court finds that there are particular circumstances which would make it unjust to impose the prescribed custodial sentence, the discount for the plea of guilty is not limited to 20% of the sentence which would have been appropriate following a contested trial.

### Mentally ordered defendants

If the offender qualifies for a hospital order under the MHA 1983, the court may make a hospital order: SC s.77 and the MHA 1983 s.37(1A)(b). **63-010**

### Triable on indictment only

A burglary committed in circumstances in which the obligation to pass a minimum sentence applies is triable only on indictment: SC s.314(4). **63-011**

# EXTENDED DETERMINATE SENTENCES (AGED 18-20 AND 21+ AT CONVICTION)

## Sentencing Code s.266–268, 306 and Sch.19

*References: Current Sentencing Practice A4; Archbold 5A-796*

### What is an extended sentence?

An extended sentence is a sentence of detention or imprisonment the term of which is equal to the aggregate of: **64-001**

(a) the appropriate custodial term; and
(b) a further period (the "*extension period*") for which the offender is to be subject to a licence: SC ss.266 and 279.

### Availability

An extended sentence of detention in a young offender institution is available in respect of an offence where: **64-002**

(a) the offence is a specified offence (see s.306(1));
(b) the offender is aged at least 18 but under 21/aged 21 or over when convicted of the offence;
(c) the court is of the opinion that there is a significant risk to members of the public of serious harm occasioned by the commission by the offender of further specified offences (see s.308);
(d) the court is not required by ss.273, s.274 or 247A, s.283, s.285 or s.285A to impose a life sentence;
(e) the court is not required by s.268B to impose a serious terrorism sentence for the offence or for an offence associated with it; and
(f) the earlier offence condition or the four-year term condition is met: SC ss.267(1) and 280(1).

### Specified offence

A specified offence is one in Pt 1 (violent offence), Pt 2 (sexual offence) or Pt 3 (terrorism offence) of Sch.18 to the Sentencing Code: SC s.308(1) and (2). See **para.64-026** for Sch.18. **64-003**

An offence contrary to s.9(1)(b) (where the offender had inflicted or attempted to inflict grievous bodily harm on another) was not listed in Sch.18 of the Sentencing Act 2020 (by contrast to the fact that an offence contrary to s.9(1)(a) was so listed): *Johnson* [2023] EWCA Crim 1609; [2024] 1 Cr. App. R. (S.) 32.

### Dangerousness test

The pre-sentence report requirements (see s.30 of the Sentencing Code) apply to the court in relation to the dangerousness test: SC ss.267(2)and 280(2). See *Assessing dangerousness* below. **64-004**

### Earlier offence condition

**64-005** The earlier offence condition is that, when the offence was committed, the offender had been convicted of an offence listed in Sch.14: SC ss.267(3) and 280(3). See **para.64-025** for Sch.14.

### Four-year term condition

**64-006** The four-year term condition is that, if the court were to impose an extended sentence, the term that it would specify as the appropriate custodial term (see s.268) would be at least four years: SC ss.267(4) and 280(4).

It is permissible to consider the totality of the offending and to aggregate the offending to satisfy the four-year requirement. It is not permissible to impose consecutive sentences to reach the four-year limit: *Pinnell* [2010] EWCA Crim 2848; [2012] 1 W.L.R. 17; [2011] 2 Cr. App. R.(S.) 30.

The decision in *Pinnell* as to the permissibility of aggregating the sentences for specified and non-specified offences to determine the custodial term of the extended sentence was confirmed in *Camara* [2022] EWCA Crim 542; [2022] Crim. L.R. 782.

### Assessing dangerousness

**64-007** **General** The following applies where the court is required to consider whether the offender poses a significant risk of serious harm to members of the public by the commission of further specified offences: SC s.308(1). This is colloquially known as the "*dangerousness test*".

The decision to make a finding on the issue of dangerousness without a pre-sentence report is one which requires a careful justification: *Allen* [2019] EWCA Crim 1772.

It will be a rare case in which an appellate court will overturn on an appeal against sentence the exercise of judicial discretion in making a finding of dangerousness, that appellate court not having conducted the trial or see the offender: *Howlett* [2019] EWCA Crim 1224; [2020] 1 Cr. App. R.(S.) 14.

**64-008** **Must take into account** The court must take into account all such information as is available to it about the nature and circumstances of the offence: SC s.308(2).

**64-009** **May take into account** The court may take into account:

(a) all such information as is available about the nature and circumstances of any other offences of which the offender has been convicted by a court anywhere in the world;
(b) any information which is before it about any pattern of behaviour of which any of the offences of which the offender has been convicted forms part; and
(c) any information about the offender which is before it: SC s.308(2).

**64-010** **Serious harm** Serious harm means death or personal injury, whether physical or psychological: SC s.306(2).

**Risk** The risk does not have to be based on the instant offence: *Green* [2007] EWCA Crim 2172; [2008] 1 Cr. App. R.(S.) 97; [2008] Crim. L.R. 66. The absence of previous offences causing serious harm requiring an extended sentence does not preclude the finding of dangerousness: *Powell* [2015] EWCA Crim 2200; [2016] 1 Cr. App. R.(S.) 49. **64-011**

### Imposing the sentence

**Determining the appropriate sentence** A finding of dangerousness does not automatically lead to the imposition of an extended sentence (in circumstances where the seriousness is not such that a life sentence is required). The court has a discretion as to whether an extended sentence is necessary: *Bourke* [2017] EWCA Crim 2150; [2018] 1 Cr. App. R.(S.) 42. A determinate sentence may provide adequate public protection alongside, e.g. sexual notification, an SHPO and the barring provisions. This will be a fact-specific decision. **64-012**

In deciding, whether to impose an extended sentence or a standard determinate sentence, the court may take into account, the early release and licence provisions in relation to the two forms of sentence: *AYO* [2022] EWCA Crim 1271; [2022] 4 W.L.R. 95.

Having decided to impose an extended sentence, the court must determine:

(a) the appropriate custodial term; and
(b) the extension period.

**Custodial term** The appropriate custodial term is the term of detention that would be imposed in respect of the offence in compliance with s.231(2) (length of discretionary custodial sentences: general provision) if the court did not impose an extended sentence: SC ss.268(2) and 281(2). **64-013**

The custodial period must be adjusted for totality in the same way as determinate sentences would be: *Totality Guideline,* p.10.

**Extended licence** The extension period must be a period of such length as the court considers necessary for the purpose of protecting members of the public from serious harm occasioned by the commission by the offender of further specified offences: SC ss.268(3) and 281(3). **64-014**

The extension period must:

(a) be at least one year; and
(b) not exceed:
    (i) five years in the case of a specified violent offence (unless sub-para (iii) applies);
    (ii) eight years in the case of a specified sexual offence or a specified terrorism offence (unless subpara.(iii) applies);
    (iii) 10 years in the case of a serious terrorism offence for which the sentence is imposed on or after 29 June 2021 (the day on which s.16 of the Counter-Terrorism and Sentencing Act 2021 came into force).

An extended licence period is different in kind from a determinate sentence. It is not tied to the seriousness of the offending; its purpose is protective. Like all sentences, it should not be longer than necessary for the relevant purpose. It should be just and proportionate, and not such as to crush the defendant: *Phillips* [2018] EWCA Crim 2008; [2019] 1 Cr. App. R.(S.) 11; [2019] Crim. L.R. 176.

The extension period is such as the court considers necessary for the purpose of protecting members of the public from serious harm caused by the offender committing further specified offences: *Cornelius* [2002] EWCA Crim 138; [2002] 2 Cr. App. R.(S.) 69; [2002] M.H.L.R. 134. The length of the extension period is a matter of judicial judgement and the Court of Appeal will only interfere where it could be demonstrated that the judge had erred in deciding what factors should be taken into account when exercising their judgement, or where the judge had reached a wholly unreasonable conclusion as to the necessary term: *ARD* [2017] EWCA Crim 1882; [2018] 1 Cr. App. R.(S.) 23; [2018] Crim. L.R. 345.

As the extension period is measured by the need for protection, it does not require adjustment for totality: *Totality Guideline,* p.10.

Further guidance is provided in *AYO* [2022] EWCA Crim 1271; [2022] 4 W.L.R. 95.

64-015 **Maximum sentence** The term of the extended sentence of detention under s.254 must not exceed the maximum term of imprisonment with which the offence is punishable in the case of a person aged 21 or over: SC ss.268(5) and 281(5).

64-016 **Explaining sentence** In *Bourke* [2017] EWCA Crim 2150; [2018] 1 Cr. App. R.(S.) 42 the court noted that where the sentencing judge considered an extended sentence unsuitable, it would have been preferable had they explained why that was so, even if that explanation were brief. The usual duty to give reasons for, and explain, the sentence applies: *Lang* [2005] EWCA Crim 2864; [2006] 1 W.L.R. 2509; [2006] 2 Cr. App. R.(S.) 3.

64-017 **Consecutive sentences** In appropriate circumstances, consecutive extended sentences may be imposed, see e.g. *Watkins* [2014] EWCA Crim 1677; [2015] 1 Cr. App. R.(S.) 6. However in such circumstances, the explanation of the sentences (and their effect) is likely to be complex, and care should be taken in determining the true position.

In *B* [2015] EWCA Crim 1295; [2015] 2 Cr. App. R.(S.) 78; [2015] Crim. L.R. 1009, the court substituted consecutive extended sentences, aggregating the licence periods resulting in a total 10-year extended licence. In *Thompson* [2018] EWCA Crim 639; [2018] 1 W.L.R. 4429; [2018] 2 Cr. App. R.(S.) 19, a five-judge court confirmed that it was permissible to impose consecutive sentences so as to take the total extended licence period beyond the five or eight-year limits provided by the Act. The court commented that it would be permissible only in exceptional circumstances, however.

It is not permissible to make the sentences partly concurrent and partly consecutive: *Francis* [2014] EWCA Crim 631; *DJ* [2015] EWCA Crim 563; [2015] 2 Cr. App. R.(S.) 16; [2015] Crim. L.R. 650.

There is no objection to imposing an extended sentence consecutive to a determinate sentence (either on the same occasion, or in addition to an existing determinate sentence): *Brown* [2006] EWCA Crim 1996; [2007] 1 Cr. App. R.(S.) 77; [2006] Crim. L.R. 1082 and *Hibbert* [2015] EWCA Crim 507; [2015] 2 Cr. App. R.(S.) 15. However, the Court of Appeal has repeatedly stated that it is undesirable to impose a determinate sentence consecutive to an extended sentence (see e.g. *Brown* and *Prior* [2014] EWCA Crim 1290). This issue was considered in *Ulhaqdad* [2017] EWCA Crim 1216; [2018] 4 W.L.R. 65; [2017] 2 Cr. App. R.(S.) 46, where the court established that the order in which a court imposed an extended sentence and a determinate sentence (where those sentences are made to run consecutively) created no practical difficulty for the prison service in relation to the calculation of sentences and release dates, etc. However, having identified no practical or principled reason for the guidance given in *Brown*, the court in *Ulhaqdad* maintained the status quo. Therefore the position remains that where extended and determinate sentences are being imposed to run consecutively, the determinate sentence should be imposed first. Two further points remain. First, that in *Prior*, the court suggested that an alternative approach was to increase the custodial term of the extended sentence and make the sentences run concurrently. Secondly, despite the guidance in *Brown*, there is nothing unlawful about imposing an extended sentence consecutive to a determinate sentence in an appropriate case: *Hibbert* [2015] EWCA Crim 507; [2015] 2 Cr. App. R.(S.) 15. However, it is submitted that the operation of the release provisions renders either approach permissible.

### Release

**Sentence imposed on or after 13 April 2015** At the 2/3 point of the custodial portion of the sentence, defendants will be referred to the Parole Board for consideration for release: CJA 2003 s.246A(3) and (4)(a). **64-018**

If the first application is unsuccessful, there must be another referral after two years. The test for the Parole Board is whether or not it is satisfied that it is no longer necessary for the protection of the public that the defendant should be confined: CJA 2003 s.246A(4)(b) and (6).

Release is automatic at the expiry of the custodial portion of the sentence: CJA 2003 s.246A(7). **64-019**

The defendant is then on licence for the aggregate of the remaining custodial portion (if there is one) and the extended licence period.

# LIFE SENTENCES—MANSLAUGHTER OF EMERGENCY WORKER

## Sentencing Act 2020 ss.274A/285A

*References: Archbold 5A-849a*

### Applicability

**Aged 18-20** Where— **64-020**

- (a) a person aged 18 or over but under 21 is convicted of a relevant offence,
- (b) the offence was committed—
  - (i) when the person was aged 16 or over, and
  - (ii) on or after 28 June 2022, and
- (c) the offence was committed against an emergency worker acting in the exercise of functions as such a worker, the court must impose a sentence of custody for life under s.272: s.274A(1).

The court may not impose a life sentence if it is of the opinion that there are exceptional circumstances which—

- (a) relate to the offence or the offender, and
- (b) justify not doing so: s.274A(1) and (2).

**Aged 21+** Where— **64-021**

- (a) a person aged 21 or over is convicted of a relevant offence,
- (b) the offence was committed—
  - (i) when the person was aged 16 or over, and
  - (ii) on or after 28 June 2022, and
- (c) the offence was committed against an emergency worker acting in the exercise of functions as such a worker, the court must impose a sentence of custody for life under s.272: s.285A(1).

The court may not impose a life sentence if it is of the opinion that there are exceptional circumstances which—

- (a) relate to the offence or the offender, and
- (b) justify not doing so: s.285A(1) and (2).

**Dangerousness** There is no requirement that the offender be found to be "*dangerous*". Therefore the fact that an offender is not dangerous is not something that, of itself, would make it unjust to pass a life sentence under ss.274A or 285A. Additionally, there is no requirement to consider whether the seriousness threshold has been passed for the purposes of the dangerousness life sentence: see, by analogy, *Attorney General's Reference (No. 27 of 2013) (Burinskas)* [2014] EWCA Crim 334; [2014] 1 W.L.R. 4209; [2014] 2 Cr. App. R.(S.) 45. **64-022**

**Setting the minimum term** A court which imposes a sentence of imprisonment (or custody) for life must fix a minimum term. The offender is not entitled to be released until they have served the minimum term. For details on setting the **64-023**

minimum term, see **LIFE SENTENCES—MINIMUM TERM (NON-MURDER CASES)** at **para.70**.

64-024 **Definitions** Circumstances in which an offence is to be taken as committed against a person acting in the exercise of functions as an emergency worker include circumstances where the offence takes place at a time when the person is not at work but is carrying out functions which, if done in work time, would have been in the exercise of functions as an emergency worker: s.274A(3).

"*Relevant offence*" means the offence of manslaughter, but does not include—

(a) manslaughter by gross negligence, or
(b) manslaughter mentioned in s.2(3) or 4(1) of the Homicide Act 1957 or s.54(7) of the Coroners and Justice Act 2009 (partial defences to murder): s.274A(4).

"*Emergency worker*" has the meaning given by s.68: s.274A(5).

An offence the sentence for which is imposed under this section is not to be regarded as an offence the sentence for which is fixed by law: s.274A(6).

EXTENDED SENTENCES: THE EARLIER OFFENCE CONDITION: OFFENCES

Part 1

*Offences under the Law of England and Wales*

The following offences to the extent that they are offences under the law of England and Wales— **64-025**

**Manslaughter**

1 Manslaughter.

**Offences against the Person Act 1861**

2 An offence under any of the following sections of the Offences against the Person Act 1861—
   (a) section 4 (soliciting murder);
   (b) section 18 (wounding with intent to cause grievous bodily harm);
   (c) section 28 (causing bodily injury by explosives);
   (d) section 29 (using explosives etc with intent to do grievous bodily harm).

**Explosive Substances Act 1883**

3 An offence under any of the following provisions of the Explosive Substances Act 1883—
   (a) section 2 (causing explosion likely to endanger life or property);
   (b) section 3 (attempt to cause explosion, or making or keeping explosive with intent to endanger life or property);
   (c) section 4 (making or possession of explosive under suspicious circumstances).

**Firearms Act 1968**

4 An offence under any of the following provisions of the Firearms Act 1968—
   (a) section 16 (possession of a firearm with intent to endanger life);
   (b) section 17(1) (use of a firearm to resist arrest);
   (c) section 18 (carrying a firearm with criminal intent).

**Theft Act 1968**

5 An offence of robbery under section 8 of the Theft Act 1968 where, at some time during the commission of the offence, the offender had in his or her possession a firearm or an imitation firearm within the meaning of the Firearms Act 1968.

**Protection of Children Act 1978**

6 An offence under section 1 of the Protection of Children Act 1978 (indecent images of children).

**Terrorism Act 2000**

7 An offence under any of the following provisions of the Terrorism Act 2000—
(a) section 54 (weapons training);
(b) section 56 (directing terrorist organisation);
(c) section 57 (possession of article for terrorist purposes);
(d) section 59 (inciting terrorism overseas) if the offender is liable on conviction on indictment to imprisonment for life.

**Anti-terrorism Crime and Security Act 2001**

8 An offence under any of the following provisions of the Anti-terrorism, Crime and Security Act 2001—
(a) section 47 (use etc of nuclear weapons);
(b) section 50 (assisting or inducing certain weapons-related acts overseas);
(c) section 113 (use of noxious substance or thing to cause harm or intimidate).

**Sexual Offences Act 2003**

9 An offence under any of the provisions of the Sexual Offences Act 2003 listed in column 1 of the following table that meets the condition (if any) listed in relation to it in column 2—

| | **Provision of the Sexual Offences Act 2003** | **Condition** |
|---|---|---|
| (a) | Section 1 (rape) | |
| (b) | Section 2 (assault by penetration) | |
| (c) | Section 4 (causing a person to engage in sexual activity without consent) | The offender is liable on conviction on indictment to imprisonment for life |
| (d) | Section 5 (rape of a child under 13) | |
| (e) | Section 6 (assault of a child under 13 by penetration) | |
| (f) | Section 7 (sexual assault of a child under 13) | |
| (g) | Section 8 (causing or inciting a child under 13 to engage in sexual activity) | |
| (h) | Section 9 (sexual activity with a child) | |
| (i) | Section 10 (causing or inciting a child to engage in sexual activity) | |

| | Provision of the Sexual Offences Act 2003 | Condition |
|---|---|---|
| (j) | Section 11 (engaging in sexual activity in the presence of a child) | |
| (k) | Section 12 (causing a child to watch a sexual act) | |
| (l) | Section 14 (arranging or facilitating commission of a child sex offence) | |
| (m) | Section 15 (meeting a child following sexual grooming etc) | |
| (n) | Section 25 (sexual activity with a child family member) | The offender is aged 18 or over at the time of the offence |
| (o) | Section 26 (inciting a child family member to engage in sexual activity) | The offender is aged 18 or over at the time of the offence |
| (p) | Section 30 (sexual activity with a person with a mental disorder impeding choice) | The offender is liable on conviction on indictment to imprisonment for life |
| (q) | Section 31 (causing or inciting a person with a mental disorder to engage in sexual activity) | The offender is liable on conviction on indictment to imprisonment for life |
| (r) | Section 34 (inducement, threat or deception to procure sexual activity with a person with a mental disorder) | The offender is liable on conviction on indictment to imprisonment for life |
| (s) | Section 35 (causing a person with a mental disorder to engage in or agree to engage in sexual activity by inducement etc) | The offender is liable on conviction on indictment to imprisonment for life |
| (t) | Section 47 (paying for sexual services of a child) | The offence is against a person aged under 16 |
| (u) | Section 48 (causing or inciting sexual exploitation of a child) | |
| (v) | Section 49 (controlling a child in relation to sexual exploitation) | |
| (w) | Section 50 (arranging or facilitating sexual exploitation of a child) | |
| (x) | Section 62 (committing an offence with intent to commit a sexual offence) | The offender is liable on conviction on indictment to imprisonment for life. |

**Domestic Violence, Crime and Victims Act 2004**

10 An offence under section 5 of the Domestic Violence, Crime and Victims Act 2004 (causing or allowing the death of a child or vulnerable adult).

**Terrorism Act 2006**

11 An offence under any of the following provisions of the Terrorism Act 2006—
(a) section 5 (preparation of terrorist acts);
(b) section 6 (training for terrorism);
(c) section 9 (making or possession of radioactive device or materials);
(d) section 10 (misuse of radioactive devices or material and misuse and damage of facilities);
(e) section 11 (terrorist threats relating to radioactive devices, materials or facilities).

**Modern Slavery Act 2015**

12 An offence under either of the following provisions of the Modern Slavery Act 2015—
(a) section 1 (slavery, servitude and forced or compulsory labour);
(b) section 2 (human trafficking).

**Murder**

13 Murder.

**Inchoate offences**

14 An inchoate offence (see section 398) in relation to an offence specified in any of the preceding paragraphs of this Part of this Schedule.

**Abolished offences**

15 Any offence that—
(a) was abolished (with or without savings) before 3 December 2012, and
(b) would, if committed on the day on which the offender is convicted of the offence referred to in section 267(1)(a) or 280(1)(a) (as appropriate), have constituted an offence specified in any of the preceding paragraphs in this Part of this Schedule.

Part 2

*Offences under service law*

16 An offence under section 70 of the Army Act 1955, section 70 of the Air Force Act 1955 or section 42 of the Naval Discipline Act 1957 as respects which the corresponding civil offence (within the meaning of the Act in question) is an offence specified in Part 1 of this Schedule.

17(1) An offence under section 42 of the Armed Forces Act 2006 as respects which the corresponding offence under the law of England and Wales (within the meaning given by that section) is an offence specified in Part 1 of this Schedule.

(2) Section 48 of the Armed Forces Act 2006 (attempts, conspiracy etc) applies for the purposes of this paragraph as if the reference in subsection (3)(b) of

that section to any of the following provisions of that Act were a reference to this paragraph.

## Part 3

*Offences under the law of Scotland, Northern Ireland or a member State other than the United Kingdom*

18 A civilian offence for which the person was convicted in Scotland, Northern Ireland or a member State other than the United Kingdom and which, if committed in England and Wales at the time of the conviction, would have constituted an offence specified in Part 1 of this Schedule.

19 A member State service offence which, if committed in England and Wales at the time of the conviction, would have constituted an offence specified in Part 1 of this Schedule.

20 In this Part of this Schedule— civilian offence means an offence other than an offence described in Part 2 of this Schedule or a member State service offence; member State service offence means an offence which was the subject of proceedings under the law of a member State, other than the United Kingdom, governing all or any of the naval, military or air forces of that State.

## Part 4

*Interpretation*

21 In this Schedule imprisonment for life includes custody for life and detention for life.

SPECIFIED OFFENCES FOR PURPOSES OF SECTION 306

Part 1
*Specified violent offences*

**Common law offences**

1 Manslaughter. **64-026**
2 Kidnapping.
3 False imprisonment.

**Offences against the Person Act 1861**

4 An offence under any of the following provisions of the Offences against the Person Act 1861—
 (a) section 4 (soliciting murder);
 (b) section 16 (threats to kill);
 (c) section 18 (wounding with intent to cause grievous bodily harm);
 (d) section 20 (malicious wounding);
 (e) section 21 (attempting to choke, suffocate or strangle in order to commit or assist in committing an indictable offence);
 (f) section 22 (using chloroform etc to commit or assist in the committing of any indictable offence);
 (g) section 23 (maliciously administering poison etc so as to endanger life or inflict grievous bodily harm);
 (h) section 27 (abandoning children);
 (i) section 28 (causing bodily injury by explosives);
 (j) section 29 (using explosives etc with intent to do grievous bodily harm);
 (k) section 30 (placing explosives with intent to do bodily injury);
 (l) section 31 (setting spring guns etc with intent to do grievous bodily harm);
 (m) section 32 (endangering the safety of railway passengers);
 (n) section 35 (injuring persons by furious driving);
 (o) section 37 (assaulting officer preserving wreck);
 (p) section 38 (assault with intent to resist arrest);
 (q) section 47 (assault occasioning actual bodily harm).

**Explosive Substances Act 1883**

5 An offence under any of the following provisions of the Explosive Substances Act 1883—
 (a) section 2 (causing explosion likely to endanger life or property);
 (b) section 3 (attempt to cause explosion, or making or keeping explosive with intent to endanger life or property);

(c) section 4 (making or possession of explosive under suspicious circumstances); [1]

(d) section 5 (punishment of accessories to offences of causing or attempting to cause explosions or making or possessing explosives) in a case where the offender is convicted on or after the day on which section 15 of the Counter-Terrorism and Sentencing Act 2021 comes into force.

**Infant Life (Preservation) Act 1929**

6 An offence under section 1 of the Infant Life (Preservation) Act 1929 (child destruction).

**Children and Young Persons Act 1933**

7 An offence under section 1 of the Children and Young Persons Act 1933 (cruelty to children).

**Infanticide Act 1938**

8 An offence under section 1 of the Infanticide Act 1938 (infanticide).

**Firearms Act 1968**

9 An offence under any of the following provisions of the Firearms Act 1968—

(a) section 16 (possession of firearm with intent to endanger life);

(b) section 16A (possession of firearm with intent to cause fear of violence);

(c) section 17(1) (use of firearm to resist arrest);

(d) section 17(2) (possession of firearm at time of committing or being arrested for offence specified in Schedule 1 to that Act);

(e) section 18 (carrying a firearm with criminal intent).

**Theft Act 1968**

10 An offence under any of the following provisions of the Theft Act 1968—

(a) section 8 (robbery or assault with intent to rob);

(b) section 9, where the offence is burglary with intent to—

(i) inflict grievous bodily harm on a person, or

(ii) do unlawful damage to a building or anything in it;

(c) section 10 (aggravated burglary);

(d) section 12A (aggravated vehicle-taking), where the offence involves an accident which caused the death of any person.

**Criminal Damage Act 1971**

11(1) An offence of arson under section 1 of the Criminal Damage Act 1971.

(2) An offence under section 1(2) of that Act (destroying or damaging property) other than an offence of arson.

---

1 Added by Counter-Terrorism and Sentencing Act 2021 c. 11 Pt 1 s.15(2) (29 June 2021 except as specified in 2021 c.11 s.50(3)(c); not yet in force otherwise).

**Biological Weapons Act 1974**

An offence under section 1 of the Biological Weapons Act 1974 (developing certain biological agents and toxins or biological weapons) in a case where the offender is convicted on or after the day on which section 15 of the Counter-Terrorism and Sentencing Act 2021 comes into force.[2]

**Taking of Hostages Act 1982**

12 An offence under section 1 of the Taking of Hostages Act 1982 (hostage-taking).

**Aviation Security Act 1982**

13 An offence under any of the following provisions of the Aviation Security Act 1982—
(a) section 1 (hijacking);
(b) section 2 (destroying, damaging or endangering safety of aircraft);
(c) section 3 (other acts endangering or likely to endanger safety of aircraft);
(d) section 4 (offences in relation to certain dangerous articles); [3]
(e) section 6(2) (inducing or assisting the commission of offences relating to safety of aircraft) in a case where the offender is convicted on or after the day on which section 15 of the Counter-Terrorism and Sentencing Act 2021 comes into force.

**Nuclear Material (Offences) Act 1983**

13A An offence under either of the following provisions of the Nuclear Material (Offences) Act 1983 in a case where the offender is convicted on or after the day on which section 15 of the Counter-Terrorism and Sentencing Act 2021 comes into force
(a) section 1B (offences relating to damage to the environment);
(b) section 2 (preparatory acts and threats).[4]

**Mental Health Act 1983**

14 An offence under section 127 of the Mental Health Act 1983 (ill-treatment of patients).

**Prohibition of Female Circumcision Act 1985**

15 An offence under section 1 of the Prohibition of Female Circumcision Act 1985 (prohibition of female circumcision).

---

2 Added by Counter-Terrorism and Sentencing Act 2021 c. 11 Pt 1 s.15(3) (June 29, 2021 except as specified in 2021 c.11 s.50(3)(c); not yet in force otherwise).

3 Added by Counter-Terrorism and Sentencing Act 2021 c. 11 Pt 1 s.15(4) (29 June 2021 except as specified in 2021 c.11 s.50(3)(c); not yet in force otherwise.)

4 Added by Counter-Terrorism and Sentencing Act 2021 c. 11 Pt 1 s.15(5) (29 June 2021 except as specified in 2021 c.11 s.50(3)(c); not yet in force otherwise).

**Public Order Act 1986**

16 An offence under any of the following provisions of the Public Order Act 1986—
(a) section 1 (riot);
(b) section 2 (violent disorder);
(c) section 3 (affray).

**Criminal Justice Act 1988**

17 An offence under section 134 of the Criminal Justice Act 1988 (torture).

**Road Traffic Act 1988**

18 An offence under any of the following provisions of the Road Traffic Act 1988—
(a) section 1 (causing death by dangerous driving);
(b) section 3ZC (causing death by driving: disqualified drivers);
(c) section 3A (causing death by careless driving when under influence of drink or drugs).

**Aviation and Maritime Security Act 1990**

19 An offence under any of the following provisions of the Aviation and Maritime Security Act 1990—
(a) section 1 (endangering safety at aerodromes);
(b) section 9 (hijacking of ships);
(c) section 10 (seizing or exercising control of fixed platforms);
(d) section 11 (destroying fixed platforms or endangering their safety);
(e) section 12 (other acts endangering or likely to endanger safe navigation);
(f) section 13 (offences involving threats); [5]
(g) section 14(4) (inducing or assisting the commission of offences relating to hijacking of ships, or destroying ships or fixed platforms or endangering their safety) in a case where the offender is convicted on or after the day on which section 15 of the Counter-Terrorism and Sentencing Act 2021 comes into force. [6]

**Channel Tunnel (Security) Order 1994**

20 An offence under Part 2 of the Channel Tunnel (Security) Order 1994 (S.I. 1994/570) (offences relating to Channel Tunnel trains and the tunnel system).

**Chemical Weapons Act 1996**

20A An offence under either of the following provisions of the Chemical Weapons

---

5 Added by Counter-Terrorism and Sentencing Act 2021 c. 11 Pt 1 s.15(6) (29 June 2021 except as specified in 2021 c.11 s.50(3)(c); not yet in force otherwise).

6 Added by Counter-Terrorism and Sentencing Act 2021 c. 11 Pt 1 s.15(6) (29 June 2021 except as specified in 2021 c.11 s.50(3)(c); not yet in force otherwise).

Act 1996 in a case where the offender is convicted on or after the day on which section 15 of the Counter-Terrorism and Sentencing Act 2021 comes into force:

(a) section 2 (use etc of chemical weapons);

(b) section 11 (premises or equipment used for producing chemical weapons).[7]

**Protection from Harassment Act 1997**

21 An offence under section 4 or 4A of the Protection from Harassment Act 1997 (putting people in fear of violence and stalking involving fear of violence or serious alarm or distress).

**Crime and Disorder Act 1998**

22(1) An offence under section 29 of the Crime and Disorder Act 1998 (racially or religiously aggravated assaults).

(2) An offence falling within section 31(1)(a) or (b) of that Act (racially or religiously aggravated offences under section 4 or 4A of the Public Order Act 1986).

**International Criminal Court Act 2001**

23 An offence under section 51 or 52 of the International Criminal Court Act 2001 (genocide, crimes against humanity, war crimes and related offences), other than one involving murder.

**Anti-terrorism, Crime and Security Act 2001**

23A An offence under any of the following provisions of the Anti-terrorism, Crime and Security Act 2001—

(a) section 47 (use etc of nuclear weapons);

(b) section 50 (assisting or inducing certain weapons-related acts overseas);

**Female Genital Mutilation Act 2003**

24 An offence under any of the following provisions of the Female Genital Mutilation Act 2003—

(a) section 1 (female genital mutilation);

(b) section 2 (assisting a girl to mutilate her own genitalia);

(c) section 3 (assisting a non-UK person to mutilate overseas a girl's genitalia).

**Domestic Violence, Crime and Victims Act 2004**

25 An offence under section 5 of the Domestic Violence, Crime and Victims Act

---

7 Added by Counter-Terrorism and Sentencing Act 2021 c. 11 Pt 1 s.15(7) (29 June 2021 except as specified in 2021 c.11 s.50(3)(c); not yet in force otherwise).

2004 (causing or allowing a child or vulnerable adult to die or suffer serious physical harm).

**Modern Slavery Act 2015**

26(1) An offence under section 1 of the Modern Slavery Act 2015 (slavery, servitude and forced or compulsory labour).

(2) An offence under section 2 of that Act (human trafficking) which is not within Part 2 of this Schedule.

**Serious Crime Act 2015**

26A An offence under section 75A of the Serious Crime Act 2015 (strangulation or suffocation).

**Space Industry Act 2018**

26B An offence under Sch.4 paras.1–5.

**Inchoate offences**

27 An inchoate offence (see section 398) in relation to an offence specified in any of the preceding paragraphs of this Part of this Schedule.

28 An inchoate offence in relation to murder.

Part 2

*Specified sexual offences*

**Sexual Offences Act 1956**

29 An offence under any of the following provisions of the Sexual Offences Act 1956—

(a) section 1 (rape);
(b) section 2 (procurement of woman by threats);
(c) section 3 (procurement of woman by false pretences);
(d) section 4 (administering drugs to obtain or facilitate intercourse);
(e) section 5 (intercourse with girl under 13);
(f) section 6 (intercourse with girl under 16);
(g) section 7 (intercourse with a defective);
(h) section 9 (procurement of a defective);
(i) section 10 or 11 (incest);
(j) section 14 (indecent assault on a woman);
(k) section 15 (indecent assault on a man);
(l) section 16 (assault with intent to commit buggery);
(m) section 17 (abduction of woman by force or for the sake of her property);
(n) section 19 (abduction of unmarried girl under 18 from parent or guardian);
(o) section 20 (abduction of unmarried girl under 16 from parent or guardian);
(p) section 21 (abduction of defective from parent or guardian);

(q) section 22 (causing prostitution of women);
(r) section 23 (procuration of girl under 21);
(s) section 24 (detention of woman in brothel);
(t) section 25 (permitting girl under 13 to use premises for intercourse;
(u) section 26 (permitting girl under 16 to use premises for intercourse);
(v) section 27 (permitting defective to use premises for intercourse);
(w) section 28 (causing or encouraging prostitution of, intercourse with, or indecent assault on, girl under 16);
(x) section 29 (causing or encouraging prostitution of defective);
(y) section 32 (soliciting by men);
(z) section 33A (keeping a brothel used for prostitution).

**Mental Health Act 1959**

30 An offence under section 128 of the Mental Health Act 1959 (sexual intercourse with patients).

**Indecency with Children Act 1960**

31 An offence under section 1 of the Indecency with Children Act 1960 (indecent conduct towards young child).

**Sexual Offences Act 1967**

32 An offence under either of the following provisions of the Sexual Offences Act 1967—
(a) section 4 (procuring others to commit homosexual acts);
(b) section 5 (living on earnings of male prostitution).

**Theft Act 1968**

33 An offence under section 9 of the Theft Act 1968 of burglary with intent to commit rape.

**Criminal Law Act 1977**

34 An offence under section 54 of the Criminal Law Act 1977 (inciting girl under 16 to have incestuous sexual intercourse).

**Protection of Children Act 1978**

35 An offence under section 1 of the Protection of Children Act 1978 (indecent photographs of children).

**Customs and Excise Management Act 1979**

36 An offence under section 170 of the Customs and Excise Management Act 1979 (penalty for fraudulent evasion of duty etc) in relation to goods prohibited to be imported under section 42 of the Customs Consolidation Act 1876 (indecent or obscene articles).

## Criminal Justice Act 1988

37 An offence under section 160 of the Criminal Justice Act 1988 (possession of indecent photograph of a child).

## Sexual Offences Act 2003

38 An offence under any of the following provisions of the Sexual Offences Act 2003—

(a) section 1 (rape);
(b) section 2 (assault by penetration);
(c) section 3 (sexual assault);
(d) section 4 (causing a person to engage in sexual activity without consent);
(e) section 5 (rape of a child under 13);
(f) section 6 (assault of a child under 13 by penetration);
(g) section 7 (sexual assault of a child under 13);
(h) section 8 (causing or inciting a child under 13 to engage in sexual activity);
(i) section 9 (sexual activity with a child);
(j) section 10 (causing or inciting a child to engage in sexual activity);
(k) section 11 (engaging in sexual activity in the presence of a child);
(l) section 12 (causing a child to watch a sexual act);
(m) section 13 (child sex offences committed by children or young persons);
(n) section 14 (arranging or facilitating commission of a child sex offence);
(o) section 15 (meeting a child following sexual grooming etc);
(p) section 15A (sexual communication with a child);
(q) section 16 (abuse of position of trust: sexual activity with a child);
(r) section 17 (abuse of position of trust: causing or inciting a child to engage in sexual activity);
(s) section 18 (abuse of position of trust: sexual activity in the presence of a child);
(t) section 19 (abuse of position of trust: causing a child to watch a sexual act);
(u) section 25 (sexual activity with a child family member);
(v) section 26 (inciting a child family member to engage in sexual activity);
(w) section 30 (sexual activity with a person with a mental disorder impeding choice);
(x) section 31 (causing or inciting a person with a mental disorder impeding choice to engage in sexual activity);
(y) section 32 (engaging in sexual activity in the presence of a person with a mental disorder impeding choice);
(z) section 33 (causing a person with a mental disorder impeding choice to watch a sexual act);
(aa) section 34 (inducement, threat or deception to procure sexual activity with a person with a mental disorder);
(ab) section 35 (causing a person with a mental disorder to engage in or agree to engage in sexual activity by inducement, threat or deception);
(ac) section 36 (engaging in sexual activity in the presence, procured by inducement, threat or deception, of a person with a mental disorder);

- (ad) section 37 (causing a person with a mental disorder to watch a sexual act by inducement, threat or deception);
- (ae) section 38 (care workers: sexual activity with a person with a mental disorder);
- (af) section 39 (care workers: causing or inciting sexual activity);
- (ag) section 40 (care workers: sexual activity in the presence of a person with a mental disorder);
- (ah) section 41 (care workers: causing a person with a mental disorder to watch a sexual act);
- (ai) section 47 (paying for sexual services of a child);
- (aj) section 48 (causing or inciting sexual exploitation of a child);
- (ak) section 49 (controlling a child in relation to sexual exploitation);
- (al) section 50 (arranging or facilitating sexual exploitation of a child);
- (am) section 52 (causing or inciting prostitution for gain);
- (an) section 53 (controlling prostitution for gain);
- (ao) section 57 (trafficking into the UK for sexual exploitation);
- (ap) section 58 (trafficking within the UK for sexual exploitation);
- (aq) section 59 (trafficking out of the UK for sexual exploitation);
- (ar) section 59A (trafficking for sexual exploitation);
- (as) section 61 (administering a substance with intent);
- (at) section 62 (committing an offence with intent to commit a sexual offence);
- (au) section 63 (trespass with intent to commit a sexual offence);
- (av) section 64 (sex with an adult relative: penetration);
- (aw) section 65 (sex with an adult relative: consenting to penetration);
- (ax) section 66 (exposure);
- (ax) section 66 (exposure);
  - (axa) section 66A (sending etc photograph or film of genitals);
  - (axb) section 66B(2) (sharing intimate photograph or film with intent to cause alarm, distress or humiliation);
  - (axc) section 66B(3) (sharing intimate photograph or film for purpose of obtaining sexual gratification);
- (ay) section 67 (voyeurism);
- (az) section 69 (intercourse with an animal);
- (ba) section 70 (sexual penetration of a corpse).

**Modern Slavery Act 2015**

39 An offence under section 2 of the Modern Slavery Act 2015 (human trafficking) committed with a view to exploitation that consists of or includes behaviour within section 3(3) of that Act (sexual exploitation).

**Inchoate offences**

40 An inchoate offence (see section 398) in relation to any offence specified in this Part of this Schedule.

## Part 3
*Specified terrorism offences*

**Terrorism Act 2000**

41 An offence under any of the following provisions of the Terrorism Act 2000—
(a) section 11 (membership of a proscribed organisation);
(b) section 12 (inviting support for a proscribed organisation);
(c) section 54 (weapons training);
(d) section 56 (directing terrorist organisation);
(e) section 57 (possession of article for terrorist purposes);
(f) section 58 (collection of information likely to be of use to a terrorist);
(g) section 58A (publishing information about members of the armed forces);
(h) section 58B (entering or remaining in a designated area);
(i) section 59 (inciting terrorism overseas).

**Anti-terrorism, Crime and Security Act 2001**

42 An offence under any of the following provisions of the Anti-terrorism, Crime and Security Act 2001—
(a) section 113 (use of noxious substance or thing to cause harm or intimidate).

**Terrorism Act 2006**

43 An offence under any of the following provisions of the Terrorism Act 2006—
(a) section 1 (encouragement of terrorism);
(b) section 2 (dissemination of terrorist publications);
(c) section 5 (preparation of terrorist acts);
(d) section 6 (training for terrorism);
(e) section 8 (attendance at a place used for terrorist training);
(f) section 9 (making or possession of radioactive device or material);
(g) section 10 (misuse of radioactive device or material for terrorist purposes etc);
(h) section 11 (terrorist threats relating to radioactive devices etc).

**Inchoate offences**

44 An inchoate offence (see section 398) in relation to any offence specified in this Part of this Schedule.

# SERIOUS TERRORISM SENTENCES (18-20 AND 21+ AT OFFENCE DATE)

## Sentencing Code ss.268A-C, 282A-C and Sch.17A

### General

A serious terrorism sentence of detention in a young offender institution or imprisonment is a sentence the term of which is equal to the aggregate of— **65-001**

(a) the appropriate custodial term (see ss.268C or 282C); and
(b) a further period (the "extension period") for which the offender is to be subject to a licence: s.268A(1) and s.282A(1).

A serious terrorism offence is an offence:

(a) specified in Pt.1 of Sch.7A; or
(b) is specified in Pt.2 of that Schedule and has been determined to have a terrorist connection under s.69: s.306(2).

### Duty to impose

The court must impose a serious terrorism sentence where the offender is convicted of an offence: **65-002**

(a) committed on or after 29 June 2021;
(b) the offender was aged 18 or over when the offence was committed;
(c) the court is of the opinion that there is a significant risk to members of the public of serious harm occasioned by the commission by the offender of further serious terrorism offences or other specified offences (see s.308 of the Sentencing Code);
(d) the court does not impose a sentence of imprisonment or custody for life; and
(e) the risk of multiple deaths condition is met: s.268B(1) and s.282B(1).

*Note: For those aged 21 or over at conviction, the sentence will be a serious terrorism sentence of imprisonment; for those aged 18-20 at conviction, the sentence will be a serious terrorism sentence of detention in a young offender institution.*

### Risk of multiple deaths

The risk of multiple deaths condition is that the court is of the opinion that— **65-003**

(a) either—
    (i) the serious terrorism offence; or
    (ii) the combination of the offence and one or more offences associated with it, was very likely to result in or contribute to (whether directly or indirectly) the deaths of at least two people as a result of an act of terrorism (within the meaning of s.1 of the Terrorism Act 2000); and
(b) the offender was, or ought to have been, aware of that likelihood;
(c) it is irrelevant for the purposes of determining whether the risk of multiple

deaths condition is met whether or not any death actually occurred: s.268B(3) and (4) and s.282B(3) and (4).

**Exceptional circumstances**

**65-004** The court is released from its obligation to impose a serious terrorism sentence where the court is of the opinion that there are exceptional circumstances which—

(a) relate to the offence or to the offender; and
(b) justify not doing so: s.268B(2) and s.282B(2).

**Custodial term**

**65-005** The appropriate custodial term is:

(a) 14 years; or
(b) if longer, the term of imprisonment that would be imposed in respect of the offence in compliance with s.231(2) (length of discretionary custodial sentences) if the court did not impose a serious terrorism sentence of imprisonment (or an extended sentence or a sentence under s.278): s.268C(2) and s.282C(2).

**Guilty plea**

**65-006** If the court imposes a serious terrorism sentence, nothing in s.268C(2) or s.282C(2) prevents the court, after taking into account the timing of the guilty plea from imposing as the appropriate custodial term a term of any length which is not less than 80% of the term which would otherwise be required: SC s.73(2A).

**Assistance to the prosecution**

**65-007** Nothing in s.268C(2) or s.282C(2) (minimum appropriate custodial term for serious terrorism sentences) affects the court's power under s.74(2) (reflecting assistance given to the prosecution in determining length of sentence) so far it relates to determining the appropriate custodial term: s.74(4A).

**Extension period**

**65-008** The extension period must be a period of such length as the court considers necessary for the purpose of protecting members of the public from serious harm occasioned by the commission by the offender of further serious terrorism offences or other specified offences and must be at least seven years and must not exceed 25 years: s.268C(3) and (4) and s.282C(3) and (4).

# LIFE SENTENCES: AGED 18–20 (CUSTODY FOR LIFE)

## Sentencing Code s.272

*References: Current Sentencing Practice A4; Archbold 5A-819*

There are a number of scenarios in which an offender aged 18–20 convicted of an offence can receive a life sentence. **66-001**

For murder and the mandatory life sentence, s.272 does not apply.

For the "*two-strikes*" life sentence, s.272 does apply.

For the "*dangerousness*" life sentence, s.272 does apply.

For the "*manslaughter of an emergency worker*" sentence, s.272 does apply.

In relation to the minimum term, where a person aged at least 18 but under 21 is convicted of an offence for which the sentence is not fixed by law, the court must sentence the offender to custody for life if:

(a) the offence is punishable in the case of a person aged 21 or over with imprisonment for life, and the court considers that a sentence for life would be appropriate; or
(b) the court is required by s.273 or 274 to impose a sentence of custody for life: SC s.272(1) and (2).

Sections 230 (threshold for imposing discretionary custodial sentence) and 231 (length of discretionary custodial sentences: general provision), in particular, apply for the purposes of subs.(2)(a): SC s.272(3).

## LIFE SENTENCES—"DANGEROUSNESS" (AGED 18–20 AND 21+)

### Sentencing Code s.274

*References: Current Sentencing Practice A4; Archbold 5A-819*

### General

**Types of life sentence** There are four types of life sentence: **67-001**

(a) dangerousness life: SC ss.274;
(b) discretionary life (the inherent jurisdiction of the court to impose a life sentence) (this section);
(c) two-strikes life: SC ss.273; and
(d) mandatory life for murder.

**Life licence** An offender sentenced to life imprisonment or custody for life will remain on licence for the rest of their life. **67-002**

### Dangerousness life

**Aged 18 or over at conviction** The court must impose a life sentence where: **67-003**

(1) the defendant is convicted of an offence within Sch.19;
(2) the court considers that there is a significant risk of serious harm occasioned by the commission by the defendant of further specified offences;
(3) the offence was committed on or after 4 April 2005; and
(4) the court considers that the seriousness of the offence, or of the offence and one or more offences associated with it, is such as to justify the imposition of a sentence of imprisonment for life: SC s.274(1) and (3).

In the case of a person aged 18–20 at conviction, the court must impose a sentence of custody for life rather than life imprisonment.

**Does the seriousness of the offence justify a life sentence?** The question as to whether or not the seriousness of the offence, or of the offence and one or more offences associated with it, was such as to justify a life sentence requires consideration of: **67-004**

(i) the seriousness of the offence itself, on its own or with other offences associated with it, which was always a matter for the judgment of the court;
(ii) the defendant's previous convictions;
(iii) the level of danger to the public posed by the defendant and whether or not there was a reliable estimate of the length of time they would remain a danger; and
(iv) the available alternative sentences: *Attorney General's Reference (No. 27 of 2013) (Burinskas)* [2014] EWCA Crim 334; [2014] 1 W.L.R. 4209; [2014] 2 Cr. App. R.(S.) 45.

### Assessing dangerousness

67-005 **General** The following applies where the court is required to consider whether the offender poses a significant risk of serious harm to members of the public by the commission of further specified offences: SC s.308(1). This is colloquially known as the "*dangerousness test*".

It will be a rare case in which an appellate court will overturn on an appeal against sentence the exercise of judicial discretion in making a finding of dangerousness, that appellate court not having conducted the trial or see the offender: *Howlett* [2019] EWCA Crim 1224; [2020] 1 Cr. App. R.(S.) 14.

67-006 **Must take into account** The court must take into account all such information as is available to it about the nature and circumstances of the offence: SC s.308(2).

67-007 **May take into account** The court may take into account:

(a) all such information as is available about the nature and circumstances of any other offences of which the offender has been convicted by a court anywhere in the world;
(b) any information which is before it about any pattern of behaviour of which any of the offences of which the offender has been convicted forms part; and
(c) any information about the offender which is before it: SC s.308(2).

67-008 **Serious harm** "*Serious harm*" means death or personal injury, whether physical or psychological: SC s.306(2).

67-009 **Risk** The risk does not have to be based on the instant offence: *Green* [2007] EWCA Crim 2172; [2008] 1 Cr. App. R.(S.) 97 (p.579). The absence of previous offences causing serious harm requiring an extended sentence does not preclude the finding of dangerousness: *Powell* [2015] EWCA Crim 2200; [2016] 1 Cr. App. R.(S.) 49.

In *Neville* [2015] EWCA Crim 1874; [2016] 1 Cr. App. R.(S.) 38; [2016] Crim. L.R. 368, the court held that a finding of dangerousness founded on unpredictability demonstrated by a long absence of serious offending prior to the instant offence was permissible.

### The correct approach

67-010 (i) consider the question of dangerousness. If the offender is not dangerous and the two-strikes life sentence does not apply, a determinate sentence should be passed. If the offender is not dangerous and the conditions for the two-strikes life sentence are satisfied then a life sentence must be imposed;
(ii) if the offender is dangerous, consider whether the seriousness of the offence and offences associated with it justify a life sentence;
(iii) if a life sentence is justified then the judge must pass a life sentence in accordance with s.274. If the two-strikes life sentence also applies, the judge should record that fact in open court;
(iv) if a life sentence is not justified, then the sentencing judge should consider whether the two-strikes like sentence applies. If it does, then a life sentence must be imposed; and

(v) if the two-strikes life sentence does not apply the judge should then consider an extended sentence. Before passing an extended sentence the judge should consider a determinate sentence: *Attorney General's Reference (No. 27 of 2013) (Burinskas)* [2014] EWCA Crim 334; [2014] 1 W.L.R. 4209; [2014] 2 Cr. App. R.(S.) 45.

Where the conditions are met, the sentence is not discretionary: *Wilder* [2023] EWCA Crim 1295; [2024] 1 Cr. App. R. (S.) 37.

**Setting the minimum term**

A court which imposes a sentence of imprisonment (or custody) for life must fix a minimum term. The offender is not entitled to be released until they have served the minimum term. For details on setting the minimum term, see **LIFE SENTENCES—MINIMUM TERM (NON-MURDER CASES)** at **para.70**. **67-011**

## Schedule 19 Offences

### Common law offences

1 Manslaughter. **67-012**
2 Kidnapping.
3 False imprisonment.

### Offences against the Person Act 1861

4 An offence under any of the following provisions of the Offences against the Person Act 1861—
   (a) section 4 (soliciting murder);
   (b) section 18 (wounding with intent to cause grievous bodily harm);
   (c) section 21 (attempting to choke, suffocate or strangle in order to commit or assist in committing an indictable offence);
   (d) section 22 (using chloroform etc to commit or assist in the committing of any indictable offence);
   (e) section 28 (causing bodily injury by explosives);
   (f) section 29 (using explosives etc with intent to do grievous bodily harm);
   (g) section 32 (endangering the safety of railway passengers).

### Explosive Substances Act 1883

5 An offence under either of the following provisions of the Explosive Substances Act 1883—
   (a) section 2 (causing explosion likely to endanger life or property);
   (b) section 3 (attempt to cause explosion, or making or keeping explosive with intent to endanger life or property).
6 An offence under section 4 of that Act (making or possession of explosive under suspicious circumstances) committed on or after 13 April 2015.

### Infant Life (Preservation) Act 1929

7 An offence under section 1 of the Infant Life (Preservation) Act 1929 (child destruction).

### Infanticide Act 1938

8 An offence under section 1 of the Infanticide Act 1938 (infanticide).

### Firearms Act 1968

9 An offence under any of the following provisions of the Firearms Act 1968—
   (a) section 16 (possession of firearm with intent to endanger life);
   (b) section 17(1) (use of firearm to resist arrest);

(c) section 17(2) (possession of firearm at time of committing or being arrested for offence specified in Schedule 1 to that Act);
(d) section 18 (carrying a firearm with criminal intent).

**Theft Act 1968**

10 An offence under either of the following provisions of the Theft Act 1968—
(a) section 8 (robbery or assault with intent to rob);
(b) section 10 (aggravated burglary).

**Criminal Damage Act 1971**

11 An offence of arson under section 1 of the Criminal Damage Act 1971.
12 An offence under section 1(2) of that Act (destroying or damaging property) other than an offence of arson.

**Taking of Hostages Act 1982**

13 An offence under section 1 of the Taking of Hostages Act 1982 (hostage-taking).

**Aviation Security Act 1982**

14 An offence under any of the following provisions of the Aviation Security Act 1982—
(a) section 1 (hijacking);
(b) section 2 (destroying, damaging or endangering safety of aircraft);
(c) section 3 (other acts endangering or likely to endanger safety of aircraft).

**Criminal Justice Act 1988**

15 An offence under section 134 of the Criminal Justice Act 1988 (torture).

**Aviation and Maritime Security Act 1990**

16 An offence under any of the following provisions of the Aviation and Maritime Security Act 1990—
(a) section 1 (endangering safety at aerodromes);
(b) section 9 (hijacking of ships);
(c) section 10 (seizing or exercising control of fixed platforms);
(d) section 11 (destroying fixed platforms or endangering their safety);
(e) section 12 (other acts endangering or likely to endanger safe navigation);
(f) section 13 (offences involving threats).

**Channel Tunnel (Security) Order 1994**

17 An offence under Part 2 of the Channel Tunnel (Security) Order 1994 (S. I. 1994/570) (offences relating to Channel Tunnel trains and the tunnel system).

**Terrorism Act 2000**

18 An offence under any of the provisions of the Terrorism Act 2000 listed in column 1 of the following table that meets the condition listed in relation to it in column 2—

| | **Provision of the Terrorism Act 2000** | **Condition** |
|---|---|---|
| (a) | Section 54 (weapons training) | The offence was committed on or after 13 April 2015 |
| (b) | Section 56 (directing terrorist organisation) | The offence was committed on or after 12 January 2010. |
| (c) | Section 59 (inciting terrorism overseas) | The offence was committed on or after 12 January 2010 and the offender is liable on conviction on indictment to imprisonment for life. |

**Anti-terrorism, Crime and Security Act 2001**

19 An offence under either of the following provisions of the Anti-terrorism, Crime and Security Act 2001 committed on or after 12 January 2010—
(a) section 47 (use etc of nuclear weapons);
(b) section 50 (assisting or inducing certain weapons-related acts overseas).

**Domestic Violence, Crime and Victims Act 2004**

19A Section 5 where the unlawful act to which the offence relates was an act that occurred, or so much of an act as occurred, on or after 28 June 2022, and the offender is liable on conviction on indictment to imprisonment for life.

**Sexual Offences Act 2003**

20 An offence under any of the provisions of the Sexual Offences Act 2003 listed in column 1 of the following table that meets the condition (if any) listed in relation to it in column 2—

| | **Provision of the Sexual Offences Act 2003** | **Condition** |
|---|---|---|
| (a) | Section 1 (rape) | |
| (b) | Section 2 (assault by penetration) | |
| (c) | Section 4 (causing a person to engage in sexual activity without consent) | The offender is liable on conviction on indictment to imprisonment for life |
| (d) | Section 5 (rape of a child under 13) | |
| (e) | Section 6 (assault of a child under 13 by penetration) | |

| | Provision of the Sexual Offences Act 2003 | Condition |
|---|---|---|
| (f) | Section 8 (causing or inciting a child under 13 to engage in sexual activity) | The offender is liable on conviction on indictment to imprisonment for life |
| (g) | Section 30 (sexual activity with a person with a mental disorder impeding choice) | The offender is liable on conviction on indictment to imprisonment for life |
| (h) | Section 31 (causing or inciting a person with a mental disorder to engage in sexual activity) | The offender is liable on conviction on indictment to imprisonment for life |
| (i) | Section 34 (inducement, threat or deception to procure sexual activity with a person with a mental disorder) | The offender is liable on conviction on indictment to imprisonment for life |
| (j) | Section 35 (causing a person with a mental disorder to engage in or agree to engage in sexual activity by inducement etc) | The offender is liable on conviction on indictment to imprisonment for life |
| (k) | Section 47 (paying for sexual services of a child) against a person aged under 16 | The offender is liable on conviction on indictment to imprisonment for life |
| (l) | Section 62 (committing an offence with intent to commit a sexual offence) | The offender is liable on conviction on indictment to imprisonment for life. |

**Terrorism Act 2006**

21 An offence under any of the provisions of the Terrorism Act 2006 listed in column 1 of the following table that meets the condition listed in relation to it in column 2—

| | Provision of the Terrorism Act 2006 | Condition |
|---|---|---|
| (a) | Section 5 (preparation of terrorist acts) | The offence was committed on or after 12 January 2010 |
| (b) | Section 6 (training for terrorism) | The offence was committed on or after 13 April 2015 |
| (c) | Section 9 (making or possession of radioactive device or material) | The offence was committed on or after 12 January 2010 |
| (d) | Section 10 (misuse of radioactive device or material for terrorist purposes etc) | The offence was committed on or after 12 January 2010 |
| (e) | Section 11 (terrorist threats relating to radioactive devices etc) | The offence was committed on or after 12 January 2010. |

# LIFE SENTENCES—COMMON LAW

*References: Current Sentencing Practice A4; Archbold 5A-819*

## Availability

Where: **68-001**

(a) the offence was committed prior to 4 April 2005; or
(b) the offence is not a Sch.19 offence, the court has an inherent jurisdiction to impose a life sentence.

Such instances are likely to be rare: *Saunders* [2013] EWCA Crim 1027; [2014] 1 Cr. App. R.(S.) 45; [2013] Crim. L.R. 930.

## Test

The decisions in *Attorney General's Reference 32 of 1996 (Whittaker)* [1997] 1 Cr. App. R.(S.) 261; [1996] Crim. L.R. 917; (1996) 93(38) L.S.G. 42 and *Chapman* [2000] 1 Cr. App. R.(S.) 377 established a two-stage test for the imposition of discretionary "*common law*" life sentences: **68-002**

(1) the offender has been convicted of a very serious offence; and
(2) there are good grounds for believing that the offender may remain a serious danger to the public for a period which cannot be reliably estimated at the date of sentence.

This test is to be preferred to the three-stage test proffered in *Hodgson* (1968) 52 Cr. App. R. 113; [1968] Crim. L.R. 46, *Ali* [2019] EWCA Crim 856; [2019] 2 Cr. App. R.(S.) 43.

## Example

Some of these offences may involve a significant risk of serious harm to the public, but are not included within the list of "specified" offences in the dangerousness provisions in the Sentencing Code. One obvious example is the offender who commits repeated offences of very serious drug supplying which justifies the imposition of the life sentence. In circumstances like these the court is not obliged to impose the sentence in accordance with ss.274 and 285, but its discretion to do so is unaffected: *Saunders* [2013] EWCA Crim 1027; [2014] 1 Cr. App. R.(S.) 45; [2013] Crim. L.R. 930 at [11]. **68-003**

# LIFE SENTENCES—"TWO STRIKES LIFE" (AGED 18-20 AND 21+)

SENTENCING CODE ss.273 AND 283 AND SCH.15

*References: Current Sentencing Practice A4; Archbold 5A-819*

## Applicability

Where: **69-001**

(a) a court is dealing with an offender for an offence ("*the index offence*") that is listed in Pt 1 of Sch.15;
(b) the index offence was committed on or after the relevant date listed in Sch.15;
(c) the offender is aged 18 or over when convicted of the index offence; and
(d) the sentence condition and the previous offence condition are met,

the court must impose a life sentence under ss.273 or 283: SC ss.273(1) and 283(1).

**Unjust to impose life sentence** The court must impose a life sentence unless the court is of the opinion that there are particular circumstances which: **69-002**

(a) relate to:
   (i) the index offence;
   (ii) the previous offence referred to in subs.(5); or
   (iii) the offender; and
(b) would make it unjust to do so in all the circumstances: SC ss.273(3) and 283(3).

## Offence condition

The previous offence condition is that: **69-003**

(a) when the index offence was committed, the offender had been convicted of an offence ("*the previous offence*") listed in Sch.15; and
(b) a relevant life sentence or a relevant sentence of detention for a determinate period was imposed on the offender for the previous offence: SC ss.273(5) and 283(5).

A "*relevant sentence*" is one which (disregarding any reduction for time spent on bail or in custody pre-sentence);

(i) is a life sentence where the offender was not eligible for release during the first five years of the sentence;
(ii) is an extended sentence where the custodial period was 10 years or more; or
(iii) is any other sentence of imprisonment or detention for determinate period of 10 years or more: SC ss.273(5)-(11) and 283(5)-(11).

A robbery may not be treated as a robbery committed by a person in possession of a firearm or imitation firearm unless it is established or admitted that the offender was party to a robbery which to their knowledge involved a firearm or imitation firearm: *Gore* [2010] EWCA Crim 369; [2010] 3 All E.R. 743; [2010] 2 Cr. App. R.(S.) 93.

**Sentence condition**

**69-004** The sentence condition is that, but for ss.273 and 283, the court would impose a custodial sentence of 10 years or more, disregarding any extension period that it would impose as a part of an extended sentence: SC ss.273(4) and 283(4).

It is permissible to aggravate the seriousness of the offence and any associated offences when considering the sentence which would otherwise be imposed for the purposes of the sentence condition: *Fernandez* [2014] EWCA Crim 2405; [2015] 1 Cr. App. R.(S.) 35.

**Dangerousness**

**69-005** There is no requirement that the offender be found to be "*dangerous*". Therefore the fact that an offender is not dangerous is not something that, of itself, would make it unjust to pass a life sentence under ss.273 or 283. Additionally, there is no requirement to consider whether the seriousness threshold has been passed for the purposes of the dangerousness life sentence: *Attorney General's Reference (No. 27 of 2013) (Burinskas)* [2014] EWCA Crim 334; [2014] 1 W.L.R. 4209; [2014] 2 Cr. App. R.(S.) 45.

**The correct approach**

**69-006**
(i) consider the question of dangerousness. If the offender is not dangerous and the two-strikes life sentence does not apply, a determinate sentence should be passed. If the offender is not dangerous and the conditions for the two-strikes life sentence are satisfied then a life sentence must be imposed;
(ii) if the offender is dangerous, consider whether the seriousness of the offence and offences associated with it justify a life sentence;
(iii) if a life sentence is justified then the judge must pass a life sentence in accordance with ss.274 and 283. If the two-strikes life sentence also applies, the judge should record that fact in open court;
(iv) if a life sentence is not justified, then the sentencing judge should consider whether the two-strikes like sentence applies. If it does, then a life sentence must be imposed; and
(v) if the two-strikes life sentence does not apply the judge should then consider an extended sentence. Before passing an extended sentence the judge should consider a determinate sentence: *Attorney General's Reference (No. 27 of 2013) (Burinskas)* [2014] EWCA Crim 334; [2014] 2 Cr. App. R.(S.) 45.

**Setting the minimum term**

**69-007** A court which imposes a sentence of imprisonment (or custody) for life must fix a minimum term. The offender is not entitled to be released until they have served the minimum term. For details on setting the minimum term, **LIFE SENTENCES—MINIMUM TERM (NON-MURDER CASES)** at **para.70**

## Life sentence for second offence: listed offences

### Part 1
*Offences under the law of England and Wales*

The following offences to the extent that they are offences under the law of England and Wales— **69-008**

| | | Offence | Specified date |
|---|---|---|---|
| *Manslaughter* | | | |
| 1 | Manslaughter | | 3 December 2012 |
| *Offences against the Person Act 1861* | | | |
| 2 | An offence under any of the following provisions of the Offences against the Person Act 1861— | | |
| | (a) | s.4 (soliciting murder) | 3 December 2012 |
| | (b) | s.18 (wounding with intent to cause grievous bodily harm) | 3 December 2012 |
| | (c) | s.28 (causing bodily injury by explosives) | 13 April 2015 |
| | (d) | s.29 (using explosives etc with intent to do grievous bodily harm) | 13 April 2015 |
| *Explosive Substances Act 1883* | | | |
| 3 | An offence under any of the following provisions of the Explosive Substances Act 1883— | | |
| | (a) | s.2 (causing explosion likely to endanger life or property) | 13 April 2015 |
| | (b) | s.3 (attempt to cause explosion, or making or keeping explosive with intent to endanger life or property) | 13 April 2015 |
| | (c) | s.4 (making or possession of explosive under suspicious circumstances) | 13 April 2015 |
| *Firearms Act 1968* | | | |
| 4 | An offence under any of the following provisions of the Firearms Act 1968— | | |
| | (a) | s.16 (possession of a firearm with intent to endanger life) | 3 December 2012 |

| | | Offence | Specified date |
|---|---|---|---|
| | (b) | s.17(1) (use of a firearm to resist arrest) | 3 December 2012 |
| | (c) | s.18 (carrying a firearm with criminal intent) | 3 December 2012 |
| *Theft Act 1968* | | | |
| 5 | An offence of robbery under s.8 of the Theft Act 1968 (robbery) where, at some time during the commission of the offence, the offender had in his or her possession a firearm or an imitation firearm within the meaning of the Firearms Act 1968 | | 3 December 2012 |
| *Protection of Children Act 1978* | | | |
| 6 | An offence under s.1 of the Protection of Children Act 1978 (indecent images of children) | | 3 December 2012 |
| *Terrorism Act 2000* | | | |
| 7 | An offence under any of the following provisions of the Terrorism Act 2000— | | |
| | (a) | s.54 (weapons training) | 13 April 2015 |
| | (b) | s.56 (directing terrorist organisation) | 3 December 2012 |
| | (c) | s.57 (possession of article for terrorist purposes) | 3 December 2012 |
| | (d) | s.59 (inciting terrorism overseas) if the offender is liable on conviction on indictment to imprisonment for life | 3 December 2012 |
| *Anti-terrorism, Crime and Security Act 2001* | | | |
| 8 | An offence under any of the following provisions of the Anti-terrorism, Crime and Security Act 2001— | | |
| | (a) | s.47 (use etc of nuclear weapons) | 3 December 2012 |
| | (b) | section 50 (assisting or inducing certain weapons-related acts overseas) | 3 December 2012 |
| | (c) | section 113 (use of noxious substance or thing to cause harm or intimidate) | 3 December 2012 |
| *Sexual Offences Act 2003* | | | |
| 9 | An offence under any of the following provisions of the Sexual Offences Act 2003— | | |
| | (a) | s.1 (rape) | 3 December 2012 |
| | (b) | s.2 (assault by penetration) | 3 December 2012 |
| | (c) | section 4 (causing a person to | 3 December 2012 |

| | | Offence | Specified date |
|---|---|---|---|
| | | engage in sexual activity without consent) if the offender is liable on conviction on indictment to imprisonment for life | |
| | (d) | s.5 (rape of a child under 13) | 3 December 2012 |
| | (e) | s.6 (assault of a child under 13 by penetration) | 3 December 2012 |
| | (f) | s.7 (sexual assault of a child under 13) | 3 December 2012 |
| | (g) | s.8 (causing or inciting a child under 13 to engage in sexual activity) | 3 December 2012 |
| | (h) | s.9 (sexual activity with a child) | 3 December 2012 |
| | (i) | s.10 (causing or inciting a child to engage in sexual activity) | 3 December 2012 |
| | (j) | s.11 (engaging in sexual activity in the presence of a child) | 3 December 2012 |
| | (k) | s.12 (causing a child to watch a sexual act) | 3 December 2012 |
| | (l) | s.14 (arranging or facilitating commission of a child sex offence) | 3 December 2012 |
| | (m) | s.15 (meeting a child following sexual grooming etc) | 3 December 2012 |
| | (n) | s.25 (sexual activity with a child family member) if the offender is aged 18 or over at the time of the offence | 3 December 2012 |
| | (o) | s.26 (inciting a child family member to engage in sexual activity) if the offender is aged 18 or over at the time of the offence | 3 December 2012 |
| | (p) | s.30 (sexual activity with a person with a mental disorder impeding choice) if the offender is liable on conviction on indictment to imprisonment for life | 3 December 2012 |
| | (q) | s.31 (causing or inciting a person with a mental disorder to engage in sexual activity) if the offender is liable on con- | 3 December 2012 |

| | | Offence | Specified date |
|---|---|---|---|
| | | viction on indictment to imprisonment for life | |
| | (r) | s.34 (inducement, threat or deception to procure sexual activity with a person with a mental disorder) if the offender is liable on conviction on indictment to imprisonment for life | 3 December 2012 |
| | (s) | s.35 (causing a person with a mental disorder to engage in or agree to engage in sexual activity by inducement etc) if the offender is liable on conviction on indictment to imprisonment for life | 3 December 2012 |
| | (t) | s.47 (paying for sexual services of a child) if the offence is against a person aged under 16 | 3 December 2012 |
| | (u) | s.48 (causing or inciting sexual 3 December 2012 exploitation of a child) | 3 December 2012 |
| | (v) | s.49 (controlling a child in relation to sexual exploitation) | 3 December 2012 |
| | (w) | s.50 (arranging or facilitating sexual exploitation of a child) | 3 December 2012 |
| | (x) | s.62 (committing an offence with intent to commit a sexual offence) if the offender is liable on conviction on indictment to imprisonment for life | 3 December 2012 |
| *Domestic Violence, Crime and Victims Act 2004* | | | |
| 10 | An offence under s.5 of the Domestic Violence, Crime and Victims Act 2004 (causing or allowing the death of a child or vulnerable adult) | | 3 December 2012 |
| *Terrorism Act 2006* | | | |
| 11 | An offence under any of the following provisions of the Terrorism Act 2006— | | |
| | (a) | s.5 of the Terrorism Act 2006 (preparation of terrorist acts) | 3 December 2012 |
| | (b) | s.6 (training for terrorism) | 13 April 2015 |
| | (c) | s.9 (making or possession of radioactive device or materials) | 3 December 2012 |

| | | Offence | Specified date |
|---|---|---|---|
| | (d) | s.10 (misuse of radioactive devices or material and misuse and damage of facilities) | 3 December 2012 |
| | (e) | s.11 (terrorist threats relating to radioactive devices, materials or facilities) | 3 December 2012 |
| *Modern Slavery Act 2015* | | | |
| 12 | An offence under either of the following provisions of the Modern Slavery Act 2015— | | |
| | (a) | s.1 (slavery, servitude and forced or compulsory labour) | 31 July 2015 |
| | (b) | s.2 of that Act (human trafficking) | 31 July 2015 |
| *Inchoate offences* | | | |
| 14 | | An inchoate offence (see section 398) in relation to an offence specified in any of the preceding paragraphs of this Part of this Schedule (a "relevant offence") | the date specified for the relevant offence |
| 15 | | An inchoate offence in relation to murder | 3 December 2012 |

## Part 2
*Further offences under the law of England and Wales*

The following offences to the extent that they are offences under the law of England and Wales—

16 Murder.

17 Any offence that—
- (a) was abolished (with or without savings) before 3 December 2012, and
- (b) would, if committed when the index offence was committed, have constituted an offence specified in Part 1 of this Schedule.

## Part 3
*Offences under service law*

18 An offence under section 70 of the Army Act 1955, section 70 of the Air Force Act 1955 or section 42 of the Naval Discipline Act 1957 as respects which the corresponding civil offence (within the meaning of the Act in question) is an offence specified in Part 1 or 2 of this Schedule.

19 (1) An offence under section 42 of the Armed Forces Act 2006 as respects which the corresponding offence under the law of England and Wales (within the meaning given by that section) is an offence specified in Part 1 or 2 of this Schedule.

(2) Section 48 of the Armed Forces Act 2006 (attempts, conspiracy etc) ap-

plies for the purposes of this paragraph as if the reference in subsection (3)(b) of that section to any of the following provisions of that Act were a reference to this paragraph.

## Part 4
### *Offences Under the Law of Scotland, Northern Ireland or a Member State Other than the United Kingdom*

20 A civilian offence for which the person was convicted in Scotland, Northern Ireland or a member State other than the United Kingdom and which, if committed in England and Wales at the time of the conviction, would have constituted an offence specified in Part 1 or 2 of this Schedule.

This is subject to paragraph 23.

21 A member State service offence which, if committed in England and Wales at the time of the conviction, would have constituted an offence specified in Part 1 or 2 of this Schedule.

This is subject to paragraph 23.

22 In this Part of this Schedule—

*"civilian offence"* means an offence other than an offence described in Part 3 of this Schedule or a member State service offence;

*"member State service offence"* means an offence which was the subject of proceedings under the law of a member State, other than the United Kingdom, governing all or any of the naval, military or air forces of that State.

23 (1) Where the index offence was committed before 13 April 2015, this Part of this Schedule has effect—

(a) as if, in paragraph 20, the reference to a civilian offence were to an offence, and

(b) with the omission of paragraphs 21 and 22.

(2) For the purposes of sub-paragraph (1), where an offence is found to have been committed—

(a) over a period of 2 or more days, or

(b) at some time during a period of 2 or more days,

it is to be taken to have been committed on the last of those days.

## Part 5
### *Interpretation*

24 (1) In this Schedule—

*"imprisonment for life"* includes custody for life and detention for life;

*"index offence"* has the same meaning as in section 273 or 283 (as appropriate).

(2) The references in Part 1 of this Schedule to offences under sections 48, 49 and 50 of the Sexual Offences Act 2003 include references to offences under those sections as they had effect before the amendments made by section 68 of the Serious Crime Act 2015 (child sexual exploitation) came into force.

## SENTENCING CODE s.323

*References: Current Sentencing Practice A4; Archbold 5A-819*

### General

**Applicability** These provisions apply where the court passes any of the following sentences: 70-001

(a) a discretionary life sentence (common law);
(b) a dangerousness life sentence;
(c) a two-strikes life sentence; and
(d) a life sentence for manslaughter of an emergency worker: SC s.323(1).

This section does not apply where the court passes a mandatory life sentence on a person convicted of murder.

**Minimum term order** Where the court imposes a life sentence and does not impose a whole life order, the court must make a minimum term order, that being a period during which the offender is ineligible for release: SC s.321(1), (2) and (4). 70-002

**Serious terrorism cases** The determination of the minimum term is subject to the requirement that the minimum term in a serious terrorism case must be at least 14 years: s.323(3). 70-003

A "*serious terrorism case*" is a case where, but for the fact that the court passes a life sentence, the court would be required by s.268B(2) or 282B(2) to impose a serious terrorism sentence (assuming for this purpose that the court is not of the opinion mentioned in s.268B(2) or 282B(2): s.323(4)).

The minimum term may be less than 14 years if the court is of the opinion that there are exceptional circumstances which (a) relate to the offence or to the offender, and (b) justify a lesser period: s.323(5).

The minimum term may be less than 14 years if the court considers it appropriate, taking into account: (a) time on remand or on a qualifying curfew, and (b) the effect that the following would, if the court had sentenced the offender under s.268B(2) or 282B(2), have had in relation to the appropriate custodial term for that sentence: (i) s.73 (reductions for guilty pleas), and (ii) s.74 (reductions for assistance to the prosecution): s.323(6).

**Whole life order** The court must make a minimum term order unless it is required to impose a whole life order: s.321(2). 70-004

The court is required to make a whole life order if:

(a) the case is within s.321(3A) or (3B), and
(b) the court is of the opinion that, because of the seriousness of—

(i) the offence, or
(ii) the combination of the offence and one or more offences associated with it, it should not make a minimum term order: s.321(3).

A case is within s.321(3A) if the offender was aged 21 or over when the offence was committed. A case is within s.321(3B) if—

(a) the offence was committed on or after the day on which s.126 of the Police, Crime, Sentencing and Courts Act 2022 came into force, and
(b) the offender was aged 18 or over but under 21 when the offence was committed.

In a case within s.321(3B), the court may arrive at the opinion set out in s.321(3)(b) only if it considers that the seriousness of the offence, or combination of offences, is exceptionally high even by the standard of offences which would normally result in a whole life order in a case within subs.(3A).

**Determining the length**

70-005 **General** The starting point is the relevant portion of the notional determinate sentence. The notional determinate sentence is the determinate term of imprisonment that would have been appropriate if a sentence of life imprisonment had not been passed.

The "*relevant portion*" of the notional determinate sentence is—

(a) where that sentence is within section 247A(2A) of the Criminal Justice Act 2003 (terrorist prisoners not entitled to early release), the term that the court would have determined as the appropriate custodial term (within the meaning given by subsection (8) of that section);
(b) where that sentence is a sentence under section 252A, 254, 265, 266, 278 or 279 (and is not within paragraph (a)), two-thirds of the term that the court would have determined as the appropriate custodial term under that section;
(c) where that sentence is any other custodial sentence, two-thirds of the term of the sentence.

70-006 **Factors to take into account** The minimum term must be the starting point adjusted as the court considers appropriate, taking into account:

(a) the seriousness of:
  (i) the offence; or
  (ii) the combination of the offence and one or more offences associated with it; and
(c) the effect that the following would have if the court had sentenced the offender to a term of imprisonment:
  (i) s.240ZA of the CJA 2003 (crediting periods of remand in custody);
  (ii) s.240A of that Act (crediting periods of remand on bail subject to certain restrictions);

  including the effect of any declaration which the court would have made under ss.325 or 327 (specifying periods of remand on bail subject to certain restrictions or in custody pending extradition): SC s.323(2).

## Combining sentences

**Consecutive indeterminate sentences** It is generally undesirable to order an indeterminate sentence to be served consecutively to any other period of imprisonment on the basis that indeterminate sentences should start on their imposition. However, where necessary the court can order an indeterminate sentence to run consecutively to an indeterminate sentence passed on an earlier occasion. The second sentence will commence on the expiration of the minimum term of the original sentence and the offender will become eligible for a parole review after serving both minimum terms: *Totality Guideline,* p.11 **70-007**

**Determinate sentence consecutive to indeterminate sentence** The court can order a determinate sentence to run consecutively to an indeterminate sentence. The determinate sentence will commence on the expiry of the minimum term of the indeterminate sentence and the offender will become eligible for a parole review after serving half of the determinate sentence: *Totality Guideline,* p.11. **70-008**

# LIFE SENTENCES—MURDER (ALL AGES)

## Sentencing Code ss.259, 275 and 322 and Sch.21

*References: Current Sentencing Practice A4 and B1; Archbold 5A-862*

### Mandatory sentences

**Aged 21 + at conviction** A person convicted of murder who is aged 21 on the date of conviction must be sentenced to imprisonment for life: Murder (Abolition of Death Penalty) Act 1965 (M(ADP)A 1965) s.1. This is unless the offender was under 18 at the date on which the offence was committed (see below). **71-001**

**Aged 18–20 at conviction** A person convicted of murder who is aged under 21 and over 18 on the date of conviction, must be sentenced to custody for life: SC s.275(1) and (2). This is unless the offender was under 18 at the date on which the offence was committed (see below). **71-002**

**Aged under 18 at date of offence** A person convicted of murder who was under 18 on the date when the offence was committed must be sentenced to be detained during Her Majesty's Pleasure, irrespective of their age on the date of conviction: SC s.259. **71-003**

### Minimum term

**Early release or whole life order** In all cases, a court which imposes a mandatory life sentence on a person convicted of murder must order that the early release provisions shall apply to them after they have served a part of the sentence specified by the court, unless the offender is over 18 and the seriousness of the offence or offences concerned is such that a "*whole life order*" must be made: SC ss.321(3) and (5). This will be determined by the seriousness of the offence. **71-004**

The court is required to make a whole life order if:

(a) the case is within s.321(3A) or (3B), and
(b) the court is of the opinion that, because of the seriousness of—
  (i) the offence, or
  (ii) the combination of the offence and one or more offences associated with it, it should not make a minimum term order: s.321(3).

A case is within s.321(3A) if the offender was aged 21 or over when the offence was committed. A case is within s.321(3B) if—

(a) the offence was committed on or after the day on which s.126 of the Police, Crime, Sentencing and Courts Act 2022 came into force, and
(b) the offender was aged 18 or over but under 21 when the offence was committed.

In a case within s.321(3B), the court may arrive at the opinion set out in s.321(3)(b) only if it considers that the seriousness of the offence, or combination of offences, is exceptionally high even by the standard of offences which would normally result in a whole life order in a case within subs.(3A).

**71-005** **Seriousness of the offence** In considering the seriousness of the offence, or of the combination of the offence and one or more offences associated with it, under:

(a) s.321(3) (determining whether to make a whole life order); or
(b) subs.(2) (determining the minimum term), the court must have regard to:
  (i) the general principles set out in Sch.21; and
  (ii) any sentencing guidelines relating to offences in general which are relevant to the case and are not incompatible with the provisions of Sch.21: SC s.322(3).

**71-006** **The starting point** There are various starting points set out in Sch.21 to the SC. They are a whole life order, 30 years, 25 years and 15 years. For those aged under 18 at the time of the offence, the starting points are set out in para.5A as follows:

| *1* | 2 | *3* | *4* |
|---|---|---|---|
| **Age of offender when offence committed** | **Starting point supplied by paragraph 3(1) had offender been 18** | **Starting point supplied by paragraph 4(1) had offender been 18** | **Starting point supplied by paragraph 5 had offender been 18** |
| *17* | 27 years | 23 years | 14 years |
| *15 or 16* | 20 years | 17 years | 10 years |
| *14 or under* | 15 years | 13 years | 8 years |

Guidance on para.5A can be found in the decision in *SK* [2022] EWCA Crim 1421; [2023] 1 Cr. App. R. (S.) 26.

For those aged 21+ at the date of the offence, para.2 sets out the cases which would normally attract a starting point of whole life order (which are cases of exceptionally high seriousness).

For those aged 18+ at the date of the offence, para.3 sets out the cases which would normally attract a starting point of 30 years (which are cases of particularly high seriousness); para.4 sets out the cases which attract a 25-year starting point; and para.5 provides that all other cases attract a 15 year starting point.

Composite guidance on whole life orders can be found in the decision in *Stewart (Ian)* [2022] EWCA Crim 1063; [2022] 4 W.L.R. 86.

Having identified an appropriate starting point in accordance with Sch.21, the court must take into account any aggravating or mitigating factors, to the extent that it has not allowed for them in its choice of starting point, and specify a minimum term which it considers appropriate to the seriousness of the offence or offences concerned. The minimum term may be of any length (whatever the starting point).

**71-007** **Minimum term** If the court makes a minimum term order, the minimum term must be such part of the offender's sentence as the court considers appropriate taking into account:

(a) the seriousness of:
  (i) the offence; or

    (ii) the combination of the offence and any one or more offences associated with it; and
- (b) the effect that the following would have if the court had sentenced the offender to a term of imprisonment:
    - (i) s.240ZA of the CJA 2003 (crediting periods of remand in custody); and
    - (ii) s.240A of that Act (crediting periods on bail subject to certain restrictions),

including the effect of any declaration that the court would have made under ss.325 or 327 (specifying periods of remand on bail subject to certain restrictions or in custody pending extradition): SC s.322(2).

An error in the number of days spent on remand (and thus to be credited against sentence) may not be remedied administratively: *Cookson* [2023] EWCA Crim 10.

**Guilty plea** Whereas a court should consider the fact that an offender has pleaded guilty to murder when deciding whether it is appropriate to order a whole life term, where a court determines that there should be a whole life minimum term, there will be no reduction for a guilty plea. **71-008**

In other circumstances:

- the court will weigh carefully the overall length of the minimum term taking into account other reductions for which the offender may be eligible so as to avoid a combination leading to an inappropriately short sentence;
- where it is appropriate to reduce the minimum term having regard to a plea of guilty, the reduction will not exceed one-sixth and will never exceed five years;
- the maximum reduction of one-sixth or five years (whichever is less) should only be given when a guilty plea has been indicated at the first stage of the proceedings. Lesser reductions should be given for guilty pleas after that point, with a maximum of one-twentieth being given for a guilty plea on the day of trial. The exceptions at F1 and F2 of the guideline apply to murder cases: *Reduction in Sentence for a Guilty Plea guideline* p.8.

**Transitional cases** In the case of a person sentenced to custody for life or imprisonment for life for an offence committed before 18 December 2003, the minimum term must not be greater than the term which under the practice followed by the Secretary of State before December 2002, the Secretary of State would have been likely to have specified: SC Sch.21. **71-009**

**Duty to explain sentence** On passing sentence, the court must state in open court, in ordinary language, its reasons for deciding on the order made, and in particular must state which of the starting points in Sch.21 it has chosen and its reasons for doing so, and why it has departed from that starting point: SC s.322(4). **71-010**

# TIME IN CUSTODY ON REMAND

## Criminal Justice Act 2003 s.240ZA

*References: Current Sentencing Practice A4, Archbold 5A-723*

### Applicability

These provisions apply to any person sentenced on or after 3 December 2012, irrespective of the date on which the offence was committed. For sentences imposed prior to that date, earlier legislation will need to be consulted. **72-001**

### To which sentences does it apply?

These provisions apply to offenders serving: **72-002**

(a) a term of imprisonment (including an activated suspended sentence order);
(b) a detention and training order (imposed on/after 28 June 2022);
(c) an extended sentence of imprisonment or detention in a young offender institution;
(d) a special custodial sentence for offenders of particular concern;
(e) a determinate sentence of detention in a young offender institution under;
(f) a determinate sentence of detention; and
(g) an extended sentence of detention: s.240ZA(1)(a) and (11).

The provisions do not apply to offenders serving sentences of life imprisonment, custody for life or detention for life.

### Extent of discount

If the offender has been remanded in custody for the offence or a related offence, the number of days for which the offender was remanded in custody count as time served as part of the sentence: CJA 2003 s.240ZA(3). **72-003**

It is immaterial whether for all or part of the period during which the defendant was remanded in custody, the defendant was also remanded in custody in connection with other offences, however a day may be counted in relation to only one sentence, and only once in relation to that sentence: CJA 2003 s.240ZA(2) and (5).

If, on any day on which the offender was remanded in custody, the offender was also detained in connection with any other matter, that day is not to count as time served: CJA 2003 s.240ZA(4).

### Court does not make an order

It is not necessary for the sentencing court to make any order in relation to time spent in custody on remand. **72-004**

### Related offences

**72-005** A related offence is an offence with which the offender was charged and which was founded on the same facts or evidence as the offence for which the sentence was imposed: CJA 2003 s.240ZA(8).

### Police detention

**72-006** Time spent in police detention does not count for the purposes of s.240ZA: *Gordon* [2007] EWCA Crim 165; [2007] 1 W.L.R. 2117; [2007] 2 Cr. App. R.(S.) 66.

### Acquittals

**72-007** In *Williams* [2021] EWCA Crim 1915; [2022] 2 Cr. App. R.(S.) 5, the court, exceptionally, made a deduction for the time the defendant spent in custody in relation to another offence in respect of which he was acquitted, in circumstances where that time would not count against the sentence for the offence in respect of which the defendant was convicted, as the offence was not a "related offence".

### Deportation

**72-008** There is no automatic right to time spent in custody pending deportation to be taken into account: *Keeley* [2018] EWCA Crim 2089; [2019] 1 Cr. App. R.(S.) 13; [2019] Crim. L.R. 172.

### Young offenders

**72-009** Time spent in local authority accommodation does not equate to being remanded in custody as defined in s.242(2)(b) of the CJA 2003 (which refers to being "*remanded to youth detention accommodation under s.91(4) of the Legal Aid, Sentencing and Punishment of Offenders Act 2012*") and therefore is not automatically deducted. Where a court intended that such time be deducted from the sentence, it does not follow that on appeal, that reduction will be made: *Anderson* [2017] EWCA Crim 2604; [2018] 2 Cr. App. R.(S.) 21; [2018] Crim. L.R. 865.

# TIME SPENT ON REMAND ON BAIL SUBJECT TO QUALIFYING CURFEW

## Sentencing Code s.325

*References: Current Sentencing Practice A4; Archbold 5A-724*

**Applicability** Section 325 of the Sentencing Code applies where: **73-001**

(a) a court passes a determinate sentence on an offender in respect of an offence (see subs.(5));
(b) the offender was remanded on bail by a court in course of or in connection with proceedings for the offence, or any related offence; and
(c) the offender's bail was subject to a qualifying curfew condition and an electronic monitoring condition ("*the relevant conditions*"): SC s.325(1).

There is nothing in s.325 that required the monitoring device to be functioning, nor the monitor to have actually been fitted before a defendant was entitled to credit: *Sothilingham* [2023] EWCA Crim 485.

### To which sentences does it apply?

For these purposes, a court passes a determinate sentence if it: **73-002**

(a) sentences the offender to imprisonment for a term; or
(b) imposes a detention and training order;
(c) passes a determinate sentence of detention in a young offender institution; or
(d) passes a determinate sentence of detention under s.250, s.252A or 254 (offenders aged under 18): SC s.325(5).

Categories (a) and (b) include extended sentences and sentences for offenders of particular concern.

However, a suspended sentence:

(a) is to be treated as a determinate sentence when it is activated under para.13(1)(a) or (b) of Sch.16; and
(b) is to be treated as being imposed by the order under which it is activated: SC s.325(6).

The provisions do not apply to offenders serving sentences of life imprisonment, custody for life, or detention for life.

### Mandatory order

Where the defendant is sentenced to a sentence of imprisonment (see above), was remanded on bail and was subject to a qualifying curfew condition and an electronic monitoring condition, the court must direct that the credit period is to count as time served by the offender as part of the sentence: SC s.325(2). **73-003**

### Extent of credit

73-004 The credit period is calculated by taking the following five steps which are outlined on the following page:

See below:

*Step 1*

Add:

(a) the day on which the offender's bail was first subject to the relevant conditions (and for this purpose a condition is not prevented from being a relevant condition by the fact that it does not apply for the whole of the day in question); and
(b) the number of other days on which the offender's bail was subject to those conditions (but exclude the last of those days if the offender spends the last part of it in custody).

*Step 2*

Deduct the number of days on which the offender, whilst on bail subject to the relevant conditions, was also:

(a) subject to any requirement imposed for the purpose of securing the electronic monitoring of the offender's compliance with a curfew requirement; or
(b) on temporary release under rules made under s.47 of the Prison Act 1952.

*Step 3*

From the remainder, deduct the number of days during that remainder on which the offender has broken either or both of the relevant conditions.

*Step 4*

Divide the result by 2.

*Step 5*

If necessary, round up to the nearest whole number.

### Exceptions

73-005 A day of the credit period counts as time served in relation to only one sentence and only once in relation to that sentence: CJA 2003 s.240(3A).

### State declaration in open court

73-006 Where the court makes a declaration under subs.(2) it must state in open court:

(a) the number of days on which the offender was subject to the relevant conditions; and

(b) the number of days (if any) which it deducted under each of steps 2 and 3: SC s.325(4).

## Form of words

In *Hoggard* [2013] EWCA Crim 1024; [2014] 1 Cr. App. R.(S.) 42; [2013] Crim. L.R. 782, the court suggested the following form of words: **73-007**

> "the defendant will receive full credit for half the time spent under curfew if the curfew qualified under the provisions of s.240A. On the information before me the total period is ... days (subject to the deduction of ... days that I have directed under Step(s) 2 and/or 3 making a total of ... days), but if this period is mistaken, this court will order an amendment of the record for the correct period to be recorded."

In *Cox* [2019] EWCA Crim 71; [2019] 4 W.L.R. 88; [2019] 2 Cr. App. R.(S.) 6, the importance of specifying the actual number of days representing the qualifying curfew period at the time of sentence was emphasised.

## Non-qualifying curfews

There is a discretion to take account of a non-qualifying curfew. For a recent example of the court holding that a judge had erred in not doing so: *Whitehouse* [2019] EWCA Crim 970; [2019] 2 Cr. App. R.(S.) 48. **73-008**

In *Cornelius* [2019] EWCA Crim 2154, the defendant had been subject to a 10-hour curfew which was not electronically monitored; the court held that it was appropriate to exercise the court's discretion and reflect that fact in the sentence imposed. **73-009**

## Definitions

An "*electronic monitoring condition*" is any electronic monitoring requirement imposed under s.2(6ZZA) of the BA 1976 for the purpose of securing the electronic monitoring of a person's compliance with a qualifying curfew condition: SC s.326(3). **73-010**

A "*qualifying curfew condition*" means a condition of bail which requires the person granted bail to remain at one or more specified places for a total of not less than nine hours in any given day: SC s.326(3).

A "*related offence*" is an offence, other than the offence for which the sentence is imposed, with which the offender was charged and the charge for which was founded on the same facts or evidence as the offence for which the sentence is imposed: SC s.326(2).

# EXTRADITED OFFENDERS

## Sentencing Code s.327; Criminal Justice Act 2003 s.243

*References: Current Sentencing Practice A4; Archbold 5A-728*

### Applicability

Section 327 applies where a court imposes a fixed-term sentence on a person who: **74-001**

(a) was tried for the offence in respect of which the sentence was imposed, or received the sentence:
  (i) after having been extradited to the UK; and
  (ii) without having first been restored or had an opportunity of leaving the UK; and
(b) was for any period kept in custody while awaiting extradition to the UK as mentioned in para.(a): SC s.327(1).

*Fixed term sentence* means:

(a) a sentence of imprisonment for a determinate term;
(b) a detention and training order;
(c) a determinate sentence of detention in a young offender institution; or
(d) a determinate sentence of detention under s.250, s.252A or 254: SC s.327(2).

### Duty to specify number of days in custody

The court by which an extradited prisoner is sentenced must specify in open court the number of days for which they were kept in custody while awaiting extradition: SC s.327(3). **74-002**

CJA 2003 s.240ZA (time on remand to count as time served) applies to days specified under SC s.327(2) as if they were days for which the prisoner was remanded in custody in connection with the offence or a related offence: CJA 2003 s.243(2A).

Where a court omits to state that days spent in custody awaiting extradition are to be credited, there is no entitlement to have those days credited and the failure of the Secretary of State for Justice (SoS) to credit such days did not render the continuing detention unlawful: *R. (Shields-McKinley) v Secretary of State for Justice and Lord Chancellor* [2017] 1 W.L.R. 3705.

### No power to disallow days

The sentencing court has no power to disallow any days spent in custody prior to extradition. **74-003**

**Discretion** There exists a discretion to modify a sentence that was otherwise law- **74-004**

ful, however cases in which that would be appropriate will be exceptional. That was because the rules laid down in the CJA 2003 (and the Sentencing Code) for the according of credit against sentence for periods spent on remand or on qualifying bail were intended to lay down a comprehensive scheme governing the issue. Parliament has also made clear that time spent on remand in cases unrelated to the case under consideration should not, prima facie, warrant any adjustment to the sentence: *Prenga* [2017] EWCA Crim 2149; [2018] 4 W.L.R. 59; [2018] 1 Cr. App. R.(S.) 41. Thus, it will be rare where cases outside of the statutory scheme will result in a discretionary reduction of time.

There is no right to have the time spent in custody awaiting deportation credited against sentence: *Keeley* [2018] EWCA Crim 2089; [2019] 1 Cr. App. R.(S.) 13; [2019] Crim. L.R. 172.

# E: SECONDARY DISPOSALS

# CRIMINAL BEHAVIOUR ORDERS

## Sentencing Code ss.330–332

*References: Current Sentencing Practice A5, Archbold 5A-925*

### General

**What is a CBO?** A "*criminal behaviour order*" is an order which, for the purpose of preventing an offender from engaging in behaviour that is likely to cause harassment, alarm or distress to any person: **75-001**

(a) prohibits the offender from doing anything described in the order;
(b) requires the offender to do anything described in the order: SC s.330.

**Threshold** Home Office Guidance (2017) stated that the CBO "*is intended for tackling the most serious and persistent offenders where their behaviour has brought them before a criminal court.*" Section 331 of the Code might on a literal construction be said to apply to a high proportion of cases in the criminal courts. It was not Parliament's intention that CBOs should become a mere matter of a box-ticking routine. As was said in *DPP v Bulmer* [2015] EWHC 2323 (Admin); [2015] 1 W.L.R. 5159; [2016] 1 Cr. App. R.(S.) 12, such orders were not lightly to be imposed; the court should proceed with a proper degree of caution and circumspection; the order must be tailored to the specific circumstances of the person on whom it was to be imposed; and assessments of proportionality were intensively fact sensitive: *Khan (Kamran)* [2018] EWCA Crim 1472; [2018] 1 W.L.R. 5419; [2018] 2 Cr. App. R.(S.) 53. **75-002**

**Relevance of ASBO caselaw** As with any order of a criminal court which has characteristics of an injunction, it is essential that the guidance set out in *Boness* [2005] EWCA Crim 2395; [2006] 1 Cr. App. R.(S.) 120; [2006] Crim. L.R. 160 at [19]–[23] in relation to anti-social behaviour orders should be borne in mind: *Khan (Kamran)* [2018] EWCA Crim 1472; [2018] 2 Cr. App. R.(S.) 53. **75-003**

**Explanation of the legislation** The court gave guidance as to the operation of the provisions in *DPP v Bulmer* [2015] EWHC 2323 (Admin); [2016] 1 Cr. App. R.(S.) 12. **75-004**

### Making the order

**Availability** A CBO is available where: **75-005**

(a) a person is convicted of an offence; and
(b) the prosecution makes an application to the court for a CBO to be made against the offender: SC s.331(1).

Additionally, as a CBO is a secondary order, the court may make a CBO only if it:

(a) does so in addition to dealing with the offender for the offence; and
(b) does not make an order for absolute discharge under s.79 in respect of the offence: SC s.331(3).

**75-006** **Test** The court may make a CBO against the offender if it:

(a) is satisfied that the offender has engaged in behaviour that caused or was likely to cause harassment, alarm or distress to any person; and
(b) considers that making the order will help in preventing the offender from engaging in such behaviour: SC s.331(2).

**75-007** **Under 18s** For offenders aged under 18 when the application is made, the prosecution must find out the views of the local youth offending team before applying: SC s.331(5).

When deciding whether making the proposed CBO would help in preventing an offender from engaging in such behaviour, a finding of fact that an offender was incapable of understanding or complying with the terms of the order, so that the only effect of the order would be to criminalise behaviour over which the offender had no control, would indicate that the order would not be helpful and would not satisfy the second condition: *Humphreys v CPS* [2019] EWHC 2794 (Admin); [2020] 1 Cr. App. R.(S.) 39.

**Procedure**

**75-008** **Evidence** For the purpose of deciding whether to make a CBO the court may consider evidence led by the prosecution and evidence led by the offender. It does not matter whether the evidence would have been admissible in the proceedings in which the offender was convicted: SC s.332(1) and (2).

**75-009** **Adjournment** The court may adjourn any proceedings on an application for a CBO even after sentencing the offender: SC s.332(3). See s.332 for further provision relating to adjournments.

It may not be appropriate for an adjourned application for a CBO to be resolved before someone other than the sentencing judge: *Maguire* [2019] EWCA Crim 1193; [2019] 2 Cr. App. R.(S.) 55; [2020] Crim. L.R. 88.

**75-010** **Findings of fact** The findings of fact giving rise to the making of the order must be recorded: *Khan (Kamran)* [2018] EWCA Crim 1472; [2018] 2 Cr. App. R.(S.) 53.

**75-011** **Explaining the order** The order must be explained to the offender. The exact terms of the order must be pronounced in open court and the written order must accurately reflect the order as pronounced. In the case of a foreign national, consideration should be given for the need for the order to be translated: *Khan (Kamran)* [2018] EWCA Crim 1472; [2018] 2 Cr. App. R.(S.) 53.

**75-012** **Parenting order** See s.8(1)(b) of the CDA 1998 for requirements and powers of a court to make a parenting order under that Act in a case where it makes a CBO against an offender aged under 18.

**How long may the order last?/when does it take effect?**

**75-013** **Effective date** The order takes effect on the day it is made, save for where on the day an order is made the offender is subject to another CBO. In such a circumstance, the new order may be made so as to take effect on the day on which the previous order ceases to have effect: SC s.334(1) and (2).

**Length: must specify** A CBO must specify the period ("*the order period*") for which it has effect: SC s.334(3). **75-014**

**Length: aged 18+ when order made** A fixed period of not less than two years, or for an indefinite period: SC s.334(5). **75-015**

**Length: aged under 18 when order made** A fixed period of not less than one year and not more than three years: SC s.334(4). **75-016**

**Prohibitions and requirements forming part of the order**

**Contents** The order may, for the purpose of preventing the offender from engaging in such behaviour: **75-017**

(a) prohibit the offender from doing anything; or
(b) require the offender to do anything, described in the order: SC s.330.

**Two or more requirements** Before including two or more requirements, the court must consider their compatibility with each other: SC s.333(3). **75-018**

**Interference with other elements of offender's life** Prohibitions and requirements in a CBO must, so far as practicable, be such as to avoid: **75-019**

(a) any interference with the times, if any, at which the offender normally works or attends school or any other educational establishment;
(b) any conflict with the requirements of any other court order to which the offender may be subject: SC s.331(4).

Prohibitions interfering with the operation of the offender's business will not contravene the legislation in an appropriate case: *Janes* [2016] EWCA Crim 676; [2016] 2 Cr. App. R.(S.) 27; [2016] Crim. L.R. 785.

The order may specify periods for which particular prohibitions or requirements have effect: SC s.334(6).

**Must specify supervising officer, etc.** A CBO that includes a requirement must specify the person who is to be responsible for supervising compliance with the requirement. The person may be an individual or an organisation: SC s.333(1). **75-020**

**Must hear from supervising officer** Before including a requirement, the court must receive evidence about its suitability and enforceability from the supervising officer: SC s.333(2). **75-021**

**The terms of the order** Prohibitions should be reasonable and proportionate; realistic and practical; and be in terms which make it easy to determine and prosecute a breach. Because an order must be precise and capable of being understood by the offender, a court should ask itself before making an order "*are the terms of this order clear so that the offender will know precisely what it is that they are prohibited from doing?*": *Khan (Kamran)* [2018] EWCA Crim 1472; [2018] 2 Cr. App. R.(S.) 53. **75-022**

75-023 **Geographical prohibitions** These should be clearly delineated (generally with the use of clearly marked maps, although there is no problem of definition in an order extending to Greater Manchester for example) and individuals whom the defendant is prohibited from contacting or associating with should be clearly identified, *Khan*. Prohibitions need not be related to the geographical area in which the behaviour giving rise to the order was conducted: *Browne-Morgan* [2016] EWCA Crim 1903; [2017] 4 W.L.R. 118; [2017] 1 Cr. App. R.(S.) 33.

75-024 **Deterrence** Deterrence can be a legitimate purpose to pursue when including prohibitions in an order: *Tofagsazan* [2020] EWCA Crim 982; [2021] 1 Cr. App. R.(S.) 24.

75-025 **Obligations on the offender** An offender must keep in touch with the person responsible for supervising compliance in relation to a requirement and notify the person of any change of address. These obligations have effect as requirements of the order: SC s.333(6).

**Review of order**

75-026 **Who is subject to a review** If:

- (a) an offender subject to a CBO will be under the age of 18 at the end of a review period (see subs.(2));
- (b) the term of the order runs until the end of that period or beyond; and
- (c) the order is not discharged before the end of that period,

a review of the operation of the order must be carried out before the end of that period: SC s.337(1).

The "*review periods*" are:

- (a) the period of 12 months beginning with:
  - (i) the day on which the CBO takes effect; or
  - (ii) if during that period the order is varied under s.336, the day on which it is varied (or most recently varied, if the order is varied more than once);
- (b) a period of 12 months beginning with:
  - (i) the day after the end of the previous review period; or
  - (ii) if during that period of 12 months the order is varied under s.336, the day on which it is varied (or most recently varied, if the order is varied more than once): SC s.337(2).

75-027 **Content of review** A review must consider:

- (a) the extent to which the offender has complied with the order;
- (b) the adequacy of any support available to the offender to help them comply with it;
- (c) any matters relevant to the question whether an application should be made for the order to be varied or discharged: SC s.337(3).

**Interim orders**

75-028 The court may make a CBO that lasts until the final hearing of the application or until further order if the court thinks it just to do so: SC s.335(2).

There is no requirement to consult the local youth offending team, that the prosecution make an application, or that the order is in addition to a sentence or conditional discharge: SC s.335(3). Subject to that, the court has the same powers whether or not the CBO is an interim order: SC s.335(4).

### Variation and discharge

**Power** An order may be varied or discharged by the court which made it on the application of the offender, or the prosecution: SC s.336(1). **75-029**

The order may only be varied or discharged by the "*court which made the order*", and accordingly the Crown Court has no power to vary or discharge a CBO made by a magistrates' court: *Potter* [2019] EWCA Crim 461; [2019] 2 Cr. App. R.(S.) 5.

**Extent of power** The power to vary an order includes power to include an additional prohibition or requirement in the order or to extend the period for which a prohibition or requirement has effect: SC s.336(4). **75-030**

**Bar on future applications** If an application by the offender is dismissed, the offender may make no further application without the consent of the court which made the order, or the agreement of the prosecution: SC s.336(2). **75-031**

If an application by the prosecution is dismissed, the prosecution may make no further application without the consent of the court which made the order, or the agreement of the offender: SC s.336(3).

### Breach

**Offence** A person who, without reasonable excuse: **75-032**

(a) does anything prohibited; or
(b) fails to do anything required by a CBO,

commits an offence: SC s.339(1).

**Maximum sentence** Five years: SC s.339(2). **75-033**

**Conditional discharge** A court may not impose a conditional discharge for a breach of a CBO: SC s.339(3). **75-034**

**Reporting restrictions** Youth Justice and Criminal Evidence Act 1999 (YJCEA 1999) s.45 (power to restrict reporting of criminal proceedings involving persons under 18) applies to proceedings for a breach of a CBO, but the CYPA 1933 s.49 does not apply: SC s.339(5). **75-035**

# DISQUALIFICATION FROM BEING THE DIRECTOR OF A COMPANY

## Company Directors Disqualification Act 1986 s.2

*References: Current Sentencing Practice A5; Archbold 5A-954*

### Power to order/test to apply

**Indictable offences** The court may make a disqualification order where a person is convicted of an indictable offence (whether on indictment or summarily) in connection with the promotion, formation, management, liquidation or striking off of a company with the receivership of a company's property or with the person being an administrative receiver of a company: Company Directors Disqualification Act 1986 (CDDA 1986) s.2(1). **76-001**

**Summary offences** Where a person is convicted of a summary offence, in consequence of a contravention of, or failure to comply with, any provision of the companies legislation requiring a return, account or other document to be filed with, delivered or sent, or notice of any matter to be given, to the registrar of companies (whether the contravention or failure is on the person's own part or on the part of any company) and during the five years ending with the date of the conviction, the person has had made against them, or has been convicted of, in total not less than three default orders and offences as specified above, the court may make a disqualification order: CDDA 1986 s.5(1)-(3). **76-002**

The offence concerned may relate to the internal management of the company, or the general conduct of its business: *Georgiou* (1988) 4 B.C.C. 322; (1988) 10 Cr. App. R.(S.) 137; [1988] Crim. L.R. 472.

It is not necessary in a criminal case for the court to consider the tests of fitness required for the purposes of an order under s.6 of the Act: see *Young* [1990] B.C.C. 549; (1990–91) 12 Cr. App. R.(S.) 262; [1990] Crim. L.R. 818.

### Making the order

The period of a disqualification order is determined by the court in the exercise of its discretion. The maximum term is 15 years (where the order is made by a magistrates' court, five years). There is no minimum period: CDDA 1986 s.2(3). **76-003**

If the offender is already subject to a disqualification order, any new order will run concurrently with the existing order: CDDA 1986 s.1(3).

The court should inform counsel of its intentions and invite them to mitigate on the question before making an order of disqualification.

### Effect of the order

A person subject to an order shall not: **76-004**

(a) be a director of a company;

(b) act as receiver of a company's property; or
(c) in any way, whether directly or indirectly, be concerned or take part in the promotion, formation or management of a company unless (in each case) they have the leave of the court; and
(d) they shall not act as an insolvency practitioner: CDDA 1986 s.1(1).

# EXCLUSION ORDERS (LICENSED PREMISES)

## Licensed Premises (Exclusion of Certain Persons) Act 1980

*References: Current Sentencing Practice A5*

*Note: The Licensed Premises (Exclusion of Certain Persons) Act 1980 is repealed by the VCRA 2006, Sch.5. That repeal was not in force on 31 October 2024.*

### Availability

If the offender has been convicted of an offence committed on licensed premises in the course of which they made resort to violence, the court may make an exclusion order: Licensed Premises (Exclusion of Certain Persons) Act 1980 (LP(ECP)A 1980) s.1(1). **77-001**

### Effect

The order prohibits the offender from entering the licensed premises specified in the order without the express consent of the licensee or their servant or agent. **77-002**

The order may be made in respect of any licensed premises, whether or not the offender has committed an offence in those premises, but all the premises to which the order applies must be specified in the order.

### Length

The court must fix the term of the order. The minimum term is three months; the maximum term is two years: LP(ECP)A 1980 s.1(3). **77-003**

### Combining sentences

An exclusion order may be made in addition to any other form of sentence or order including a discharge. An exclusion order may not be made as the only sentence of order for the offence: LP(ECP)A 1980 s.1(2). **77-004**

# FEMALE GENITAL MUTILATION PROTECTION ORDERS

## Female Genital Mutilation Act 2003 Sch.2

*References: Current Sentencing Practice A5*

### Making the order

**Power** The court before which there are criminal proceedings in England and Wales for a genital mutilation offence may make an FGM protection order (without an application being made to it) if: 78-001

(a) the court considers that an FGM protection order should be made to protect a girl (whether or not the victim of the offence in relation to the criminal proceedings); and
(b) a person who would be a respondent to any proceedings for an FGM protection order is a defendant in the criminal proceedings: Female Genital Mutilation Act 2003 (FGMA 2003) Sch.2 para.3.

Genital mutilation offence means an offence under the FGMA 2003 ss.1, 2 or 3: FGMA 2003 Sch.2 para.17(1).

**Contents of the order** An FGM protection order may contain: 78-002

(a) such prohibitions, restrictions or requirements; and
(b) such other terms, as the court considers appropriate for the purposes of the order: FGMA 2003 Sch.2 para.1(3).

The terms of an FGM protection order may, in particular, relate to:

(a) conduct outside England and Wales as well as (or instead of) conduct within England and Wales;
(b) respondents who are, or may become, involved in other respects as well as (or instead of) respondents who commit or attempt to commit, or may commit or attempt to commit, a genital mutilation offence against a girl; and
(c) other persons who are, or may become, involved in other respects as well as respondents of any kind: FGMA 2003 Sch.2 para.1(4).

### Variation

**Power to vary on application** The court may vary or discharge an FGM protection order on an application by: 78-003

(a) the prosecution or the defendant;
(b) the girl being protected by the order; or
(c) any person affected by the order: FGMA 2003 Sch.2 para.6(1).

**Power to vary of own motion** The court may vary or discharge a "criminal" FGM protection order even though no application has been made to the court: FGMA 2003 Sch.2 para.6(3). 78-004

**Breach**

78-005 **Offence** A person who without reasonable excuse does anything that the person is prohibited from doing by an FGM protection order is guilty of an offence: FGMA 2003 Sch.2 para.4(1).

Where an individual is convicted of an offence, the conduct forming the basis of the conviction is not punishable as a contempt of court: FGMA 2003 Sch.2 para.4(3).

78-006 **Penalty** The maximum penalty for breaching an order is five years' imprisonment: FGMA 2003 Sch.2 para.4(5).

# FOOTBALL BANNING ORDERS

## Football Spectators Act 1989 ss.14-14J

*References: Current Sentencing Practice A5; Archbold 5A-964*

### General

**Purpose** The order is not designed as a punishment (although it will have that effect), it is designed as a preventive measure: *Doyle* [2012] EWCA Crim 995; [2013] 1 Cr. App. R.(S.) 36; [2012] Crim. L.R. 636. **79-001**

**Effect** A banning order prohibits the offender from attending a regulated football match in England and Wales, and requires them to report when required to a police station when football matches are being played outside England and Wales. A banning order may include other requirements. The order must require the offender to surrender their passport in connection with matches played outside England and Wales: Football Spectators Act 1989 (FSA 1989) s.14(4). **79-002**

### Making the order

**Combination with other orders** A banning order may be made only in addition to any other form of sentence or in addition to a conditional discharge: FSA 1989 s.14(4)(a). **79-003**

**Duty to make an order** Where an offender has been convicted of a relevant offence (see below), the court must make a banning order in respect of the offender unless the court considers that there are particular circumstances relating to the offence or to the offender which would make it unjust in all the circumstances to do so: FSA 1989 s.14A(2). **79-004**

*NB. This applies to offences committed on or after 29 June 2022. For offences prior to that date, see the 2022 edition of this work.*

**State reasons where order not made** Where the court does not make a banning order it must state in open court the reasons for not doing so: FSA 1989 s.14A(3). **79-005**

**Length of the order** If the offender receives an immediate custodial sentence, the banning order must be for at least six years and not more than 10 years. In all other cases, the banning order must be for at least three years and not more than five years. **79-006**

**Limiting the order to specific teams** It is not permissible to make an order restricted to certain football teams: *Commissioner of Police of the Metropolis v Thorpe* [2015] EWHC 3339 (Admin); [2016] 4 W.L.R. 7; [2016] 1 Cr. App. R.(S.) 46. **79-007**

## Relevant offences

**79-008** The following offences are relevant offences:

- (a) any offence under the FSA 1989 ss.14J(1), 19(6), 20(10) or; 21C(2);
- (b) any offence under ss.2 or 2A of the Sporting Events (Control of Alcohol, etc.) Act 1985 (alcohol, containers and fireworks) committed by the accused at any regulated football match or while entering or trying to enter the ground;
- (c) any offence under s.4, 4A or s.5 of the POA 1986 (fear or provocation of violence, or harassment, alarm or distress) or any provision of Pt III of that Act (racial hatred) committed at any premises while the accused was at, or was entering or leaving or trying to enter or leave, the premises;
- (d) any offence involving the use or threat of violence by the accused towards another person committed during a period relevant to a regulated football match at any premises while the accused was at, or was entering or leaving or trying to enter or leave, the premises;
- (e) any offence involving the use or threat of violence towards property committed during a period relevant to a regulated football match at any premises while the accused was at, or was entering or leaving or trying to enter or leave, the premises;
- (f) any offence involving the use, carrying or possession of an offensive weapon or a firearm committed during a period relevant to a regulated football match at any premises while the accused was at, or was entering or leaving or trying to enter or leave, the premises;
- (g) any offence under s.12 of the Licensing Act 1872 (persons found drunk in public places, etc.) of being found drunk in a highway or other public place committed while the accused was on a journey to or from a regulated football match applies in respect of which the court makes a declaration of relevance;
- (h) any offence under s.91(1) of the Criminal Justice Act 1967 (disorderly behaviour while drunk in a public place) committed in a highway or other public place while the accused was on a journey to or from a regulated football match in respect of which the court makes a declaration of relevance;
- (j) any offence under s.1 of the Sporting Events (Control of Alcohol, etc.) Act 1985 (alcohol on coaches or trains to or from sporting events) committed while the accused was on a journey to or from a regulated football match in respect of which the court makes a declaration of relevance;
- (k) any offence under s.4A or s.5 of the POA 1986 (harassment, alarm or distress) or any provision of Pt III of that Act (racial hatred) committed while the accused was on a journey to or from a regulated football match in respect of which the court makes a declaration of relevance;
- (l) any offence under ss.4 or 5 of the RTA 1988 (driving, etc. when under the influence of drink or drugs or with an alcohol concentration above the prescribed limit) committed while the accused was on a journey to or from a regulated football match in respects of which the court makes a declaration of relevance;
- (m) any offence involving the use or threat of violence by the accused towards another person committed while one or each of them was on a journey to

or from a regulated football match in respect of which the court makes a declaration of relevance;

(n) any offence involving the use or threat of violence towards property committed while the accused was on a journey to or from a regulated football match in respect of which the court makes a declaration of relevance;

(o) any offence involving the use, carrying or possession of an offensive weapon or a firearm committed while the accused was on a journey to or from a regulated football match in respect of which the court makes a declaration of relevance;

(p) any offence under the Football (Offences) Act 1991;

(q) any other offence under s.4, 4A or s.5 of the POA 1986 (fear or provocation of violence, or harassment, alarm or distress) which does not fall within (c) or (k) above was committed during a period relevant to a regulated football match in respect of which the court makes a declaration that the offence related to that match or to that match and any other football match which took place during that period;

(r) any other offence involving the use or threat of violence by the accused towards another person which does not fall within (d) or (m) above was committed during a period relevant to a regulated football match in respect of which the court makes a declaration that the offence related to that match or to that match and any other football match which took place during that period;

(s) any other offence involving the use or threat of violence towards property which does not fall within (e) or (n) above was committed during a period relevant to a regulated football match in respect of which the court makes a declaration that the offence related to that match or to that match and any other football match which took place during that period;

(t) any other offence involving the use, carrying or possession of an offensive weapon which does not fall within (f) or (o) above was committed during a period relevant to a regulated football match in respect of which the court makes a declaration that the offence related to that match or to that match and any other football match which took place during that period;

(u) any offence under s.166 of the CJPOA 1994 (sale of tickets by unauthorised persons) which relates to tickets for a football match;

(v) any offence under any provision of Pt 3 or 3A of the Public Order Act 1986 ′ (hatred by reference to race etc.)—
    (i) which does not fall within para.(c) or (k), and
    (ii) as respects which the court makes a declaration that the offence related to a football match, to a football organisation or to a person whom the accused knew or believed to have a prescribed connection with a football organisation,

(w) any offence under s.31 of the Crime and Disorder Act 1998 (racially or religiously aggravated public order offences) as respects which the court makes a declaration that the offence related to a football match, to a football organisation or to a person whom the accused knew or believed to have a prescribed connection with a football organisation,

(x) any offence under s.1 of the Malicious Communications Act 1988 (offence of sending letter, distress or anxiety)—
    (i) which does not fall within paragr.(d), (e), (m), (n), (r) or (s),
    (ii) as respects which the court has stated that the offence is aggravated

by hostility of any of the types mentioned in s.66(1)) of the Sentencing Code (racial hostility etc.), and

(iii) as respects which the court makes a declaration that the offence related to a football match, to a football organisation or to a person whom the accused knew or believed to have a prescribed connection with a football organisation,

(y) any offence under s.127(1) of the Communications Act 2003 (improper use of public telecommunications network)—

(i) which does not fall within par.(d), (e), (m), (n), (r) or (s),

(ii) as respects which the court has stated that the offence is aggravated by hostility of any of the types mentioned in s.66(1) of the Sentencing Code (racial hostility etc.), and

(iii) as respects which the court makes a declaration that the offence related to a football match, to a football organisation or to a person whom the accused knew or believed to have a prescribed connection with a football organisation.

(z) any offence under s.4(3) or 5 of the Misuse of Drugs Act 1971 (supply or possession etc. of controlled substances) committed by the accused, in relation to a Class A drug, as defined in s.2(1)(b) of that Act, at any football match to which this Schedule applies or while entering or trying to enter the ground (offences committed on/after 10 November 2022).

(z) any offence under s.179 (false communications) or 181 (threatening communications) of the Online Safety Act 2023—

(i) which does not fall within paragraph (d), (e), (m), (n), (r) or (s);

(ii) as respects which the court has stated that the offence is aggravated by hostility of any of the types mentioned in s.66(1) of the Sentencing Code (racial hostility etc); and

(iii) as respects which the court makes a declaration that the offence related to a football match, to a football organisation or to a person whom the accused knew or believed to have a prescribed connection with a football organisation.

*[A second sub-paragraph (z) was inserted on 31 January 2024 by the Online Safety Act 2023 (Commencement No. 3) Regulations 2024 (SI 2024/31), and the Online Safety Act 2023 s.191 and Sch.14, para.1. The numbering (duplicating sub-paragraph (z)) appears to be in error.]*

**79-009** **"Period relevant"** The period relevant to a football match is the period beginning 24 hours before the start of the match, or the advertised start, and ending 24 hours after the end of the match. If the match does not take place, the period is the period beginning 24 hours before the time at which it was advertised to start, and ending 24 hours after that time.

**79-010** **"Regulated football match"** A regulated football match is an association football match in which one or both of the participating teams represents a club which is for the time being a member (whether a full or associate member) of the Football League, the Football Association Premier League or the Football Conference, or represents a club from outside England and Wales, or represents a country or territory; and which is either played at a sports ground which is designated by order under s.1(1) of the Safety of Sports Grounds Act 1975, or registered with the Football League or the Football Association Premier League as the home ground of a club which is a member of the Football League or the Football Association Premier League at the time the match is played; or is played in the Football Association Cup (other than in a preliminary or qualifying round): FSA 1989 s.14(2) and The Football Spectators (Prescription) Order 2004 (SI 2004/2409) art.3(3).

**"Regulated football organisation"** "Regulated football organisation" means an organisation (whether in the UK or elsewhere) which— **79-011**

(a) relates to association football, and
(b) is a prescribed organisation or an organisation of a prescribed description: FSA 1989 s.14(2A).

In the schedule, "*football organisation*" means an organisation which is a regulated football organisation for the purposes of Pt 2 of the Act: FSA 1989 Sch.1 para.4.

**Declarations of relevance**

**Definition** A declaration by a court that an offence **79-012**

(a) related to football matches,
(b) related to one or more particular football matches,
(c) related to a football organisation, or
(d) related to a person whom the defendant knew or believed to have a prescribed connection with a football organisation: FSA 1989 s.23(5).

**Notice must be served** The court may not make a declaration of relevance unless the prosecutor gave notice to the defendant five days before the first day of the trial that it was proposed to show that **79-013**

(a) related to football matches,
(b) related to one or more particular football matches,
(c) related to a football organisation, or
(d) related to a person whom the defendant knew or believed to have a prescribed connection with a football organisation, as the case may be, unless the offender consents to waive the requirement or the court is satisfied that the interests of justice do not require more notice to be given: FSA 1989 s.23(1) and (2).

**Failure to make a declaration** The failure to make a declaration of relevance does not render a football banning order invalid: *DPP v Beaumont* [2008] EWHC 523 (Admin); [2008] 1 W.L.R. 2186; [2008] 2 Cr. App. R.(S.) 98. **79-014**

**Declarations serve no purpose** There appears to be no purpose in a declaration of relevance in the present state of the legislation: *Boggild* [2011] EWCA Crim 1928; [2012] 1 W.L.R. 1298; [2012] 1 Cr. App. R.(S.) 81, (*obiter*). **79-015**

A football banning order may only be made in respect of a relevant offence. There are two routes to satisfying that criterion: first, that the offence is deemed to automatically "*relate*" to football matches; and secondly, an offence for which may or may not relate to a football match, for which it is necessary to make a determination. The purpose therefore appears to be to safeguard against the imposition of orders in cases where the offence coincidentally occurred during a period relevant to a football match. However, an offence which coincidentally occurred during a period relevant to a football match would presumably fail the "*reasonable grounds*" test in FSA 1989 s.14A(1) and (2) and so the declaration appears to be without purpose as noted in *Boggild*.

**Notice requirements**

**79-016** An order must require the person subject to the order to report initially at a police station specified in the order within the period of five days beginning with the day on which the order is made: FSA 1989 s.14E(2).

An order must require the person subject to the order to give notification of:

(a) a change of any of their names;
(b) the first use by them after the making of the order of a name for themself that was not disclosed by them at the time of the making of the order;
(c) a change of their home address;
(d) their acquisition of a temporary address;
(e) a change of their temporary address or their ceasing to have one;
(f) them becoming aware of the loss of their passport;
(g) receipt by them of a new passport;
(h) an appeal made by them in relation to the order;
(i) an application made by them under s.14H(2) for termination of the order; and
(j) an appeal made by them under s.23(3) against the making of a declaration of relevance in respect of an offence of which they have been convicted: FSA 1989 s.14E(3).

**Appeals**

**79-017** A defendant may appeal against the making of a declaration of relevance: FSA 1989 s.23(3).

The prosecution may appeal against the failure of a court to make a banning order: FSA 1989 s.14A(5A).

**Termination or variation**

**79-018** An application to terminate the order may be made once the period of two thirds of the length of the order has expired, FSA 1989 s.14H(1). Upon an application by the person subject to the order, the person who applied for the order or the prosecutor in relation to the order may be varied so as to impose, omit or replace or omit any requirements: FSA 1989 s.14G(2).

**Breach**

**79-019** A failure to comply with a requirement of a football banning order constitutes an offence to which a maximum sentence of six months' imprisonment and/or a level 5 fine applies: FSA 1989 s.14J.

# PSYCHOACTIVE SUBSTANCES—PROHIBITION ORDERS

PSYCHOACTIVE SUBSTANCES ACT 2016 ss.17–22

*References: Current Sentencing Practice A5; Archbold 27-131*

## General

Prohibition order means an order prohibiting the person against whom it is made from carrying on any prohibited activity or a prohibited activity of a description specified in the order: PSA 2016 s.17(1). **80-001**

Prohibited activity means any of the following activities:

(a) producing a psychoactive substance that is likely to be consumed by individuals for its psychoactive effects;
(b) supplying such a substance;
(c) offering to supply such a substance;
(d) importing such a substance;
(e) exporting such a substance; and
(f) assisting or encouraging the carrying on of a prohibited activity listed in any of paras (a) to (e): PSA 2016 s.12(1).

But this is subject to the list of exceptions to offences, see PSA 2016 s.11.

The sections of the PSA 2016 pertinent to prohibition orders were commenced on 26 May 2016 (see The Psychoactive Substances Act 2016 (Commencement) Regulations 2016 (SI 2016/553)) with no transitional provisions.

## Making the order

**Availability** The order is available where the court is dealing with a person who has been convicted of a relevant offence: PSA 2016 s.19(1). **80-002**

A relevant offence means:

(a) an offence under any of ss.4 to 8 of the PSA 2016;
(b) an offence of attempting or conspiring to commit an offence under any of ss.4 to 8;
(c) an offence under Pt 2 of the SCA 2007 in relation to an offence under any of ss.4 to 8;
(d) an offence of inciting a person to commit an offence under any of ss.4 to 8; and
(e) an offence of aiding, abetting, counselling or procuring the commission of an offence under any of ss.4 to 8: PSA 2016 s.19(5).

A prohibition order may not be made except:

(a) in addition to a sentence imposed in respect of the offence concerned, or

(b) in addition to an order discharging the person conditionally: PSA 2016 s.19(2).

80-003 **Test to apply** The court may only make the order if it considers it necessary and proportionate for the purpose of preventing the person from carrying on any prohibited activity: PSA 2016 s.19(1).

80-004 **Effect of making prohibition order on existing prohibition notice** If a court makes a prohibition order under this section, any prohibition notice that has previously been given to the person against whom the order is made is to be treated as having been withdrawn: PSA 2016 s.19(3).

**Extent and contents of the order**

80-005 **Nature** The order may make prohibitions, restrictions or requirements: PSA 2016 s.22(1).

80-006 **Test for prohibitions, etc.** The order may only include prohibitions, restrictions or requirement which the court considers to be appropriate: PSA 2016 s.22(1).

80-007 **Mandatory prohibition** Every order will include a prohibition on carrying on any prohibited activity or a prohibited activity of a description specified in the order: PSA 2016 s.17(1) and 22(1).

**Sample prohibitions**

80-008
(a) prohibitions or restrictions on, or requirements in relation to, the person's business dealings (including the conduct of the person's business over the internet);
(b) a requirement to hand over for disposal an item belonging to the person that the court is satisfied:
  (i) is a psychoactive substance; or
  (ii) has been, or is likely to be, used in the carrying on of a prohibited activity;
(c) a prohibition on access to premises owned, occupied, leased, controlled or operated by the person for a specified period not exceeding three months (an "*access prohibition*"): PSA 2016 s.22(3), (4) and (6).

A person (other than a mortgagee not in possession) "*owns*" premises in England and Wales or Northern Ireland if:

(a) the person is entitled to dispose of the fee simple in the premises, whether in possession or reversion; or
(b) the person holds or is entitled to the rents and profits of the premises under a lease that (when granted) was for a term of not less than three years: PSA 2016 ss.14(6) and 22(11).

80-009 **Items handed over for disposal** Such items may not be disposed of:

(a) before the end of the period within which an appeal may be made against the imposition of the requirement (ignoring any power to appeal out of time); or

(b) if such an appeal is made, before it is determined or otherwise dealt with: PSA 2016 s.22(5).

**Access prohibitions** An access prohibition may: 80-010

(a) prohibit access by all persons, or by all persons except those specified, or by all persons except those of a specified description;
(b) prohibit access at all times, or at all times except those specified;
(c) prohibit access in all circumstances, or in all circumstances except those specified;
(d) be made in respect of the whole or any part of the premises; or
(e) include provision about access to a part of the building or structure of which the premises form part: PSA 2016 s.22(8) and (9).

Specified means specified in the prohibition order: PSA 2016 s.22(10).

## Variation

**On application** The court may vary or discharge a prohibition order or a premises order on the application of: 80-011

(a) the person who applied for the order (if any);
(b) the person against whom the order was made; or
(c) any other person who is significantly adversely affected by the order: PSA 2016 s.28(1).

The court may vary or discharge the order on the application of:

(a) in the case of an order made in England and Wales, the chief officer of police for a police area or the chief constable of the British Transport Police Force;
(b) in the case of an order made in England and Wales or Northern Ireland, the Director General of the National Crime Agency; or
(c) in the case of an order made in England and Wales or Northern Ireland, the Secretary of State by whom general customs functions are exercisable: PSA 2016 s.28(2).

Where the order imposed an access condition and an application for the variation of the order is made by the person who applied for the order, or by a chief constable, the director of the NCA or the Secretary of State (see s.28(2)), before the expiry of the period for which the access prohibition has effect, the court may extend or further extend the access condition so long as it does not have effect for a period exceeding six months: PSA 2016 s.28(3)-(5).

**On conviction** Where a court is dealing with a person who has been convicted of: 80-012

(a) a relevant offence and against whom a prohibition order has previously been made; or
(b) an offence under s.26 of failing to comply with a prohibition order,

the court may vary the order: PSA 2016 s.29(1) and (2).

An order may not be varied except:

(a) in addition to a sentence imposed in respect of the offence concerned; or
(b) in addition to an order discharging the person conditionally or, in Scotland, discharging the person absolutely: PSA 2016 s.29(4).

**Appeals**

80-013 **Against orders** A person against whom a prohibition order is made on conviction for a relevant offence may appeal against the making of the order as if it were a sentence passed on the person for the offence referred to in s.19(1) (to the extent it would not otherwise be so appealable): PSA 2016 s.30(5).

80-014 **Against variations of orders made on conviction** A person against whom a prohibition order has been made may appeal against a variation of the order made on conviction as if the varied order were a sentence passed on the person for the offence referred to in s.29(1) (to the extent it would not otherwise be so appealable): PSA 2016 s.31(7).

80-015 **Against variations of orders made on application** A person against whom the order was made, or a person significantly affected by the order may appeal against the decision in relation to the variation/discharge of the order: PSA 2016 s.31(2).

A decision made by a youth court or magistrates' court may be appealed to the Crown Court; a decision made by the Crown Court may be appealed to the Court of Appeal, PSA 2016 s.31(1). The appeal must be made within 28 days from the date of the decision: PSA 2016 s.31(4).

On an appeal the court hearing the appeal may (to the extent it would not otherwise have power to do so) make such orders as may be necessary to give effect to its determination of the appeal, and may also make such incidental or consequential orders as appear to it to be just: PSA 2016 s.31(5).

**Breach of a prohibition order/access condition**

80-016 **Prohibition order: offence** A person against whom a prohibition order or a premises order is made commits an offence by failing to comply with the order: PSA 2016 s.26(1).

80-017 **Prohibition order: defence** A person does not commit an offence if:

(a) they took all reasonable steps to comply with the order; or
(b) there is some other reasonable excuse for the failure to comply: PSA 2016 s.26(3).

80-018 **Prohibition order: penalty** The maximum term of imprisonment upon summary conviction is 12 months (subject to the limit on magistrates' court sentencing powers): PSA 2016 s.26(2).

80-019 **Access condition: offences** A person, other than the person against whom the order was made, who without reasonable excuse remains on or enters premises in contravention of the access prohibition commits an offence: PSA 2016 s.27(2).

A person who without reasonable excuse obstructs an authorised person acting in relation to enforcement of an access condition (see s.23) commits an offence: PSA 2016 s.27(3).

**Access condition: penalty** A person guilty of an access condition offence may, on summary conviction, be sentenced to imprisonment not exceeding 51 weeks (subject to the limit on magistrates' courts sentencing powers) or a fine or both: PSA 2016 s.27(4). **80-020**

# RESTRAINING ORDERS

## Sentencing Code ss.359–364 and Protection from Harrassment Act 1997 s.5A

*References: Current Sentencing Practice A5; Archbold 19-357b*

### Post-conviction orders

**What is a restraining order?** A restraining order means an order made under s.360 against a person which prohibits the person from doing anything described in the order: SC s.359(1). **81-001**

**Availability** A restraining order is available where: **81-002**

(a) a court is dealing with an offender for an offence; and
(b) the court makes the order in addition to dealing with the offender for the offence: SC s.306(1) and (3).

This means that the court must impose another sentence (a primary order) for a restraining order to be available; a restraining order cannot be the sole disposal imposed.

A person who is unfit to plead but has been found to have done the act alleged may not be made subject to a restraining order; such a finding is neither a conviction nor an acquittal: *Chinegwundoh* [2015] EWCA Crim 109; [2015] 1 W.L.R. 2818; [2015] 1 Cr. App. R.(S.) 61.

**Contents of the order** The order may prohibit the defendant from doing anything described in the order: SC s.359(1). This can include, for instance, a requirement to notify the police of entry into a particular county 48 hours prior to doing so: *Conlon* [2017] EWCA Crim 2450; [2018] 1 Cr. App. R.(S.) 38 or even a prohibition from entering a town: *R* [2019] EWCA Crim 2238; [2020] 2 Cr. App. R.(S.) 3. **81-003**

**Test to apply** The order may only be made for the purpose of protecting the victim(s) of the offence, or any other person mentioned in the order, from conduct which amounts to harassment, or will cause fear of violence: SC s.306(2). This means that there must be an identifiable victim or identifiable person to be protected and this must be specified in the order. **81-004**

Harassing a person includes alarming the person or causing the person distress: SC s.364.

"*Conduct*" includes speech: PHA 1997 s.7(4).

**Considerations** A court should take into account the views of the person to be protected by such an order as to whether or not an order should be made. It could not be said that there would never be a case where it would be inappropriate to make a restraining order, even though the subject of the order did not seek one, but the **81-005**

views of the victim would clearly be relevant. Nor could it be said that a court must have direct evidence of the views of the victim. That might prove impossible. The court might be able to draw a proper inference as to those views, or may conclude that a restraining order should be made whatever the views of the victim, although clearly, if a victim did not want an order to be made because she wanted to have contact with the defendant, that might make such an order impractical. In normal circumstances, the views of the victim should be obtained. It was the responsibility of the prosecution to ensure that the necessary enquiries were made: *Khellaf* [2016] EWCA Crim 1297; [2017] 1 Cr. App. R.(S.) 1.

81-006 **Evidence** Both the prosecution and the defence may lead, as further evidence, any evidence that would be admissible in proceedings for an injunction under s.3 of the 1997 Act: SC s.362.

81-007 **Length of the order** The order may be for a specified period or until further order: SC s.359(2).

81-008 **Wording of the order** As with all other behaviour/preventive orders, the wording of the order must be specific, clear, and capable of being understood.

81-009 **Varying or discharging the order** The prosecutor, the defendant or any other person mentioned in the order may apply to the court which made the order for it to be varied or discharged by a further order. Any person mentioned in the order is entitled to be heard on the hearing of an application to vary or discharge the order: SC s.361(1).

Any person mentioned in the order is entitled to be heard on the hearing of an application to vary the order: SC s.361(2).

There is no hard-edged requirement for a complainant to prove there had been a change of circumstances since the restraining order was made on a first application to vary an order and it should remain open to a complainant who considered at the sentencing stage the court had underestimated the necessary duration or other terms of a restraining order to ask the court to revisit the matter: *Jackson* [2021] EWCA Crim 901; [2021] 4 W.L.R. 93; [2022] 1 Cr. App. R.(S.) 21.

**Breach**

81-010 A breach of an order, without reasonable excuse, is punishable with imprisonment not exceeding five years, or a fine or both: SC s.363(1) and (2).

**Orders made following an acquittal**

81-011 **Availability** A court may make a restraining order following an acquittal: Protection from Harassment Act 1997 (PHA 1997) s.5A(1).

A person who is unfit to plead but has been found to have done the act alleged may not be made subject to a restraining order; such a finding is neither a conviction nor an acquittal: *Chinegwundoh* [2015] EWCA Crim 109; [2015] 1 Cr. App. R. (S.) 61.

81-012 **Test to apply** An order may be made where the court considers it necessary to protect a person from harassment by the defendant: PHA 1997 s.5A(1).

It is necessary to find that the defendant is likely to pursue a course of conduct which amounts to harassment within the meaning of s.1 of the PHA 1997. Pursuit of a course of conduct requires intention: *Smith* [2012] EWCA Crim 2566; [2013] 1 W.L.R. 1399; [2013] 2 Cr. App. R.(S.) 28.

Harassing a person includes alarming the person or causing the person distress: SC s.364.

"*Conduct*" includes speech: SC s.364.

A "*course of conduct*" must involve at least two occasions in relation to a single person, and at least once each, in relation two or more persons: PHA 1997 s.7(3).

A restraining order on acquittal does not require proof that the substantive offence had occurred; it required only that the court considers it necessary to make an order "to protect a person from harassment by the defendant". The test does not directly concern the nature of the subjective fears of the person or persons, whom the proposed restraining order is to protect, or require proof of actual fear of harassment on their part, rather, it required the court on the evidence to consider the restraining order necessary for their protection: *Oshosanya* [2022] EWCA Crim 1794; [2023] 1 Cr. App. R. (S.) 34.

**Evidence** Both the prosecution and the defence may lead, as further evidence, any evidence that would be admissible in proceedings for an injunction under s.3 of the Act: PHA 1997 s.5A(2). **81-013**

**Procedure** The question of consenting to an order should and could only properly arise after notice of an intention to make an application which identified the evidence upon which the prosecution contends that a restraining order is necessary, in compliance with the Crim PR, had been served. An expression of consent before then could only be a consent in principle and did not obviate the need for the evidence upon which the Crown intends to rely to be identified: *McCarren* [2023] EWCA Crim 1233; [2024] 1 Cr. App. R. (S.) 27. **81-014**

**Length of the order** The order may be for a specified period or until further order: PHA 1997 s.5A(2). **81-015**

**Wording of the order** As with all other behaviour/preventive orders, the wording of the order must be specific, clear, and capable of being understood. **81-016**

**Varying or discharging the order** The prosecutor, the defendant or any other person mentioned in the order may apply to the court which made the order for it to be varied or discharged by a further order. Any person mentioned in the order is entitled to be heard on the hearing of an application to vary or discharge the order: PHA 1997 s.5A(2). **81-017**

Any person mentioned in the order is entitled to be heard on the hearing of an application to vary the order: PHA 1997 s.5A(2).

There is no hard-edged requirement for a complainant to prove there had been a change of circumstances since the restraining order was made on a first application to vary an order and it should remain open to a complainant who considered at the sentencing stage the court had underestimated the necessary duration or other terms of a restraining order to ask the court to revisit the matter: *Jackson* [2021] EWCA Crim 901; [2022] 1 Cr. App. R.(S.) 21.

81-018 **Appeals** Where the Court of Appeal quashes a conviction, it may remit the case to the Crown Court to consider whether to make a restraining order: PHA 1997 s.5A(3).

Where the Crown Court allows an appeal against a conviction in the magistrates' court, the Crown Court may make a restraining order: PHA 1997 s.5A(4).

A person made subject to a restraining order on acquittal has the same right of appeal as if they had been convicted of an offence and the order had been made under the Sentencing Code: PHA 1997 s.5A(5).

**Breach**

81-019 A breach of an order under s.5A of the PHA 1997 is punishable with imprisonment not exceeding five years, or a fine or both: PHA 1997 s.5A(2).

No offence is committed if the act of doing something prohibited under the order was done with a reasonable excuse: PHA 1997 s.5A(2).

# SERIOUS CRIME PREVENTION ORDERS

## Serious Crime Prevention Order Act 2007 ss.1–43

*References: Current Sentencing Practice A5; Archbold 5A-987*

### Availability

**General** A serious crime prevention order (SCPO) is available: **82-001**

(a) for an offence committed on or after 6 April 2008;
(b) for an offence committed before 6 April 2008, where the conviction and sentence occur after that date.

However, an SCPO is not available where the conviction occurs before 6 April 2008 but where the sentence is imposed after that date: SCA 2007 Sch.13 para.2.

An order may be made only in addition to the sentence is respect of the offence concerned, or in addition to a conditional discharge or absolute discharge: SCA 2007 s.19(7).

An SCPO may be made against an individual, a body corporate, a partnership or an unincorporated association: SCA 2007 s.5.

Given the international reach and cross-border nature of serious crime, it would be surprising if Parliament did not intend the SCPO regime to extend to conduct abroad: *Juul v Chief Constable of Dyfed-Powys Police* [2024] EWHC 193 (Admin); [2024] 4 W.L.R. 16.

**Offences** An SCPO is available for a "*serious offence*", that is one specified in **82-002** SCA 2007 Sch.1.

Additionally, the court may treat any offence as if it were a specified offence if it considers the offence to be "*sufficiently serious*" to be treated as if it were a specified offence: SCA 2007 s.2(2)(b).

**Timing** The Serious Crime Act 2007 does not create a jurisdictional time limit **82-003** for the making of an application for a serious crime prevention order and therefore the fact that a court has concluded sentencing (and confiscation proceedings) does not render it functus officio in relation to the making of a serious crime prevention order.

However, Crim PR rr.31.1 and 31.11 require that applications are made "*as soon as practicable*" (albeit that the court may extend time). When considering such an issue, the court will consider any prejudice to the defendant: *Adams* [2021] EWCA Crim 1525; [2022] 1 W.L.R. 1736; [2022] 2 Cr. App. R.(S.) 3.

### The hearing

**Application** An SCPO may be made only on an application by the Director of **82-004** Public Prosecutions, the Director of Revenue and Customs prosecutions, or the

Director of the Serious Fraud Office: SCA 2007 s.8. A Chief Officer of Police may make an application for an SCPO in a case which is terrorism related: SCA 2007 s.8 and 8A.

82-005 **Right of others to be heard** The Crown Court must give an opportunity to a person other than the offender to make representations, if that person applies to do so, if it considers that the making of an SCPO would be likely to have a significant adverse effect on that person: SCA 2007 s.9(4).

82-006 **Nature of the proceedings** Proceedings in the Crown Court in relation to serious crime prevention orders are civil proceedings and the standard of proof to be applied is the civil standard of proof. The court is not restricted to considering evidence that would have been admissible in the criminal proceedings in which the person concerned was convicted and may adjourn any proceedings in relation to an SCPO even after sentencing the person concerned.

82-007 **Extent of the order** An SCPO is binding on a person only if they are present or represented at the proceedings at which the order is made, or a notice setting out the terms of the order has been served on them: SCA 2007 s.9(4).

### Making the order

82-008 **Power** The Crown Court may make an SCPO where person aged 18 or over is convicted of a "*serious offence*" or has been convicted of a "*serious offence*" by a magistrates' court and committed to the Crown Court to be dealt with for the offence: SCA 2007 s.19(1).

82-009 **Test to apply** The court may make an order where it has reasonable grounds to believe that the order would protect the public by preventing, restricting or disrupting involvement by the person in serious crime in England and Wales: SCA 2007 s.19(2).

### Contents of the order

82-010 **Prohibitions and requirements** The order may contain such prohibitions, restrictions or requirements as the court considers appropriate for protecting the public by preventing, restricting or disrupting involvement by the person concerned in serious crime: SCA 2007 s.19(5).

Examples of prohibitions, restrictions or requirements that may be imposed on individuals include prohibitions or restrictions on, or requirements in relation to:

(a) an individual's financial, property or business dealings or holdings;
(b) an individual's working arrangements;
(c) the means by which an individual communicates or associates with others, or the persons with whom they communicate or associate;
(d) the premises to which an individual has access;
(e) the use of any premises or item by an individual; and
(f) an individual's travel (whether within the UK, between the UK and other places or otherwise): SCA 2007 s.5(3).

82-011 **Financial reporting orders** The power to make a financial reporting order was repealed in 2015 and consolidated into the SCPO.

**Must specify start-date** An SCPO must specify when it is to come into force and when it is to cease to be in force: SCA 2007 s.16(1). **82-012**

**Length of the order** An order may not be in force for more than five years beginning with the date on which it comes into force. Different provisions of the order may come into force or cease to be in force on different dates: SCA 2007 s.16(2) and (3). **82-013**

## Effect of an order

An SCPO may not require a person to answer questions or provide information orally or to answer any privileged question, or provide any privileged information or documents. An order may not require a person to produce any excluded material (Police and Criminal Evidence Act 1984 s.11). An order may not require a person to produce information or documents in respect of which they owe an obligation of confidence by virtue of carrying on a banking business unless the person to whom the obligation of confidence is owed consents to the disclosure or production or the order contains a requirement to disclose information or produce documents of this kind. An order may not require a person to answer any question, provide any information or produce any document if the disclosure concerned is prohibited under any other enactment: SCA 2007 ss.11-14. **82-014**

## Varying orders

**Upon conviction** Where a person, subject to an SCPO: **82-015**

(a) has been convicted by or before a magistrates' court of having committed a serious offence in England and Wales and has been committed to the Crown Court to be dealt with; or
(b) has been convicted by or before the Crown Court of having committed a serious offence in England and Wales, the Crown Court may vary the order if the court has reasonable grounds to believe that the terms of the order as varied would protect the public by preventing, restricting or disrupting involvement by the person in serious crime in England and Wales, in addition to dealing with the person in relation to the offence: SCA 2007 s.20(1) and (2).

A variation on conviction may only be made in addition to a sentence or imposition of a discharge: SCA 2007 s.20(6).

**Upon breach** Where a person: **82-016**

(a) has been convicted by or before a magistrates' court of having committed an offence under SCA 2007 s.25 in relation to an SCPO and has been committed to the Crown Court to be dealt with; or
(b) has been convicted by or before the Crown Court of having committed an offence under s.25 in relation to an SCPO, the court may, in addition to imposing a sentence or a discharge in respect of the breach, vary or replace the order if it has reasonable grounds to believe that the terms of the order as varied, or the new order, would protect the public by preventing, restricting or disrupting involvement by the person in serious crime in England and Wales: SCA 2007 s.21(1) and (2).

The Crown Court may vary an SCPO which has been made by the High Court: SCA 2007 s.22(1).

### Extending orders where person charged with serious offence/breach

**82-017** Where a person is charged with a serious offence or an offence of breaching an SCPO, the authority may apply to the court to vary the order until:

(a) following the conviction for the offence, the order is varied or a new order imposed;
(b) the person is acquitted;
(c) the charge is withdrawn; or
(d) the proceedings are discontinued: SCA 2007 s.22E(4).

### Appeals

**82-018** **Right to appeal** A person who is subject to an SCPO, or an authority who has applied for an order, may appeal to the Court of Appeal in relation to a decision in relation to an SCPO. A person who has been given the opportunity to make representations in respect of an order may also appeal to the Court of Appeal: SCA 2007 Sch.1.

SCH.1

**Drug trafficking**

1(1) An offence under any of the following provisions of the Misuse of Drugs Act 1971— **82-019**

(a) section 4(2) or (3) (unlawful production or supply of controlled drugs);
(b) section 5(3) (possession of controlled drug with intent to supply);
(ba) section 6 (restriction of cultivation of cannabis plant);
(c) section 8 (permitting etc. certain activities relating to controlled drugs);
(d) section 20 (assisting in or inducing the commission outside the United Kingdom of an offence punishable under a corresponding law).

(2) An offence under any of the following provisions of the Customs and Excise Management Act 1979 if it is committed in connection with a prohibition or restriction on importation or exportation which has effect by virtue of section 3 of the Misuse of Drugs Act 1971—

(a) section 50(2) or (3) (improper importation of goods);
(b) section 68(2) (exportation of prohibited or restricted goods);
(c) section 170 (fraudulent evasion of duty etc.).

(3) An offence under either of the following provisions of the Criminal Justice (International Co-operation) Act 1990—

(a) section 12 (manufacture or supply of a substance for the time being specified in Schedule 2 to that Act);
(b) section 19 (using a ship for illicit traffic in controlled drugs).

**Psychoactive substances**

(1ZA) An offence under any of the following provisions of the Psychoactive Substances Act 2016—

(a) section 4 (producing a psychoactive substance);
(b) section 5 (supplying, or offering to supply, a psychoactive substance);
(c) section 7 (possession of psychoactive substance with intent to supply);
(d) section 8 (importing or exporting a psychoactive substance).

**Slavery etc.**

(1A) An offence under section 1 of the Modern Slavery Act 2015 (slavery, servitude and forced or compulsory labour).

**People trafficking**

2(1) An offence under section 25, 25A or 25B of the Immigration Act 1971 (assisting unlawful immigration etc.).

(2) An offence under any of sections 57 to 59A of the Sexual Offences Act 2003 (trafficking for sexual exploitation).

(3) An offence under section 4 of the Asylum and Immigration (Treatment of Claimants, etc.) Act 2004 (c. 19) (trafficking people for exploitation).

**Terrorism**

2A An offence for the time being listed in section 41(1) of the Counter Terrorism Act 2008 (offences to which Part 4 of that Act applies: terrorism offences).

**Firearms offences**

3(1) An offence under any of the following provisions of the Firearms Act 1968—
  (a) section 1(1) (possession etc of firearms or ammunition without certificate);
  (b) section 2(1) (possession etc of shot gun without certificate);
  (c) section 3(1) (dealing etc in firearms or ammunition by way of trade or business without being registered);
  (d) section 5(1), (1A) or (2A) (possession, manufacture etc of prohibited weapons).
(2) An offence under either of the following provisions of the Customs and Excise Management Act 1979 if it is committed in connection with a firearm or ammunition—
  (a) section 68(2) (exportation of prohibited or restricted goods);
  (b) section 170 (fraudulent evasion of duty etc).
(3) (1) In sub-paragraph (2) "firearm" and "ammunition" have the same meanings as in section 57 of the Firearms Act 1968.

**Prostitution and child sex**

4(1) An offence under section 33A of the Sexual Offences Act 1956 (c. 69) (keeping a brothel used for prostitution).
(2) An offence under any of the following provisions of the Sexual Offences Act 2003—
  (a) section 14 (arranging or facilitating commission of a child sex offence);
  (b) section 48 (causing or inciting sexual exploitation of a child);
  (c) section 49 controlling a child in relation to sexual exploitation;
  (d) section 50 (arranging or facilitating sexual exploitation of a child);
  (e) section 52 (causing or inciting prostitution for gain);
  (f) section 53 (controlling prostitution for gain).

**Armed robbery etc.**

5(1) An offence under section 8(1) of the Theft Act 1968 (c. 60) (robbery) where the use or threat of force involves a firearm, an imitation firearm or an offensive weapon.
(2) An offence at common law of an assault with intent to rob where the assault involves a firearm, imitation firearm or an offensive weapon.
(3) In this paragraph—firearm has the meaning given by section 57(1) of the Firearms Act 1968; imitation firearm has the meaning given by section 57(4) of that Act; offensive weapon means any weapon to which section 141 of the Criminal Justice Act 1988 (offensive weapons) applies.

**Money laundering**

6 An offence under any of the following provisions of the Proceeds of Crime Act 2002—
- (a) section 327 (concealing etc. criminal property);
- (b) section 328 (facilitating the acquisition etc. of criminal property by or on behalf of another);
- (c) section 329 (acquisition, use and possession of criminal property).

**Fraud**

7(1) An offence under section 17 of the Theft Act 1968 (false accounting).
(2) An offence under any of the following provisions of the Fraud Act 2006—
- (a) section 1 (fraud by false representation, failing to disclose information or abuse of position);
- (b) section 6 (possession etc. of articles for use in frauds);
- (c) section 7 (making or supplying articles for use in frauds);
- (d) section 9 (participating in fraudulent business carried on by sole trader etc.);
- (e) section 11 (obtaining services dishonestly).

(3) An offence at common law of conspiracy to defraud.

**Offences in relation to public revenue**

8(1) An offence under section 170 of the Customs and Excise Management Act 1979 (fraudulent evasion of duty etc.) so far as not falling within paragraph 1(2)(c) or 3(1)(b) above.
(2) An offence under section 72 of the Value Added Tax Act 1994 (fraudulent evasion of VAT etc.).
(3) An offence under section 106A of the Taxes Management Act 1970 (fraudulent evasion of income tax).
(4) An offence under section 35 of the Tax Credits Act 2002 (tax credit fraud).
(5) An offence at common law of cheating in relation to the public revenue.

**Bribery**

9 An offence under any of the following provisions of the Bribery Act 2010—
- (a) section 1 (offences of bribing another person);
- (b) section 2 (offences relating to being bribed);
- (c) section 6 (bribery of foreign public officials).

**Counterfeiting**

10 An offence under any of the following provisions of the Forgery and Counterfeiting Act 1981—
- (a) section 14 (making counterfeit notes or coins);
- (b) section 15 (passing etc. counterfeit notes or coins);
- (c) section 16 (having custody or control of counterfeit notes or coins);
- (d) section 17 (making or having custody or control of counterfeiting materials or implements).

11(1) An offence under section 21 of the Theft Act 1968 (blackmail).

(2) An offence under section 12(1) or (2) of the Gangmasters (Licensing) Act 2004 (acting as a gangmaster other than under the authority of a licence, possession of false documents, etc.).

**Computer misuse**

11A An offence under any of the following provisions of the Computer Misuse Act 1990—
- (a) section 1 (unauthorised access to computer material);
- (b) section 2 (unauthorised access with intent to commit or facilitate commission of further offences);
- (c) section 3 (unauthorised acts with intent to impair, or with recklessness as to impairing, operation of computer etc);
- (d) section 3ZA (unauthorised acts causing, or creating risk of, serious damage to human welfare etc);
- (e) section 3A (making, supplying or obtaining articles for use in offence under section 1, 3 or 3ZA).

**Intellectual property**

12(1) An offence under any of the following provisions of the Copyright, Designs and Patents Act 1988—
- (a) section 107(1)(a), (b), (d)(iv) or (e) (making, importing or distributing an article which infringes copyright);
- (b) section 198(1)(a), (b) or (d)(iii) (making, importing or distributing an illicit recording);
- (c) section 297A (making or dealing etc. in unauthorised decoders).
- (2) An offence under section 92(1), (2) or (3) of the Trade Marks Act 1994 (unauthorised use of trade mark etc.).

**Environment**

13(1) An offence under section 1 of the Salmon and Freshwater Fisheries Act 1975 (fishing … with prohibited implements etc.).

(2) An offence under section 14 of the Wildlife and Countryside Act 1981 (introduction of new species etc.).

(3) An offence under section 33 of the Environmental Protection Act 1990 (prohibition on unauthorised or harmful deposit, treatment or disposal etc. of waste).

(4) An offence under paragraph 1(2) of Schedule 1 to the Control of Trade in Endangered Species Regulations 2018 (S.I. 2018/703).

(5) An offence under paragraph 2 of that Schedule which consists of the conduct specified in the table in that paragraph as the subject matter of Article 16(1)(c) or (d) of Council Regulation (EC) No 338/97 on the protection of species of wild fauna and flora by regulating trade therein.

**Organised crime**

13A An offence under section 45 of the Serious Crime Act 2015 (participating in activities of organised crime group).

**Sanctions legislation**

13B(1) An offence under an instrument made under section 2(2) of the European Communities Act 1972 for the purpose of implementing, or otherwise in relation to, EU obligations created or arising by or under an EU financial sanctions Regulation.

(2) An offence under an Act or under subordinate legislation where the offence was created for the purpose of implementing a UN financial sanctions Resolution.

(3) An offence under paragraph 7 of Schedule 3 to the Anti-terrorism, Crime and Security Act 2001 (freezing orders).

(4) An offence under paragraph 30 or 30A of Schedule 7 to the Counter-Terrorism Act 2008 where the offence relates to a requirement of the kind mentioned in paragraph 13 of that Schedule.

(5) An offence under paragraph 31 of Schedule 7 to the Counter-Terrorism Act 2008.

(5A) An offence under regulations made under section 1 of the Sanctions and Anti-Money Laundering Act 2018.

(6) In this paragraph—

*"EU financial sanctions Regulation"* and "UN financial sanctions Resolution" have the same meanings as in Part 8 of the Policing and Crime Act 2017 (see section 143 of that Act);

*"subordinate legislation"* has the same meaning as in the Interpretation Act 1978.

**Inchoate offences**

14(1) An offence of attempting or conspiring the commission of an offence specified or described in this Part of this Schedule.

(2) An offence under Part 2 of this Act (encouraging or assisting) where the offence (or one of the offences) which the person in question intends or believes would be committed is an offence specified or described in this Part of this Schedule.

(3) An offence of aiding, abetting, counselling or procuring the commission of an offence specified or described in this Part of this Schedule.

(4) The references in sub-paragraphs (1) to (3) to offences specified or described in this Part of this Schedule do not include the offence at common law of conspiracy to defraud.

**Earlier offences**

15(1) This Part of this Schedule (apart from paragraph 14(2)) has effect, in its application to conduct before the passing of this Act, as if the offences specified or described in this Part included any corresponding offences under the law in force at the time of the conduct.

(2) Paragraph 14(2) has effect, in its application to conduct before the passing of this Act or before the coming into force of section 59 of this Act, as if the offence specified or described in that provision were an offence of inciting the commission of an offence specified or described in this Part of this Schedule.

## Scope of offences

16 Where this Part of this Schedule refers to offences which are offences under the law of England and Wales and another country, the reference is to be read as limited to the offences so far as they are offences under the law of England and Wales.

*Note: The court may treat any other offence as if it were a specified offence if it considers the offence to be sufficiently serious to be treated as if it were a specified offence, SCA 2007 s.2(2)(b).*

# SERIOUS DISRUPTION PREVENTION ORDER

## Public Order Act 2023 ss.20–33

*References: Archbold 5A-1029a*

### Availability

A serious disruption prevention order is available where: **82A-001**

(a) a person aged 18 or over ("P") is convicted of an offence ("the current offence") which was committed on or after 5 April 2024; and
(b) the prosecution applies for a serious disruption prevention order to be made in respect of P: s.20(1), POA 2023.

The court may make a serious disruption prevention order in respect of P only if it is made in addition to:

(a) a sentence imposed in respect of the current offence; or
(b) an order discharging P conditionally: s.20(7).

### Test to apply

**The test** The court may be a serious disruption prevention order where: **82A-002**

(a) the court is satisfied on the balance of probabilities that the current offence is a protest-related offence;
(b) the condition in subs.(3) is met; and
(c) the court considers it necessary to make the order for a purpose mentioned in subs.(5).

**Protest related offence** A "protest-related offence" means an offence which is directly related to a protest: POA 2023, s.32. **82A-003**

**Condition in subsection (3)** The condition in s.20(3) is that the court is satisfied on the balance of probabilities that: **82A-004**

(a) within the relevant period,[1] P has:
  (i) committed another protest-related offence for which P was convicted; or
  (ii) committed a protest-related breach of an injunction for which P was found in contempt of court.
(b) the current offence and P's conduct mentioned in paragraph (a):
  (i) relate to different protests; or
  (ii) took place on different days, and

---

[1] "the relevant period" means the period of five years ending with the day on which P is convicted of the current offence; but P's conduct may be taken into account for the purposes of this section only if it took place:
(a) on or after the day on which this section comes into force; and
(b) when P was aged 16 or over: s.20(4).

(c) P's conduct mentioned in paragraph (a) has not been taken into account when making any previous serious disruption prevention order in respect of P.

82A-005 **Protest related breach** A "protest-related breach", in relation to an injunction, means a breach which is directly related to a protest: POA 2023, s.32.

82A-006 **The purposes** The purposes listed in s.20(5) are:

(a) to prevent P from committing a protest-related offence or a protest-related breach of an injunction;
(b) to prevent P from carrying out activities related to a protest that result in, or are likely to result in, serious disruption to two or more individuals, or to an organisation, in England and Wales;
(c) to prevent P from causing or contributing to:
  (i) the commission by any other person of a protest-related offence or a protest-related breach of an injunction; or
  (ii) the carrying out by any other person of activities related to a protest that result in, or are likely to result in, serious disruption to two or more individuals, or to an organisation, in England and Wales.
(d) to protect two or more individuals, or an organisation, in England and Wales from the risk of serious disruption arising from:
  (i) a protest-related offence;
  (ii) a protest-related breach of an injunction; or
  (iii) activities related to a protest.

**Making the order**

82A-007 **Evidence** For the purpose of deciding whether to make a serious disruption prevention order the court may consider evidence led by the prosecution or P: s.20(8).

It does not matter whether the evidence would have been admissible in the proceedings for the current offence: s.20(9)

82A-008 **When to make the order** The court may adjourn any proceedings on an application for a serious disruption prevention order even after sentencing P: s.20(10).

82A-009 **Explanation of the order** On making a serious disruption prevention order the court must in ordinary language explain to P the effects of the order: s.20(14).

82A-010 **Contents** A serious disruption prevention order made in respect of a person must specify:

(a) the reasons for making the order; and
(b) the penalties which may be imposed on the person for breaching the order: s.26.

**Contents of orders**

82A-011 **General** A serious disruption prevention order under this section is an order which, for a purpose mentioned in subs.(5) (see above):

(a) requires P to do anything described in the order;
(b) prohibits P from doing anything described in the order: s.20(6).

A serious disruption prevention order may specify periods for which particular requirements or prohibitions have effect: s.25(5).

**Prohibitions/Requirements** The only requirements and prohibitions that may be imposed on a person by a serious disruption prevention order are those which the court making the order thinks are necessary for a purpose mentioned in s.20(5) (see above): s.22(1). **82A-012**

The requirements imposed on a person ("P") by a serious disruption prevention order may, in particular, have the effect of requiring P:

(a) to present themselves to a particular person at a particular place at, or between, particular times on particular days;
(b) to remain at a particular place for particular periods: s.22(2).

The prohibitions imposed on a person ("P") by a serious disruption prevention order may, in particular, have the effect of prohibiting P from:

(a) being in or entering a particular place or area;
(b) being in or entering a particular place or area between particular times on particular days;
(c) being in or entering a particular place or area between particular times on any day;
(d) being with particular persons;
(e) participating in particular activities;
(f) having particular articles with them;
(g) using the internet to facilitate or encourage persons to:
    (i) commit a protest-related offence or a protest-related breach of an injunction, or
    (ii) carry out activities related to a protest that result in, or are likely to result in, serious disruption to two or more individuals, or to an organisation, in England and Wales: s.22(4).

A serious disruption prevention order which imposes prohibitions on a person may include exceptions from those prohibitions: s.22(6).

The requirements or prohibitions which are imposed on a person by a serious disruption prevention order must, so far as practicable, be such as to avoid:

(a) any conflict with the person's religious beliefs; and
(b) any interference with the times, if any, at which the person normally works or attends any educational establishment: s.22(8).

A serious disruption prevention order which imposes on a person ("P") a requirement, other than a notification requirement under s.24, must specify a person who is to be responsible for supervising compliance with the requirement. That person may be an individual or an organisation: s.23(1) and (2).

Before including such a requirement, the court must receive evidence about its suitability and enforceability from:

(a) the individual to be specified, if an individual is to be specified;

(b) an individual representing the organisation to be specified, if an organisation is to be specified: s.23(3).

Before including two or more such requirements, the court must consider their compatibility with each other: s.23(4).

82A-013 **Duty upon person subject to the order** Where a person subject to an order ('P') is subject to a requirement in a serious disruption prevention order, other than a notification requirement under s.24, P must:

(a) keep in touch with the person specified under s.23(1) in relation to that requirement, in accordance with any instructions given by that person from time to time; and
(b) notify that person of any change of P's home address: s.23(7).

Those obligations have effect as if they were requirements imposed on P by the order: s.23(8).

82A-014 **Notification** Section 24 makes provision for notification requirements.

82A-015 **Length of the order** A serious disruption prevention order must specify the period for which it has effect, which must be a fixed period of not less than one week and not more than two years: s.25(2).

The order takes effect upon the day on which it is made: s.25(1), however the order may make provision that it is not to take effect until an offender is released from custody (remand or a sentence) or ceases to be on licence: s.25(3) and (4).

82A-016 **Variation, renewal and discharge** Section 28 makes provision for the variation, renewal and discharge of orders.

82A-017 **Appeals** Section 29 makes provision for appeals against orders.

82A-018 **Breach/failure to comply** Where a serious disruption prevention order has effect in respect of a person ("P"), P commits an offence if P:

(a) fails without reasonable excuse to do anything P is required to do by the order;
(b) without reasonable excuse does anything P is prohibited from doing by the order; or
(c) notifies to the police, in purported compliance with the order, any information which P knows to be false: s.27(1).

The maximum penalty is that which applies to summary offences: s.27(2).

# SEXUAL HARM PREVENTION ORDERS

## SENTENCING CODE ss.343–358

*References: Current Sentencing Practice A5; Archbold 272*

### Post-conviction orders

This section deals only with the power to make an order on conviction. For powers to make an order on application or following a finding under the Criminal Procedure (Insanity) Act 1964, see the SOA 2003 ss.103A-K. **83-001**

### What is an SHPO?

A "*sexual harm prevention order*" means an order under this Chapter made in respect of an offender which prohibits the offender from doing anything described in the order: SC s.343. **83-002**

### Differences with previous (SOPO) regime

Note that by contrast to the SOPO regime, the SHPO regime employs a lower test for imposition and defines a child as a person under 18, not under 16: see *Parsons Morgan* [2017] EWCA Crim 2163; [2018] 1 W.L.R. 2409; [2018] 1 Cr. App. R.(S.) 43 for details. **83-003**

### Making the order

**Availability** A court may make an order where it deals with the defendant in respect of: **83-004**

- (a) an offence listed in the SOA 2003 Sch.3 or 5;
- (b) a finding that the defendant is not guilty of an offence listed in Sch.3 or 5 by reason of insanity; or
- (c) a finding that the defendant is under a disability and has done the act charged against them in respect of an offence listed in Sch.3 or 5: SC s.345(1).

Schedule 3 to the SOA 2003 is to be read as though any condition subject to which an offence is so listed that relates:

- (a) to the way in which the defendant is dealt with in respect of an offence so listed or a relevant finding (as defined by the SOA 2003 s.132(9)); or
- (b) to the age of any person,

is omitted: SC s.345(2).

**Test** Where an SHPO is available to a court, the court may make such an order only if satisfied that it is necessary to do so for the purpose of: **83-005**

- (a) protecting the public or any particular members of the public from sexual harm from the offender; or
- (b) protecting children or vulnerable adults generally, or any particular children

or vulnerable adults, from sexual harm from the offender outside the UK: SC s.346.

"*Sexual harm*" from a person means physical or psychological harm caused:

(a) by the person committing one or more offences listed in Sch.3 to the SOA 2003 (sexual offences for the purposes of Pt 2 of that Act); or
(b) (in the context of harm outside the UK) by the person doing, outside the UK, anything which would constitute an offence listed in that schedule if done in any part of the UK: SC s.344(1).

Where an offence listed in Sch.3 to the SOA 2003 is listed subject to a condition that relates:

(a) to the way in which the offender is dealt with in respect of an offence so listed; or
(b) to the age of any person,

that condition is to be disregarded in determining for the purposes of subs.(1) whether the offence is listed in that schedule: SC s.344(2).

Where, on an application for an SHPO, there was doubt as to whether an offence had been sexually motivated, the court had to determine whether it could be satisfied that it was necessary to make an SHPO for the purposes of protecting the public or any particular members of the public from sexual harm from the offender, conducting a *Newton*-type hearing if necessary: *AB* [2019] EWCA Crim 2480; [2020] 1 Cr. App. R.(S.) 67.

The focus of the test is on the harm risked by the offender committing a Sch.3 offence (or if outside the UK, would fall within Sch.3): *Davidoff* [2022] EWCA Crim 1253; [2023] 1 Cr. App. R. (S.) 22.

83-006 **Defendant subject to earlier order** Where a court makes an SHPO in relation to an offender who is already subject to:

(a) an SHPO; or
(b) an order under s.103A of the SOA 2003 (SHPOs under that Act),

the earlier order ceases to have effect: SC s.349(1).

Where a court makes an SHPO in relation to an offender who is already subject to:

(a) a sexual offences prevention order under s.104 of the SOA 2003; or
(b) a foreign travel order under s.114 of that Act,

the earlier order ceases to have effect (whichever part of the UK it was made in) unless the court orders otherwise: SC s.349(2).

83-007 **Offender under 18** See s.8(1)(b) of the CDA 1998 for powers of a court to make a parenting order under that Act in a case where it makes an SHPO in respect of an offender aged under 18.

## Contents of the order

**Prohibitions** An SHPO prohibits the defendant from doing anything described in the order: SC s.343. **83-008**

An SHPO must specify:

(a) the prohibitions included in the order; and
(b) for each prohibition, the period for which it is to have effect (the "prohibition period"): SC s.347(1).

Any conflict between the SHPO and condition upon release on licence should be avoided: *McLellan; Bingley* [2017] EWCA Crim 1464; [2018] 1 W.L.R. 2969; [2018] 1 Cr. App. R.(S.) 18. Nor should there be a conflict with the notification regime: *Sokolowski* [2017] EWCA Crim 1903; [2018] 4 W.L.R. 126; [2018] 1 Cr. App. R.(S.) 30.

As to the contents of prohibitions, including issues concerning blanket bans on internet usage, age, risk management software, cloud storage and encryption, see *Parsons Morgan* [2017] EWCA Crim 2163; [2018] 1 Cr. App. R.(S.) 43.

Prohibitions should be proportionate and necessary in the individual case. It is insufficient for the prosecution to assert that the prohibitions are necessary on a "safety first" approach: *Sokolowski* [2017] EWCA Crim 1903; [2018] 1 Cr. App. R.(S.) 30.

An SHPO may only be made to protect *people* and so, an order may not properly contain terms which restricts or prohibits an offender's contact with animals: *Kish* [2022] EWCA Crim 1161; [2023] 1 W.L.R. 2407.

A polygraph requirement, if properly considered and drafted, would not breach arts 6 or 8 of the ECHR: *David* [2023] EWCA Crim 1561; [2024] 1 Cr. App. R. (S.) 44. The court underlined the fact that it was incumbent upon a sentencing judge to address expressly the requirements of s.343 of the Sentencing Act 2020, and also to give reasons as to why such an order is necessary for the specified purposes and why it was proportionate and sufficiently clear.

**Evidence** There is no requirement that there had always to be "evidence" before the judge to demonstrate the need for a given restriction before it could be included in a SHPO. A sound basis for concluding that a restriction was necessary might derive from assertions of fact made by the prosecution coupled with a guilty plea, or some further admissions or submissions made by or on behalf of the defendant, or from an inference drawn by the judge from facts that had been conceded or proved: *Lea* [2021] EWCA Crim 65; [2021] 4 W.L.R. 3. **83-009**

**Length of prohibitions** The prohibition period must be for a fixed period of not less than five years or for an indefinite period. The order may specify that some of its prohibitions have effect until further order and some for a fixed period. Different periods for different prohibitions may be specified: SC s.347(2) and (3). The period of the order must be clearly identified (and thus, an order which had purported to run from the appellant's release from custody was insufficiently certain as it was unclear from when it would begin): *Pearson* [2021] EWCA Crim 784. **83-010**

83-011 **Test for prohibitions** The only prohibitions that may be included in an SHPO are those necessary for the purpose of:

(a) protecting the public or any particular members of the public from sexual harm from the offender; or
(b) protecting children or vulnerable adults generally, or any particular children or vulnerable adults, from sexual harm from the offender outside the UK: SC s.343(2).

Prohibitions which merely replicate the barring scheme should be avoided: *Begg* [2019] EWCA Crim 1578; [2020] 1 Cr. App. R.(S.) 30.

83-012 **Foreign travel prohibition** A prohibition on foreign travel contained in an order must be for a fixed period of not more than five years: SC s.348(1). The order may be extended for a further period (of no more than five years each time): SC s.348(2).

A prohibition on foreign travel is one that prohibits travel to any country outside the UK, to any country outside the UK as specified or other than specified. Where an order prohibits travel to any country outside the UK, the order must also require the defendant to surrender all their passports: SC s.348(3) and (4).

**Variations, renewals and discharges**

83-013 **Who may apply** The following persons may apply to a court to vary, discharge or renew an order:

(a) the defendant;
(b) the chief officer of police for the area in which the defendant resides; or
(c) a chief officer of police who believes that the defendant is in, or is intending to come to that officer's police area: SC s.350(1) and (2).

83-014 **Renewing or varying an order** An order may be renewed or varied so as to impose additional prohibitions on the defendant only if it is necessary to do so for the purpose of:

(a) protecting the public or any particular members of the public from sexual harm from the defendant; or
(b) protecting children or vulnerable adults generally, or any particular children or vulnerable adults, from sexual harm from the defendant outside the UK.

Any renewed or varied order may contain only such prohibitions as are necessary for this purpose: SC s.350(6). A variation must have some proper basis, it must not be an illegitimate attempt to appeal: *Cheyne* [2019] EWCA Crim 182; [2019] 2 Cr. App. R.(S.) 14.

83-015 **Discharging an order** The court must not discharge an order before the end of five years beginning with the day on which the order was made, without the consent of the defendant and:

(a) where the application is made by a chief officer of police, that chief officer; or
(b) in any other case, the chief officer of police for the area in which the defendant resides: SC s.350(7).

## Interim orders

An interim order is not available upon conviction. **83-016**

## Notification requirements

**Subject to notification requirements** Where an SHPO is made in respect of a defendant who was subject to notification requirements under the SOA 2003 immediately before the making of the order, and the defendant would cease to be subject to those notification requirements while the order has effect, the defendant remains subject to the notification requirements: SC s.352(1). **83-017**

**Length of SHPO** As to the existence of any correlation between the length of the notification requirements that applied automatically on conviction and the length of any SHPO imposed: **83-018**

(i) there is no requirement of principle that the duration of an SHPO should not exceed the duration of the applicable notification requirements;
(ii) as with any sentence, an SHPO should not be made for longer than was necessary;
(iii) an SHPO should not be made for an indefinite period (rather than a fixed period) unless the court was satisfied of the need to do so. An indefinite SHPO should not be made without careful consideration or as a default option. Ordinarily, as a matter of good practice, a court should explain, however briefly, the justification for making an indefinite SHPO, although there were cases where that justification would be obvious; and
(iv) all concerned should be alert to the fact that the effect of an SHPO of longer duration than the statutory notification requirements had the effect of extending the operation of those notification requirements; an indefinite SHPO would result in indefinite notification requirements. Notification requirements had practical consequences for those subject to them and any inadvertent extension was to be avoided: *McLellan; Bingley* [2017] EWCA Crim 1464; [2018] 1 Cr. App. R.(S.) 18.

**Not subject to notification requirements** Where an SHPO is made in respect of a defendant who was not subject to notification requirements under SOA 2003 immediately before the making of the order, the order causes the defendant to become subject to the notification requirements under SOA 2003 from the making of the order until the order (as renewed from time to time) ceases to have effect: SC s.352(2). **83-019**

## Appeals

**Against the making of an order** A defendant may appeal against the making of an order "*as if the order were a sentence*": SC s.353. **83-020**

**Against the variation, etc. of an order** A defendant may appeal against the variation, renewal or discharge, or the refusal to make such an order: **83-021**

(a) where the application for such an order was made to the Crown Court, to the Court of Appeal; and
(b) in any other case, to the Crown Court: SC s.353.

**Breach**

83-022 **Offence** A person who, without reasonable excuse, does anything prohibited by an SHPO, commits an offence. This includes a requirement to surrender all passports where a foreign travel prohibition prohibiting travel to any country outside the UK is included in an order: SC s.354(1) and (3).

83-023 **Maximum sentence** Five years' imprisonment: SC s.354(4).

83-024 **Cannot impose conditional discharge** Where an individual is sentenced for breaching their SHPO, the court may not impose a conditional discharge: SC s.354(5).

# SLAVERY AND TRAFFICKING REPARATION ORDERS

## Modern Slavery Act 2015 s.8

*References: Current Sentencing Practice A5; Archbold 19-446*

### General

**What is a slavery and trafficking reparation order?** A slavery and trafficking reparation order is an order requiring the person against whom it is made to pay compensation to the victim of a relevant offence for any harm resulting from that offence: MSA 2015 s.9(1). **84-001**

### Availability

The court may make a slavery and trafficking reparation order against a person: **84-002**

(1) if the person has been convicted of an offence under MSA 2015 ss.1, 2 or 4, and a confiscation order is made against the person in respect of the offence;
(2) if a confiscation order is made against a person by virtue of s.28 of the POCA 2002 (defendants who abscond during proceedings) and the person is later convicted of an offence under MSA 2015 ss.1, 2 or 4; or
(3) in addition to dealing with the person in any other way in respect of an offence under MSA 2015 ss.1, 2 or 4: MSA 2015 s.8(1)-(3).

The court may not make a slavery and trafficking reputation order in addition to a compensation order: MSA 2015 s.10(1).

The court may make a slavery and trafficking reparation order against the person even if the person has been sentenced for the offence before the confiscation order is made: MSA 2015 s.8(4).

### Duty to consider making an order in all cases

In any case in which the court has power to make a slavery and trafficking reparation order it must consider whether to make such an order (whether or not an application for such an order is made), and if it does not make an order, give reasons: MSA 2015 s.8(7). **84-003**

### Making the order

**Means** The court must consider the means of the individual when determining whether or not to make a slavery and trafficking reparation order: MSA 2015 s.8(5). **84-004**

In determining the amount to be paid by the person under a slavery and trafficking reparation order the court must have regard to the person's means: MSA 2015 s.9(5).

If the court considers that it would be appropriate both to impose a fine and to make a slavery and trafficking reparation order, but the person has insufficient means to pay both an appropriate fine and appropriate compensation under such an order, the court must give preference to compensation (although it may impose a fine as well): MSA 2015 s.8(6).

### Determining the amount

84-005 The amount of the compensation is to be such amount as the court considers appropriate having regard to any evidence and to any representations made by or on behalf of the person or the prosecutor, but the amount of the compensation payable under the slavery and trafficking reparation order (or if more than one order is made in the same proceedings, the total amount of the compensation payable under those orders) must not exceed the amount the person is required to pay under the confiscation order: MSA 2015 s.9(3) and (4).

In determining the amount to be paid by the person under a slavery and trafficking reparation order the court must have regard to the person's means: MSA 2015 s.9(5).

### Variation and appeals

84-006 **Appeals and reviews** Sections 141, 143 and 144 of the Sentencing Code (appeals, review, etc. of compensation orders) apply to slavery and trafficking reparation orders: MSA 2015 s.10(3).

84-007 **Varying confiscation orders** If the court varies a confiscation order so as to increase the amount required to be paid under that order, it may also vary any slavery and trafficking reparation order made by virtue of the confiscation order so as to increase the amount required to be paid under the slavery and trafficking reparation order: MSA 2015 s.10(4).

Where the order is made by virtue of the confiscation order and some or all of the amount required to be paid under it has not been paid and the court varies a confiscation order so as to reduce the amount required to be paid under that order, it may also vary any relevant slavery and trafficking reparation order so as to reduce the amount which remains to be paid under that order or discharge any relevant slavery and trafficking reparation order: MSA 2015 s.10(5) and (7).

84-008 **Discharging confiscation orders** Where the order is made by virtue of the confiscation order and some or all of the amount required to be paid under it has not been paid and the court discharges a confiscation order, it may also discharge any relevant slavery and trafficking reparation order: MSA 2015 s.10(6) and (7).

84-009 **Court of Appeal** If, on an appeal, the Court of Appeal:

- (a) quashes a confiscation order, it must also quash any slavery and trafficking reparation order made by virtue of the confiscation order;
- (b) varies a confiscation order, it may also vary any slavery and trafficking reparation order made by virtue of the confiscation order; or
- (c) makes a confiscation order, it may make any slavery and trafficking reparation order that could have been made under s.8 above by virtue of the confiscation order: MSA 2015 s.10(8).

# TRAVEL RESTRICTION ORDERS

## Criminal Justice and Police Act 2001 ss.33–34

*References: Current Sentencing Practice A5; Archbold 5A-1032*

### General

**Applicability** Where a court: 85-001

(a) convicts an offender of a drug trafficking offence committed on or after 1 April 2002; and
(b) determines that it would be appropriate to impose a sentence of imprisonment of four years or more; the court must consider whether it would be appropriate to make a travel restriction order in relation to the offender: Criminal Justice and Police Act 2001 (CJPA 2001) s.33(1) and (2).

**Drug trafficking offence** This means an offence under: 85-002

(a) MDA 1971 ss.4(2), 4(3), 20;
(b) CEMA 1979 ss.50(2), 50(3), 68(2), 170, in connection with a prohibition or restriction on importation or exportation, see MDA 1971 s.3;
(c) CLA 1971 s.1 (or common law conspiracy) in respect of the offences listed in (a) and (b);
(d) CAA 1981 s.1 in respect of the offences listed in (a) and (b); or
(e) MDA 1971 s.19 (or inciting at common law) of the offences listed in (a) and (b): CJPA 2001 s.34(1).

Possession with intent to supply, and money laundering offences, are not included.

### Making the order

**Duty to make an order** If the court determines that it would be appropriate to make an order, the court must make such travel restriction order as it thinks suitable in all the circumstance: CJPA 2001 s.33(1) and (2). 85-003

**Must give reasons if not making an order** If the court determines that it is not appropriate to make a travel restriction order, it must state its reasons for not making one: CJPA 2001 s.33(1) and (2). 85-004

**Start date of the order** The order begins on the day on which the offender is released from prison: CJPA 2001 s.33(3)(a). 85-005

**Minimum length** A travel restriction order must be for at least two years: CJPA 2001 s.33(3)(b). 85-006

**Effect of the order** A travel restriction order prohibits the offender from leaving the UK at any time during the period beginning with their release from custody and continuing to the end of the period specified by the court: CJPA 2001 s.33(3). 85-007

A travel restriction order may contain a direction to the offender to deliver up, or cause to be delivered up, to the court any UK passport held by them: CJPA 2001 s.33(4).

**Revoking or amending the order**

**85-008** The defendant may apply, to the court that imposed the order, for the order to be revoked or suspended: CJPA 2001 s.35(1).

**85-009** **When may the application be made?** The application may be made at any time which after the end of the minimum period, and not less than three months after the making of any previous application for the revocation of the prohibition: CJPA 2001 s.35(1).

**85-010** **Minimum period** The minimum period is:

(a) in the case of an order for four years or less, a period of two years;
(b) in the case of an order for more than four years but less than 10 years, a period of four years; and
(c) in any other case is a period of five years: CJPA 2001 s.35(7).

**85-011** **Test: revocation** A court must not revoke a travel restriction order unless it considers that it is appropriate to do so in all the circumstances of the case and having regard, in particular the offender's character, their conduct since the making of the order, and the offences of which they were convicted on the occasion on which the order was made: CJPA 2001 s.35(2).

**85-012** **Test: suspension** A court must not suspend a travel restriction order for any period unless it is satisfied that there are exceptional circumstances that justify the suspension on compassionate grounds, in particular having regard to the offender's character, their conduct since the making of the order, the offences of which they were convicted on the occasion on which the order was made and any other circumstances of the case that the court considers relevant: CJPA 2001 s.35(3) and (4).

# PROSECUTION COSTS

## Prosecution of Offences Act 1985 s.18

*References: Archbold 6-22*

### General

**Power** Where: 86-001

(a) any person is convicted of an offence by a magistrates' court;
(b) the Crown Court dismisses an appeal against such a conviction or against the sentence imposed on that conviction; or
(c) any person is convicted of an offence before the Crown Court;

the court may make such order as to the costs to be paid by the accused to the prosecutor as it considers just and reasonable: Prosecution of Offences Act 1985 (POA 1985) s.18(1).

**No order where financial order does not exceed £5** Where any person is convicted of an offence before a magistrates' court and: 86-002

(a) the court orders payment of any sum as a fine, penalty, forfeiture or compensation; and
(b) the sum so ordered to be paid does not exceed £5,

the court shall not order the accused to pay any costs under this section unless in the particular circumstances of the case it considers it right to do so: POA 1985 s.18(4).

**Guilty plea** The fact that an offender has pleaded guilty is a material factor in considering whether to order them to pay the costs of the prosecution, but it does not necessarily mean that an order is inappropriate: *Matthews* (1979) 1 Cr. App. R.(S.) 346. 86-003

**Either-way offences** An offender should not be ordered to pay costs simply because they have refused to consent to summary trial: *Hayden* [1975] 1 W.L.R. 852; [1975] 2 All E.R. 558; (1974) 60 Cr. App. R. 304. 86-004

### Making the order

**Means** An offender should not be ordered to pay costs unless the court is satisfied that they have the means to pay the costs ordered, or will have the means within a reasonable time: *Ahmed* [1997] 2 Cr. App. R.(S.) 8. 86-005

**Combining costs order with custody** An offender who is sentenced to custody should not be ordered to pay costs unless they have the means to pay immediately, or good prospects of employment on release: *Gaston* [1971] 1 W.L.R. 85; (1971) 55 Cr. App. R. 88. 86-006

**Consider overall effect of financial penalties** The fact that the amount of costs 86-007 is greater than the amount of a fine imposed for the offence is not necessarily a ground for objecting to the order, but the court should consider the overall effect of any combination of financial penalties: *Glenister* unreported 28 November 1975.

**Imprisonment in default**

**86-008** The court does not fix any term of imprisonment in default, but may allow time for payment or fix payment by instalments: *Bunce* (1978) 66 Cr. App. R. 109; [1978] Crim. L.R. 236.

# CONFISCATION ORDER—PROCEEDS OF CRIME ACT 2002

## PROCEEDS OF CRIME ACT 2002

*References: Archbold 5B*

### Preliminary matters

**Applicability** The POCA 2002 applies where all offences were committed on or after 24 March 2003, The Proceeds of Crime Act 2002 (Commencement No. 5, Transitional Provisions, Savings and Amendment) Order 2003 (SI 2003/333) para.3(1). Where an offence has been committed over a period of two or more days, or at some time during a period of two or more days, it is taken to have been committed on the earliest of those days. **87-001**

### Conditions

(1) A confiscation order is available where the defendant has either been: **87-002**
   (a) convicted of an offence or offences in proceedings before the Crown Court; or
   (b) committed to the Crown Court for sentence in respect of an offence or offences under s.70 POCA 2002.

(2) The court must proceed with a view to a confiscation order if it is asked to do so by the prosecutor, or if the court believes "it is appropriate for it to do so": POCA 2002 s.6(1)-(3)

**Absconded defendants** Where the defendant has absconded: **87-003**

(a) and either before or after doing so, they are convicted of an offence or offences in proceedings before the Crown Court; or
(b) after being committed to the Crown Court for sentence in respect of an offence or offences under any provision of sections 14 to 20 of the Sentencing Code; or
(c) after being committed to the Crown Court in respect of an offence or offences under section 70 below (committal with a view to a confiscation order being considered) and the prosecution apply to proceed under section 6, and the Court think it is appropriate to do so, proceedings may be undertaken under section 6: s.27(2) and (3).

See section 27 for details of the modification of the procedure.

**Postponement** The court may proceed with the confiscation hearing before sentencing the defendant for the offence(s) or may postpone the confiscation proceedings for a specified period: POCA 2002 s.14(1). This period may be extended, but not beyond the permitted period: POCA 2002 s.14(2) and (3). The permitted period is two years from the date of conviction: POCA 2002 s.14(5). However that limit does not apply where there are exceptional circumstances: POCA 2002 s.14(3). A postponement or extension may be made on application by the defence or prosecution, or by the court of its own motion: POCA 2002 s.14(7). **87-004**

If the court has postponed confiscation proceedings it may proceed to sentence the defendant (see *Sentencing the Defendant for the Offence* para.**87-020**).

87-005 **Civil proceedings** If the court believes that any victim of the offence has initiated, or intends to initiate, civil proceedings against the defendant, it is not bound to institute confiscation proceedings, but may do so in its discretion: POCA 2002 s.6(6).

**(1) Criminal lifestyle**

87-006 If the Crown Court embarks on confiscation proceedings, it must first decide whether the defendant has a "criminal lifestyle": POCA 2002 s.6(4)(a).

(1) A person has a "*criminal lifestyle*" if either:
  (a) they are convicted of one of the offences specified in POCA 2002 Sch.2; or
  (b) the offence constitutes "*conduct forming part of a course of criminal activity*"; or
  (c) if the offence was committed over a period of at least six months and the defendant has benefited from the conduct, POCA 2002 s.75(2).

An offence constitutes part of a course of criminal conduct if either:

(a) the defendant has been convicted in the same proceedings of at least four offences, they have benefited from at least four offences, and their "*relevant benefit*" is at least £5,000; or
(b) the defendant has been convicted on at least two separate occasions during the period of six years ending with a day when the proceedings for the present offence were started and has benefited from the offences in respect of which they were convicted on both of those occasions, and the "relevant benefit" amounts to at least £5,000: POCA 2002 s.75(3) and (4).

The latest offence must have been committed on or after 24 March 2003, but it is not necessary that the two earlier offences should have been if the offender has a criminal lifestyle, see (2A) below; otherwise see (2B).

87-007 **(2A) Offender has a criminal lifestyle** If the court decides that the defendant has a "*criminal lifestyle*" it must decide whether they have benefited from their "*general criminal conduct*": POCA 2002 s.6(4)(b).

"General criminal conduct" is "*all his criminal conduct*", and it is immaterial whether the conduct occurred before or after the passing of the Act or whether property constituting a benefit from conduct was obtained before or after the passing of the Act: POCA 2002 s.76(2).

87-008 **Assumptions** In making this decision, the court must make any of the assumptions required by s.10 which apply, unless the assumption is "*shown to be incorrect*" or there would be a "*serious risk of injustice*" if the assumption were made: POCA 2002 s.10(1) and (6).

(1) The first assumption is that any property transferred to the defendant within the period of six years ending on the day on which proceedings were started against the defendant was obtained by them as a result of their general criminal conduct.

(2) The second assumption is that any property held by the defendant at any time after the date of conviction was obtained by them as a result of their general criminal conduct.
(3) The third assumption is that any expenditure incurred by the defendant within a period of six years ending with the date on which the proceedings were started against them were met from property obtained by them as a result of their general criminal conduct.
(4) The fourth assumption is that any property obtained or assumed to have been obtained by the defendant was free of any other interest in the property: POCA 2002 s.10(2)-(5).

**(2B) Offender does not have a criminal lifestyle** If the court decides that the defendant does not have a "*criminal lifestyle*", the court must then decide whether the defendant has benefited from their "*particular criminal conduct*": POCA 2002 s.6(4)(c). **87-009**

Particular criminal conduct of the defendant is all his criminal conduct which falls within the following paragraphs—

(a) conduct which constitutes the offence or offences concerned;
(b) conduct which constitutes offences of which he was convicted in the same proceedings as those in which he was convicted of the offence or offences concerned;
(c) conduct which constitutes offences which the court will be taking into consideration in deciding his sentence for the offence or offences concerned: POCA 2002 s.76(3).

Benefit arising from offences committed before 24 March 2003, and which are taken into consideration, must be disregarded.

**Standard of proof** Any question arising in connection with whether the defendant has a criminal lifestyle or whether they have benefited from their general or particular criminal conduct must be decided on a balance of probabilities: POCA 2002 s.6(7). **87-010**

**Benefit figure and available amount**

The court must then determine the benefit derived: POCA 2002 s.8. The benefit is the total value of property or advantage gained, not the net profit after deductions for expenses, etc.: *May* [2008] UKHL 28; [2008] 2 W.L.R. 1131; [2009] 1 Cr. App. R.(S.) 31. **87-011**

The court must make an order for the amount which it has assessed to be the defendant's benefit, unless either:

(a) it believes that a victim of the offence has started or intends to start civil proceedings against the defendant (in which case the amount of the order is such amount "*as the court believes is just*", but the amount must not exceed the amount of the defendant's benefit; or
(b) the defendant shows that the "*available amount*" is less than the benefit (in

which case the amount of the confiscation order is either the "available amount" itself, or a nominal amount).

The *"available amount"* includes the total of the values of all *"free property"* held by the defendant at the time the confiscation order is made, and the total value of all *"tainted gifts"*: POCA 2002 s.83. See also POCA 2002 s.9.

Section 6(5)(b) does not enable the Crown Court to carry out a general balancing exercise as between the statutory aim of the 2002 Act and other interests, for example the potential hardship or injustice to third parties: *Morrison* [2019] EWCA Crim 351 ; [2019] 4 All E.R. 181; [2019] 2 Cr. App. R.(S.) 25.

**87-012** When determining the issue of third party interests under s.10A, in *Forte* [2020] EWCA Crim 1455; [2021] 4 W.L.R. 26; [2021] Crim. L.R. 601, the court stated at [12]:

*"The lack of a prescriptive procedural structure means that judges dealing with the determination of the property rights of non-parties to confiscation proceedings under s.10A of the Act will be careful to ensure that the procedures adopted are fair and enable an accurate determination of the issue. Article 6 of the EHCR applies to protect the fair trial rights of such people."*

That principle extends beyond procedural fairness and courts must be careful to apply the relevant law properly and to explain any decision to deprive a third party of property which they claimed to own clearly: *Ruto* [2021] EWCA Crim 1669; [2022] 2 Cr. App. R.(S.) 2.

**Procedure**

**87-013** The court will set a timetable for the key procedural steps. A suggested standard timetable is as follows:

(a) s.18 request for information (prosecution) served;
(b) s.17 response (defence) (four weeks later);
(c) s.16 statement (prosecution) (four to six weeks after s.17 response);
(d) response to s.16 statement (defence) (four to six weeks after s.16 statement);
(e) any further response (prosecution) (four to six weeks after response to s.16 statement); and
(f) list for mention; if the order can be agreed, that can be achieved at the mention; if the order cannot be agreed, the timetable for a contested hearing can be set at the mention.

**87-014** **Prosecution** If the Crown Court is proceeding with a view to a confiscation order on the application of the prosecutor, the prosecutor must give the Crown Court a statement of information: POCA 2002 s.16(1). If the Crown Court is proceeding with a view to confiscation on its own initiative, it may order the prosecutor to give such a statement: POCA 2002 s.16(2).

**87-015** **Defence** Where a statement of information has been given to the court and a copy served on the defendant, the Crown Court may order the defendant to indicate to what extent they accept the allegations made in the statement, and in so far as they do not accept an allegation, "*to give particulars of any matters he proposes to rely* *on*": POCA 2002 s.17(1). If the defendant accepts any allegation, the Crown Court may treat that acceptance as conclusive: POCA 2002 s.17(2). If the defendant fails to comply with an order, they may be treated as accepting every allegation in the statement of information other than an allegation in respect of which they have complied with the requirement, or an allegation that they have benefited from their general or particular criminal conduct: POCA 2002 s.17(3). No acceptance of an allegation by the defendant is admissible in evidence in proceedings for an offence: POCA 2002 s.17(6).

The Crown Court may order the defendant to give it the "*information specified in the order*": POCA 2002 s.18(2). There is no restriction on the kind of information which may be specified. If the defendant fails "*without reasonable excuse*" to comply with an order, the court "may draw such inference as it believes is appropriate" from the failure: POCA 2002 s.18(4).

**Other orders to be made after confiscation order imposed**

When the Crown Court makes a confiscation order it must make the following orders: **87-016**

**Enforcement receiver**

(a) appoint receiver (ss.50-55) The court may appoint an "enforcement receiver" on the application of the prosecutor; **87-017**
(b) empower the receiver The court must confer on the enforcement receiver the powers under s.51; or
(c) transfer from management receiver to enforcement receiver (s.64) Where a receiver has been appointed in connection with a restraint order, and the Crown Court makes a confiscation order and a receiver is appointed under s.50, the Crown Court must order the "*management receiver*" appointed in connection with the restraint order to transfer to the "enforcement receiver" appointed in connection with the confiscation order all property held by the first receiver by virtue of the exercise of their powers.

**Allow time for payment (s.11)** If the defendant shows that they need time to pay the order, the court may make an order allowing the payment to be made within a specified period which must not exceed three months from the day on which the confiscation order is made: POCA 2002 s.11(1)-(3). **87-018**

If the defendant makes a further application to the Crown Court within the specified period and court believes that there are "*exceptional circumstances*" it may make an order extending the period. The extended period must not extend beyond six months from the day on which the confiscation order was made: POCA 2002 s.11(4)-(6).

An order extending the period may be made after the end of the specified period to which it relates, but it must not be made after the period of six months beginning with the date of the confiscation order has expired: POCA 2002 s.11(6).

It is not open to the Crown Court to make an order allowing 12 months for payment on the defendant's initial application, even though the defendant shows that there are exceptional circumstances in which this would be appropriate. The defendant must make a further application within the six-month period.

87-019 **Fix term of imprisonment in default (s.35)** Sections 129(1) to (3) and (5) and 132(1) to (4) of the Sentencing Code apply as if the amount ordered to be paid were a fine imposed on the defendant. Where a court fixes a term under s.129 of the Sentencing Code in respect of an amount to be paid under a confiscation order, the maximum terms are those set out in the table below.

| **Amount** | **Maximum term** |
|---|---|
| £10,000 or less | 6 months |
| More than £10,000 but no more than £500,000 | 5 years |
| More than £500,000 but no more than £1 million | 7 years |
| More than £1 million | 14 years |

The prosecution cannot appeal against the making of a default order: *Mills* [2018] EWCA Crim 944; [2019] 1 W.L.R. 192; [2018] 2 Cr. App. R.(S.) 32.

**Sentencing the defendant for the offence (ss.13, 15, 71)**

87-020 The defendant cannot claim that their sentence should be mitigated because a confiscation order has been made.

87-021 **Before sentencing** The court must take account of the confiscation order before imposing:

- (i) a fine;
- (ii) an order involving payment by the defendant, other than a compensation order or an unlawful profit order;
- (iii) a deprivation order under the PCC(S)A 2000;
- (iv) a forfeiture order under the MDA 1971; or
- (v) a forfeiture order under the TA 2000: POCA 2002 s.13(2).

87-022 **Postponement** If the court has postponed confiscation proceedings it may proceed to sentence the defendant, however during the postponement period, it must not impose:

- (i) a fine;
- (ii) a compensation order;
- (iii) an unlawful profit order;
- (iv) a deprivation order under the Sentencing Code;
- (v) a forfeiture order under the MDA 1971;
- (vi) a forfeiture order under the TA 2000; or
- (vii) the statutory surcharge: POCA 2002 s.15(2).

It appears that the court may impose a slavery and trafficking reparation order, however, it is suggested that such is simply a missed consequential amendment and that when postponing confiscation proceedings, such an order should not be made prior to the imposition of the confiscation order.

Where the defendant has been sentenced and subsequently a confiscation order is made following a postponement, the sentence originally passed may be varied by the addition of:

(i) a fine;
(ii) a compensation order;
(iii) an unlawful profit order;
(iv) a deprivation order under the Sentencing Code;
(v) a forfeiture order under MDA 1971; or
(vi) a forfeiture order under TA 2000 within 28 days starting with the last day of the period of postponement. This does not necessarily mean the day on which the confiscation order is actually made: POCA 200 s.15(3)-(4).

**Compensation** A court which has made a confiscation order may leave the confiscation order out of account in deciding whether to make a compensation order in favour of the victim of the offence and in deciding the amount of the order: POCA 2002 s.13(2). It is open to the Crown Court to make a confiscation order and a compensation order in respect of the same offence, even though this means that the defendant will be required to pay twice the amount involved in the offence, see *Copley* (1979) 1 Cr. App. R.(S.) 55 for a related decision. **87-023**

**Sentencing powers** If the defendant has been committed for sentence under s.70 for an either-way offence, the powers of the Crown Court to deal with the offender for the offence depend on whether the magistrates' court at the time of committal stated in accordance with s.70(5) that it would have committed the defendant for sentence under s.14(2) of the Sentencing Code. If it did, the Crown Court must inquire into the circumstances of the case and may deal with the defendant in any way in which it could deal with them if they had just been convicted of the offence on indictment: POCA 2002 s.71(1) and (2). **87-024**

If the magistrates' court did not make a statement under s.70(5) in respect of an either-way offence, or the offence is not an either-way offence, the Crown Court, having inquired into the circumstances of the case, may deal with the defendant in any way in which the magistrates' court could deal with them if it had just convicted them of the offence: POCA 2002 s.71(3).

### Enforcing the default term (ss.35–39)

All questions relating to serving the default term will be dealt with in the magistrates' court, in the same way as a fine, subject to the amendments made by s.35(3) to the normal procedure: POCA 2002 s.35. **87-025**

# CONFISCATION FLOWCHART

## CONFISCATION FLOW CHART

88-001

### Proceeds of Crime Act 2002

### 1. Preliminary Matters

The Crown Court must proceed under s.6 if the defendant is:

(a) convicted of an offence in proceedings before the Crown Court;

(b) committed to the Crown Court for sentence under the PCC(S)A 3, 3A , 3B, 3C,4, 4A or 6; or

(c) committed to the Crown Court under s.70 of POCA.

AND

*either*

Section 6(3)(a): The prosecutor asks the court to proceed under s.6.

*or*

Section 6(3)(b): The court believes it is appropriate to proceed under s.6.

The court may order (at this stage or at any time) that the defendant provide information to the court to help it in carrying out its functions (including functions under s.10A) (s.18(2), CrimPR 2020 r33.13(2)(a)).

The prosecutor MUST give the court a statement of information within the period the court orders (s.16(1), CrimPR 2020 r33.13(2)(b)).

The court may order the prosecutor to give the court a statement of information within a period ordered by the court (s.16(2), CrimPR 2020 r33.13 CrimPR 2020 r33.13(2)(b)).

If the prosecutor provides a statement of information, the court may order D (1) to indicate within a given period the extent to which he accepts each allegation and (2) to give particulars he proposes to rely on where he does not accept an allegation (s.17(1), CrimPR 2020, r33.13(2)(c).

Normally the court should proceed to consider making a confiscation order before sentencing for the offence. It must do so before imposing the victim surcharge, a fine, compensation, forfeiture, or deprivation order s.13(2)(3)). It may (*and often does*) sentence D before making a confiscation order (s.14(1)(a)).

The court may postpone s.6 proceedings for a specified period of up to two years from the date of conviction (s.14(1)(b), (5). Any extension beyond two years requires exceptional circumstances (s.14(4) or if D has appealed his conviction (s.14(5)).

## 2. The Hearing

S.6 Hearing. Decide whether D has a criminal lifestyle (s.6(4)(a); s.75; Sch.2) on balance of probabilities s.6(7).

*D has a criminal lifestyle*

Decide whether D has benefited from his general criminal conduct (s..6(4)(b); s.8) on balance of probabilities.

*D does not have a criminal lifestyle*

Decide whether D has benefited from his particular criminal conduct (s.6(4)(c); s.8) on balance of probabilities.

If D has benefited:

Consider application of the four s.10 assumptions – decide the recoverable amount (s.6(5); s.9) on balance of probabilities (s.6(7)).

If D has benefited

Do not apply the s.10 assumptions – decide the recoverable amount (s.6(5); s.9) on balance of probabilities (s.6(7)).

If D had benefited there is usually a DUTY to make a confiscation order (s.6(5)(b)).

But it is only a POWER to make an order where the court believes any victim has started or intends to start proceedings against D (s.6(6)).

Determine the recoverable amount. This should be the sum assessed as D's benefit, unless D can show that his available assets are worth less in which case the recoverable amount should be limited to the value of his net assets. If D has no assets, make a nominal order (s.7).

Where is appears that there is property held by D that is likely to be realised or otherwise used to satisfy the order and a person other than D holds, or may hold, an interest in the property, the court may determine the extent of D's interest (s.10A).

When making an Order the Court must consider "proportionality" in accordance with s.6(5).

The whole amount to be paid is due immediately (s.11(1)). However, the court may allow payment over a specified period of up to three months from the confiscation order (s.11(2), (3)); or of up to six months, on D's application, if despite having made all reasonable efforts he is unable to pay the amount specified by the date specified (s.11(4)(5)(6)). The extension period should be as short as it can be (s.11(7)) and may apply to sums represented by any or all of the defendant's assets (s.11(2)).

Sentence to be served in default of payment must be set (s.35 POCA; s.258(2B) CJA 2003); and consider whether it is appropriate to make any order for the purpose of ensuring that the confiscation order is effective (Compliance Order – s.13A), in particular whether any restriction or prohibition on D's travel outside the UK ought to be imposed (s.13A(4)).

Proceed to sentence for the offence(s), taking the confiscation order into account before fining or making orders within s.13(3), but otherwise leaving the confiscation order out of account (s.13(4)). If both confiscation and compensation orders are made, and D lacks the means to pay both in full, then compensation can be paid out of the sum recovered under the confisation order (s.13(5)(6).

**This flowchart has been produced by HHJ Michael Hopmeier and HHJ Alexander Mills.**

# F: CHILDREN AND YOUNG PERSONS

# PURPOSES OF SENTENCING—YOUNG OFFENDERS

## Crime and Disorder Act 1998 s.37; Children and Young Persons Act 1933 s.44

*References: Current Sentencing Practice A6; Archbold 5A-1072*

### General aim

It is the principal aim of the youth justice system to prevent offending by children and young persons, and in addition to any other duty to which they are subject, it shall be the duty of all persons and bodies carrying out functions in relation to the youth justice system to have regard to that aim: CDA 1998 s.37(1). **89-001**

The court in *ZA* [2023] EWCA Crim 596 gave guidance on the approach to sentencing children. In particular:

a) that sentencing children and young people was a difficult and time-consuming endeavour, and that full and accurate sentencing notes from prosecution and the defence were critical, directing the judge to the necessary guidance.
b) It will generally be unhelpful for the prosecution to start by directing the court straight to para.6.46 of the overarching Children guideline (which contained a suggestion that an appropriate custodial sentence for a youth may be "half to two-thirds of the adult sentence"). Reference should be made to the previous sections.
c) The Criminal Practice Directions addressed court familiarisation, ground rules hearings, court dress, where young people are to be located in the courtroom, and how sentencing hearings are to be managed. Reference should be made to s.6.4.
d) Further guidance was to be found in the "Children and Young People in the Crown Court Bench Book" ("Youth Bench Book"), published by the Judicial College.
e) Rule 25.16(7)(b)(iii) of the Criminal Procedure Rules required judges to explain their sentence in a way that the defendant can understand. When sentencing a child or young person, this means taking care to explain the sentence, and the reasons for it to them, in a way and using words that they can easily grasp.

### Duty to have regard to welfare

Every court in dealing with a child or young person who is brought before it, either as an offender or otherwise, shall have regard to the welfare of the child or young person and shall in a proper case take steps for removing them from undesirable surroundings, and for securing that proper provision is made for their education and training: CYPA 1933 s.44(1). **89-002**

**Purposes of sentencing (not in force)**

**89-003** A court dealing with an offender aged under 18 must have regard to the prevention of offending (or reoffending) by persons aged under 18, the welfare of the offender, and the following purposes of sentencing:

(a) the punishment of offenders;
(b) the reform and rehabilitation of offenders;
(c) the protection of the public; and
(d) the making of reparation by offenders to persons affected by their offences: SC Sch.22 para.3.

The provision contains similar exclusions to those listed in the corresponding adult provision.

*This provision was not in force on 31 October 2024.*

# REMITTING A JUVENILE FOR SENTENCE

Sentencing Code ss.25–29

*References: Current Sentencing Practice A6; Archbold 5A-270*

See **para.22**. **90-001**

## REPARATION ORDERS

### SENTENCING CODE ss.109–116

The reparation order was repealed with effect from 28 June 2022. It is still available for convictions preceding that date. See the 2022 edition of this work for details. 91-001

# REFERRAL ORDERS

## Sentencing Code ss.83–108

*References: Current Sentencing Practice A6; Archbold 5A-1091*

### General

**What is a referral order?** A *"referral order"* means an order: **92-001**

(a) which requires an offender to attend each of the meetings of a youth offender panel established for the offender by a youth offending team; and
(b) by virtue of which the offender is required to comply, for a particular period, with a programme of behaviour to be agreed between the offender and the panel in accordance with this Part (which takes effect as a youth offender contract): SC s.83(1).

**Availability** A referral order is available to a court dealing with an offender for an offence where: **92-002**

(a) the court is a youth court or other magistrates' court;
(b) the offender is aged under 18 when convicted;
(c) neither the offence nor any connected offence is an offence the sentence for which is fixed by law;
(d) the court is not proposing to:
    (i) impose a custodial sentence; or
    (ii) make a hospital order (within the meaning of the MHA 1983),
    in respect of the offence or any connected offence;
(e) the court is not proposing to make:
    (i) an order for absolute discharge; or
    (ii) an order for conditional discharge, in respect of the offence; and
(f) the offender pleaded guilty to the offence or to any connected offence: SC s.84(1).

A referral order is not available unless the court has been notified by the Secretary of State that arrangements for the implementation of referral orders are available in the area in which it appears to the court that the offender resides or will reside (and the notice has not been withdrawn): SC s.84(2).

The youth court has exclusive jurisdiction to make a referral order; s.66 of the CA 2003 (which enables certain judicial office holders to exercise the powers of a DJ (MC)) does not provide the Crown Court or the Court of Appeal (Criminal Division) with the jurisdiction to impose a referral order as neither court would be sitting as a youth court when exercising those powers: *Ntim* [2019] EWCA Crim 311.

**Mandatory order** Where a referral order is available: **92-003**

(a) the court must make a referral order if the compulsory referral conditions are met; or
(b) otherwise, the court may make a referral order: SC s.85(1).

The compulsory referral conditions are met where:

(a) the offence is an imprisonable offence;
(b) the offender pleaded guilty to the offence and to any connected offence; and
(c) the offender has never been:
  (i) convicted by or before a court in the UK of any offence other than the offence and any connected offence; or
  (ii) convicted by or before a court in another Member State of any offence: SC s.85(2).

92-004 **Discretionary order** Where a referral order is available the court may make a referral order: SC s.85(1).

92-005 **Guidance** The Ministry of Justice and the Youth Justice Board released guidance on referral orders (October 2018).[1]

**Making the order**

92-006 **Contents** A referral order must specify the youth offending team responsible for implementing the order, require the offender to attend meetings of the panel established by the team, and specify the period during which the contract is to have effect: SC s.86(1).

92-007 **Length of the order** The order must be not less than three months and not more than 12 months: SC s.86(2).

92-008 **Duty to explain order and effect of breach** The court must explain the effect of the order and the consequences of non-compliance or breach: SC s.86(4).

92-009 **Multiple offences** Where a court imposes referral orders in relation to two or more offences, the referral orders have the effect of referring the offender to a single youth offender panel: SC s.88(1) and (2). Multiple referral orders may be made to run consecutively, but the total period cannot extend beyond 12 months: SC s.88(4) and (5).

In dealing with the offender for any connected offence, the court must:

(a) sentence the offender by making a referral order; or
(b) make an order for absolute discharge: SC s.89(2).

92-010 **Parental orders (to attend meetings)** The court may order the offender's parent or a representative of the local authority to attend meetings of the panel: SC s.90.

**Duties of the offender**

92-011 The offender must attend meetings of the panel and reach an agreement on a programme of behaviour aimed at preventing re-offending by the offender. The agreement takes effect as a "*youth offender contract*": SC s.83(1).

If the offender does not agree with the panel within a reasonable time, or fails

---

[1] Ministry of Justice, *Referral Order Guidance* (2018), *https://assets.publishing.service.gov.uk/media/5bbb2aabed915d23b049e137/referral-order-guidance-9-october-2018.pdf*.

to sign the contract, or fails to comply with the contract, or if there is a change in the offender's circumstances, the panel may refer the offender back to the court: SC s.98.

## Combining sentences

**Prohibited orders** In dealing with the offender in respect of the offence or any connected offence, the court may not: 92-012

(a) order the offender to pay a fine;
(b) make any of the following orders:
  (i) a YRO;
  (ii) an order under s.1(2A) of the Street Offences Act 1959;
  (iii) a reparation order; or
  (iv) an order for conditional discharge: SC s.89(3).

The court may not make:

(a) an order binding the offender over to keep the peace or to be of good behaviour; or
(b) an order under s.376 (binding over of parent or guardian), in connection with the offence or any connected offence: SC s.89(4).

Where the mandatory referral order conditions are satisfied, the court may not make an order deferring sentence: SC s.4(2). However, the court may remand for mental health reports or commit to Crown Court for a restriction order under the MHA 1983 ss.35, 38, 43 or 44, remit the offender to another court under SC s.25, or adjourn for inquiries under the MCA 1980 s.10(3): SC s.89(5).

**Permitted orders** It appears that the court may, alongside a referral order, impose: 92-013

(a) a compensation order under SC s.133;
(b) a deprivation order under SC s.153;
(c) a disqualification order under RTOA 1988 ss.34 or 35 or SC s.163 or 164; or
(d) a parenting order after considering a report from an appropriate officer under SC s.366(3).

**Remitting to Youth Court** The Crown Court is required to remit the case to the relevant Youth Court "unless satisfied that it would be undesirable to do so". Sometimes, it might not be desirable to do so, including where: 92-014

(1) a trial judge would be better apprised of the facts;
(2) there was the risk of disparity of co-defendants being sentenced in separate courts; and
(3) remittance might result in delay, a duplication of procedures, and fruitless expense: *Dillon* [2017] EWCA Crim 2671; [2019] 1 Cr. App. R.(S.) 22.

## Referrals back to court for breach, etc.

The offender must be referred back to the court by the panel: 92-015

(a) if it considers there is no prospect of agreement being reached: SC s.98(3);
(b) where the offender fails to sign the youth offender contract: SC s.98(4); or

(c) at the final meeting where the panel conclude that the contract has not been satisfactorily completed: SC s.101(5).

The offender may be referred back to the court by the panel:

(a) where the offender fails to attend a meeting: SC s.92(3);
(b) by the panel where the offender has breached the youth offender contract, having discussed the breach with the offender: SC s.100(3);
(c) if, at a progress meeting, the contract is varied and agreed, but the offender does not sign the contract: SC s.100(6);
(d) at the request of the offender, where the panel consider this is or soon will be a change in circumstances: SC s.100(8); or
(e) where it considers that, due to circumstances that have arisen since the making of the order, it is in the interests of justice that the order be revoked (this includes good behaviour by the offender): SC s.102(2).

92-016 **Re-sentencing powers** If the offender is referred back to the court, and the court is satisfied that the panel was entitled to make any finding of fact that it did make, and that the panel reasonably exercised its discretion, the court:

(a) may revoke the order: SC Sch.4 para.7(2); or
(b) may revoke the order and re-sentence: SC Sch.4 para.7(2) and (4);

Where the offender has been referred back to court under ss.92(3), 100(3) or 101(5), the court:

(a) may extend the period for which the contract has effect so that the total period does not exceed 12 months: SC Sch.4 para.9(1) and (2); or
(b) extended the period (so that the total period does not exceed 12 months) or impose a fine of not exceeding £2,500: SC Sch.4 para.9(4).

92-017 **Commission of offence during referral period** If the offender is convicted of an offence committed after the referral order was made, any court may revoke the referral order and re-sentence: SC Sch.4 para.17.

If the offender is convicted of an offence committed after the referral order was made, a magistrates' court may sentence the offender for the new offence by making an order extending the length of the compliance period, but not to more than 12 months: SC Sch.4 para.15(3).

# YOUTH REHABILITATION ORDERS

## SENTENCING CODE ss.173–199

*References: Current Sentencing Practice A6; Archbold 5A-1111*

### The different types of order

There are three types of YRO, a basic order and two enhanced orders: **93-001**

(a) the basic order, imposing one or more requirements (see below);
(b) YRO with intensive supervision and surveillance; and
(c) a YRO with fostering.

A "youth rehabilitation order" means an order imposing one or more youth rehabilitation requirements: SC s.173(1).

A "*youth rehabilitation order with intensive supervision and surveillance*" means a YRO which imposes:

(a) an extended activity requirement;
(b) a supervision requirement; and
(c) a curfew requirement (and, accordingly, if so required by para.19(3) of Sch.6, an electronic compliance monitoring requirement); and
(d) in relation to an order made on or after 3 July 2023, an electronic whereabouts monitoring requirement, unless para.48 of Sch.6[1] prevents such a requirement from being imposed: SC s.175(1).

A YRO with intensive supervision and surveillance:

(a) may impose other youth rehabilitation requirements; but
(b) may not impose a fostering requirement: SC s.175(2).

A "*youth rehabilitation order with fostering*" means a YRO which imposes:

(a) a fostering requirement; and
(b) a supervision requirement: SC s.176(1). A YRO with fostering may also impose other requirements: SC s.176(2).

### Availability and power to order

**Basic order: availability** A YRO is available to a court by or before which an offender is convicted of an offence if the offender is aged under 18 at the time of the conviction: SC s.177(1). **93-002**

This is subject to two restrictions:

(1) a YRO is not available if a mandatory sentence requirement applies in relation to the offence (see s.399):

---

1 Paragraph 48 concerns practical arrangements for securing the monitoring.

(a) because the sentence is fixed by law; or
(b) by virtue of:
   (i) s.258 or s.258A (required sentence of detention for life; dangerousness or manslaughter of emergency worker); or
   (ii) s.311 (minimum sentence for certain offences involving firearms that are prohibited weapons);[2] and

(2) that a YRO is not available where the court also imposes a hospital order or guardianship order (s.37(8) of the MHA 1983): SC s.177(2) and (3).

A court must not make a YRO in respect of an offender at a time when:

(a) another YRO; or
(b) a reparation order, is in force in respect of the offender, unless when it makes the order it revokes the earlier order: SC s.181(4)-(5).

93-003 **Basic order: test** A YRO may be made only if the court is of the opinion that the offence or the combination of the offence and one or more offences associated with it was serious enough to warrant a YRO: SC s.179(2).

In forming its opinion for these purposes, the court must take into account all the information that is available to it about the circumstances of the offence, or of it and any associated offence or offences, including any aggravating or mitigating factors: SC s.179(3). The pre-sentence report requirements apply to the court in relation to forming that opinion: SC s.179(4).

93-004 **YRO with fostering/intensive supervision: availability** These orders are available where the court is dealing with the offender for an offence which is punishable with imprisonment: SC s.178(1).

93-005 **YRO with fostering/intensive supervision and surveillance: test** The court must not make an order unless:

(a) the court is of the opinion that the offence, or the combination of the offence and one or more offences associated with it, was so serious that, but for the availability of a YRO with Fostering or Intensive Supervision and Surveillance, a custodial sentence would be appropriate (or, if the offender was aged under 12 at the time of conviction, would be appropriate if the offender had been aged 12); and
(b) if the offender was aged under 15 at the time of conviction, the court is of the opinion that the offender is a persistent offender: SC s.180(2).

In forming its opinion for these purposes, the court must take into account all the information that is available to it about the circumstances of the offence, or of it and any associated offence or offences, including any aggravating or mitigating factors: SC s.180(3). The pre-sentence report requirements apply to the court in relation to forming that opinion: SC s.180(4).

---

[2] This is subject to s.74 and Ch.4 of Pt 12 of the Sentencing Code (reduction of sentence for assistance to prosecution).

## Making the order: general

**Reports** Before making a YRO, the court must obtain and consider information about the offender's family circumstances and the likely effect of the order on those circumstances: SC s.179(6). 93-006

**Compatibility/suitability of requirements** The particular youth rehabilitation requirement or combination of youth rehabilitation requirements imposed by the order must, in the opinion of the court, be the most suitable for the offender: SC s.186(3). 93-007

The pre-sentence report requirements apply to the court in relation to forming any opinion on whether a particular youth rehabilitation requirement or combination of youth rehabilitation requirements is suitable for the offender: SC s.186(4). In forming its opinion for these purposes, the court may take into account any information about the offender which is before it: SC s.186(5).

The requirements must so far as is practicable avoid conflict with the offender's religious beliefs, avoid any interference with the times at which the offender normally works or attends any school or educational establishment, and avoid any conflict with the requirements of any other youth rehabilitation order to which the offender is subject: SC s.186(10)-(11).

**Multiple offences** If the court makes an order of any of the following kinds in respect of one of the offences: 93-008

(a) a YRO with intensive supervision and surveillance;
(b) a YRO with fostering; or
(c) any other YRO,

it may not make a YRO of another of those kinds in respect of the other offence, or any of the other offences: SC s.183(2).

See s.183 for further provision regarding concurrent and consecutive sentences.

**Credit for remand time** In determining the restrictions on liberty to be imposed by a YRO the court may have regard to any period for which the offender has been remanded in custody in connection with the offence or any other offence the charge for which was founded on the same facts or evidence: SC s.182(1). 93-009

**Guilty plea** Where a court is considering sentence for an offence for which a custodial sentence is justified, a guilty plea may be one of the factors that persuades a court that it can properly impose a YRO instead and no further adjustment to the sentence needs to be made to fulfil the obligation to give credit for that plea. 93-010

**Length of the order** A YRO must specify a date, not more than three years after the date on which the order takes effect, by which all the requirements in it must have been complied with: SC s.187(1) and (2). 93-011

An order which imposes two or more different requirements may also specify a date or dates in relation to compliance with any one or more of them; the last such date must be the date by which all the requirements must be satisfied: SC s.187(3).

**Effect of the order** A YRO takes effect on the day on which it is made: SC 93-012 s.198(1). But a court may order that the order is to take effect at a later date: SC s.198(2).

If the offender is subject to a DTO, the court may order the YRO to take effect when the offender is released from custody under supervision, or at the expiry of the term of the detention and training order: SC s.181(1)-(3).

93-013 **Magistrates' courts supervision** Where the Crown Court makes a YRO (otherwise than on appeal from the magistrates' courts) the Crown Court may include a direction that the order is to be subject to magistrates' court supervision: SC s.189(2).

**Making the order: YRO with ISS/fostering**

93-014 **Intensive supervision and surveillance** If the court makes a YRO with intensive supervision and surveillance, the order may include an extended activity requirement of not more than 180 days, and must make a supervision requirement and a curfew requirement with an electronic monitoring requirement, where such a requirement is required.

A YRO with intensive supervision and surveillance may include other types of requirement: except a fostering requirement, CJIA 2008 Sch.1 para.3.

In the case of a YRO with intensive supervision and surveillance, the date specified must not be earlier than six months after the date on which the order takes effect: SC s.187(2).

93-015 **Fostering requirement** A fostering requirement is a requirement that, for a period specified in the order, the offender must reside with a local authority foster parent: SC Sch.6 para.26(1).

A court may not impose a fostering requirement unless:

(a) The court is satisfied that:
  (i) the behaviour which constituted the offence was due to a significant extent to the circumstances in which the offender was living; and
  (ii) imposing that requirement would assist in the offender's rehabilitation;
(b) the court has been notified by the Secretary of State that arrangements for implementing such a requirement are available in the area of the local authority which is to place the offender with a local authority foster parent (and the notice has not been withdrawn);
(c) it has consulted the offender's parents or guardians (unless it is impracticable to do so), and it has consulted the local authority which is to place the offender with a local authority foster parent; and
(d) the offender was legally represented at the relevant time in court; (but this does not apply where a right to representation for the purposes of the proceedings was withdrawn because of the offender's conduct; or the offender refused or failed to apply for representation after being informed of

the right to apply and having had the opportunity to do so): SC Sch.6 para.27.

A YRO which imposes a fostering requirement must also impose a supervision requirement: SC s.176(1)(b).

The period specified must end no later than 12 months beginning with the date on which the requirement first has effect and not include any period after the offender has reached the age of 18: SC Sch.6 para.26(3). **93-016**

A fostering requirement may not be included in a YRO with intensive supervision and surveillance or a youth rehabilitation: SC s.185(3).

## Requirements

The following requirements may be included in a YRO. **93-017**

**Activity requirement** An activity requirement is a requirement that the offender must participate in specified activities at a specified place or places, or participate in one or more residential exercises for a continuous period or periods of the number or numbers of days to be specified in the order, or engage in activities in accordance with instructions of the responsible officer on the number of days specified in the order: SC Sch.6 para.1(1) and (2). **93-018**

The total number of days specified in an activity requirement must not in aggregate exceed 90: SC Sch.6 para.1(3).

An extended activity requirement is an activity requirement for which the aggregate number of days specified in the YRO under paras 3, 4, 5 and 6 is greater than 90. Where a YRO imposes an extended activity requirement, the aggregate number of days specified in the order under those paragraphs must not exceed 180: SC Sch.6 para.2.

An extended activity requirement is not available for a YRO other than a YRO with intensive supervision and surveillance: SC s.185(1). **93-019**

See Pt 1 of Sch.6 to the Sentencing Code for further provision regarding activity requirements.

**Attendance centre requirement** An attendance centre requirement is a requirement that the offender must attend at an attendance centre specified in the order for such number of hours as may be so specified: SC Sch.6 para.14(1). **93-020**

If the offender is aged 16 or over at the time of conviction, the aggregate number of hours for which the offender may be required to attend at an attendance centre must be not less than 12, and not more than 36: SC Sch.6 para.14(3).

If the offender is aged 14 or over but under 16 at the time of conviction, the aggregate number of hours for which the offender may be required to attend at an attendance centre must be not less than 12, and not more than 24: SC Sch.6 para.14(3).

**93-021** If the offender is aged under 14 at the time of conviction, the aggregate number of hours for which the offender may be required to attend at an attendance centre must not be more than 12: SC Sch.6 para.14(3).

A court may not include an attendance centre requirement in a youth rehabilitation order unless it has been notified by the Secretary of State that an attendance centre is available for persons of the offender's description, and provision can be made at the centre for the offender. The court must be satisfied that the attendance centre proposed is reasonably accessible to the offender, having regard to the means of access available to the offender and any other circumstances: SC Sch.6 para.15.

**93-022** **Curfew requirement** A curfew requirement is a requirement that the offender must remain, for periods specified in the order, at a place so specified: SC Sch.6 para.18(1).

A curfew requirement may specify different places or different periods for different days, but may not specify periods which amount to less than two hours or more than 20 hours in any day and so long as the total does not exceed 112 hours in any seven day period: SC Sch.6 para.18(3) and (4).

A curfew requirement may not specify periods which fall outside the period of 12 months beginning with the day on which the requirement first takes effect: SC Sch.6 para.18(5).

**93-023** Before making a YRO imposing a curfew requirement, the court must obtain and consider information about the place proposed to be specified in the order (including information as to the attitude of persons likely to be affected by the enforced presence there of the offender): SC Sch.6 para.19.

Where a curfew requirement is made, the order must also include an electronic compliance monitoring requirement, unless the court considers it inappropriate for the order to include an electronic monitoring requirement, or it will not be practicable to secure that the monitoring takes place, without the consent of some person other than the offender, and that person does not consent to the inclusion of the electronic monitoring requirement: SC Sch.6 para.19(3).

**93-024** **Drug testing requirement** A drug testing requirement is a requirement that the offender must, during the treatment period of a drug treatment requirement, provide samples in accordance with instructions given by the responsible officer or the treatment provider for the purpose of ascertaining whether there is any drug in the offender's body: SC Sch.6 para.34(1).

A court may not include a drug testing requirement in a YRO unless:

(a) the court has been notified by the Secretary of State that arrangements for implementing drug testing requirements are in force in the local justice area in which the offender resides or is to reside;
(b) the order also imposes a drug treatment requirement; and
(c) the offender has expressed willingness to comply with the requirement: SC Sch.6 para.35.

A drug testing requirement must specify for each month the minimum number of occasions on which samples are to be provided, and may specify times at which and circumstances in which the responsible officer or treatment provider may require samples to be provided, and descriptions of the samples which may be so required: SC Sch.6 para.34(2).

A drug testing requirement must provide for the results of tests carried out otherwise than by the responsible officer on samples provided by the offender in pursuance of the requirement to be communicated to the responsible officer: SC Sch.6 para.34(3).

**Drug treatment requirement** A drug treatment requirement is a requirement that the offender must submit, during a period or periods specified in the order, to treatment, by or under the direction of a treatment provider with a view to the reduction or elimination of the offender's dependency on, or propensity to misuse, drugs: SC Sch.6 para.31(1). **93-025**

The treatment required may be treatment as a resident in such institution or place as may be specified in the order, or treatment as a non-resident at such institution or place, and at such intervals, as may be so specified. The nature of the treatment is not specified in the order: SC Sch.6 para.31(1) and (3).

A court must not make a drug treatment requirement unless:

(a) it is satisfied that the offender is dependent on, or has a propensity to misuse, drugs, and that the offender's dependency or propensity is such as requires and may be susceptible to treatment;
(b) the court has been notified by the Secretary of State that arrangements for implementing drug treatment requirements are in force in the local justice area in which the offender resides or is to reside; and
(c) the court is satisfied that arrangements have been or can be made for the treatment intended to be specified in the order;
(d) the requirement has been recommended to the court as suitable for the offender by a member of a youth offending team, an officer of a local probation board or an officer of a provider of probation services; and
(e) the offender must express willingness to comply with the requirement: SC Sch.6 para.32.

**Education requirement** An education requirement is a requirement that the offender must comply, during a period or periods specified in the order, with approved education arrangements made for the time being by the offender's parent or guardian, and approved by the local education authority specified in the order: SC Sch.6 para.39(1). **93-026**

A court may not include an education requirement in a YRO unless:

(a) it has consulted the local education authority proposed to be specified in the order with regard to the proposal to include the requirement;
(b) it is satisfied that, in the view of that local education authority, arrangements exist for the offender to receive efficient full-time education suitable to the offender's age, ability, aptitude and special educational needs (if any); and
(c) that, having regard to the circumstances of the case, the inclusion of the education requirement is necessary for securing the good conduct of the of-

fender or for preventing the commission of further offences: SC Sch.6 para.40.

Any period specified in a YRO as a period during which an offender must comply with approved education arrangements must not include any period after the offender ceases to be a person to whom Pt I of the Education and Skills Act 2008 applies, or if later, ceases to be of compulsory school age: SC Sch.6 para.39(2) and (4).

93-027 **Electronic monitoring requirement** There are two electronic monitoring requirements that may now be imposed as part of a YRO.

The conventional electronic compliance monitoring requirement is a requirement for securing the electronic monitoring of the offender's compliance with other requirements imposed by the order during a period specified in the order or determined by the responsible officer in accordance with the order. Thus, if a YRO does not impose at least one other requirement this requirement is not available: SC s.185(4).

Additionally, there is an "Electronic whereabouts monitoring requirement", being piloted from 3 July 2022 to 3 January 2025 (see the Police, Crime, Sentencing and Courts Act 2022 (Youth Rehabilitation Order With Intensive Supervision and Surveillance) Piloting Regulations 2023 (SI 2023/705)). It is available in specified local authority areas in London, the North-East, West Midlands and Wales. An "electronic whereabouts monitoring requirement" means a requirement to submit to electronic monitoring of the offender's whereabouts (otherwise than for the purpose of monitoring the offender's compliance with any other requirement included in the order) during a period specified in the order: SC Sch.6 para.45.

Where it is proposed to make an electronic monitoring requirement, but there is a person (other than the offender) without whose co-operation it will not be practicable to secure that the monitoring takes place, the requirement may not be included in the order without that person's consent: SC Sch.6 para.44(1).

A youth rehabilitation order which imposes an electronic monitoring requirement must include provision for making a person of a description specified in an order made by the Secretary of State responsible for the monitoring: SC Sch.6 para.42.

93-028 A court may not make an electronic monitoring requirement unless the court has been notified by the Secretary of State that arrangements for electronic monitoring of offenders are available in the local justice area proposed to be specified in the order, and in the area in which the relevant place is situated, and is satisfied that the necessary provision can be made under the arrangements currently available: SC Sch.6 para.44.

The offender must (in particular)—

- (a) submit, as required from time to time by the responsible officer or the person responsible for the monitoring, to—
  - (i) being fitted with, or installation of, any necessary apparatus, and
  - (ii) inspection or repair of any apparatus fitted or installed for the purposes of the monitoring,

(b) not interfere with, or with the working of, any apparatus fitted or installed for the purposes of the monitoring, and
(c) take any steps required by the responsible officer, or the person responsible for the monitoring, for the purpose of keeping in working order any apparatus fitted or installed for the purposes of the monitoring: SC Sch.6 para.43A.

**Exclusion requirement** An exclusion requirement is a provision prohibiting the offender from entering a place or area specified in the order for a period so specified, which must not exceed three months: SC Sch.6 para.20(1) and (3). **93-029**

An exclusion requirement may provide for the prohibition to operate only during the periods specified in the order, and may specify different places for different periods or days: SC Sch.6 para.20(4).

Where an exclusion requirement is made, the order must also include an electronic monitoring requirement, unless the court considers it inappropriate for the order to include an electronic monitoring requirement, or it will not be practicable to secure that the monitoring takes place, without the consent of some person other than the offender, and that person does not consent to the inclusion of the electronic monitoring requirement: SC Sch.6 para.21.

**Intoxicating substance treatment requirement** An intoxicating substance treatment requirement is a requirement that the offender must submit, during a period or periods specified in the order, to treatment, by or under the direction of a specified qualified person with a view to the reduction or elimination of the offender's dependency on or propensity to misuse intoxicating substances: SC Sch.6 para.36(1). **93-030**

A court may not include an intoxicating substance treatment requirement in a youth rehabilitation order unless it is satisfied that:

(a) the offender is dependent on, or has a propensity to misuse, intoxicating substances, and that the offender's dependency or propensity is such as requires and may be susceptible to treatment;
(b) arrangements have been or can be made for the treatment intended to be specified in the order;
(c) the requirement has been recommended to the court as suitable for the offender by a member of a youth offending team, an officer of a local probation board or an officer of a provider of probation services; and
(d) the offender has expressed willingness to comply with the requirement: SC Sch.6 para.37.

The treatment required must be treatment as a resident in an institution or place specified in the order, or treatment as a non-resident in a specified institution or place, at specified intervals; the nature of the treatment is not specified: SC Sch.6 para.36(3).

**Local authority residence requirement** A local authority residence requirement is a requirement that, during the period specified in the order, the offender must reside in accommodation provided by or on behalf of a local authority specified in the order for the purposes of the requirement: SC Sch.6 para.24(1). **93-031**

The period for which the offender must reside in local authority accommodation must not be longer than six months, and must not include any period after the offender has reached the age of 18: SC Sch.6 para.24(4)

An order containing a local authority residence requirement may also stipulate that the offender is not to reside with a person specified in the order: SC Sch.6 para.24(2).

**93-032** A court may not make a local authority residence requirement unless:

(a) it is satisfied that the behaviour which constituted the offence was due to a significant extent to the circumstances in which the offender was living, and that the imposition of that requirement will assist in the offender's rehabilitation;
(b) it has consulted a parent or guardian of the offender (unless it is impracticable to consult such a person), and the local authority which is to receive the offender; or
(c) the offender was legally represented at the relevant time in court; (but this does not apply where a right to representation for the purposes of the proceedings was withdrawn because of the offender's conduct; or the offender refused or failed to apply for representation after being informed of the right to apply and having had the opportunity to do so): SC Sch.6 para.25.

A local authority residence requirement must specify, as the local authority which is to receive the offender, the local authority in whose area the offender resides or is to reside: SC Sch.6 para.24(3)(b).

**93-033** **Mental health treatment requirement** A mental health treatment requirement is a requirement that the offender must submit, during a period or periods specified in the order, to treatment by or under the direction of a registered medical practitioner or a chartered psychologist (or both, for different periods) with a view to the improvement of the offender's mental condition: SC Sch.6 para.28(1).

The treatment required must be treatment as a resident patient in an independent hospital or care home, or a hospital within the meaning of the MHA 1983, but not in hospital premises where high security psychiatric services are provided, treatment as a non-resident patient at such institution or place as may be specified in the order, or treatment by or under the direction of such registered medical practitioner or chartered psychologist (or both) as may be so specified. The nature of the treatment is not specified in the order: SC Sch.6 para.28.

A court may not make a mental health treatment requirement unless:

(a) the court is satisfied that the mental condition of the offender:
    (i) is such as requires and may be susceptible to treatment; but
    (ii) is not such as to warrant the making of a hospital order or guardianship order within the meaning of that Act;
(b) the court is satisfied that arrangements have been or can be made for the treatment intended to be specified in the order (including, where the offender is to be required to submit to treatment as a resident patient, arrangements for the reception of the offender); and

(c) the offender has expressed willingness to comply with the requirement: SC Sch.6 para.29.

**Programme requirement** A programme requirement is a requirement that the offender must participate in a systematic programme of activities specified in the order at a place or places so specified on such number of days as may be so specified: SC Sch.6 para.12(1). **93-034**

A programme requirement may require the offender to reside at any place specified in the order for any period so specified if it is necessary for the offender to reside there for that period in order to participate in the programme: SC Sch.6 para.12(1).

A youth rehabilitation order which imposes a programme requirement must specify:

(a) the programme;
(b) the place or places at which the offender is required to participate in it;
(c) the number of days on which the offender is required to participate in it; and
(d) if the programme has a residential component:
    (i) the place where the offender is required to reside for the purposes of the residential component; and
    (ii) the period for which the offender is required to reside there: SC Sch.6 para.12(2).

A court may not include a programme requirement in a YRO unless the programme has been recommended to the court by:

(a) a member of a youth offending team;
(b) an officer of a local probation board; or
(c) an officer of a provider of probation services, as being suitable for the offender, and the court is satisfied that the programme is available at the place or places proposed to be specified: SC Sch.6 para.13(1).

A court may not include a programme requirement in a YRO if compliance with that requirement would involve the co-operation of a person other than the offender and the offender's responsible officer, unless that other person consents to its inclusion: SC Sch.6 para.13(2).

**Prohibited activity requirement** A prohibited activity requirement is a requirement that the offender must refrain from participating in activities specified in the order, on a day or days specified during a period specified in the order: SC Sch.6 para.16(1). **93-035**

A court may not include a prohibited activity requirement in a YRO unless it has consulted a member of a youth offending team, an officer of a local probation board, or an officer of a provider of probation services: SC Sch.6 para.17.

The requirements that may be included in a YRO include a requirement that the offender does not possess, use or carry a firearm: SC Sch.6 para.16(3).

The primary function is not to punish the offender but to prevent, or at least to reduce, the risk of further offending: *J* [2008] EWCA Crim 2002.

93-036 **Residence requirement** A residence requirement is a requirement that, during the period specified in the order, the offender must reside with an individual specified in the order, or at a place specified in the order: SC Sch.6 para.22(1).

A residence requirement that the offender reside with an individual may not be made unless that individual has consented to the requirement: SC Sch.6 para.23(1).

A requirement that the offender reside at a specified place may not be made unless the offender was aged 16 or over at the time of conviction: SC Sch.4 para.23(2).

93-037 Before making a requirement that the offender reside at a specified place, the court must consider the home surroundings of the offender: SC Sch.6 para.23(3).

The court may not specify a hostel or other institution as the place where an offender must reside except on the recommendation of a member of a youth offending team, an officer of a local probation board, an officer of a provider of probation services, or a social worker of a local authority: SC Sch.6 para.23(4).

93-038 **Supervision requirement** A supervision requirement is a requirement that the offender must attend appointments with the responsible officer or another person determined by the responsible officer, at such times and places as may be determined by the responsible officer: SC Sch.6 para.9.

93-039 **Unpaid work requirement** An unpaid work requirement is a requirement that the offender must perform unpaid work: SC Sch.6 para.10.

The number of hours or work must be not less than 40, and not more than 240: SC Sch.6 para.10(3).

A court may not impose an unpaid work requirement unless:

(a) after hearing (if the court thinks necessary) an appropriate officer, the court is satisfied that the offender is a suitable person to perform work under such a requirement; and
(b) the court is satisfied that provision for the offender to work under such a requirement can be made: SC Sch.6 para.11.

The work must be performed at such times as the responsible officer may specify in instructions. The work must be performed during the period of 12 months beginning with the day on which the order takes effect. A YRO imposing an unpaid work requirement remains in force until the offender has worked under it for the number of hours specified in it, unless the order is revoked: SC s.198(5).

An unpaid work requirement is not available for a YRO in respect of an offence unless the offender is aged 16 or 17 when convicted of the offence: SC s.185(2).

**Revocation of order**

93-040 **Application** If an application is made by the offender or responsible officer to the appropriate court, and it appears to the court to be in the interests of justice to do so, having regard to circumstances which have arisen since the order was made, the court may either revoke the order, or revoke the order, and deal with the offender, for the offence in respect of which the order was made, in any way in which the court could have dealt with the offender for that offence: SC Sch.7 para.12 and 13.

**Good progress** The circumstances in which a YRO may be revoked include the offender's making good progress or responding satisfactorily to supervision or treatment: SC Sch.7 para.12 and 13. **93-041**

**Partial compliance** If the court revokes the order and deals with the offender for the original offence, the court must take into account the extent to which the offender has complied with the requirements of the order: SC Sch.7 para.12 and 13. **93-042**

**Breach: failure to comply**

An order can be "*breached*" either by a failure to comply with a requirement imposed under the order, or by a conviction for an offence committed during the currency of the order. **93-043**

**Requirements involving treatment** If the order imposes a mental health treatment requirement, a drug treatment requirement, or an intoxicating substance treatment requirement, the offender is not to be treated as having failed to comply with the order on the ground only that the offender had refused to undergo any surgical, electrical or other treatment, if in the opinion of the court, the refusal was reasonable having regard to all the circumstances: SC Sch.7 para.8. **93-044**

**Youth Court** If it is proved to the satisfaction of a youth court or magistrates' court that an offender subject to a YRO has failed without reasonable excuse to comply with the YRO, the court may deal with the offender by: **93-045**

(a) ordering the offender to pay a fine not exceeding £2,500;
(b) by amending the terms of the order so as to impose any requirement which could have been included in the order when it was made in addition to, or in substitution for any requirement or requirements already imposed by the order; or
(c) by dealing with the offender, for the offence in respect of which the order was made, in any way in which the court could have dealt with the offender for that offence: SC Sch.7 para.6.

If the court amends the order and imposes a new requirement, the period for compliance with the order may be extended by up to six months, unless the period has previously been extended: SC Sch.7 paras 6 and 10.

If the order does not contain an unpaid work requirement, the court may add an unpaid work requirement with a requirement to perform between 20 and 240 hours' work: SC Sch.7 para.10(7).

The court may not add to an existing YRO an extended activity requirement, or a fostering requirement, if the order does not already impose such a requirement: SC Sch.7 para.10(8). **93-046**

If the order imposes a fostering requirement, the court may impose a new fostering requirement ending not later than 18 months from the date on which the original order was made: SC Sch.7 para.10(9) and (10).

If the court resentences the offender for the offence (under para.c) above, the court must take into account the extent to which the offender has complied with the order; the order must be revoked: SC Sch.7 para.6.

93-047 If the court is resentencing the offender and the offender has wilfully and persistently failed to comply with a YRO, the court may impose a youth rehabilitation order with intensive supervision and surveillance: SC Sch.7 para.11.

If the original order is a youth rehabilitation order with intensive supervision and surveillance, and the offence for which it was imposed was punishable with imprisonment, the court may impose a custodial sentence notwithstanding the general restrictions on imposing discretionary custodial sentences: SC Sch.7 para.11(4).

If the order is a youth rehabilitation order with intensive supervision and surveillance which was imposed following the breach of an earlier order, and the original offence was not punishable with imprisonment, the court may deal with the offender by making a DTO for a term not exceeding four months: SC Sch.7 para.11(5).

93-048 **Crown Court** Where an offender appears or is brought before the Crown Court and it is proved to the satisfaction of that court that the offender has failed without reasonable excuse to comply with the youth rehabilitation order, the court may:

- (a) order the offender to pay a fine not exceeding £2,500;
- (b) amend the terms of the order so as to impose any requirement which could have been included in the order when it was made, in addition to, or in substitution for, any requirement or requirements already imposed by the order; or
- (c) deal with the offender, for the offence in respect of which the order was made, in any way in which the Crown Court could have dealt with the offender for that offence: SC Sch.7 para.7.

If the court amends the order and imposes a new requirement, the period for compliance with the order may be extended by up to six months, unless the period has previously been extended: SC Sch.7 para.7 and 10.

If the court resentences the offender for the offence, it must take into account the extent to which the offender has complied with the order. The order must be revoked: SC Sch.7 para.7 and 10.

93-049 If the original order imposes a fostering requirement, the court may substitute a new fostering requirement ending not later than 18 months from the date on which the original order was made: SC Sch.7 paras.8–10.

If the order does not contain an unpaid work requirement, the court may add an unpaid work requirement requiring the offender to perform between 20 and 240 hours' work. The court may not impose an extended activity requirement, or a fostering requirement, if the order does not already impose such a requirement: SC Sch.7 para.10(7).

If the offender has wilfully and persistently failed to comply with an order, and the court is dealing with the offender for the original offence, the court may impose a YRO with intensive supervision and surveillance: SC Sch.7 para.11(2).

If the order is a YRO with intensive supervision and surveillance, and the offence for which it was imposed was punishable with imprisonment, the court may impose a custodial sentence notwithstanding the general restrictions on imposing discretionary custodial sentences: SC Sch.7 para.11(3). **93-050**

If the order is a YRO with intensive supervision and surveillance which was imposed following the breach of an earlier order, and the original offence was not punishable with imprisonment, the court may deal with the offender by making a DTO for a term not exceeding four months: SC Sch.7 para.4.

**Breach: conviction of further offence**

**Youth Court** Where an order: **93-051**

(a) is in force and;
(b) the offender is convicted of an offence by a youth court or other magistrates' court;
(c) and the order was made by a youth court or other magistrates' court, or was made by the Crown Court with a direction that further proceedings should be in the youth court or magistrates' court; and
(d) the court is dealing with the offender for the further offence, the court may revoke the order and may deal with the offender, for the offence in respect of which the order was made, in any way in which it could have dealt with the offender for that offence: SC Sch.7 para.21 and 22.

The court must not revoke the order and deal with the offender for the original offence, unless it considers that it would be in the interests of justice to do so, having regard to circumstances which have arisen since the YRO was made: SC Sch.7 para.21.

The sentencing court must take into account the extent to which the offender has complied with the order: SC Sch.7 para.21(5).

If the YRO was made by the Crown Court, the youth court or magistrates' court may commit the offender in custody, or on bail to the Crown Court: SC Sch.7 para.22(4).

**Crown Court** If an offender: **93-052**

(a) appears before the Crown Court while an order is in force, having been committed by the magistrates' court to the Crown Court for sentence; or
(b) is convicted by the Crown Court of an offence while an order is in force, the Crown Court may revoke the order and may deal with the offender, for the offence in respect of which the order was made, in any way in which the court which made the order could have dealt with the offender for that offence: SC Sch.7 para.23(1) and (2).

The Crown Court must not deal with the offender for the original offence unless it considers that it would be in the interests of justice to do so, having regard to circumstances which have arisen since the YRO was made: SC Sch.7 para.23(2).

The Crown Court must take into account the extent to which the offender has complied with the order: SC Sch.7 para.23(5).

If the offender has been committed to the Crown Court to be dealt with in respect of a YRO following a conviction by a youth court or magistrates' court, the Crown Court may deal with the offender for the later offence in any way which the youth court or magistrates' court could have dealt with the offender for that offence: SC Sch.7 para.23(6).

# DETENTION AND TRAINING ORDERS

## Sentencing Code ss.233–248

*References: Current Sentencing Practice A6; Archbold 5A-1119*

### General

**What is a detention and training order?** A DTO in respect of an offender is an order that the offender is subject, for the term specified in the order, to a period of detention and training followed by a period of supervision: SC s.233. **94-001**

**Availability** A DTO is available where a court is dealing with an offender for an offence if: **94-002**

(a) the offender was aged under 18, but at least 12, when convicted;
(b) the offence is an imprisonable offence; and
(c) the court is not required to pass:
  (i) a sentence of detention under s.250 (see s.249(2));
  (ii) a serious terrorism sentence; or
  (iii) a sentence of detention during Her Majesty's pleasure under s.259: SC s.234(1).

A DTO is a custodial sentence and the criteria for the imposition of a custodial sentence must be satisfied. (See **CUSTODIAL SENTENCES—GENERAL PRINCIPLES, para.50**.)

Note that in certain circumstances, a court is required to impose a DTO; see the **MANDATORY MINIMUM SENTENCE**: SC ss.312, 315.

### Age restrictions

The order is available for offenders aged 12–17 at conviction, subject to the following restrictions. **94-003**

If the offender is under 15, in addition the court must be of the opinion that the offender is a "persistent offender": SC s.235(3).

If the offender is under 12, in addition to being of the opinion that the offender is a persistent offender, the court must be of the opinion that only a custodial sentence would be adequate to protect the public from further offending by the offender and the offence must have been committed on or after the appointed day: SC Sch.22 para.27. No day had been appointed for this purpose by 31 October 2024 and so a DTO remains unavailable for those aged under 12.

### Length

**Maximum** The maximum term of a detention and training order is two years, but it may not exceed the maximum term of imprisonment that the Crown Court could (in the case of an offender aged 21 or over) impose for the offence: SC s.236(2). **94-004**

A detention and training order must be for at least four months and not more than 24 months: SC s.236(1).

The powers of the youth court to impose detention and training orders are not restricted to those of a magistrates' court; a youth court can impose a sentence of two years' custody in the form of a DTO.

Any period in excess of 24 months is automatically remitted: SC s.238(2).

94-005 **Time on remand/curfew** Any time spent on remand or on qualifying bail is automatically deducted from the period of detention and training by virtue of s.240ZA and Criminal Justice Act 2003 of the CJA 2003.

**The effect of the sentence**

94-006 **Detention** An offender must serve the period of detention and training under a detention and training order in such youth detention accommodation as may be determined by the Secretary of State: SC s.241(1).

94-007 **Supervision under the order** At the half-way point of the sentence, the offender will be released from custody and the supervision period will begin: SC s.241(2).

The supervision period ends at the expiry of the term of the order: SC s.242(1).

94-008 **Additional supervision** Where the offender is aged 18 or over at the half-way point of the sentence, the term of the order is less than 12 months, and the offence for which the sentence was imposed was committed on or after 1 February 2015, there is an additional 12-month period of supervision: SC s.247.

94-009 **Combining sentences** If the offender is convicted of more than one offence, or is convicted of offences while the offender is subject to an existing detention and training order, the court may pass consecutive detention and training orders, so long as the aggregate of the orders to which the offender is subject does not exceed two years: SC s.238.

A court cannot order that a DTO is to commence upon the expiration of the term of a DTO under which the supervision period has already commenced; otherwise, the court may do so: SC s.237(3).

Section 237(4) of the Sentencing Act 2020 permits a court to impose a detention and training order to run consecutively to an order for detention under s.250. However, that power is open to the court only where the offender was already "subject to" the s.250 sentence of detention (i.e. already serving that sentence); it did not permit the court to impose both sentences on the same occasion: *Kovalkov* [2023] EWCA Crim 1509; [2024] 1 Cr. App. R. (S.) 47.

**Breach**

94-010 **Offence committed after release** If an offender who has been released from a DTO commits an offence punishable with imprisonment during the period between their release and the end of the term of the order, the court which sentences them for that offence may order the offender to be detained for the whole or any part of a period equivalent to the period which remained of the original order on the date the offence was committed: SC Sch.12 para.7.

There are therefore two elements to the new sentence: (1) the sentence for the new offence; and (2) the period of detention for the breach.

Any period of detention imposed for the new offence must be imposed concurrently with any period of detention imposed for the breach, and the detention for the breach must be ordered to begin immediately: SC Sch.12 para.7(6) and *McGeechan* [2019] EWCA Crim 235; [2019] 2 Cr. App. R.(S.) 12; [2019] Crim. L.R. 554.

Where a court makes a further DTO in respect of an offender who has been sentenced to a DTO from which they have been released, the length of the original DTO is disregarded for the purposes of the two year aggregate limit: SC Sch.12 para.7(6). It is uncertain whether a period of renewed detention is relevant for calculating the aggregate for this purpose.

### Breach of supervision requirement

If an offender fails to comply with a supervision requirement, they may be **94-011** brought before the appropriate youth court who may order them:

(a) to be detained for a period not exceeding the remainder of the order or three months, whichever is the less;
(b) to be subject to supervision for a period not exceeding the remainder of the order or three months, whichever is the less; or
(c) a fine not exceeding level 3 on the standard scale: SC Sch.12 para.3.

# DETENTION FOR SPECIFIED PERIOD (SECTION 250)

## SENTENCING CODE s.250

*References: Current Sentencing Practice A6; Archbold 5A-1208*

### Availability

The power to impose detention under s.250 applies where a person aged under 18 is convicted on indictment of: **95-001**

(1) an offence punishable in the case of a person aged 21 or over with imprisonment for 14 years or more, not being an offence the sentence for which is fixed by law;
(2) an offence under ss.3, 13, 25 or 26 of the SOA 2003;
(3) an offence listed in Sch.20 to the Sentencing Code: SC s.249(1);
(4) but the court is not required to impose a serious terrorism sentence.

**Test** The power may be exercised only if the court is of the opinion that neither a YRO nor a DTO is suitable: SC s.251(2). **95-002**

A DTO is a custodial sentence and the criteria for the imposition of a custodial sentence must be satisfied: SC s.251(3). (See **CUSTODIAL SENTENCES: GENERAL PRINCIPLES, para.50.**)

**Detention and training order not available** Cases involving offenders under 15 for whom a DTO is not available will only rarely attract a period of detention under s.91; the more rarely if the offender is under 12. The usual sentence will be a non-custodial disposal: *R. (W) v Thetford Youth Justices* [2002] EWHC 1252 (Admin); [2003] 1 Cr. App. R.(S.) 67; [2002] Crim. L.R. 681. **95-003**

### Making the order

**Maximum length** The period of detention specified in the sentence must not exceed: **95-004**

(a) the maximum term of imprisonment with which the offence is punishable in the case of a person aged 21 or over; or
(b) life, if the offence is punishable with imprisonment for life in the case of a person aged 21 or over: SC s.252(2).

### Minimum length

There is no statutory minimum period. A sentence of detention for less than two years may be passed in appropriate circumstances: *R. (W) v Southampton Youth Court* [2002] EWCA 1640 (Admin); [2003] 1 Cr. App. R.(S.) 87. Such an occurrence is likely to be rare, however: *R. (D) v Manchester Youth Court* [2001] EWHC Admin 869; [2002] 1 Cr. App. R.(S.) 135. **95-005**

### Multiple offences

95-006 Where the offender is to be sentenced for a number of associated offences, the court may pass a single sentence of detention which is commensurate with the seriousness of all the associated offences (including those for which detention under s.91 is not available) and impose no separate penalty for the other offences, provided that the other offences do not attract mandatory sentences: *Mills* [1998] 1 W.L.R. 363; [1998] 1 All E.R. 874; [1998] 2 Cr. App. R.(S.) 128.

Section 237(4) of the Sentencing Act 2020 permits a court to impose a detention and training order to run consecutively to an order for detention under s.250. However, that power is open to the court only where the offender was already "subject to" the s.250 sentence of detention (i.e. already serving that sentence); it did not permit the court to impose both sentences on the same occasion: *Kovalkov* [2023] EWCA Crim 1509; [2024] 1 Cr. App. R. (S.) 47.

### Time on remand

95-007 The CJA 2003 does not exclude the crediting of time spent on remand to local authority accommodation, however the only means by which this could be effected is in the calculation of the sentence. The deduction cannot be made administratively: *A* [2019] EWCA Crim 106; [2019] 4 W.L.R. 45; [2019] 2 Cr. App. R.(S.) 11.

### Release

95-008 An offender sentenced to detention under s.250 is subject to the same provisions relating to early release as one sentenced to imprisonment, namely at the halfway point. Where the sentence is less than 12 months, there will be a minimum period of three months' supervision immediately following release: CJA 2003 s.256B.

## Detention under section 250 and minimum sentences: firearms offences

### Part 1
*Offences*

1 An offence under section 5(1)(a), (ab), (aba), (ac), (ad), (ae), (af) or (c) of the Firearms Act 1968 (offence of having in possession, purchasing or acquiring, weapon or ammunition) committed on or after 22 January 2004. **95-009**

2 An offence under section 5(1A)(a) of the Firearms Act 1968 (offence of having in possession, purchasing or acquiring firearm disguised as another object) committed on or after 22 January 2004.

3 An offence under section 5(2A) of the Firearms Act 1968 (manufacture, sale or transfer of firearm or ammunition, or possession etc for sale or transfer) committed in respect of a relevant firearm or relevant ammunition.

4 (1) An offence under any of the provisions of the Firearms Act 1968 listed in sub-paragraph (2) committed on or after 6 April 2007 in respect of a relevant firearm or relevant ammunition.

(2) Those provisions are—

section 16A (possession of firearm with intent to cause fear or violence);
section 17 (use of firearm to resist arrest);
section 18 (carrying firearm with criminal intent);
section 19 (carrying a firearm in a public place);
section 20(1) (trespassing in a building with firearm).

5 An offence under section 28 of the Violent Crime Reduction Act 2006 (using someone to mind a weapon), where the dangerous weapon in respect of which the offence was committed was a relevant firearm.

### Part 2
*Interpretation of Schedule*

6 In this Schedule—

*"relevant firearm"* means a firearm specified in any of the following provisions of section 5 of the Firearms Act 1968 (weapons subject to general prohibition)—

(a) subsection (1)(a), (ab), (aba), (ac), (ad), (ae) or (af);
(b) subsection (1A)(a);

*"relevant ammunition"* means ammunition specified in subsection (1)(c) of that section.

For this purpose, *"firearm"* and *"ammunition"* have the same meanings as in the Firearms Act 1968.

# SPECIAL CUSTODIAL SENTENCE FOR CERTAIN TERRORIST OFFENDERS OF PARTICULAR CONCERN

*References: Sentencing Code s.252A and Sch.13*

## General

A special custodial sentence for certain terrorist offenders of particular concern must be equal to the aggregate of— **97-001**

(a) the appropriate custodial term; and
(b) a further period of one year for which the offender is to be subject to a licence,

and must not exceed the maximum term of imprisonment with which the offence is punishable in the case of a person aged 21 or over: s.252A(4).

**Availability** Where: **97-002**

(a) a person aged under 18 is convicted of an offence committed on or after 29 June 2021 listed in Pt 1 of Sch.13 (offences involving or connected with terrorism), [1] and
(b) the court does not impose a sentence of detention for life (under s.250) or an extended sentence of detention (under s.254) for the offence (or for an offence associated with it); and
(c) the court would, apart from this section, impose a custodial sentence,

it must impose a special custodial sentence for certain terrorist offenders of particular concern: s.252A(1) to (3).

In determining for the purposes of (c) above whether it would impose a custodial sentence, the court must disregard any restriction on its power to impose such a sentence by reference to the age of the offender: s.252A(2).

**Length of custodial term** The "*appropriate custodial term*" is the term that, in the opinion of the court, ensures that the sentence is appropriate: s.252A(5). **97-003**

---

1 See Sch.13 **para.58-008**

# EXTENDED SENTENCES

## Sentencing Code s.254 and Sch.18

*References: Current Sentencing Practice: A6; Archbold: 5A-1217*

### What is an extended sentence?

An extended sentence of detention under this section is a sentence of detention the term of which is equal to the aggregate of: **98-001**

(a) the appropriate custodial term (see s.256); and
(b) a further period (the "*extension period*") for which the offender is to be subject to a licence: SC s.254.

### Availability

An extended sentence is available where a court is dealing with an offender for an offence if: **98-002**

(a) the offence:
   (i) is a specified offence (see s.306(1)); and
   (ii) is one for which a sentence of detention is available under s.250 or 252A (see the table in s.249(1) and s.252A(1)(a) and (b));
(b) the offender is aged under 18 when convicted;
(c) the court is of the opinion that there is a significant risk to members of the public of serious harm occasioned by the commission by the offender of further specified offences (see s.308);
(d) the court is not required by s.258 or s.258A to impose a sentence of detention for life under s.250; and
(e) if the court were to impose an extended sentence, the term that it would specify as the appropriate custodial term (see s.256) would be at least four years: SC s.255(1).

### Dangerousness test

The pre-sentence report requirements (see s.30 of the Sentencing Code) apply to the court in relation to the dangerousness test: SC s.255(2). **98-003**

### Specified offence

A specified offence is one in Pt 1 (violent offence), Pt 2 (sexual offence) or Pt 3 (terrorism offence) of Sch.18 to the Sentencing Code: SC s.308(1) and (2). See **para.64-026** for Sch.18. **98-004**

### Four-year term condition

It is permissible to consider the totality of the offending and to aggregate the offending to satisfy the four-year requirement. It is not permissible to impose consecutive sentences to reach the four-year limit: *Pinnell* [2010] EWCA Crim 2848; [2012] 1 W.L.R. 17; [2011] 2 Cr. App. R.(S.) 30. **98-005**

The decision in *Pinnell* as to the permissibility of aggregating the sentences for specified and non-specified offences to determine the custodial term of the extended sentence was confirmed in *Camara* [2022] EWCA Crim 542; [2022] Crim. L.R. 782.

**Assessing dangerousness**

98-006 **General** The following applies where the court is required to consider whether the offender poses a significant risk of serious harm to members of the public by the commission of further specified offences: SC s.308(1). This is colloquially known as the "dangerousness test".

It will be a rare case in which an appellate court will overturn on an appeal against sentence the exercise of judicial discretion in making a finding of dangerousness, that appellate court not having conducted the trial or see the offender: *Howlett* [2019] EWCA Crim 1224; [2020] 1 Cr. App. R.(S.) 14.

98-007 **Must take into account** The court must take into account all such information as is available to it about the nature and circumstances of the offence: SC s.308(2).

98-008 **May take into account** The court may take into account:

(a) all such information as is available about the nature and circumstances of any other offences of which the offender has been convicted by a court anywhere in the world;
(b) any information which is before it about any pattern of behaviour of which any of the offences of which the offender has been convicted forms part; and
(c) any information about the offender which is before it: SC s.308(2).

98-009 **Serious harm** *"Serious harm"* means death or personal injury, whether physical or psychological: SC s.306(2).

98-010 **Risk** The risk does not have to be based on the instant offence: *Green* [2007] EWCA Crim 2172; [2008] 1 Cr. App. R.(S.) 97 (p.579; [2008] Crim. L.R. 66). The absence of previous offences causing serious harm requiring an extended sentence does not preclude the finding of dangerousness: *Powell* [2015] EWCA Crim 2200; [2016] 1 Cr. App. R.(S.) 49.

**Imposing the sentence**

98-011 **Determining the appropriate sentence** A finding of dangerousness does not automatically lead to the imposition of an extended sentence (in circumstances where the seriousness is not such that a life sentence is required). The court has a discretion as to whether an extended sentence is necessary: *Bourke* [2017] EWCA Crim 2150; [2018] 1 Cr. App. R.(S.) 42. A determinate sentence may provide adequate public protection alongside, e.g. sexual notification, an SHPO and the barring provisions. This will be a fact-specific decision.

The court must determine:

(a) the appropriate custodial term; and
(b) the extension period,

of an extended sentence of detention under s.254 to be imposed on an offender in respect of an offence: SC s.256(1).

**Custodial term** The appropriate custodial term is the term of detention that would be imposed in respect of the offence in compliance with s.231(2) (length of discretionary custodial sentences: general provision) if the court did not impose an extended sentence: SC s.256(2). **98-012**

**Extended licence** The extension period must be a period of such length as the court considers necessary for the purpose of protecting members of the public from serious harm occasioned by the commission by the offender of further specified offences: SC s.256(3). **98-013**

The extension period must:

(a) be at least one year; and
(b) not exceed:
    (i) five years in the case of a specified violent offence (unless sub para. (iii) applies);
    (ii) eight years in the case of a specified sexual offence or a specified terrorism offence (unless sub para. (iii) applies);
    (iii) 10 years in the case of a serious terrorism offence for which the sentence is imposed on or after 29 June 2021 (the day on which s.16 of the Counter-Terrorism and Sentencing Act 2021 came into force).

An extended licence period is different in kind from a determinate sentence. It is not tied to the seriousness of the offending; its purpose is protective. Like all sentences, it should not be longer than necessary for the relevant purpose. It should be just and proportionate, and not such as to crush the defendant: *Phillips* [2018] EWCA Crim 2008; [2019] 1 Cr. App. R.(S.) 11; [2019] Crim. L.R. 176.

An extended licence period is not tied to the seriousness of the offending; its purpose is protective. Like all sentences, it should not be longer than necessary for the relevant purpose. It should be just and proportionate, and not such as to crush the defendant: *Phillips* [2018] EWCA Crim 2008; [2019] 1 Cr. App. R.(S.) 11. **98-014**

The extension period is such as the court considers necessary for the purpose of protecting members of the public from serious harm caused by the offender committing further specified offences: *Cornelius* [2002] EWCA Crim 138; [2002] 2 Cr. App. R.(S.) 69; [2002] M.H.L.R. 134. The length of the extension period is a matter of judicial judgement and the Court of Appeal will only interfere where it could be demonstrated that the judge had erred in deciding what factors should be taken into account when exercising their judgement or where the judge had reached a wholly unreasonable conclusion as to the necessary term: *ARD* [2017] EWCA Crim 1882; [2018] 1 Cr. App. R.(S.) 23; [2018] Crim. L.R. 345.

As the extension period is measured by the need for protection, it does not require adjustment for totality, *Totality Guideline*, p.10.

**Maximum sentence** The term of the extended sentence of detention under s.254 must not exceed the maximum term of imprisonment with which the offence is punishable in the case of a person aged 21 or over: SC s.256(5). **98-015**

An extended licence period is different in kind from a determinate sentence. It is not tied to the seriousness of the offending; its purpose is protective. Like all sentences, it should not be longer than necessary for the relevant purpose. It should be just and proportionate, and not such as to crush the defendant: *Phillips* [2018] EWCA Crim 2008; [2019] 1 Cr. App. R.(S.) 11.

An extended licence period is not tied to the seriousness of the offending; its purpose is protective. Like all sentences, it should not be longer than necessary for the relevant purpose. It should be just and proportionate, and not such as to crush the defendant: *Phillips* [2018] EWCA Crim 2008; [2019] 1 Cr. App. R.(S.) 11.

**98-016** **Explaining sentence** In *Bourke* [2017] EWCA Crim 2150; [2018] 1 Cr. App. R.(S.) 42 the court noted that where the sentencing judge considered an extended sentence unsuitable, it would have been preferable had they explained why that was so, even if that explanation were brief. The usual duty to give reasons for, and explain, the sentence applies: *Lang* [2005] EWCA Crim 2864; [2006] 1 W.L.R. 2509; [2006] 2 Cr. App. R.(S.) 3.

**98-017** **Consecutive sentences** In appropriate circumstances, consecutive extended sentences may be imposed, see e.g. *Watkins* [2014] EWCA Crim 1677; [2015] 1 Cr. App. R.(S.) 6. However in such circumstances, the explanation of the sentences (and their effect) is likely to be complex, and care should be taken in determining the true position.

In *B* [2015] EWCA Crim 1295; [2015] 2 Cr. App. R.(S.) 78; [2015] Crim. L.R. 1009, the court substituted consecutive extended sentences, aggregating the licence periods resulting in a total 10-year extended licence. In *Thompson* [2018] EWCA Crim 639; [2018] 1 W.L.R. 4429; [2018] 2 Cr.App.R (S.) 19, a five-judge court confirmed that it was permissible to impose consecutive sentences so as to take the total extended licence period beyond the five or eight-year limits provided by the Act. The court commented that it would be permissible only in exceptional circumstances, however.

It is not permissible to make the sentences partly concurrent and partly consecutive: *Francis* [2014] EWCA Crim 631; *DJ* [2015] EWCA Crim 563; [2015] 2 Cr. App. R.(S.) 16; [2015] Crim. L.R. 650.

**98-018** There is no objection to imposing an extended sentence consecutive to a determinate sentence (either on the same occasion, or in addition to an existing determinate sentence): *Brown* [2006] EWCA Crim 1996; [2007] 1 Cr. App. R.(S.) 77; [2006] Crim. L.R. 1082 and *Hibbert* [2015] EWCA Crim 507; [2015] 2 Cr. App. R.(S.) 15. However, the Court of Appeal has repeatedly stated that it is undesirable to impose a determinate sentence consecutive to an extended sentence (see e.g. *Brown* and *Prior* [2014] EWCA Crim 1290). This issue was considered in *Ulhaqdad* [2017] EWCA Crim 1216, where the court established that the order in which a court imposed an extended sentence and a determinate sentence (where those sentences are made to run consecutively) created no practical difficulty for the prison service in relation to the calculation of sentences and release dates, etc. However, having identified no practical or principled reason for the guidance given in *Brown*, the court in *Ulhaqdad* maintained the status quo. Therefore the position remains that where extended and determinate sentences are being imposed to run consecutively, the determinate sentence should be imposed first. Two further points remain. First, that in *Prior*, the court suggested that an alternative approach was to increase the custodial term of the extended sentence and make the sentences run concurrently. Secondly, despite the guidance in *Brown*, there is nothing unlawful about imposing an extended sentence consecutive to a determinate sentence in an appropriate case: *Hibbert* [2015] EWCA Crim 507; [2015] 2 Cr. App. R.(S.) 15. However, it is submitted that the operation of the release provisions renders either approach permissible.

**Offender subject to DTO** Where the court imposes an extended sentence of detention under s.254 in the case of an offender who is subject to a relevant DTO, and the offender has not at any time been released for supervision under the relevant DTO, the court may order that the extended sentence of detention is to take effect at the time when the offender would otherwise be released for supervision under the relevant detention and training order: SC s.257(1) and (2). **98-019**

Otherwise, the extended sentence of detention takes effect at the beginning of the day on which it is passed: SC s.257(3).

**Release**

**Sentence imposed on or after 13 April 2015** At the 2/3 point of the custodial portion of the sentence, defendants will be referred to the Parole Board for consideration for release: CJA 2003 s.246A(3) and (4)(a). **98-020**

If the first application is unsuccessful, there must be another referral after two years. The test for the Parole Board is whether or not it is satisfied that it is no longer necessary for the protection of the public that the defendant should be confined: CJA 2003 s.246A(4)(b) and (6).

Release is automatic at the expiry of the custodial portion of the sentence: CJA 2003 s.246A(7).

The defendant is then on licence for the aggregate of the remaining custodial portion (if there is one) and the extended licence period.

# LIFE SENTENCE—DANGEROUSNESS

## Sentencing Code s.258 and Sch.19

References: *Current Sentencing Practice A6; Archbold 5A-1235*

### General

**Types of life sentence** There are three types of life sentence available to a court sentencing an offender aged under 18: 99-001

(a) dangerousness life: SC s.258 (this section);
(b) discretionary life (the inherent jurisdiction of the court to impose a life sentence); and
(c) mandatory life for murder: SC s.259.

**Life licence** An offender sentenced to detention for life will remain on licence for the rest of their life. 99-002

**Availability** A life sentence is available under ss.250 and 258 where: 99-003

(a) a person aged under 18 is convicted of a Sch.19 offence;
(b) the court considers that the seriousness of:
    (i) the offence; or
    (ii) the offence and one or more offences associated with it, is such as to justify the imposition of a sentence of detention for life; and
(c) the court is of the opinion that there is a significant risk to members of the public of serious harm occasioned by the commission by the offender of further specified offences: SC s.258(1) and (2).

**Does the seriousness of the offence justify a life sentence?** The question as to whether or not the seriousness of the offence, or of the offence and one or more offences associated with it, was such as to justify a life sentence required consideration of: 99-004

(i) the seriousness of the offence itself, on its own or with other offences associated with it, which was always a matter for the judgment of the court;
(ii) the defendant's previous convictions;
(iii) the level of danger to the public posed by the defendant and whether or not there was a reliable estimate of the length of time they would remain a danger; and
(iv) the available alternative sentences: *Attorney General's Reference (No. 27 of 2013) (Burinskas)* [2014] EWCA Crim 334; [2014] 1 W.L.R. 4209; [2014] 2 Cr. App. R.(S.) 45.

### Assessing dangerousness

**General** The following applies where the court is required to consider whether the offender poses a significant risk of serious harm to members of the public by 99-005 the commission of further specified offences: SC s.308(1). This is colloquially known as the "dangerousness test".

It will be a rare case in which an appellate court will overturn on an appeal against sentence the exercise of judicial discretion in making a finding of dangerousness, that appellate court not having conducted the trial or see the offender: *Howlett* [2019] EWCA Crim 1224; [2020] 1 Cr. App. R.(S.) 14.

99-006 **Must take into account** The court must take into account all such information as is available to it about the nature and circumstances of the offence: SC s.308(2).

99-007 **May take into account** The court may take into account:

(a) all such information as is available about the nature and circumstances of any other offences of which the offender has been convicted by a court anywhere in the world;
(b) any information which is before it about any pattern of behaviour of which any of the offences of which the offender has been convicted forms part; and
(c) any information about the offender which is before it: SC s.308(2).

99-008 **Serious harm** *"Serious harm"* means death or personal injury, whether physical or psychological: SC s.306(2).

99-009 **Risk** The risk does not have to be based on the instant offence: *Green* [2007] EWCA Crim 2172; [2008] 1 Cr. App. R.(S.) 97; [2008] Crim. L.R. 66. The absence of previous offences causing serious harm requiring an extended sentence does not preclude the finding of dangerousness: *Powell* [2015] EWCA Crim 2200; [2016] 1 Cr. App. R.(S.) 49.

In *Neville* [2015] EWCA Crim 1874; [2016] 1 Cr. App. R.(S.) 38; [2016] Crim. L.R. 368, the court held that a finding of dangerousness founded on unpredictability demonstrated by a long absence of serious offending prior to the instant offence was permissible.

**The correct approach**

99-010 (i) consider the question of dangerousness. If the offender is not dangerous, a determinate sentence should be passed;
(ii) if the offender is dangerous, consider whether the seriousness of the offence and offences associated with it justify a life sentence;
(iii) if a life sentence is justified then the judge must pass a life sentence in accordance with ss.274;
(iv) if the two-strikes life sentence does not apply the judge should then consider an extended sentence. Before passing an extended sentence the judge should consider a determinate sentence: *Attorney General's Reference (No.27 of 2013) (Burinskas)* [2014] EWCA Crim 334; [2014] 2 Cr. App. R.(S.) 45 (amended to reflect the position for those aged under 18).

Where the conditions are met, the sentence is not discretionary: *Wilder* [2023] EWCA Crim 1295; [2024] 1 Cr. App. R. (S.) 37.

### Setting the minimum term

**General** A court which imposes a sentence of imprisonment (or custody) for life must fix a minimum term in accordance with SC s.321. The offender is not entitled to be released until they have served the minimum term. For details on setting the minimum term, see **LIFE SENTENCES—MINIMUM TERM (NON-MURDER CASES)** at **para.70**. **99-011**

### Not a sentence fixed by law

An offence the sentence for which is imposed under s.258 is not to be regarded as an offence the sentence for which is fixed by law: SC s.258(4). **99-012**

## Schedule 19 Offences

### Common law offences

1 Manslaughter. 100-001
2 Kidnapping.
3 False imprisonment.

### Offences against the Person Act 1861

4 An offence under any of the following provisions of the Offences against the Person Act 1861—
(a) section 4 (soliciting murder);
(b) section 18 (wounding with intent to cause grievous bodily harm);
(c) section 21 (attempting to choke, suffocate or strangle in order to commit or assist in committing an indictable offence);
(d) section 22 (using chloroform etc to commit or assist in the committing of any indictable offence);
(e) section 28 (causing bodily injury by explosives);
(f) section 29 (using explosives etc with intent to do grievous bodily harm);
(g) section 32 (endangering the safety of railway passengers).

### Explosive Substances Act 1883

5 An offence under either of the following provisions of the Explosive Substances Act 1883—
(a) section 2 (causing explosion likely to endanger life or property);
(b) section 3 (attempt to cause explosion, or making or keeping explosive with intent to endanger life or property).
6 An offence under section 4 of that Act (making or possession of explosive under suspicious circumstances) committed on or after 13 April 2015.

### Infant Life (Preservation) Act 1929

7 An offence under section 1 of the Infant Life (Preservation) Act 1929 (child destruction).

### Infanticide Act 1938

8 An offence under section 1 of the Infanticide Act 1938 (infanticide).

### Firearms Act 1968

9 An offence under any of the following provisions of the Firearms Act 1968—
(a) section 16 (possession of firearm with intent to endanger life);
(b) section 17(1) (use of firearm to resist arrest);

(c) section 17(2) (possession of firearm at time of committing or being arrested for offence specified in Schedule 1 to that Act);
(d) section 18 (carrying a firearm with criminal intent).

**Theft Act 1968**

10 An offence under either of the following provisions of the Theft Act 1968—
(a) section 8 (robbery or assault with intent to rob);
(b) section 10 (aggravated burglary).

**Criminal Damage Act 1971**

11 An offence of arson under section 1 of the Criminal Damage Act 1971.
12 An offence under section 1(2) of that Act (destroying or damaging property) other than an offence of arson.

**Taking of Hostages Act 1982**

13 An offence under section 1 of the Taking of Hostages Act 1982 (hostage-taking).

**Aviation Security Act 1982**

14 An offence under any of the following provisions of the Aviation Security Act 1982—
(a) section 1 (hijacking);
(b) section 2 (destroying, damaging or endangering safety of aircraft);
(c) section 3 (other acts endangering or likely to endanger safety of aircraft).

**Criminal Justice Act 1988**

15 An offence under section 134 of the Criminal Justice Act 1988 (torture).

**Aviation and Maritime Security Act 1990**

16 An offence under any of the following provisions of the Aviation and Maritime Security Act 1990—
(a) section 1 (endangering safety at aerodromes);
(b) section 9 (hijacking of ships);
(c) section 10 (seizing or exercising control of fixed platforms);
(d) section 11 (destroying fixed platforms or endangering their safety);
(e) section 12 (other acts endangering or likely to endanger safe navigation);
(f) section 13 (offences involving threats).

**Channel Tunnel (Security) Order 1994**

17 An offence under Part 2 of the Channel Tunnel (Security) Order 1994 (S. I. 1994/570) (offences relating to Channel Tunnel trains and the tunnel system).

**Terrorism Act 2000**

18 An offence under any of the provisions of the Terrorism Act 2000 listed in column 1 of the following table that meets the condition listed in relation to it in column 2—

| | Provision of the Terrorism Act 2000 | Condition |
|---|---|---|
| (a) | Section 54 (weapons training) | The offence was committed on or after 13 April 2015 |
| (b) | Section 56 (directing terrorist organisation) | The offence was committed on or after 12 January 2010. |
| (c) | Section 59 (inciting terrorism overseas) | The offence was committed on or after 12 January 2010 and the offender is liable on conviction on indictment to imprisonment for life. |

**Anti-terrorism, Crime and Security Act 2001**

19 An offence under either of the following provisions of the Anti-terrorism, Crime and Security Act 2001 committed on or after 12 January 2010—
(a) section 47 (use etc of nuclear weapons);
(b) section 50 (assisting or inducing certain weapons-related acts overseas).

**Sexual Offences Act 2003**

20 An offence under any of the provisions of the Sexual Offences Act 2003 listed in column 1 of the following table that meets the condition (if any) listed in relation to it in column 2—

| | Provision of the Sexual Offences Act 2003 | Condition |
|---|---|---|
| (a) | Section 1 (rape) | |
| (b) | Section 2 (assault by penetration) | |
| (c) | Section 4 (causing a person to engage in sexual activity without consent) | The offender is liable on conviction on indictment to imprisonment for life |
| (d) | Section 5 (rape of a child under 13) | |
| (e) | Section 6 (assault of a child under 13 by penetration) | |
| (f) | Section 8 (causing or inciting a child under 13 to engage in sexual activity) | The offender is liable on conviction on indictment to imprisonment for life |
| (g) | Section 30 (sexual activity with a person with a mental disorder impeding choice) | The offender is liable on conviction on indictment to imprisonment for life |

| | Provision of the Sexual Offences Act 2003 | Condition |
|---|---|---|
| (h) | Section 31 (causing or inciting a person with a mental disorder to engage in sexual activity) | The offender is liable on conviction on indictment to imprisonment for life |
| (i) | Section 34 (inducement, threat or deception to procure sexual activity with a person with a mental disorder) | The offender is liable on conviction on indictment to imprisonment for life |
| (j) | Section 35 (causing a person with a mental disorder to engage in or agree to engage in sexual activity by inducement etc) | The offender is liable on conviction on indictment to imprisonment for life |
| (k) | Section 47 (paying for sexual services of a child) against a person aged under 16 | The offender is liable on conviction on indictment to imprisonment for life |
| (l) | Section 62 (committing an offence with intent to commit a sexual offence) | The offender is liable on conviction on indictment to imprisonment for life. |

**Terrorism Act 2006**

**100-002** 21 An offence under any of the provisions of the Terrorism Act 2006 listed in column 1 of the following table that meets the condition listed in relation to it in column 2—

| | Provision of the Terrorism Act 2006 | Condition |
|---|---|---|
| (a) | Section 5 (preparation of terrorist acts) | The offence was committed on or after 12 January 2010 |
| (b) | Section 6 (training for terrorism) | The offence was committed on or after 13 April 2015 |
| (c) | Section 9 (making or possession of radioactive device or material) | The offence was committed on or after 12 January 2010 |
| (d) | Section 10 (misuse of radioactive device or material for terrorist purposes etc) | The offence was committed on or after 12 January 2010 |
| (e) | Section 11 (terrorist threats relating to radioactive devices etc) | The offence was committed on or after 12 January 2010. |

# LIFE SENTENCE—COMMON LAW

*References: Archbold 5A-1238*

## Availability

Where: 101-001

(a) the offence was committed prior to 4 April 2005; or
(b) the offence is not a Sch.19 offence, the court has an inherent jurisdiction to impose a life sentence.

Such instances are likely to be rare: *Saunders* [2013] EWCA Crim 1027; [2014] 1 Cr. App. R.(S.) 45; [2013] Crim. L.R. 930.

## Test

The decisions in *Attorney General's Reference 32 of 1996 (Whittaker)* [1997] 1 Cr. App. R.(S.) 261; [1996] Crim. L.R. 917; (1996) 93(38) L.S.G. 4 and *Chapman* [2000] Cr. App. R.(S.) 377 established a two-stage test for the imposition of discretionary "common law" life sentences: 101-002

(1) the offender has been convicted of a very serious offence; and
(2) there are good grounds for believing that the offender may remain a serious danger to the public for a period which cannot be reliably estimated at the date of sentence.

This test is to be preferred to the three-stage test proffered in *Hodgson* (1968) 52 Cr. App. R. 113; [1968] Crim. L.R. 46, *Ali* [2019] EWCA Crim 856; [2019] 2 Cr. App. R.(S.) 43.

## Example

Some of these offences may involve a significant risk of serious harm to the public, but are not included within the list of "*specified*" offences in the dangerousness provisions in the Sentencing Code. One obvious example is the offender who commits repeated offences of very serious drug importation/supply which justifies the imposition of the life sentence. In circumstances like these the court is not obliged to impose the sentence in accordance with s.258 but its discretion to do so is unaffected: *Saunders* [2013] EWCA Crim 1027; [2014] 1 Cr. App. R.(S.) 45; [2013] Crim. L.R. 930 at [11]. 101-003

# DETENTION IN DEFAULT OR FOR CONTEMPT

## PCC(S)A 2000 s.108

### Availability

In any case where a court would have power to commit a person aged at least 18 and under 21 to prison in default of payment of a fine or other sum of money, or for contempt, or any kindred offence, the court may commit the person to be detained for a term not exceeding the appropriate term of imprisonment: see PCC(S)A 2000 s.108. **102-001**

The court may not commit a person to be detained unless it is of the opinion that no other method of dealing with them is appropriate, and in forming that opinion the court must take into account all such information about the default or contempt as is available to it and may take into account any information about the person which is before it: PCC(S)A 2000 s.108(3).

### Magistrates' courts

If a magistrates' court commits a person to be detained, it must state in open court the reason for its opinion that no other method of dealing with them is appropriate and cause that reason to be specified in the warrant of commitment: PCC(S)A 2000 s.108(4). **102-002**

# PARENTING ORDERS

## Sentencing Code ss.365-375 and Crime and Disorder Act 1998 S.8

*References: Current Sentencing Practice A6; Archbold 5A-1258*

### General

**What is a parenting order? Sentencing Code** A parenting order made under the Sentencing Code is an order which requires the person in respect of whom it is made ("*the parent*"): 103-001

(a) to comply, for a period of not more than 12 months, with requirements specified in the order; and
(b) to attend, for a concurrent period of not more than three months, such counselling or guidance programme as may be specified in directions given by the responsible officer: SC s.365.

**What is a parenting order? CDA 1998** A parenting order is an order which requires the parent: 103-002

(a) to comply with such requirements as are specified in the order; and
(b) to attend such counselling or guidance programme as may be specified in directions given by the responsible officer: CDA 1998 s.8(4).

**Different types of order** There are various different orders: 103-003

(a) where a person aged under 18 is convicted of an offence (SC s.366);
(b) where the parent or guardian fails to attend a meeting under s.90 of the Sentencing Code (referral order: youth offender panel) (SC s.368);
(c) where the parent or guardian is convicted of an offence under the EA 1996 ss.443 or 444 (SC, s.369); and
(d) where the court sentencing a person under the age of 18 has also imposed a CBO or SHPO (CDA 1998 s.8).

### Post-conviction order

**Availability** A parenting order under this section is available to a court by or before which an offender aged under 18 is convicted of an offence: SC s.366(1). 103-004

**Power/duty to impose** If the offender is aged under 16 at the time of conviction, the court must: 103-005

(a) make a parenting order under this section in respect of a parent or guardian of the offender if it is satisfied that the order would be desirable in the interests of preventing the commission of any further offence by the offender; or
(b) state in open court that it is not so satisfied, and why not. This does not apply if the court makes a referral order in respect of the offender: SC s.366(3).

If the offender is aged 16 or 17 at the time of conviction, the court may make a parenting order under this section in respect of a parent or guardian of the offender if it is satisfied that the order would be desirable in the interests of preventing the commission of any further offence by the offender: SC s.366(4).

**103-006 Requirements** The requirements that the court may specify in the order under s.365(1)(a) are requirements that it considers desirable in the interests of preventing the commission of any further offence by the offender: SC s.366(6).

If the order contains a requirement under s.365(1)(b) and the court is satisfied that:

(a) the attendance of the parent or guardian at a residential course is likely to be more effective than that person's attendance at a non-residential course in preventing the commission of any further offence by the offender; and
(b) any interference with family life which is likely to result from the parent's or guardian's attendance at a residential course is proportionate in all the circumstances,

the court may provide in the order that a counselling or guidance programme which the parent or guardian is required to attend by virtue of the requirement may be or include a residential course: SC s.366(7).

**103-007 Reports, etc.** Before making a parenting order under this section in respect of a parent or guardian of an offender aged under 16, the court must obtain and consider information about:

(a) the offender's family circumstances; and
(b) the likely effect of the order on those circumstances: SC s.366(8).

**103-008 Referral order** See s.367 of the Sentencing Code for provision about where the court proposes to impose both a parenting order and a referral order.

**Order following failure to attend referral order meetings**

**103-009 Availability** A parenting order under this section is available to a youth court where:

(a) an offender has been referred to a youth offender panel; and
(b) a parent or guardian of the offender is referred by the panel to the youth court under s.93 in respect of a failure to comply with an order under s.90 (order requiring attendance at meetings of panel): SC s.368(1).

**103-010 Test** Where a parenting order under this section is available, the youth court may make such an order if it is satisfied that:

(a) the parent or guardian has failed without reasonable excuse to comply with the order under s.90; and
(b) the parenting order would be desirable in the interests of preventing the commission of any further offence by the offender: SC s.368(2).

**103-011 Requirements** The requirements that the court may specify in the order under s.365(1)(a) are requirements that it considers desirable in the interests of preventing the commission of any further offence by the offender: SC s.368(4).

If the order contains a requirement under s.365(1)(b) and the court is satisfied that:

(a) the attendance of the parent or guardian at a residential course is likely to be more effective than that person's attendance at a non-residential course in preventing the commission of any further offence by the offender; and
(b) any interference with family life which is likely to result from the parent's or guardian's attendance at a residential course is proportionate in all the circumstances,

the court may provide in the order that a counselling or guidance programme which the parent or guardian is required to attend by virtue of the requirement may be or include a residential course: SC s.368(5).

**Reports, etc.** Before making a parenting order under this section in respect of a parent or guardian of an offender aged under 16, the court must obtain and consider information about: **103-012**

(a) the offender's family circumstances; and
(b) the likely effect of the order on those circumstances: SC s.368(6).

**Education Act 1996 order**

**Availability** A parenting order under this section is available to the court by or before which an offender is convicted of an offence under: **103-013**

(a) s.443 of the EA 1996 (failure to comply with school attendance order); or
(b) s.444 of that Act (failure to secure regular attendance at school of registered pupil): SC s.369(1).

**Requirements** The requirements that the court may specify under s.365(1)(a) are requirements that it considers desirable in the interests of preventing the commission of any further offence under s.443 or 444 of the EA 1996: SC s.369(4). **103-014**

If the order contains a requirement under s.365(1)(b) and the court is satisfied that:

(a) the attendance of that offender at a residential course is likely to be more effective than the offender's attendance at a non-residential course in preventing the commission of any further offence under ss.443 or 444 of the EA 1996; and
(b) any interference with family life which is likely to result from that person's attendance at a residential course is proportionate in all the circumstances,

the court may provide in the order that a counselling or guidance programme which the offender is required to attend by virtue of the requirement may be or include a residential course: SC s.369(5).

**Reports, etc.** Before making a parenting order under this section in a case where the offence related to a person aged under 16, the court must obtain and consider information about: **103-015**

(a) that person's family circumstances; and
(b) the likely effect of the order on those circumstances: SC s.369(6).

## Order following CBO or SHPO

103-016 **Availability** A parenting order is available where a CBO or an SHPO is made in respect of a child or young person: CDA 1998 s.8(1)(b).

103-017 **Test** An order may be imposed where "the relevant condition" is satisfied. The relevant condition is that the parenting order would be desirable in the interests of preventing in the case of a CBO or SHPO, any repetition of the kind of behaviour which led to the order being made: CDA 1998 s.8(6).

Where the child or young person is also convicted of an offence, the court must make a parenting order: CDA 1998 s.8(2) and 9(1).

There is no duty to make an order where the court makes a referral order in respect of the offence, CDA 1998 s.9(1A). However, the court may make both a referral order and a parenting order after considering a report from an appropriate officer.

103-018 **Reports, etc.** Before making a parenting order where the child or young person is aged under 16 and is made subject to a CBO or an SHPO, or is convicted of an offence: CDA 1998 s.9(2).

103-019 **Duty to give reasons when not making an order** If the court is not satisfied that the relevant condition is met, it shall state in open court that it is not and why it is not: CDA 1998 s.9(1).

103-020 **Arrangements must be in place** A court shall not make a parenting order unless it has been notified by the Secretary of State that arrangements for implementing such orders are available in the area in which it appears to the court that the parent resides or will reside and the notice has not been withdrawn: CDA 1998 s.8(3).

## Making the order (all orders)

103-021 **Arrangements must be in place** A parenting order may not be made unless the court has been notified by the Secretary of State that arrangements for implementing such orders are available in the area in which it appears to the court that the parent resides or will reside and the notice has not been withdrawn: SC s.370 and CDA 1998 s.8(3).

103-022 **Requirements** Requirements specified in a parenting order under this Chapter must, as far as practicable, be such as to avoid:

(a) any conflict with the parent's religious beliefs; and
(b) any interference with the times, if any, at which the parent normally works or attends an educational establishment: SC s.372 and CDA 1998 s.9(4).

103-023 **Explain effect of order** Before making a parenting order, a court must explain to the parent in ordinary language:

(a) the effect of the order and of the requirements proposed to be included in it;
(b) the consequences which may follow (under s.375) if the parent fails to comply with those requirements; and

(c) that the court has power to review the order on the application either of the parent or of the responsible officer: SC s.372(3) and CDA 1998 s.9(3).

**Consent** The consent of the parent or guardian is not required. **103-024**

**Length** The order may not last for more than 12 months; any counselling or guidance may not exceed a concurrent period of three months: SC s.365(1) and CDA 1998 s.8(4). **103-025**

# PARENTS AND GUARDIANS

## Sentencing Code ss.128, 378 and 380

*References: Current Sentencing Practice A6; Archbold 5A-1255*

This section contains information on: 104-001

(a) fines/financial orders paid by parent/guardian;
(b) financial circumstances orders; and
(c) bind overs of parent/guardian.

### Fine/compensation/costs/surcharge to be paid by parent/guardian

**Under 16s** Where a person under 16 is found guilty of an offence, and the court considers that the matter should be dealt with by means of a fine, costs or compensation order, the court must order the fine, costs or compensation order to be paid by the offender's parent or guardian, unless the parent or guardian cannot be found or it would be unreasonable to make an order for payment: SC ss.380(1) and (2) and 381. 104-002

Where a court would otherwise order a child or young person to pay the statutory surcharge, the court must order that the surcharge be paid by the parent or guardian of the child or young person instead of by the child or young person himself, unless the court is satisfied, unless the parent or guardian cannot be found or it would be unreasonable to make an order for payment: SC ss.42(4) and 380(1) and (2).

**Those aged 16–18** Where a person over 16 but under 18 is found guilty of an offence, and the court considers that the matter should be dealt with by means of a fine, costs or compensation order, the court may order the fine, costs or compensation order to be paid by the offender's parent or guardian, unless the parent or guardian cannot be found or it would be unreasonable to make an order for payment: SC ss.380(1) and (2) and 381. 104-003

Where a court would otherwise order a child or young person to pay the statutory surcharge, the court may order that the surcharge be paid by the parent or guardian of the child or young person instead of by the child or young person themselves, unless the court is satisfied, unless the parent or guardian cannot be found or it would be unreasonable to make an order for payment: SC ss.42(4) and 380(1) and (2).

**The parent or guardian must be given the opportunity to be heard** The parent or guardian must be given the opportunity to be heard before the order is made, unless they have been required to attend and have failed to do so: SC s.380(3). 104-004

**Means** In considering the means of the offender for the purpose of such an order, the court should consider the means of the parent or guardian, rather than the means of the offender: SC ss.124, 125 and 128(4). There is no requirement to consider the means of a local authority: SC s.128(7). 104-005

**104-006 Adverse findings forming the basis of an order** A court should not make an order against a parent or guardian on the basis that the offender has been neglected unless there is evidence of such neglect. The court should not base a finding adverse to a parent or guardian on information disclosed by the parent or guardian for the purposes of a pre-sentence report: *Lenihan v West Yorks. Metropolitan Police* (1981) 3 Cr. App. R.(S.) 42.

**104-007 Offender in local authority care** Where the offender is in the care of a local authority, or living in local authority accommodation, and the local authority has parental responsibility, the court may make an order against the local authority: SC ss.380 and 404.

An order should not be made against a local authority unless the local authority has failed to do everything that it reasonably could have done to protect the public from the offender, and there is a causative link between the failure and the offence: *D (A Minor) v DPP* (1995) 16 Cr. App. R.(S.) 1040; (1996) 160 J.P. 275; [1995] Crim. L.R. 748.

**104-008 Appeals** A parent or guardian may appeal to the Crown Court against an order under s.380 made by a magistrates' court: SC s.380(5). A parent or guardian may appeal to the Court of Appeal against an order under s.380 made by the Crown Court, as if the offender had been convicted on indictment and the order were a sentence passed on their conviction: SC s.380(6).

**Financial circumstances order**

**104-009** Before making an order under s.380, (power to order parent or guardian to pay fine/costs/compensation/surcharge) against the parent or guardian of an individual who has been convicted of an offence, the court may make a financial circumstances order with respect to the parent or (as the case may be) guardian: SC s.128(5). See **FINANCIAL CIRCUMSTANCES ORDERS, para.26** for more details.

For the purposes of any order under s.380, where:

(a) the parent or guardian of an offender aged under 18:
   (i) has failed to comply with a financial circumstances order imposed by virtue of s.35(4); or
   (ii) has otherwise failed to co-operate with the court in its inquiry into the parent's or guardian's financial circumstances; and
(b) the court considers that it has insufficient information to make a proper determination of the parent's or guardian's financial circumstances, the court may make such determination as it thinks fit: SC s.382(1).

**Bind over of parent/guardian**

**104-010 Powers** The court has the power to:

(a) with the consent of the offender's parent or guardian, to order the parent or guardian to enter into a recognisance to take proper care of them and exercise proper control over them;
(b) if the parent or guardian refuses consent and the court considers the refusal unreasonable, to order the parent or guardian to pay a fine not exceeding £1,000; and

(c) where the court has imposed a YRO upon the offender, it may include in the recognisance a provision that the offender's parent or guardian ensure that the offender complies with the requirements of that sentence: SC s.376(2) and (6).

**Test** Where an offender under the age of 16 is found guilty of an offence, the court must bind over the parent or guardian, if it is satisfied that this would be desirable in the interests of preventing further offences by the offender: SC s.376(4). Otherwise, the power is a discretionary power. **104-011**

**Duty to explain where order not made** Where the offender is aged under 16 and the court fails to exercise this power, it must state in open court that it is not satisfied that this would be desirable in the interests of preventing further offences by the offender and provide reasons: SC s.376(4)(b). **104-012**

**Recognisance** The recognisance may be in an amount not exceeding £1,000: SC s.376(8). **104-013**

**Length of the order** The bind over may not be for a period exceeding three years, or until the offender's 18th birthday, whichever is the shorter: SC s.376(7). **104-014**

**Fixing the amount** Before fixing the amount of the recognisance, the court must take into account the means of the parent or guardian, so far as they appear or are known: SC s.376(9). **104-015**

**Appeals** A parent or guardian may appeal to the Crown Court against an order under s.376 made by a magistrates' court: SC s.377. A parent or guardian may appeal to the Court of Appeal against an order under s.376 made by the Crown Court, as if they had been convicted on indictment and the order were a sentence passed on their conviction: SC s.377. **104-016**

# G: CONSEQUENCES OF CONVICTION

# SEXUAL OFFENDERS—NOTIFICATION REQUIREMENTS

## Sexual Offences Act 2003 s.80

*References: Current Sentencing Practice A7; Archbold 246*

### General

**Nature of the obligation** Notification is not part of a sentence: *Longworth* [2006] UKHL 1; [2006] 1 W.L.R. 313; [2006] 2 Cr. App. R.(S.) 62. It can therefore not be appealed. **105-001**

**Applicability** A person is subject to the notification requirements of the SOA 2003 if: **105-002**

(a) they are convicted of an offence listed in Sch.3;
(b) they are found not guilty of such an offence by reason of insanity;
(c) they are found to be under a disability and to have done the act charged against them in respect of such an offence; or
(d) they are cautioned in respect of such an offence: SOA 2003 s.80(1).

**The types of offences in Sch.3** There are three types of offences listed in Sch.3: **105-003**

(1) those with a sentencing condition (e.g. the offence is listed only where a sentence of, or more severe than, X is imposed);
(2) those with an offence condition (e.g. the offence is listed only where the offence is committed in a manner specified in the schedule, such as the victim being under a certain age); and
(3) those without an offence condition or a sentencing condition.

**Start date** Notification begins on the date of the conviction (or finding etc.): SOA 2003 s.82(1) and (6). This is subject to the offence being one which has a sentencing condition and therefore the requirements of the provisions will only be met (and therefore notification begins) once sentence is imposed: SOA 2003 s.82(6) and 132. **105-004**

### The notification period:

The periods during which the offender is liable to the notification requirements are as follows: **105-005**

| *Description* | *Period* |
|---|---|
| A person who, in respect of the offence, is or has been sentenced to imprisonment for life or for a term of 30 months or more | An indefinite period beginning with the relevant date |
| A person who, in respect of the offence or finding, is or has been admitted to a hospital subject to a restriction order | An indefinite period beginning with that date |

| | |
|---|---|
| A person who, in respect of the offence, is or has been sentenced to imprisonment for a term of more than six months but less than 30 months | 10 years beginning with that date |
| A person who, in respect of the offence, is or has been sentenced to imprisonment for a term of six months or less | Seven years beginning with that date |
| A person who, in respect of the offence or finding, is or has been admitted to a hospital without being subject to a restriction order | Seven years beginning with that date |
| A person who has been cautioned | Two years beginning with that date |
| A person in whose case an order for conditional discharge is made in respect of the offence | The period of conditional discharge |
| A person of any other description | Five years beginning with the relevant date |

105-006 **Those under 18** Where a person is under 18 on the relevant date, the determinate periods are one half of those specified as fixed length periods: SOA 2003 s.82(1) and (2).

Where an offender under 18 is convicted of an offence within the scope of Sch.3 and sentenced in a manner which results in an obligation to notify, the court may direct that obligation shall be treated as an obligation of the parent: SOA 2003 s.89(1).

**Particular circumstances**

105-007 **Suspended sentence order** The length of the notification period is determined by the length of the period of imprisonment (or detention) that is subject to the suspended sentence order: SC s.289.

105-008 **Detention and training orders** If an offender under 18 is sentenced to a detention and training order, the relevant period for the purpose of determining their liability to the notification requirements is the custodial part of the order (normally half of the term of the order). A person sentenced to a DTO where the total order is more than 12 months is liable to the requirements for a period of five years; if the total order is for any period not exceeding 12 months, the period of liability is three and a half years: SOA 2003 s.131.

105-009 **Community orders** Where a community order with an unpaid work requirement is imposed (which states that the unpaid work must be completed within 12 months), notwithstanding the fact that the offender may complete the unpaid work sooner, notification requirements will apply as the order was made for 12 months: *Davison* [2008] EWCA Crim 2795; [2009] 2 Cr. App. R.(S.) 13; [2009] Crim. L.R. 208.

105-010 **Absolute discharge** An absolute discharge does not attract notification requirements. However in such cases the offender is required to comply with the notification requirements from the date of conviction to the date of the imposition of the absolute discharge: Home Office Guidance on Pt 2 of the Sexual Offences Act 2003 (March 2023).[1]

**Sexual Harm Prevention Orders** For the effect of an SHPO on existing notification requirements, see **SEXUAL HARM PREVENTION ORDERS, para.83** **105-011**

**Re-sentencing** Where an offender is sentenced for a scheduled offence but, by virtue of that sentence is not subject to the notification regime, but upon breaching that sentence is re-sentenced to a sentence to which the notification regime does apply, the offender will then become subject to the notification regime upon the imposition of the new sentence: *Rawlinson* [2018] EWCA Crim 2825; [2019] 1 W.L.R. 2565; [2019] 1 Cr. App. R.(S.) 51. **105-012**

**Start date** Notification begins on the date of the conviction (or finding, etc.): SOA 2003 s.82(1) and (6).This is unless the offence listed in Sch.3 to the Act has a "sentence condition"; in such cases, notification begins on the day on which the sentence condition is satisfied: SOA 2003 s.132(3). **105-013**

**Consecutive terms** Where the offender is sentenced to terms which are wholly or partly consecutive, the table applies to the effective length of the aggregate terms: SOA 2003 s.82(3) and (4). **105-014**

**Reviews of indefinite notification requirements**

A person subject to indefinite notification requirements may apply for a review to the relevant chief officer of police with an appeal from that decision to the magistrates' court. No application may be made until after 15 years from the person's first notification (eight years for a person aged under 18): The Sexual Offences Act 2003 (Remedial) Order 2012 (SI 2012/1883). **105-015**

---

1 *https://assets.publishing.service.gov.uk/government/uploads/system/uploads/attachment_data/file/1148607/Part_2_Guidance_March_2023_FINAL_3003.pdf.*

# AUTOMATIC BARRING

## Safeguarding Vulnerable Groups Act 2006

*References: Archbold 5A-1309*

### General

Barring is not an order of the court, it is an automatic consequence of a conviction for certain offences. The offender's name will be included on the children and/or adult barred list, by the Disclosure and Barring Service (DBS). **106-001**

**Court's duties** The court before which the offender is convicted must inform the person at the time they are convicted that the Service will include them in the barred list concerned: CrimPR 2020 r.28.3(1). **106-002**

**Types of barring** There are two types of barring; automatic and discretionary. Automatic barring is contingent upon a caution or conviction for a listed offence (see below). Discretionary barring usually follows from a referral by a third party, e.g. an employer, and is not dealt with in this text. **106-003**

**The lists** There are two lists; the child list and the adult list. A person included on the adult and/or child barred lists is prohibited from regulated activity in relation to adults or children, see Safeguarding Vulnerable Groups Act 2006 (SVGA 2006) Sch.3 para.2. **106-004**

**Those aged under 18** Automatic barring applies only to those aged 18+ at the time of the commission of the offence: SVGA 2006 Sch.3 para.24(4). A defendant aged under 18 at the time of the offence will not be automatically barred, but the DBS may consider barring the defendant under the discretionary barring powers. **106-005**

### The triggering offences

There are two types of triggering offence: **106-006**

(a) automatic inclusion offences, where the defendant has no right to make representations; and
(b) automatic inclusion offences, where the defendant has a right to make representations before they are included in the list.

### Automatic inclusion offences with no right to make representations

For automatic inclusion offences with no right to make representations, the DBS will inform the person in writing of their inclusion in the adult and/or child barred lists. **106-007**

### Automatic inclusion offences with a right to make representations

For automatic inclusion offences with the right to make representations, if the person satisfies the "*test for regulated activity*" (see SVGA 2006 Sch.3 para.2), the **106-008**

DBS will seek representations from the person and consider any representations prior to making a barring decision. If no representations are received the person will be barred. The person will be informed in writing whether or not they are barred.

The list of offences can be found in The Safeguarding Vulnerable Groups Act 2006 (Prescribed Criteria and Miscellaneous Provisions) Regulations 2009 (SI 2009/37) rr.3–6 and Sch.1.

**Any "connected offence" of the listed offences**

**106-009** *"Connected offence"* means any offence of attempting, conspiring or incitement to commit that offence, or aiding, abetting, counselling or procuring the commission of the offence.

It is uncertain whether the reference to incitement in this provision includes a reference to offences contrary to the SCA 2007 ss.44, 45 and 46.

**106-010 Offence of engaging in regulated activity whilst earred** An individual commits an offence if they:

(a) seek to engage in regulated activity from which they are barred;
(b) offer to engage in regulated activity from which they are barred; or
(c) engage in regulated activity from which they are barred.

The offence is triable either way and the maximum sentence is five years: SVGA 2006 s.7.

# TERRORIST OFFENDERS—NOTIFICATION REQUIREMENTS

## Counter-Terrorism Act 2008 ss.44 and 45

*References: Archbold 25-215*

### Notification requirements

**Applicability** Notification requirements apply to a person who: **107-001**

- (a) has been convicted of an offence to which CTA 2008 Pt 4 applies; and
- (b) was aged 16 or over when sentenced; and
- (c) has been sentenced to:
  - (i) imprisonment or custody for life;
  - (ii) imprisonment or detention in a young offender institution for a term of 12 months or more;
  - (iii) imprisonment for public protection/detention for public protection under the CJA 2003 s.225;
  - (iv) detention for life or for a period of 12 months or more under PCC(S)A 2000 s.91 or s.250 of the Sentencing Code;
  - (v) a DTO for a term of 12 months or more;
  - (vi) detention for public protection under the CJA 2003 s.226;
  - (vii) an extended sentence of detention; or
  - (viii) detention during Her Majesty's pleasure: CTA 2008 s.44 and 45(1).

Notification requirements also apply to a person who has been:

- (a) convicted of an offence to which the CTA 2008 Pt 4 applies which carries a maximum term of imprisonment of 12 months or more;
- (b) found not guilty by reason of insanity of such an offence; or
- (c) found to be under a disability and to have done the act charged against them in respect of such an offence, and made subject in respect of the offence to a hospital order: CTA 2008 s.44 and 45(2).

No express provision is made for suspended sentence orders, however sexual offenders notification applies to suspended sentence orders and so it may be that terrorist notification is interpreted in the same way.

### Offences to which CTA 2008 Pt 4 applies

- (1) TA 2000 ss.11, 12, 15-18, 38B, 54, 56-61 and an offence in respect of which there is jurisdiction by virtue of ss.62-63D; **107-002**
- (2) Anti-terrorism, Crime and Security Act 2001(ATCSA 2001) s.113;
- (3) TA 2006 ss.1, 2, 5, 6, 8-11 and an offence in respect of which there is jurisdiction by virtue of s.17;
- (4) any ancillary offence in relation to an offence listed in (1)–(3) above. An "*ancillary offence*" is:
  - (a) an offence of aiding, abetting, counselling or procuring the commission of the offence;
  - (b) an offence under the SCA 2007 Pt 2 in relation to the offence; or

(c) attempting or conspiring to commit the offence, CTA 2008 s.94;

(5) offences as to which a court has determined the offence had a terrorist connection: CTA 2008 s.94.

**107-003 The notification periods** The period for which the notification requirements apply are as follows: CTA 2008 s.53.

| Description | Period |
|---|---|
| Offender aged 18 at the time of conviction and sentenced to an indeterminate sentence or a determinate sentence of 10 years or more | 30 years |
| Offender aged 18 at the time of conviction and sentenced to a term of at least five years but less than 10 years | 15 years |
| All other cases | 10 years |

**107-004 Must notify defendant** The court must tell the defendant that notification requirements apply, and under which legislation: CrimPR 2020 r.28.3.

**107-005 When does notification begin?** The notification period begins on the day the person is dealt with for the offence: CTA 2008 s.53(4).

**107-006 When does notification expire?** In determining whether the notification period has expired, any period when the person was in custody on remand or serving a sentence or imprisonment or detention, or detained in a hospital, or under the Immigration Acts is disregarded: CTA 2008 53(7).

**107-007 Appeals** A person who becomes liable to notification requirements may appeal against the determination that the offence has a terrorist connection as if that determination was a sentence: CTA 2003 s.42(2).

# DEPORTATION

## Immigration Act 1971 s.6 and Sch.3 and UK Borders Act 2007 s.32

*References: Current Sentencing Practice A7; Archbold 5A-1049, 5A-1319*

### Introduction

For the purposes of sentencing, there are two types of deportation; the "*automatic liability to deportation*" regime and the "*recommendation for deportation*" regime. **108-001**

Other sentencing powers are not to be used to remove offenders from the UK: *R. (Dragoman) v Camberwell Green Magistrates' Court* [2012] EWHC 4105 (Admin); (2013) 177 J.P. 372; [2013] A.C.D. 61.

Notwithstanding the below, it is the Secretary of State's policy that no EU citizen be deported unless the term of imprisonment imposed is two years or more: *Kluxen* [2010] EWCA Crim 1081; [2011] 1 W.L.R. 218; [2011] 1 Cr. App. R.(S.) 39.

### Automatic liability to deportation

**Duty to deport** The Secretary of State must make a deportation order in respect of a foreign criminal. A foreign criminal means a person who: **108-002**

- (a) is not a British citizen;
- (b) is convicted of an offence in the UK; and
- (c) satisfies one of the following conditions:
  - (i) is sentenced to a period of imprisonment of at least 12 months, or;
  - (ii) the offence is an offence specified by the Secretary of State under the Nationality, Immigration and Asylum Act 2002 (NIAA 2002) s.2(4)(a), and the person is sentenced to a period of imprisonment: UK Borders Act 2007 (UKBA 2007) s.32(1) and (5).

The second condition was not in force on 31 October 2024.

**Do not rearrange sentences to avoid liability** As a matter of principle it would not be right to reduce an otherwise appropriate sentence so as to avoid the provisions of the UKBA 2007 because: **108-003**

- (a) sentences are intended to be commensurate with the seriousness of the offence;
- (b) when passing sentence a judge is neither entitled nor obliged to reach a contrived result so as to avoid the operation of a statutory provision; and
- (c) automatic deportation provisions are not a penalty included in the sentence: *Mintchev* [2011] EWCA Crim 499; [2011] 2 Cr. App. R.(S.) 81; [2011] Crim. L.R. 483.

Note however, that in *Hakimzadeh* [2009] EWCA Crim 959; [2010] 1 Cr. App. R.(S.) 10; [2009] Crim. L.R. 676 where the defence suggested the sentences be rearranged to avoid the deportation provisions, relying upon the age of the offending and the fact that "deportation was never in the judge's mind", the Court of Appeal acceded to the request.

The decision in *Mintchev* was applied in *Alkidar* [2019] EWCA Crim 330 where the court described an alternative approach as "fundamentally flawed".

An argument that the sentence (and the concomitant liability to deportation) would have a disproportionate effect on the offender's family such that it was contrary to art.8 of the European Convention on Human Rights (ECHR) is not available as a matter of principle; what matters is the proper length of the sentence to be imposed: *Malik* [2020] EWCA Crim 957; [2021] 1 Cr. App. R.(S.) 7.

108-004 **Definition of "12 months' imprisonment"** A "period of imprisonment of at least 12 months" does not include:

(a) a suspended sentence (unless a court subsequently orders that the sentence or any part of it is to take effect); and
(b) a person who is sentenced to a period of at least 12 months' only by virtue of being sentenced to consecutive sentences.

However, it does include a person sentenced to detention or to be detained in an institution other than a prison and any indeterminate period, provided it could last for more than 12 months: UKBA 2007 s.38(1).

108-005 **Exceptions** There are a series of exceptions to the duty to make a deportation order. These include:

(a) where the Secretary of State thinks that the foreign criminal was aged under 18 at the date of conviction;
(b) where the deportation order would breach a person's Convention rights, or the UK's obligations under the Refugee Convention;
(c) where the removal of the foreign criminal from the UK in pursuance of a deportation order would breach rights of the foreign criminal under the EU treaties;
(d) where certain provisions of the EA 2003 apply; or
(e) where certain orders or directions under the MHA 1983 apply (including s.37, 45A, and 47): UKBA 2007 s.33.

The existence of an exception does not prevent the making of a deportation order, see UKBA 2007 s.33(7).

### Recommendations for deportation

108-006 **No recommendation where automatic liability exists** A court should not make a recommendation for deportation in the case of an offender who is liable to automatic deportation as no useful purpose would be served: *Kluxen* [2010] EWCA Crim 1081; [2011] 1 Cr. App. R.(S.) 39.

108-007 **Availability** A court may recommend for deportation an offender aged 17 on the day of conviction if they are not a British citizen and have been convicted of an offence punishable with imprisonment: IA 1971 s.3(6) and 6(1).

The offender is deemed to have attained the age of 17 at the date of their conviction if on considering any evidence they appear to have done so to the court: IA 1971 s.6(3)(a).

If any question arises as to whether any person is a British citizen, or is entitled to any exemption, the person claiming to be a British citizen or to be entitled to any exemption must prove that they are: IA 1971 s.3(8).

**Irish and Commonwealth citizens** The principal classes of persons exempted from liability to deportation are Commonwealth citizens and citizens of the Republic of Ireland who: 108-008

(a) had that status in 1973; and
(b) were then ordinarily resident in the UK; and
(c) had been ordinarily resident in the UK during the five years prior to the conviction: IA 1971 s.7(1).

**Principles** The following principles have been identified: 108-009

(a) the principal criterion for recommending deportation is the extent to which the offender will represent a potential detriment to the UK if they remain in the country: *Nazari* [1980] 1 W.L.R. 1366; [1980] 3 All E.R. 880; (1980) 71 Cr. App. R. 87;
(b) the court is primarily concerned with the offender's expected future behaviour, as evidenced by their offence and previous record, see e.g. *Benabbas* [2005] EWCA Crim 2113;
(c) the court is not concerned with the political situation or conditions in the offender's home country: *Nazari* [1980] 1 W.L.R. 1366; (1980) 71 Cr. App. R. 87;
(d) the fact that the offender is living on social security benefit is not a relevant consideration: *Serry* (1980) 2 Cr. App. R.(S.) 336;
(e) the fact that the offender is not lawfully in the UK is not a relevant consideration, except in cases where they have secured admission to the UK by fraudulent means, see e.g. *Benabbas* [2005] EWCA Crim 2113;
(f) the court should not take into account the Convention Rights of the offender; the effect that a recommendation might have on innocent persons not before the court; the provisions of art.28 of Dir.2004/38; or the Immigration (European Economic Area) Regulations 2006 (SI 2006/1003): *Carmona* [2006] EWCA Crim 508; [2006] 2 Cr. App. R.(S.) 102;
(g) the courts have no desire to break up a family, and in making the decision as to whether or not a recommendation is appropriate, the court should consider the effect upon those not before the court: *Nazari* [1980] 1 W.L.R. 1366; (1980) 71 Cr. App. R. 87. However, that statement is not to be interpreted literally and the court will uphold a recommendation in an appropriate case: *Carmona* [2006] EWCA Crim 508; [2006] 2 Cr. App. R.(S.) 102; and
(h) the making of a recommendation does not justify a reduction in sentence, as the recommendation is not part of the punishment of the offender: *Carmona* [2006] EWCA Crim 508; [2006] 2 Cr. App. R.(S.) 102.

**Recommendations will now be rare** A court should not normally make a recommendation in respect of an offender unless at least one of their offences justifies a 108-010 sentence of 12 months' imprisonment or detention: *Kluxen* [2010] EWCA Crim 1081; [2011] 1 Cr. App. R.(S.) 39.

108-011 **Full inquiry** The court must not make a recommendation without a full inquiry into the relevant circumstances: *Nazari* [1980] 1 W.L.R. 1366; (1980) 71 Cr. App. R. 87.

108-012 **Judge must warn counsel** The judge should warn counsel if they are considering making recommendation for deportation so that the advocate can make submissions: *Carmona* [2006] EWCA Crim 508; [2006] 2 Cr. App. R.(S.) 102.

108-013 **Duty to give reasons** The court must give reasons for making a recommendation for deportation, if it does so: *Carmona* [2006] EWCA Crim 508; [2006] 2 Cr. App. R.(S.) 102.

108-014 **Procedural requirements** The court may not recommend the offender for deportation unless they have been given seven days' notice in writing setting out the definition of a British citizen and explaining the exemptions from liability to be recommended for deportation. The court may adjourn to enable the required notice to be served: IA 1971 s.6(2).

Failure to comply with this requirement does not necessarily mean that any recommendation will be quashed on appeal: *Abdi* [2007] EWCA Crim 1913; [2008] 1 Cr. App. R.(S.) 87; [2007] Crim. L.R. 992.

# H: NON-RECENT OFFENCES

# NON-RECENT OFFENCES

*References: Current Sentencing Practice: A8; Archbold 5A-1333*

The approach to non-recent offences can be divided into two stages: **109-001**

(1) determining the sentencing powers of the court; and
(2) determining the appropriate sentence.

The proper approach is set out in detail in *Ahmed* [2023] EWCA Crim 281; [2023] 1 W.L.R. 1858.

**(1) Determining the sentencing powers of the court** As to the sentencing powers of the court, the first thing to note is that the maximum sentence applicable at the time of the offence must be observed. In terms of the type of sentence available, or the procedural requirements around the sentencing exercise, for convictions on or after the commencement of the Sentencing Code, that Code will apply—thus, the court has the power to impose the modern/current forms of custodial sentences, community sentences and behaviour orders.

**(2) Determining the appropriate sentence** In relation to determining the appropriate sentence, the approach endorsed by the Court of Appeal (Criminal Division) has been to apply current practice (whether that be in the form of sentencing guidelines or authorities from the Court of Appeal (Criminal Division)) with "measured reference". It is suggested that measured reference is designed to reflect the passage of time.

The Sentencing Council's Sexual Offences Guideline, Annex B states:

When sentencing sexual offences under the Sexual Offences Act 1956, or other legislation pre-dating the 2003 Act, the court should apply the following principles:[1] **109-002**

1. The offender must be sentenced in accordance with the sentencing regime applicable at the date of sentence. Under [s.63 of the Sentencing Code], the court must have regard to the statutory purposes of sentencing and must base the sentencing exercise on its assessment of the seriousness of the offence.
2. The sentence is limited to the maximum sentence available at the date of the commission of the offence. If the maximum sentence has been reduced, the lower maximum will be applicable.
3. The court should have regard to any applicable sentencing guidelines for equivalent offences under the Sexual Offences Act 2003 (2003 Act). Where the offence, if committed on the day on which the offender was convicted, would have constituted an offence contrary to s.5 or s.6 of the 2003 Act, (ss.268 and 278 of the Sentencing Code (special custodial sentence for certain offenders of particular concern) apply).
4. The seriousness of the offence, assessed by the culpability of the offender and the harm caused or intended, is the main consideration for the court. The

1 *R. v H* [2011] EWCA Crim 2753; [2012] 1 W.L.R. 1416; [2012] 2 Cr. App. R. (S.) 21.

court should not seek to establish the likely sentence had the offender been convicted shortly after the date of the offence.

5. When assessing the culpability of the offender, the court should have regard to relevant culpability factors set out in any applicable guideline.
6. The court must assess carefully the harm done to the victim based on the facts available to it, having regard to relevant harm factors set out in any applicable guideline. Consideration of the circumstances which brought the offence to light will be of importance.
7. The court must consider the relevance of the passage of time carefully as it has the potential to aggravate or mitigate the seriousness of the offence. It will be an aggravating factor where the offender has continued to commit sexual offences against the victim or others or has continued to prevent the victim reporting the offence.
8. Where there is an absence of further offending over a long period of time, especially combined with evidence of good character, this may be treated by the court as a mitigating factor. However, as with offences dealt with under the 2003 Act, previous good character/exemplary conduct is different from having no previous convictions. The more serious the offence, the less the weight which should normally be attributed to this factor. Where previous good character/exemplary conduct has been used to facilitate the offence, this mitigation should not normally be allowed and such conduct may constitute an aggravating factor.
9. If the offender was very young and immature at the time of the offence, depending on the circumstances of the offence, this may be regarded as personal mitigation.
10. If the offender made admissions at the time of the offence that were not investigated, this is likely to be regarded as personal mitigation. Even greater mitigation is available to the offender who reported himself to the police and/or made early admissions.
11. A reduction for an early guilty plea should be made in the usual manner.

That guidance has since been endorsed in *Forbes* [2016] EWCA Crim 1388; [2017] 1 W.L.R. 53. The court clarified that the task is not to ascertain what sentence would have been imposed if the defendant had been sentenced shortly after the offence, and that "measured reference" to the modern guidelines meant "have regard to" and that a sentencing judge should not simply apply the relevant guideline applicable at the date of sentence, subject to any lower statutory maximum sentence applicable at the date the offence was committed, but use the guideline in a measured and reflective manner to arrive at the appropriate sentence.

The court in *Ahmed*, provided the following guidance in cases where the offender had crossed a relevant age threshold between the date of the offence and the conviction:

i) whatever may be the offender's age at the time of conviction and sentence, the Children guideline was relevant and had to be followed unless the court was satisfied that it would be contrary to the interests of justice to do so;
ii) the court had to have regard to (though was not necessarily restricted by: see (v), the maximum sentence that was available in the case of the offender at or shortly after the time of their offending;
iii) the court must take as its starting point, the sentence that it considered was

likely to have been imposed if the child had been sentenced shortly after the offence;

iv) if, in all the circumstances of the case, the child could not, in law, have been sentenced (at the time of their offending) to any form of custody, then no custodial sentence may be imposed;

v) where some form of custody was available, the court was not necessarily bound by the maximum applicable to the child offender. The court should, however, only exceed that maximum where there was good reason to do so. The mere fact that the offender had now attained adulthood was not in itself a good reason. It was very difficult to think of circumstances in which a good reason could properly be found; and

vi) the starting point taken in accordance with point (iii) would not necessarily be the end point. Subsequent events may enable the court to be sure that the culpability of the child offender was higher, or lower, than would likely have been apparent at the time of the offending.

# I: MENTAL HEALTH DISPOSALS

# MENTAL HEALTH—GENERALLY

*References: Current Sentencing Practice A8; Archbold 5A-1333*

## Relevance of mental health

Mental health conditions and disorders might be relevant to sentencing in a number of ways. First, the impact of a mental health condition or disorder at the time of the offence might be relevant to the assessment of the offender's culpability in committing the offence. Where the offender's mental condition had been exacerbated by a failure to take prescribed medication, or by "self-medication" with controlled drugs or alcohol, the sentencer must consider whether the offender's conduct was wilful or arose, for example, from a lack of insight into their condition. **110-001**

Secondly, the offender's mental health at the time of sentence might be relevant to the decision about the type of sentence imposed and, where a custodial sentence was necessary, the length of that sentence and whether or not this could be suspended.

Thirdly, mental health conditions and disorders might be relevant to an assessment of whether or not the offender was considered "dangerous".

Fourthly, they might need to be taken into account in ensuring that the effect of the court's sentence was clearly understood by the offender and in ensuring that the requirements of a community order or an ancillary order were capable of being fulfilled by the offender: *PS* [2019] EWCA Crim 2286; [2020] 4 W.L.R. 13; [2020] 2 Cr. App. R.(S.) 9.

## Sentencing Guidelines

Reference should be made to the *Sentencing Persons with Mental Disorders, developmental disorders, or neurological impairments Definitive Guideline*. The mental health of the offender is also a factor that sentencers are required to consider at Step 1 or Step 2 of the sentencing process set out in offence-specific guidelines. Sentencing an offender who suffered from a mental disorder or learning disability necessarily required a close focus on the mental health of the individual offender (both at the time of the offence and at the time of sentence), as well as on the facts and circumstances of the specific offence. In some cases, the fact that the offender suffered from a mental health condition or disorder might have little or no effect on the sentencing outcome. In others, it might have a substantial impact. Where a custodial sentence was unavoidable, it could cause the sentencer to move substantially down within the appropriate guideline category range, or even into a lower category range, in order to reach a just and proportionate sentence. Where this was so, a sentence or two in explanation of those choices should be included in the sentencing remarks: *PS* [2019] EWCA Crim 2286;[2020] 4 W.L.R. 13; [2020] 2 Cr. App. R.(S.) 9. **110-002**

## Pre-sentence reports

It was important, when commissioning pre-sentence, psychiatric or psychological reports, that the issues to which the reports were relevant should be clearly **110-003** identified. The younger the offender, and the more serious the offence, the more likely it was that the court would need the assistance of expert reports. Where reports obtained post-conviction revealed features of the offender's mental health that were relevant, but which conflicted with the case that the offender had advanced at trial, in accordance with established principles, the sentencer had to form their own view as to the proper basis for sentence while remaining true to the jury's verdict: *PS* [2019] EWCA Crim 2286; [2020] 2 Cr. App. R.(S.) 9.

# HOSPITAL ORDERS

## Mental Health Act 1983 s.37

*References: Current Sentencing Practice A9; Archbold 5A-1394*

### Availability

Where a person has been convicted of an offence punishable by imprisonment which is not one where the sentence is fixed by law: MHA 1983 s.37(1). **111-001**

The statute refers to orders in respect of those aged 14+ but there appears no restriction for those aged 10–14.

### Order in which the court should approach the issue

In a case where the medical evidence suggests that D is suffering from a mental disorder, that the offending is wholly or in significant part attributable to that disorder, and that treatment is available, and where the court considers that a hospital order with or without restrictions may be appropriate, it must address the issues in the following order: **111-002**

(i) can the mental disorder be appropriately dealt with by a hospital and limitation direction, under the terms of s.45A;
(ii) if it can, and if D was aged 21 at the time of conviction, it should make such a direction under s.45A;
(iii) if not, consider whether the medical evidence fulfils the requirements for a hospital order under s.37(2)(a), and (where applicable) for a restriction order under s.41, and consider whether such an order is the "most suitable method of disposing of the case" under s.37(2)(b);
(iv) the wording of s.37(2)(b) requires a court, when deciding on suitability, to have regard to "other available methods of dealing with" D. Relevant to this is the power to transfer an offender from prison to hospital for treatment, under s.47; and
(v) if the court determines that a hospital order is the most suitable method of dealing with D, the order should normally be made without considering an interim order under s.38 unless there is clear evidence that such an order is needed: *Vowles* [2015] EWCA Crim 45; [2015] 1 W.L.R. 5131; [2015] 2 Cr. App. R.(S.) 6.

*Vowles* was further considered in *Edwards* [2018] EWCA Crim 595; [2018] 4 W.L.R. 64; [2018] 2 Cr. App. R. (S.) 17 in which the court noted that a level of misunderstanding of the guidance offered in *Vowles* had arisen as to the order in which a sentencing judge should approach the making of a s.37 or a s.45A order and the precedence allegedly given in *Vowles* to a s.45A order. The court stated that the position was clear that s.45A and the judgment in *Vowles* did not provide a "default" setting of imprisonment; that the sentencing judge should first consider if a hospital order may be appropriate under s.37(2)(a); if so, before making such an order, the court had to consider all the powers at its disposal including a s.45A order; therefore consideration of a s.45A order must come before the making of a hospital order because a disposal under s.45A includes a penal element and the court must have "sound reasons" for departing from the usual course of imposing a sentence with a penal element.

### Test

**111-003** (1) The court may make a hospital order provided that it is satisfied on the written or oral evidence of two medical practitioners that the offender is suffering from mental disorder and the court is satisfied that the mental disorder from which they are suffering is of a nature or degree which makes it appropriate for them to be detained in a hospital for medical treatment: MHA 1983 s.37(1) and (2).

(2) The court must be of the opinion, having regard to all the circumstances including the nature of the offence and the character and antecedents of the offender, and to the other means of dealing with them that the most suitable means of dealing with the case is by means of a hospital order: MHA 1983 s.37(2).

(3) A hospital order may not be made unless the court is satisfied that arrangements have been made for their admission to a hospital within 28 days of the making of the order: MHA 1983 s.37(4).

### Oral evidence

**111-004** Evidence may not be received by telephone where the court wishes to impose a restriction order in addition to a hospital order: *Clark* [2015] EWCA Crim 2192; [2016] 1 Cr. App. R.(S.) 52; [2016] M.H.L.R. 219.

### Discretion

**111-005** There is a discretion whether to make an order: *Nafei* [2004] EWCA Crim 3238; [2005] 2 Cr. App. R.(S.) 24; [2005] Crim. L.R. 409.

### Requesting information

**111-006** The court may request any regional health authority to furnish such information as the authority has or can reasonably obtain with respect to hospitals in its region or elsewhere at which arrangements could be made for the admission of the offender: MHA 1983 s.39(1).

### Contents of the order

**111-007** The order must specify the hospital to which the offender is to be admitted and the form or forms of mental disorder from which the offender is suffering: MHA 1983 s.37(1).

### Minimum sentences

**111-008** A hospital order may be made despite the fact that the offender would otherwise qualify for a required minimum sentence (see s.399 of the Sentencing Code): MHA 1983 s.37(1A).

## Hospital order made in absence of offender

A court may make a hospital order in the case of an offender subject to an interim hospital order in the absence of the offender, provided that they are represented by a legal representative and their legal representative is given the opportunity to be heard: MHA 1983 s.38(2). **111-009**

## Release

Where an order was made under ss.37 and 41, the First-tier Tribunal (Mental Health) would decide when the offender should be released: *Edwards*. **111-010**

# RESTRICTION ORDERS

## Mental Health Act 1983 s.41

*References: Current Sentencing Practice A9; Archbold 5A-1405*

### Availability

A restriction order may be made only in conjunction with a hospital order: MHA 1983 s.41(1). (See **HOSPITAL ORDERS, para.111**.) **112-001**

### Oral evidence

A restriction order may be made only if at least one of the medical practitioners whose evidence has been taken into account has given evidence orally before the court: MHA 1983 s.41(2). Evidence may not be received by telephone: *Clark* [2015] EWCA Crim 2192; [2016] 1 Cr. App. R.(S.) 52; [2016] M.H.L.R. 219. **112-002**

### Test to apply

The Crown Court may make a restriction order if it makes a hospital order in respect of the offender and it appears to the court, having regard to the nature of the offence, the antecedents of the offender and the risk of them committing further offences if set at large, that is necessary for the protection of the public from serious harm to do so: MHA 1983 s.41(1). **112-003**

In deciding whether to make a restriction order, the court is concerned with the seriousness of the harm which will result if the offender reoffends, rather than with the risk of reoffending.

The seriousness of the offence committed by the offender is not necessarily important for this purpose. An offender convicted of a relatively minor offence may properly be subjected to a restriction order if they suffer from a mental disorder and are dangerous. An offender convicted of a serious offence should not be subjected to a restriction order unless they are likely to commit further offences which will involve a risk of serious harm to the public.

It is not necessary that the offender should be dangerous to the public as a whole; it is sufficient if they are dangerous to a particular section of the public, or to a particular person. **112-004**

The harm to which the public would be exposed if the offender were at large need not necessarily be personal injury.

It is the responsibility of the court, and not that of the medical witnesses, to determine whether a restriction order is appropriate.

# HOSPITAL ORDERS—INTERIM

## Mental Health Act 1983 s.38

*References: Current Sentencing Practice A9; Archbold 5A-1390*

### Availability

An order may be made where a person is convicted of an offence punishable with imprisonment which is not one fixed by law: MHA 1983 s.38(1). The statute refers to orders in respect of those aged 14+ and there appears no restriction for those aged 10–14. **113-001**

### Order in which the issues should be considered

See this section in **HOSPITAL ORDERS, para.111.** **113-002**

### Test

The court may make an interim hospital order provided that it is satisfied on the written or oral evidence of two medical practitioners that the offender is suffering from mental disorder and there is reason to suppose that the mental disorder from which the offender is suffering is such that it may be appropriate for a hospital order to be made in their case: MHA 1983 s.38(1). **113-003**

An interim hospital order may be made only if a hospital place is available.

One of the practitioners on whose evidence the order is based must be employed at the hospital to be specified in the order: MHA 1983 s.38(3).

An order may not be made unless the court is satisfied that arrangements have been made for the offender's admission to the hospital specified within 28 days of the making of the order: MHA 1983 s.38(4).

### Oral evidence

Evidence may not be received by telephone: *Clark* [2015] EWCA Crim 2192; [2016] 1 Cr. App. R.(S.) 52; [2016] M.H.L.R. 219. **113-004**

### Directions

The court must give directions for the conveyance of the offender and their detention in a place of safety pending their admission to hospital: MHA 1983 s.38(4). **113-005**

### Length

An interim hospital order may be made for any period not exceeding 12 weeks in the first instance: MHA 1983 s.38(5). **113-006**

### Renewing an order

**113-007** The order may be renewed for further periods of 28 days at a time, if the court is satisfied that the continuation of the order is warranted. The order may not continue for more than 12 months in all: MHA 1983 s.38(5).

An interim hospital order may be renewed in the absence of the offender provided that they are represented by a legal representative and their legal representative is given the opportunity to be heard. At the conclusion of the interim order the offender must be sentenced or dealt with by means of a hospital order or otherwise: MHA 1983 s.38(6).

### Duty to terminate the order

**113-008** The order must be terminated if the court makes a hospital order or decides after considering the evidence of the responsible medical officer to deal with the case in some other way: MHA 1983 s.38(5)(a).

### Hospital order made in absence of offender

**113-009** A court may make a hospital order in the case of an offender subject to an interim hospital order in the absence of the offender, provided that they are represented by a legal representative and their legal representative is given the opportunity to be heard: MHA 1983 s.38(2).

# HOSPITAL AND LIMITATION DIRECTION (HYBRID ORDERS)

## Mental Health Act 1983 ss.45A, 45B

*References: Current Sentencing Practice A9; Archbold 5A-1415*

### General

A "*hybrid order*" is an order which combines a hospital order (with restriction) and a sentence of imprisonment. The offender is sentenced to custody but removed to hospital for treatment. **114-001**

In *Nelson* [2020] EWCA Crim 1615; [2021] M.H.L.R. 219 the court observed that s.45A orders were particularly appropriate in two situations: the first was where, notwithstanding the existence of the mental disorder, a penal element to the sentence was appropriate; and the second was where the offender had a mental disorder but there were real doubts that he would comply with any treatment requirements in hospital, meaning that the hospital would be looking after an offender (who might be dangerous) who was not being treated.

### Availability

A direction under s.45A is not available for those under 21 at conviction: *Fort* [2013] EWCA Crim 2332; [2014] 2 Cr. App. R.(S.) 24; [2014] M.H.L.R. 334. **114-002**

### Order in which the court should approach the issue

In a case where the medical evidence suggests that D is suffering from a mental disorder, that the offending is wholly or in significant part attributable to that disorder, and that treatment is available, and where the court considers that a hospital order with or without restrictions may be appropriate, it must address the issues in the following order: **114-003**

(i) can the mental disorder be appropriately dealt with by a hospital and limitation direction, under the terms of s.45A?
(ii) if it can, and if D was aged 21 at the time of conviction, it should make such a direction under s.45A;
(iii) if not, consider whether the medical evidence fulfils the requirements for a hospital order under s.37(2)(a), and (where applicable) for a restriction order under s.41, and consider whether such an order is the "most suitable method of disposing of the case" under s.37(2)(b);
(iv) the wording of s.37(2)(b) requires a court, when deciding on suitability, to have regard to "other available methods of dealing with" D. Relevant to this is the power to transfer an offender from prison to hospital for treatment, under s.47; and
(v) if the court determines that a hospital order is the most suitable method of dealing with D, the order should normally be made without considering an interim order under s.38 unless there is clear evidence that such an order is needed: *Vowles* [2015] EWCA Crim 45; [2015] 1 W.L.R. 5131; [2015] 2 Cr. App. R.(S.) 6.

*Vowles* was further considered in *Edwards* [2018] EWCA Crim 595; [2018] 4 W.L.R. 64; [2018] 2 Cr. App. R.(S.) 17 in which the court noted that a level of misunderstanding of the guidance offered in *Vowles* had arisen as to the order in which a sentencing judge should approach the making of a s.37 or a s.45A order and the precedence allegedly given in *Vowles* to a s.45A order. The court stated that the position was clear that s.45A and the judgment in *Vowles* did not provide a "default setting of imprisonment; that the sentencing judge should first consider if a hospital order may be appropriate under s.37(2)(a); if so, before making such an order, the court had to consider all the powers at its disposal including a s.45A order; therefore consideration of a s.45A order must come before the making of a hospital order because a disposal under s.45A includes a penal element and the court must have "*sound reasons*" for departing from the usual course of imposing a sentence with a penal element.

**Test**

**114-004** A court which passes a sentence of imprisonment for an offence other than murder on an offender may make a hospital and limitation direction, if the court is satisfied on the evidence of two medical practitioners (one of whom must give evidence orally) that:

(a) the offender is suffering from a mental disorder;
(b) the disorder is of a nature or degree which makes it appropriate for them to be detained in a hospital for medical treatment; or
(c) appropriate medical treatment is available for them: MHA 1983 s.45A(1), (2) and (4).

The hospital must be specified in the direction, and the court must be satisfied that the offender will be admitted to the hospital within 28 days of the making of the order: MHA 1983 s.45A(5).

**Oral evidence**

**114-005** Evidence may not be received by telephone: *Clark* [2015] EWCA Crim 2192; [2016] 1 Cr. App. R.(S.) 52; [2016] M.H.L.R. 219.

**Effect**

**114-006** The order must direct that the offender:

(a) be removed to a hospital; and
(b) be subject to the restrictions set out in MHA 1983 s.41: MHA 1983 s.45A(3).

An offender subject to a hospital and limitation direction will be treated as if they had been sentenced to imprisonment and transferred to hospital by order of the Secretary of State(SoS): MHA 1983 s.45B.

**Combining sentences**

**114-007** A hospital and limitation direction may be made in conjunction with a determinate sentence of imprisonment, a discretionary sentence of life imprisonment or an automatic sentence of life imprisonment. It may not be made in conjunction with a mandatory life sentence imposed for murder: MHA 1983 s.45A(1).

**Release**

**General** Where an order was made under ss.37 and 41, the First-tier Tribunal (Mental Health) would decide when the offender should be released. However, for s.45A orders, the release regime differed depending on whether or not an offender was serving a determinate or indeterminate sentence of imprisonment. **114-008**

**Determinate sentences** If a s.45A patient's health improved to such an extent that their responsible clinician or the tribunal notified the SoS that the patient no longer required treatment in hospital under the MHA 1983, the SoS would generally remit the patient to prison under s.50(1) of the 1983 Act to serve the rest of their sentence. On the offender's arrival in prison, the s.45A order would cease to have effect and they would be released from prison in the usual way. If there had been no improvement at the automatic release date, the limitation direction aspect of s.45A fell away. At that point, the patient remained in hospital but was treated as though they were subject to an unrestricted hospital order, meaning that the point at which they were discharged from hospital was a matter for the clinicians with no input from the SoS: *Edwards*. **114-009**

**Indeterminate sentences** If a s.45A patient's health improved to such an extent that their responsible clinician or the tribunal notified the SoS that the patient no longer required treatment in hospital under the MHA 1983, the SoS would generally remit the patient to prison under s.50(1). On the offender's arrival in prison, the s.45A order would cease to have any effect whatsoever. Release would be considered by the Parole Board. **114-010**

If a s.45A patient had passed the expiry of their minimum term and the tribunal then notified the SoS that they were ready for conditional discharge, the SoS could notify the tribunal that they should be so discharged (s.74(2)). In that case, the offender would be subject to mental health supervision and recall in the usual way. However, the SoS would, in practice, refer the offender to the Parole Board: *Edwards*.

## GUARDIANSHIP ORDERS

### Mental Health Act 1983 s.37

*References: Current Sentencing Practice A9; Archbold 5A-1394*

**Availability**

The court may make a guardianship order provided that the offender is aged 16 or older: MHA 1983 s.37(2). **115-001**

**Test**

(1) The court is satisfied on the written or oral evidence of two medical practitioners that the offender is suffering from a mental disorder and the court is satisfied that the mental disorder from which they are suffering is of a nature or degree which warrants their reception into guardianship: MHA 1983 s.37(2). **115-002**
(2) The court must be of the opinion, having regard to all the circumstances, including the nature of the offence and the character and antecedents of the offender that the most suitable method of disposing of the case is by means of a guardianship order: MHA 1983 s.37(2).
(3) A guardianship order may not be made unless the court is satisfied that the local authority or other person concerned is willing to receive the offender into guardianship: MHA 1983 s.37(6).

**Evidence may not be received by telephone**

Evidence may not be received by telephone: *Clark* [2015] EWCA Crim 2192; [2016] 1 Cr. App. R.(S.) 52; [2016] M.H.L.R. 219. **115-003**

**Contents of the order**

The order must specify the form or forms of mental disorder from which the offender is suffering. At least two practitioners must agree that the offender is suffering from the same form of mental disorder. **115-004**

**Combining sentences**

The court may not impose a sentence of imprisonment, impose a fine or make a community order but may make such other forms of order as may be appropriate: MHA 1983 s.37(8). **115-005**

# FITNESS TO PLEAD/NOT GUILTY BY REASON OF INSANITY (CROWN COURT)

## Criminal Procedure (Insanity) Act 1964 s.5

*References: Current Sentencing Practice A9; Archbold 5A-1423*

### General

**Applicability** Where findings are recorded that a person: 116-001

(a) is under a disability and that they did the act or made the omission charged against them; or
(b) a special verdict is returned that the accused is not guilty by reason of insanity; the court is limited in how it shall dispose of the individual: Criminal Procedure (Insanity) Act 1964 (CP(I)A 1964) s.5(1).

**Disposals** The court shall impose one of the following orders: 116-002

(a) a hospital order (with or without a restriction order);
(b) a supervision order; or
(c) an order for absolute discharge: CP(I)A 1964 s.5(2).

**Murder** Where the offence to which the findings relate is an offence for which the sentence is fixed by law, and the court has power to make a hospital order, the court must make a hospital order with a restriction order: CP(I)A 1964 s.5(3). 116-003

### Supervision order

**Definition** *"Supervision order"* means an order which requires the person in respect of whom it is made ("the supervised person") to be under the supervision of a social worker, an officer of a local probation board or an officer of a provider of probation services ("the supervising officer") for a period specified in the order of not more than two years: CP(I)A 1964 Sch.1A para.1(1). 116-004

**Test** The court must not make a supervision order unless it is satisfied that, having regard to all the circumstances of the case, the making of such an order is the most suitable means of dealing with the person: CP(I)A 1964 Sch.1A para.2(1). 116-005

**Requirements** The court must not make a supervision order unless it is satisfied that the supervising officer intended to be specified in the order is willing to undertake the supervision, and that arrangements have been made for the treatment intended to be specified in the order: CP(I)A 1964 Sch.1A para.2(2). 116-006

**Treatment** A supervision order may include a requirement that the supervised person shall, during the whole or part of the period specified in the order, submit to treatment by or under the direction of a registered medical practitioner with a view to the improvement of their mental condition. 116-007

A treatment requirement may be imposed only if the court is satisfied on the written or oral evidence of two or more registered medical practitioners that the mental condition of the supervised person is such as requires and may be susceptible to treatment, but is not such as to warrant the making of a hospital order.

The treatment required may be treatment as a non-resident patient at a specified institution or place and treatment by or under the direction of a specified registered medical practitioner: CP(I)A 1964 Sch.1A para.4(1)–(4).

**116-008** **Residence** A supervision order may include requirements as to the residence of the supervised person: CP(I)A 1964 Sch.1A para.3.

**116-009** **Explaining the order** Before making a supervision order, the court must explain in ordinary language the effect of the order and that a magistrates' court has power to review the order on the application either of the supervised person or of the supervising officer: CP(I)A 1964 Sch.1A para.3(2).

**Hospital order**

**116-010** A hospital order under the CP(I)A 1964 s.5 has the same meaning as under the MHA 1983 s.37. The Criminal Procedure (Insanity) Act 1964 s.5A makes modifications to s.37 for the purposes of enabling a court to impose a hospital order following a finding as specified in s.5.

See **HOSPITAL ORDERS, para.111** for more details.

**Absolute discharge**

**116-011** An order for absolute discharge may be made if the court considers it is the most suitable disposal in all the circumstances of the case: CP(I)A 1964 Sch.1A para.5(3A).

# J: MATTERS ARISING POST-SENTENCE

# ALTERATION OF SENTENCE (VARYING/RESCINDING A SENTENCE)

Sentencing Code s.385; Magistrates' Courts Act 1980 s.142

*References: Current Sentencing Practice A10; Archbold 5A-1433*

## General

As a general rule, the power to vary a sentence should be exercised only in open court and in the presence of the offender after hearing their counsel, who should be advised of the nature of the alteration which the court proposes to make: *May* (1981) 3 Cr. App. R.(S.) 165; [1981] Crim. L.R. 729. The case must be properly listed so that all interested parties may attend: *Perkins* [2013] EWCA Crim 323, [2013] 2 Cr. App. R.(S.) 72; [2013] Crim. L.R. 533. **117-001**

## Crown Court

**Power** The Crown Court may vary or rescind a sentence which it has imposed, or an order which it has made, within specified time limits: SC s.385(2). **117-002**

The power may not be exercised in relation to any sentence or order if an appeal, or an application for leave to appeal, against that sentence or order has been determined: SC s.385(3).

**Test** The judge should apply a flexible test balancing the public with the private interest. The test was no longer the old "*affront to the appearance of justice*" test though, where such an affront existed, a judge may still take this into account in deciding whether to use the slip rule. More broadly, there was a public interest in legal certainty and finality and a sentence should not be increased unless it would lead to a material change in the sentence. Otherwise, there would be a risk of a perception of needless tinkering for no discernible good reason: *George* [2019] EWCA Crim 2177; [2020] 4 W.L.R. 41; [2020] 2 Cr. App. R.(S.) 2. **117-003**

**Same judge must alter/vary/rescind** The Crown Court must be constituted as it was when the original sentence was imposed or order was made, except that if the court included one or more justices of the peace, one or all of them may be omitted: SC s.385(4). **117-004**

**Time limit** The time limit for the Crown Court is 56 days beginning with the day on which the sentence was imposed or the order was made. Where orders have been made on different dates in respect of the same conviction the period of 56 days begins to run on the day on which the particular order which it is proposed to vary was made: SC s.385(2). **117-005**

The relevant time limit must be strictly observed: *Commissioners of Customs and Excise v Menocal* [1980] A.C. 598; [1979] 2 W.L.R. 876; (1979) 69 Cr. App. R. 148.

There is no power to extend the time limit: *Attorney General's Reference (No.79 of 2015) (Nguyen)* [2016] EWCA Crim 448; [2016] 4 W.L.R. 99; [2016] 2 Cr. App. R.(S.) 18.

**117-006 Adjournments** If the Crown Court rescinds a sentence within the permitted period for variation or rescission, without imposing a further sentence, it may adjourn sentence for such period as may be appropriate, without regard to the time limit: *Gordon* [2007] EWCA Crim 165; [2007] 1 W.L.R. 2117; [2007] 2 Cr. App. R.(S.) 66.

**117-007 General approach** The general state of the law is as follows:

(a) where an error had occurred in the factual basis of sentence, this should be pointed out to the court as soon as possible and consideration should be given to correcting this at the earliest opportunity, preferably by revisiting sentence on the same day rather than on a subsequent day;
(b) a judge should not use the slip rule simply because there was a change of mind about the nature or length of sentence but the slip rule was available where the judge was persuaded that they had made a material error in the sentencing process whether of fact or of law. It was relevant in considering whether or not they had made a material error that the error might be corrected by the Court of Appeal on the Attorney General's application;
(c) the sooner the slip rule was invoked in such a case the better. The passage of time from the first decision to its revision was a material consideration as to how the power should be exercised (but there was a 56-day cut off in any event);
(d) a judge should not be unduly influenced by the prospect of a reference being made to change a sentence that they thought was right at the time by the mere threat of a review by the Attorney General. If the judge concluded that the sentence was not wrong in principle and was not unduly lenient, they should not change their mind simply because there was the possibility of a reference. The judge could then use the opportunity at the further sentencing hearing to give any further explanations for the original decision for the sentence;
(e) sentencing and re-sentencing should take place in the presence of the appellant and administrative convenience should not be allowed to degrade that principle. But, if for one reason or another, the appellant could not be brought to court within the 56-day period, there was a discretion to proceed in their absence so long as there was an advocate who could fully represent the appellant in the sense of who was properly instructed as to the relevant facts and was able to assist the court to make pertinent submissions on the facts and the law (as clearly W's advocate was able to do on the date of the re-sentence); and
(f) although *Nodjoumi* no longer identified the basic rule in such cases, the appearance of justice and the impact of the change on a defendant where an error had not been induced by anything that they had said or done were relevant considerations and, in appropriate cases, could be reflected in a modest discount to the proposed revised sentence to reflect that fact: *Warren* [2017] EWCA Crim 226; [2017] 4 W.L.R. 71; [2017] 2 Cr. App. R.(S.) 5.

A variation is permissible where a judge concludes on reflection, not merely that they wish to be more punitive or more lenient, but that the approach taken in a sentence was wrong in principle, indeed wrong as to an important aspect of sentence, such as the protection of the public: *O'Connor* [2018] EWCA Crim 1417; [2018] 2 Cr. App. R. (S.) 49.

The question is one of "materiality", which took into account both the nature and extent of the error of fact or law which had been made and the impact of that error upon the increase in the sentence. There was an obvious connection between the two since not every error of law or fact (even if it seemed prima facie serious) would lead to a material increase in sentence. If the error would not lead to a material increase in sentence, then the power should not be exercised. If the error was relevant to an "important" component of the law or guidelines relating to sentencing, then this would militate in favour of using the slip rule: *George* [2019] EWCA Crim 2177; [2020] 2 Cr. App. R.(S.) 2.

**Double jeopardy** In balancing the strong public interest in the imposition of correct and appropriate sentences against a justifiable sense of grievance on the part of a defendant who was brought back to court to be re-sentenced, a court can substantially address the interest of that defendant by the conferral of an appropriate level of discount to the new sentence that the judge considers should be imposed: *George* [2019] EWCA Crim 2177; [2020] 2 Cr. App. R.(S.) 2. **117-008**

**Nature of variation** The power is not limited to the correction of slips of the tongue or minor errors made when sentence was originally passed. **117-009**

There is no restriction on the nature of the variation in sentence which may be made. In appropriate circumstances the court may substitute a sentence or order which is more severe than the sentence originally passed: *Commissioners of Customs and Excise v Menocal* [1980] A.C. 598; (1979) 69 Cr. App. R. 148. See *Judge considers original sentence too lenient*, below.

Where a sentence has been imposed on the basis of a factual error, the sentence may be increased: *Warren* [2017] EWCA Crim 226; [2017] 2 Cr. App. R.(S.) 2.

### Varying the sentence outside the permitted period

Where a sentence has been passed or order made which is defective in form, it may be permissible to correct the error after the expiration of the relevant time limit, so long as the correction can be treated as a matter of form rather than substance: *Saville* [1981] Q.B. 12; [1980] 3 W.L.R. 151; (1980) 2 Cr. App. R.(S.) 26. **117-010**

The scope of the power to vary a sentence outside of the statutory period appears to have been narrowed by *D* [2014] EWCA Crim 2340; [2015] 1 Cr. App. R.(S.) 23; [2015] Crim. L.R. 227, in which the Court of Appeal held that a judge had not been entitled to vary an extended sentence to correct a defect in the way in which the sentence had been articulated, notwithstanding the fact that the defendant would not have been adversely affected by the variation.

### Magistrates' courts

**Power** A magistrates' court may vary or rescind a sentence or order at any time after the sentence has been passed or the order made, unless the Crown Court or the High Court has determined an appeal against the sentence or the conviction on which it is based: MCA 1980 s.142(1) and (1A). **117-011**

**117-012 Time limit** There is no time limit for magistrates' courts, see e.g. *Holmes v Liverpool City Justices* [2004] EWHC 3131 (Admin); (2005) 169 J.P. 306; [2005] A.C.D. 37.

**117-013 Defendant sentenced in Crown Court** The power is of no application once the defendant had been sentenced in the Crown Court: *H v DPP* [2021] EWHC 147 (Admin); [2021] 1 W.L.R. 2721; [2021] 1 Cr. App. R. 23.

**Particular situations**

**117-014 Bogus mitigation** Where the court has been persuaded to pass a particular form of sentence, or a sentence of a particular length, on the basis of the existence of specific mitigating factors, the court may review the sentence and substitute a more severe sentence if it subsequently appears that the court has been misled and that the mitigating factors did not exist: *McLean* (1988) 10 Cr. App. R.(S.) 18. Such a decision should not be made without proper inquiry and giving the offender an opportunity to dispute the allegation that they have deceived the court.

**117-015 Judge considers original sentence too lenient** The court may increase a sentence merely where it considers that the original sentence was providing considerations of fairness to the defendant and public interest in passing an appropriate, lawful sentence had to be weighed: *G* [2016] EWCA Crim 541; [2016] 4 W.L.R. 124; [2016] 2 Cr. App. R.(S.) 17. As to this "flexible" approach, see also *Jama* [2009] EWCA Crim 2109. There is no objection to reducing a sentence because on second thoughts it appears to have been too severe.

**117-016 Misbehaviour in the dock** It is wrong to vary a sentence which has been passed on the ground that the offender has reacted to the sentence by misbehaving in the dock and addressing abusive comments to the judge or other persons present: *Powell* (1985) 7 Cr. App. R.(S.) 247; [1985] Crim. L.R. 802.

**117-017 Part of sentencing postponed** Where the Crown Court passes part of a sentence and expressly postpones passing some other part of the sentence, the time limits do not apply, see **ADJOURNMENT—POST CONVICTION, para.23.**

**117-018 Multiple variations** It is not clear whether a sentence which has been varied once can be varied a second time.

# RELEASE FROM CUSTODIAL SENTENCES

## Criminal Justice Act 2003 ss.243A–264

*References: Current Sentencing Practice A10; Archbold 5A-1460*

### General

**Applicability** These provisions apply to all prisoners sentenced on or after 3 December 2012, irrespective of the date on which the offence for which they were sentenced was committed unless otherwise stated. **118-001**

### Unconditional release

**Applicability** Unconditional release applies to: **118-002**

(a) a prisoner serving a sentence of a term of one day;
(b) a prisoner serving a term of less than 12 months who is aged under 18 on the last day of the requisite custodial period; or
(c) a prisoner serving sentence of less than 12 months imposed before 1 February 2015: CJA 2003 s.243A. However, this does not apply to a person who has been referred to the Parole Board under CJA 2003 s.244ZB. This general rule is now subject to a modification. An offender is - unless the fall within one of the exceptions set out below, entitlement to release will be at 40% of the custodial term. See SI 2024/844 for details.

Offenders entitled to unconditional release must be released after serving one-half of the sentence. There is no licence period: CJA 2003 s.243A. However, this does not apply to a person who has been referred to the Parole Board under CJA 2003 s.244ZB.

**Concurrent/consecutive sentences** Where more than one sentence is imposed and the aggregate terms are less than 12 months and s.243A requires release to be unconditional in respect of each of those sentences, release will be unconditional: CJA 2003 s.264(3B). Otherwise, release will be on licence. **118-003**

### Release on licence

**General rule** Subject to the exceptions identified below the general rule is that prisoners who are not entitled to unconditional release must be released on licence after serving half of the sentence imposed by the court (the "requisite custodial period") and will remain on licence until the end of the whole term of the sentence: CJA 2003 ss.244 and 249(1). However, this does not apply to a person who has been referred to the Parole Board under CJA 2003 s.244ZB. This general rule is now subject to a modification. An offender is - unless the fall within one of the exceptions set out below, entitlement to release will be at 40% of the custodial term. See SI 2024/844 for details. **118-004**

**Sentences of four years or more but less than seven years** The general rule is subject to the exception in cases where the offence is: **118-005**

(a) manslaughter;
(b) soliciting murder;
(c) wounding with intent to cause grievous bodily harm;
(d) ancillary offences in connection with (a)–(c);
(e) inchoate offences in relation to murder; or
(f) specified in Pt 2 of that Schedule (sexual offences), and for which a life sentence was available at the time the sentence was imposed.

In those circumstances, the offender is entitled to be released at the two-thirds point of the sentence: CJA 2003 s.244ZA. In multiple offence cases, this applies only where the individual sentence is seven years or more (and not to shorter consecutive sentences each less than seven years but where the cumulative total is more than seven years): *AB* [2021] EWCA Crim 692; [2022] 1 Cr. App. R.(S.) 13; [2021] Crim. L.R. 706, decided in relation to SI 2020/158.

118-006 **Sentences of seven years or more** The general rule is subject to the exception in cases where the offence is listed within Pts 1 or 2 of Sch.15 to the CJA 2003 (violent and sexual offences) which have a maximum sentence of life imprisonment and the sentence imposed is one of seven years or more. In those circumstances, the offender is entitled to be released at the two-thirds point of the sentence: CJA 2003 s.244ZA is to be read as a reference to two-thirds: . In multiple offence cases, this applies only where the individual sentence is seven years or more (and not to shorter consecutive sentences each less than seven years but where the cumulative total is more than seven years): *AB* [2021] EWCA Crim 692; [2022] 1 Cr. App. R.(S.) 13, decided in relation to SI 2020/158.

118-007 **Terrorist offenders** The general rule is also subject to an exception created by Terrorist Offenders (Restriction of Early Release) Act 2020, which inserted a new s.247A into the CJA 2003. The effect is that offences listed in Pts I or II of Sch.19ZA to the CJA 2003.

Unless the offender's sentence was

(a) an extended sentence or serious terrorism sentence;

(b) imposed on or after 29 June 2021;

(c) imposed for an offence specified in Pt I of Sch.19ZA, or Pt III and determined to have a terrorist connection,

the offender must serve two-thirds of the custodial period before consideration for release by the Parole Board and must be released at the expiry of the custodial term: s.247A(2A)-(8).

118-008 **Extended sentence terrorist offenders** Offenders who are serving extended determinate sentences for offences listed in Pt I of Sch.19ZA to the Sentencing Code or offences listed in Pt II of that Schedule in respect of which the court has determined a terrorist connection, there is no eligibility for release; release is automatic at the expiry of the custodial term: s.247A(2A) and (7).

118-009 **Serious terrorism sentence offenders** Offenders who are serving extended determinate sentences for offences listed in Pt I of Sch.19ZA to the Sentencing Code or offences listed in Pt II of that Schedule in respect of which the court has determined a terrorist connection, there is no eligibility for release; release is automatic at the expiry of the custodial term: s.247A(2A) and (7).

**Extended sentences** Offenders serving sentences imposed under ss.254 (under 18), 266 (18–20) and 279 (over 20) will serve two-thirds of the custodial term before being considered for release by the Parole Board. The offender must be released at the expiry of the custodial term: CJA 2003 s.246A. The balance of the sentence will be served on licence. This is subject to the exception in relation to certain terrorist offences, see above. **118-010**

**Offenders of particular concern** Offenders serving sentences imposed under ss.265, s.252A, or s.278 will serve two-thirds of the custodial term before being considered for release by the Parole Board. The offender must be released at the expiry of the custodial term: CJA 2003 s.244A. The balance of the sentence will be served on licence. This is subject to the exception in relation to certain terrorist offences, see above. **118-011**

**Life sentences** Offenders serving life sentences in respect of which the court imposed a minimum term order will be considered for release by the Parole Board at the expiry of the minimum term. There is no entitlement to release. If released, the offender will spend the remainder of their life on licence: C(S)A 1997 s.28. **118-012**

**Licence conditions** Where a fixed term prisoner serving a sentence of 12 months or more is released on licence, the licence must include the standard conditions prescribed by the Secretary of State and such other conditions as may be specified. It may also include conditions relating to drug testing or electronic monitoring: CJA 2003 s.250(4). **118-013**

**Recommending licence conditions** When a court passes a sentence of imprisonment or detention in a young offender institution for 12 months or more it may "recommend any particular conditions which in its view should be included in any licence granted to the offender": SC s.328. **118-014**

The recommendation is not binding on the Secretary of State and does not form part of the sentence "for any purpose": SC s.328(3). It is therefore not subject to appeal. The recommendation will be considered by the Secretary of State when the offender is released at the half-way point in the sentence, or if they are released on licence at any other stage — under the home detention curfew scheme, or on compassionate grounds.

**Release on compassionate grounds**

The Secretary of State may release a fixed term prisoner where exceptional circumstances exist that justify their release on compassionate grounds: CJA 2003 s.248. **118-014A**

**Referral to Parole Board**

The Secretary of State may refer prisoners who would otherwise be eligible for automatic release to the Parole Board where the Secretary of State believes on reasonable grounds that the prisoner would, if released, pose a significant risk to **118-015** members of the public of serious harm occasioned by the commission of murder or a specified offence within the meaning of s.306 of the Sentencing Code: CJA 2003 ss.244ZB-C.

**Post sentence supervision**

**118-016 Young offenders** Those who:

(a) are aged under 18 on the last day of the requisite custodial period (the half-way stage of the total sentence) serving a sentence of s.91 detention of a period of less than 12 months; or
(b) are serving a sentence of detention under ss.250 or 262 of less than 12 months for an offence committed prior to 1 February 2015,

are subject to a supervision period beginning on their release and ending three months later: CJA 2003 s.256B.

**118-017 Young offenders: breach** If it is proved to the satisfaction of the court that the offender has failed to comply with requirements under s.256B(6), the court may:

(a) order the offender to be detained, in prison or such youth detention accommodation as the Secretary of State may determine, for such period, not exceeding 30 days, as the court may specify; or
(b) order the offender to pay a fine not exceeding level 3 on the standard scale: CJA 2003 s.256C(4).

**118-018 Adults** Those who are serving sentences of more than one day but less than two years who a) are 18 or over on the last day of the requisite custodial period, b) are not serving extended sentences or sentences for offenders of particular concern, c) are not serving sentences for an offence committed before 1 February 2015, are subject to supervision beginning on the expiry of the sentence and ending 12 months later: CJA 2003 s.256AA.

**118-019 Adults: breach** If it is proved to the satisfaction of the court that the person has failed without reasonable excuse to comply with a supervision requirement imposed under s.256AA, the court may:

(a) order the person to be committed to prison for a period not exceeding 14 days;
(b) order the person to pay a fine not exceeding level 3 on the standard scale; or
(c) make a "supervision default order" imposing on the person:
    (i) an unpaid work requirement; or
    (ii) a curfew requirement: CJA 2003 s.256AC(4).

Under a supervision default order:

(a) an unpaid work requirement may be for 20–60 hours;
(b) a curfew order may be for 2–16 hours per day and must require the person

to remain at the specified place or places on at least 20 days: CJA 2003 Sch.19A para.3(4).

## Home Detention Curfew (HDC)

**Eligibility** Prisoners serving determinate custodial sentences where: **118-020**

a) the requisite custodial period (i.e. half of the total sentence) is at least six weeks; and
b) the prisoner has served both:
   (i) at least four weeks of that period; and
   (ii) at least one half of that period.

The effect is that HDC only applies to prisoners whose sentences are at least 12 weeks: CJA 2003 246(1) and (2).

**The effect** Where the conditions are met, a prisoner may be released up to 135 days before the date on which they would be otherwise entitled to be released (the half-way point in their sentence): CJA 2003 s.246(1)(a). **118-021**

**Exclusions** The home detention curfew scheme does not apply to: **118-022**

(a) offenders sentenced to four years' imprisonment or more;
(b) extended sentences of imprisonment or detention; or
(c) those subject to the notification requirements under SOA 2003 Pt 2;
(d) those subject to a hospital order, hospital direction or transfer direction;
(e) prisoners whose sentence was imposed in a case where they failed to comply with a curfew requirement of a community order;
(f) prisoners liable to removal from the UK;
(g) certain prisoners who have been recalled or returned to prison; and
(h) cases where due to time spent in custody prior to sentence, the interval between the date of sentence and the expiration of the requisite custodial period is less than 14 days: CJA 2003 s.246(4).

Prison Service Instructions 43/2012 sets out at Annex B a list of offences for which prisoners will be deemed to be unsuitable for a home detention curfew (HDC). It will then be for the prisoner to show that there are exceptional circumstances in order to be considered for release. Such offences include manslaughter, possession of an offensive weapon and racially or religiously aggravated offences under CDA 1998 ss.29 to 32.

**Release** An offender serving a sentence of 12 months or more who is released under this scheme must be subject to the standard licence conditions and to a curfew condition; they may also be subject to other conditions of a kind prescribed by the Secretary of State, CJA 2003 s.250(4). The licence remains for the duration of the sentence: CJA 2003 s.249. **118-023**

The curfew condition remains in force until the day on which the offender would otherwise be entitled to be released from custody: CJA 2003 s.253(3). It must require that the offender remains at a specified place for periods of not less than nine hours each day, and must provide for electronic monitoring of their whereabouts during the specified periods: CJA 2003 s.253(1) and (2).

## Recall

**118-024 Licence recall** The Secretary of State may revoke the licence of a person who has been released on licence and recall them to custody. No particular conditions must be specified before this power is exercised: CJA 2003 s.254(1).

On their return to custody, the prisoner must be informed of the reason for their recall and may make representations about their recall: CJA 2003 s.254(2).

Prisoners who are not serving extended sentences will qualify for automatic release after 28 days from the date of return to custody if the Secretary of State is satisfied that the person will not present a risk of serious harm to members of the public if released at the end of that period: CJA 2003 s.255A(4).

**118-025** The case must be referred to the Parole Board: CJA 2003 ss.255B(4) and 255C(4)(a). If the Board does not recommend their immediate release, the Board must either fix a date for their release or fix a date for the next review of their case. The review must take place not later than one year after the decision to fix the date has been made: CJA 2003 s.256. If the prisoner is not recommended for release at a later review, they will remain in custody until the end of the sentence.

When sentencing for the commission of an offence committed during the currency of release on licence, there is a distinction to be drawn (for the purposes of treating the breach of the licence as an aggravating factor) between an offender being recalled solely as a result of the commission of the "new" offence and being recalled for that reason in addition to the offender manager determining that it was no longer safe for the offender to be at liberty: *Christie* [2019] EWCA Crim 1386; [2019] 2 Cr. App. R.(S.) 54.

**118-026 HDC recall** A person released on home detention curfew may have their licence revoked if they fail to comply with any condition of their licence, or if their whereabouts can no longer be monitored electronically: CJA 2003 s.255(1).

They must be informed of the reasons for the revocation and may make representations about the revocation to the Secretary of State, but they do not have the right to ask for their case to be reviewed by the Parole Board: CJA 2003 s.255(2).

If the Secretary of State does not reverse their decision to revoke the licence, the prisoner will remain in custody until the date on which they would otherwise have been released.

## Concurrent and consecutive sentences

**118-027** Where an offender is sentenced to terms of imprisonment which are wholly or partly concurrent, the offender does not become eligible for or entitled to be released from any of the sentences before the date on which they would be eligible for or entitled to be released from each of the other sentences: CJA 2003 s.263.

Where an offender is sentenced to consecutive terms, the aggregate of which is 12 months or more, whether they are imposed on the same occasion or different occasions, they are not entitled to be released until they have served half of the aggregate term, and will remain on licence until the end of the aggregate term: CJA 2003 s.264(3).

Where more than one sentence is imposed and the aggregate terms are less than 12 months and s.243A requires release to be unconditional in respect of each of those sentences, release will be unconditional: CJA 2003 s.264(3B). Otherwise, release will be on licence.

See **CONCURRENT AND CONSECUTIVE SENTENCES, para.17**.

# K: BREACH OF COMMUNITY ORDERS AND SUSPENDED SENTENCES

## RE-SENTENCING—GENERAL

### Sentencing Code s.402

*References: Archbold 5A-1496b*

**Sentencing Code, s.402** **119-001**

(1) Where under this Code a court has power to re-sentence an offender for an offence, the court may deal with the offender in any way in which it could deal with the offender:
  (a) if the offender had just been convicted by or before it of the offence; and
  (b) in a case where the offender was aged under 18 when in fact convicted of the offence, as if the offender were the same age as when in fact convicted.

(2) But where under this Code the Crown Court has power to re-sentence an offender for an offence and subs.(3) applies, the power of the Crown Court is power to deal with the offender in any way in which a magistrates' court could deal with the offender for the offence if:
  (a) the offender had just been convicted by the magistrates' court of the offence; and
  (b) in a case where the offender was aged under 18 when in fact convicted of the offence, the offender were the same age as when in fact convicted.

(3) This subsection applies where:
  (a) the Crown Court's power to re-sentence the offender for the offence is exercisable:
    (i) where the Crown Court revokes another order previously made in respect of the offence; or
    (ii) where an order for conditional discharge has previously been made in respect of the offence, by virtue of a further offence committed during the period of conditional discharge; and
  (b) the previous order was made:
    (i) by a magistrates' court; or
    (ii) by the Crown Court in circumstances where its powers to deal with the offender for the offence were those (however expressed) which would have been exercisable by a magistrates' court on convicting the offender of the offence.

# COMMUNITY ORDERS—BREACH OF

## Sentencing Code Sch.10

*References: Current Sentencing Practice A10; Archbold 5A-1507*

There are two types of breach: **120-001**

(a) a failure to comply with a requirement of the order; and
(b) the commission of a further offence during the currency of the order.

### Failure to comply with requirement of order: magistrates' courts

**Powers** Where it is proved to a magistrates' court that an offender subject to a community order has failed without reasonable excuse to comply with any of the requirements of the relevant order, the court must either: **120-002**

(a) impose more onerous requirements than the original order;
(b) impose a fine not exceeding £2,500;
(c) if the order was made by a magistrates' court, deal with the offender, for the offence in respect of which the order was made, in any manner in which it could deal with the offender if they had just been convicted by the court of the offence: SC Sch.10 para.10(1), (2) and (5).

Where it is proved to a magistrates' court that an offender subject to a community order has failed without reasonable excuse to comply with any of the requirements of the relevant order, and the court is dealing with the offender under para.(c) above (i.e. re-sentencing the offender for the original offence) and the offender has wilfully and persistently failed to comply with the terms of the order, the court may impose a custodial sentence even if it is not of the opinion 30 mentioned in s.230(2) (general restriction on imposing discretionary custodial sentences): SC Sch.10 para.10(1), (2), (5)(c) and (9).

**Partial compliance** In dealing with the offender, the court must take into account the extent to which the offender has complied with the requirements of the relevant order: SC Sch.10 para.10(7). **120-003**

However, there is a distinction to be drawn between requirements intended to be therapeutic in nature and those intended to be punitive in nature. In *Wolstenholme* [2016] EWCA Crim 638; [2016] 2 Cr. App. R.(S.) 19 the court found that making no reduction for partial compliance with a requirement the purpose of which was therapeutic rather than punitive was justified.

**Revoke order if re-sentencing** If the magistrates' court deals with the offender for the offence, (i.e. re-sentences the offender) it must revoke the order: SC Sch.10 para.10(10). **120-004**

**Can commit to Crown Court** If the community order was made by the Crown Court, the magistrates' court may commit the offender to the Crown Court, as an alternative to (a)–(c) above: SC Sch.10 para.10(3). **120-005**

**Failure to comply with requirement of order: Crown Court**

**120-006 Powers** When the offender appears before the Crown Court, the breach of the order must be proved to the satisfaction of the Crown Court. If the breach is proved, the Crown Court must:

(a) amend the terms of the order so as to impose more onerous requirements which the Crown Court could impose if it were then making the order;
(b) impose a fine not exceeding £2,500;
  (ba) if the community order qualifies for special procedures for the purposes of this paragraph, by ordering the offender to be committed to prison for such period not exceeding 28 days as the court considers appropriate;
(c) deal with them, for the offence in respect of which the order was made, in any way in which they could have been dealt with for that offence by the court which made the order;
(d) where:
  (i) the original offence was not an offence punishable by imprisonment;
  (ii) the offender is aged 18 or over; and
  (iii) the offender has wilfully and persistently failed to comply with the requirements of the order,

  deal with him, in respect of the original offence, by imposing a sentence of imprisonment (or detention in a young offender institution): SC Sch.10 para.11.

**120-007 Partial compliance** In dealing with the offender, the court must take into account the extent to which the offender has complied with the requirements of the relevant order: CJA 2003 Sch.8 para.10(2): SC Sch.10 para.10(7).

**120-008 Revoke order if re-sentencing** If the court deals with the offender for the offence, it must revoke the order: CJA 2003 Sch.8 para.10(5): SC Sch.10 para.10(10).

**Conviction for further offence: magistrates' courts**

**120-009 Powers** If an offender in respect of whom a community order made by a magistrates' court is in force is convicted by magistrates' court, and the magistrates' court considers it in the interests of justice to do so, the magistrates' court may either:

(a) simply revoke the community order; or
(b) revoke the order and deal with the offender in any way in which they could have been dealt with by the court which made the order: SC Sch.10 para.23.

**120-010 Commit to Crown Court** If an offender in respect of whom a community order made by the Crown Court is in force is convicted by magistrates' court, the magistrates' court may commit the offender to the Crown Court: SC Sch.10 para.24.

**Conviction for further offence: Crown Court**

**120-011 Powers** If an offender who is subject to a community order (whether imposed by the Crown Court or magistrates' court) appears before the Crown Court having been:

(a) committed by the magistrates' court following a conviction by the magistrates' court; or
(b) convicted of an offence before the Crown Court while they are subject to a community order, and where the Crown Court considers it is in the interests of justice to do so, the Crown Court may either:
    (i) revoke the order; or
    (ii) revoke the order and deal with the order in any way in which the offender could have been dealt with by the court which made the order: SC Sch.10 para.25(2).

The power to deal with the offender depends on the offender being convicted of the new offence while the order is still in force; it does not arise where the conviction is obtained after the order has expired of an offence committed while the order was current: SC Sch.10 para.25(1).

Where the court revokes a community order and re-sentences a defendant (where the community order had been made in respect of a summary-only offence, and where the Crown Court is sentencing the offender for another summary-only offence) the Crown Court is constrained by s.133(1) of the MCA 1980 with the effect that the sentences in respect of the summary-only offences are limited to a total period of six months' imprisonment: *Palmer* [2019] EWCA Crim 2231; [2020] 1 Cr. App. R.(S.) 54.

**Partial compliance**

In dealing with the offender, the court must take into account the extent to which the offender has complied with the requirements of the relevant order: SC Sch.10 para.11(4). **120-012**

**Revoke order if re-sentencing**

In dealing with the offender, the court must take into account the extent to which the offender has complied with the requirements of the relevant order: SC Sch.10 para.11(4). **120-013**

**Defendant crosses age threshold**

See **RE-SENTENCING: GENERAL** at **para.119**. **120-014**

# SUSPENDED SENTENCES—BREACH OF

## Sentencing Code Sch.16

*References: Current Sentencing Practice A10; Archbold 5A-1522*

### Breach: general

A "breach" of a suspended sentence order may occur either by a failure to comply with a community requirement during the supervision period, or by the commission of an offence during the operational period. **121-001**

As these two periods may be different in any particular case, it will be important to ensure that the relevant event took place during the relevant period.

Considerations of the principle of totality are "in play" when the court considers the activation of a suspended sentence order: *Attorney General's Reference (Usherwood)* [2018] EWCA Crim 1156; [2018] 2 Cr. App. R.(S.) 39.

A suspended sentence order can only be activated once: *Rashid* [2022] EWCA Crim 328.

### Failure to comply with requirements

**Warning** The responsible officer will first give the defendant a warning where they are of the opinion that the defendant has without reasonable excuse failed to comply with the order: SC Sch.16 para.6. **121-002**

**Failure to comply after warning** If at any point in the 12 months following the date on which the warning was given, the responsible officer is of the opinion that the defendant has without reasonable excuse failed to comply with the order, breach proceedings are mandatory and the defendant's case will be considered by an enforcement officer who, if appropriate, will cause the offender to be brought before the court: SC Sch.16 para.6 and 7. **121-003**

**Powers upon breach** If it is proved to the satisfaction of the court that the defendant has failed to comply with any of the community requirements of the order without reasonable excuse, the court must: **121-004**

(a) order the sentence to take effect with the original term unaltered; or
(b) order the sentence to take effect with the term reduced: SC Sch.16 paras 13 and 14.

If the court considers it would be unjust in all the circumstances to activate the term in full or in part, it must state its reasons and take one of the following courses:

(a) in a case where the suspended sentence order qualifies for special procedures for the purposes of this paragraph, the court is dealing with the case by virtue of para.10 or 12(2) and the offender is aged 18 or over, the court may order the offender to be committed to prison for such period not exceeding 28 days as the court considers appropriate;

(b) order the defendant to pay a fine not exceeding £2,500;
(c) in the case of an order with community requirements:
  (i) impose more onerous community requirements;
  (ii) extend the supervision period (but not beyond the operational period and not exceeding the two-year maximum);
  (iii) extend the operational period (not exceeding the two-year maximum); and
(d) in the case of an order without community requirements:
  (i) extend the operational period (not exceeding the two-year maximum): SC Sch.16 paras 13 and 14.

**Further offence**

**121-005 Which court deals with the breach?** If the offender is convicted of an offence committed during the operational period of a suspended sentence (other than one that has taken effect):

(a) where the offender is before the Crown Court, the Crown Court may deal with the offender in respect of the breach irrespective of which court made the original order;
(b) where the offender is before the magistrates' court and the suspended sentence was passed by a magistrates' court, then the magistrates' court must deal with the offender in respect of the breach; or
(c) where the offender is before the magistrates' court, the suspended sentence was passed by the Crown Court, and the offender is convicted by a magistrates' court of the further offence, the magistrates' court may commit them to the Crown Court to be dealt with: SC Sch.16 paras 11 and 12.

If the magistrates' court does not commit the offender to the Crown Court, it must notify the Crown Court of the conviction: SC Sch.16 para.11(2).

**121-006 Powers on breach** Where the court has power to deal with the breach of the suspended sentence order, the court must:

(a) order the sentence to take effect with the original term unaltered; or
(b) order the sentence to take effect with the term reduced: SC Sch.16 paras 13 and 14.

If the court considers it would be unjust in all the circumstances to activate the term in full or in part, it must state its reasons and take one of the following courses:

(a) order the defendant to pay a fine not exceeding £2,500;
(b) in the case of an order with community requirements:
  (i) impose more onerous community requirements;
  (ii) extend the supervision period (but not beyond the operational period and not exceeding the two-year maximum);
  (iii) extend the operational period (not exceeding the two-year maximum); and
(c) in the case of an order without community requirements:
  (i) extend the operational period (not exceeding the two-year maximum): SC Sch.16 paras 13 and 14.

**121-007 Presumption of consecutive sentences** The court must activate the custodial sentence unless it would be unjust in all the circumstances to do so. The predominant factor in determining whether activation is unjust relates to the level of compliance with the suspended sentence order and the facts/nature of any new offence: *Breach Offences: Definitive Guideline*.

**New offence less serious** Where the new offence is less serious than the offence for which the suspended sentence order was imposed, the court should activate the sentence of the suspended sentence order with a reduced term, or amending the order: *Breach Offences: Definitive Guideline*. **121-008**

**Cannot revoke the order** There is no power to revoke the order and impose a custodial sentence of greater length than the sentence which was suspended. **121-009**

**Conviction for offence committed before suspended sentence imposed** Where an offender who is subject to a suspended sentence appears for sentence for an offence committed before the suspended sentence was imposed, the court has no power to order the suspended sentence to take effect, to impose more onerous requirements or extend the operational period, but may cancel the community requirement of the suspended sentence order on the application of the offender or responsible officer: SC Sch.16 para.22. **121-010**

# L: APPEALS

# APPEALS

## Magistrates' Courts Act 1980 s.108; Criminal Appeal Act 1968 Ss.9 and 11

*References: Current Sentencing Practice A11; Archbold 7-119*

### From the magistrates' court

**Right to appeal** There is a right of appeal to the Crown Court. The hearing takes the form of a re-hearing. The Crown Court may therefore impose a sentence greater than that imposed by the magistrates' court: MCA 1980 s.108(1) and the Senior Courts Act 1981 (SCA 1981) ss.48 and 79. **122-001**

**Time limits** The notice of appeal must be served within 21 days of the sentence. Extensions of time may be sought and must be supported by reasons: CrimPR r.34.2. **122-002**

**Powers** On appeal the Crown Court may confirm, reverse or vary the decision appealed against any part of the decision appealed against, including a determination not to impose a separate penalty in respect of an offence, may remit the matter with its opinion, or make any order the magistrates' court could have made: SCA 1981 s.48(1) and (5). **122-003**

### From the Crown Court

**Applications for leave** An appeal notice must be in the form specified in the Criminal Practice Directions, see CrimPR r.39.3. **122-004**

It is not possible to appeal against the mandatory life sentence for murder. It is however possible to appeal against the length of the minimum term: CAA 1968 s.9(1) and (1A).

The single judge may give leave on limited grounds or against part of a sentence only. See *Hyde* [2016] EWCA Crim 1031; [2016] 1 W.L.R. 4020; [2016] 2 Cr. App. R.(S.) 39 for guidance given by the court on the proper approach to a consideration of applications for leave to appeal.

**CACD targets** The following target times are set for the hearing of appeals. Target times will run from the receipt of the appeal by the Registrar, as being ready for hearing: **122-005**

| Nature of appeal | From receipt by listing officer to fixing of hearing date | From fixing of hearing date to hearing | Total time from receipt by listing officer to hearing |
|---|---|---|---|
| Sentence Appeal | 14 days | 14 days | 28 days |
| Conviction Appeal | 21 days | 42 days | 63 days |

| Nature of appeal | From receipt by listing officer to fixing of hearing date | From fixing of hearing date to hearing | Total time from receipt by listing officer to hearing |
|---|---|---|---|
| Conviction Appeal where witness to attend | 28 days | 52 days | 80 days |

122-006 **Time limits** Notice of appeal is to be given within 28 days from the date on which the sentence is passed: CAA 1968 s.18(1) and (2).

Extensions of time may be sought and it is the practice of the Registrar to require an application for an extension of time to be made when submitting the notice of appeal. The application for an extension of time must always be supported by reasons why the notice was not submitted within the time limit: *Guide to Commencing Proceedings in the Court of Appeal* para.A3–3.

122-007 **Test and powers** On an appeal against sentence the Court of Appeal, if they consider that the appellant should be sentenced differently for an offence for which they were dealt with by the court below may:

(a) quash any sentence or order which is the subject of the appeal; and
(b) in place of it pass such sentence or make such order as they think appropriate for the case and as the court below had power to pass or make when dealing with them for the offence;

but the court shall so exercise their powers under this subsection that, taking the case as a whole, the appellant is not more severely dealt with on appeal than they were dealt with by the court below: CAA 1968 s.11(3).

In practice the court considers whether or not the sentence is wrong in principle or manifestly excessive.

The court has the power to re-open an appeal in order to correct an error that led to the quashing of a sentence which had in fact been lawfully imposed in circumstances where at the appeal hearing the court had proceeded on the basis of a factual error: *Yasain* [2015] EWCA Crim 1277; [2015] 3 W.L.R. 1571; [2016] 1 Cr. App. R.(S.) 7.

122-008 The jurisdiction identified in *Yasain* is very limited and is not available in cases where it is alleged that the proper construction of the legislation was misunderstood and has been recognised as having been misunderstood in subsequent litigation.

The appropriate procedure (until the Crim PR makes provision) is:

(i) if a party (whether prosecutor or defendant) wishes the Court of Appeal (Criminal Division) to re-open a final determination of the court based on the implicit jurisdiction identified in *Yasain* it must:
  (a) apply in writing for permission to re-open the decision, as soon as practicable after becoming aware of the grounds for doing so; and
  (b) serve the application on the Registrar and all other parties to the proceedings;

(ii) the application must specify the decision which the applicant wishes to re-open and provide reasons identifying:
   (a) the circumstances which make it necessary for the court to re-open that decision in order to avoid real injustice;
   (b) what makes those circumstances exceptional and thus appropriate for the decision to be re-opened notwithstanding the interests of other parties to the proceedings and the importance of finality;
   (c) an explanation and reasons for the absence of any alternative effective remedy and for any lapse of time in making the application having discovered the facts which form the grounds for so doing;

(iii) on receipt of an effective application, the Registrar will refer the application to the full court for determination on paper. There is no right to an oral hearing unless the full court so directs; and

(iv) the court must not give permission to re-open a final determination unless each other party to the proceedings has had an opportunity to make representations. In making any such representations, the prosecution has a duty to obtain the views of any victim or the family of such a victim: *Hockey* [2017] EWCA Crim 742; [2018] 1 W.L.R. 343; [2017] 2 Cr. App. R.(S.) 31.

**Function of the court** The Court of Appeal (Criminal Division) is, in relation to sentencing, a court of review. Its function is to review sentences passed below and not to conduct a sentencing hearing. However, it is also clear that s.23 of the Criminal Appeal Act 1968 permits the court to receive fresh evidence on appeal against sentence, provided the conditions set out in the section are met. There are circumstances where the court will consider updates to information placed before the sentencing judge without the conditions in s.23 being applied, but otherwise s.23 is of general application to all sentencing appeals: *Rogers* [2016] EWCA Crim 801; [2017] 1 W.L.R. 481; [2016] 2 Cr. App. R.(S.) 36. **122-009**

**Updated information not before sentencing judge** Exceptions to s.23 will include updated pre-sentence and prison reports on conduct in prison after sentence, but not fresh psychiatric or psychological evidence in support of an argument that a finding of dangerousness ought not to have been made or a hospital order should have been made: *Rogers* [2016] EWCA Crim 801; [2017] 1 W.L.R. 481; [2016] 2 Cr. App. R.(S.) 36; [2019] Crim. L.R. 548. **122-010**

**Loss of time** Both the court and the single judge have power, in their discretion under ss.29 and 31 of the CAA 1968 to direct that part of the time during which an applicant is in custody after lodging their notice of application for leave to appeal should not count towards sentence: *CPD 2015* [2015] EWCA Crim 1567 Loss of time 39E.1. **122-011**

**Prohibition on dealing with appellant more severely** On appeal against sentence, a defendant may not be dealt with more severely than they were dealt with at the Crown Court: CAA 1968 s.11(3). **122-012**

In *Thompson* [2018] EWCA Crim 639; [2018] 1 W.L.R. 4429; [2018] 2 Cr. App. R.(S.) 19 (five-judge court) the court observed that the limit of the power on appeal was that the court had to be satisfied that, taking the case as a whole, an appellant was not being dealt with more severely on appeal. That required a detailed **122-013** consideration of the impact of the sentence to be imposed in substitution for the original sentence, which had to involve considerations of entitlement to automatic release, parole eligibility and licence. Emphasis was placed on entitlement to release, rather than eligibility for release. The court commented that if a custodial sentence was reduced, the addition of non-custodial orders (such as disqualification from driving or sexual offences prevention orders) might be considered but, in every case, save where the substituted sentence was "*ameliorative and remedial*", that sentence had to be tested for its severity (or potential punitive effect) when compared to the original sentence. For further discussion, see [2018] Crim. L.R. 593 and *Archbold Review* (2018) 7 4-7.

More recently, the court appears to have weakened the emphasis placed on the entitlement to release in *Thompson* and decisions such as *KPR* [2018] EWCA Crim 2537; [2019] 1 Cr. App. R.(S.) 36; [2019] Crim. L.R. 548 and *B* [2018] EWCA Crim 2733; [2019] 1 W.L.R. 2550 suggest a return to the approach of considering the proposed sentence in the round to assess whether or not it is to be regarded as being more severe. See [2019] Crim. L.R. 548 for commentary.

# ATTORNEY GENERAL'S REFERENCES

## Criminal Justice Act 1988 s.36

*References: Current Sentencing Practice A11; Archbold 7-437*

### General

**Function** The function of s.36 of the 1988 Act is not to provide a general right of appeal to the prosecution. It is a means of ensuring by judicious selection of cases, that issues of principle in relation to sentencing can be resolved, and sentences corrected, in cases where public confidence in sentencing could otherwise be undermined: *Reynolds* [2007] EWCA Crim 538; [2008] 1 W.L.R. 1075; [2007] 2 Cr. App. R.(S.) 87. **123-001**

**Availability** If it appears to the Attorney General: **123-002**

(a) that the sentencing of a person in a proceeding in the Crown Court has been unduly lenient; and
(b) that the case is one to which this Part of this Act applies, they may, with the leave of the Court of Appeal, refer the case to them for them to review the sentencing of that person: CJA 1988 s.36(1).

"*Unduly lenient*" includes a situation where in the view of the Attorney General a judge has:

(a) erred in law as to their powers of sentencing; or
(b) failed to impose a mandatory sentence requirement listed in s.399(b) or (c) of the Sentencing Code, namely that:
    (i) the court is obliged by one of the following provisions to pass a sentence of detention for life, custody for life or imprisonment for life:
        (1) s.258, 274 or 285 (life sentence for certain dangerous offenders);
        (2) s.273 or 283 (life sentence for second listed offence), or
    (ii) a sentence is required by one of the following provisions and the court is not of the opinion mentioned in that provision:
        (1) s.311(2) (minimum sentence for certain offences involving firearms that are prohibited weapons);
        (2) s.312(2) (minimum sentence for offence of threatening with weapon or bladed article);
        (3) s.313(2) (minimum sentence of seven years for third class A drug trafficking offence);
        (4) s.314(2) (minimum sentence of three years for third domestic burglary); or
        (5) s.315(2) (minimum sentence for repeat offence involving weapon or bladed article): CJA 1988 s.36(2).

**Approach** In *AG's Ref (O'Neill)* [2021] EWCA Crim 1427; [2022] 1 Cr. App. R. (S.) 49, the respondent submitted that the follow principles could be discerned from the authorities; the Crown and court appeared to accept that proposition: **123-003**

1. The judge at first instance is particularly well placed to assess the weight to be given to competing factors in considering sentence.
2. A sentence is only unduly lenient where it falls outside the range of sentences which the judge at first instance might reasonably consider appropriate.
3. Leave to refer a sentence should only be granted by the court in exceptional circumstances and not in borderline cases.
4. Section 36 of the 1988 Act is designed to deal with cases where judges have fallen into "*gross error*".

## CRIMINAL JUSTICE ACT 1988 (REVIEWS OF SENTENCING) ORDER 2006 (SI 2006/1116)

### Cases to which the scheme applies

*Criminal Justice Act 1988 (Reviews of Sentencing) Order 2006 (SI 2006/1116)* **123-004**

*Note: In addition to the offences listed in this SI, the unduly lenient sentence scheme applies to all offences triable only on indictment, CJA 1988 s.35(3)(b)(i).*

The list of cases to which the ULS scheme applies is as follows:

1 Any case tried on indictment—
  (a) following a notice of transfer given under s.4 of the CJA 1987 (notices of transfer and designated authorities); or
  (b) in which one or more of the counts in respect of which sentence is passed relates to a charge which was dismissed under s.6(1) of the CJA 1987 (applications for dismissal) and on which further proceedings were brought by means of preferment of a voluntary bill of indictment.

1A Any case tried on indictment—
  (a) following a notice given under s.51B of the CDA 1998 (notices in serious or complex fraud cases); or
  (b) following such a notice, in which one or more of the counts in respect of which sentence is passed relates to a charge—
    (i) which was dismissed under para.2 of Sch.3 to the CDA 1998 (applications for dismissal); and
    (ii) on which further proceedings were brought by means of the preferment of a voluntary bill of indictment.

2 Any case in which sentence is passed on a person for one of the following offences:
  (a) an offence under s.16 of the OaPA 1861 (threats to kill);
  (b) an offence under s.5(1) of the CLAA 1885 (defilement of a girl between 14 and 17);
  (c) an offence under s.1 of the CYPA 1933 (cruelty to persons under 16) or s.20 of the CYPA (NI) 1968 (cruelty to persons under 16);
  (d) an offence under s.6 of the SOA 1956 (unlawful sexual intercourse with a girl under 16), ss.14 or 15 of that Act (indecent assault on a woman or on a man), s.52 of the OaPA 1861 (indecent assault upon a female), or art.21 of the CJ (NI) Order 2003 (indecent assault on a male);
  (e) an offence under s.1 of the IWCA 1960 or s.22 of the CYPA (NI) 1968 (indecent conduct with a child);
  (f) an offence under ss.4(2) or (3) (production or supply of a controlled drug), s.5(3) (possession of a controlled drug with intent to supply) or s.6(2) (cultivation of cannabis plant) of the MDA 1971;
  (g) an offence under s.54 of the CLA 1977 or art.9 of the CJ (NI) Order 1980 (inciting a girl under 16 to have incestuous sexual intercourse);
  (ga) an offence under s.1 of the Protection of Children Act 1978 (indecent photographs of children);

- (h) an offence under ss.50(2) or (3), s.68(2) or s.170(1) or (2) of the CEMA 1979, insofar as those offences are in connection with a prohibition or restriction on importation or exportation of either:
  - (i) a controlled drug within the meaning of s.2 of the MDA 1971, such prohibition or restriction having effect by virtue of s.3 of that Act; or
  - (ii) an article prohibited by virtue of s.42 of the CCA 1876 but only insofar as it relates to or depicts a person under the age of 16; (ha) an offence under s.160 of the Criminal Justice Act 1988 (possession of indecent photograph of child);
- (hb) an offence under s.4 (putting people in fear of violence) or s.4A (stalking involving fear of violence or serious alarm or distress) of the Protection from Harassment Act 1997;
- (i) offences under ss.29, 30, 31(a), 31(b) and 32 of the Crime and Disorder Act 1998 (racially or religiously aggravated assaults; racially or religiously aggravated criminal damage; racially or religiously aggravated public order offences; racially or religiously aggravated harassment etc);
- (j) an offence under s.4 of the AI(ToC)A 2004 (trafficking people for exploitation);
- (k) an offence under s.71 of the CoJA 2009 (slavery, servitude and forced or compulsory labour);
- (ka) an offence under s.76 of the Serious Crime Act 2015 (controlling or coercive behaviour in an intimate or family relationship);
- (l) an offence under s.1 (slavery, servitude and forced or compulsory labour), 2 (human trafficking) or 4 (committing an offence with intent to commit a human trafficking offence) of the MDA 2015.

(3) Any case in which sentence is passed on a person for an offence under one of the following sections of the Sexual Offences Act 2003

- (a) s.3 (sexual assault);
- (b) s.4 (causing a person to engage in sexual activity without consent);
- (c) s.7 (sexual assault of a child under 13);
- (d) s.8 (causing or inciting a child under 13 to engage in sexual activity);
- (e) s.9 (sexual activity with a child);
- (f) s.10 (causing or inciting a child to engage in sexual activity);
- (g) s.11 (engaging in sexual activity in the presence of a child);
- (h) s.12 (causing a child to watch a sexual act);
- (i) s.14 (arranging or facilitating commission of a child sex offence);
- (j) s.15 (meeting a child following sexual grooming etc.);
- (ja) s.16 (abuse of position of trust: sexual activity with a child);
- (jb) s.17 (abuse of position of trust: causing or inciting a child to engage in sexual activity);
- (jc) s.18 (abuse of position of trust: sexual activity in the presence of a child);
- (jd) s.19 (abuse of position of trust: causing a child to watch a sexual act);
- (k) s.25 (sexual activity with a child family member);
- (ka) s.26 (inciting a child family member to engage in sexual activity);
- (kb) s.30 (sexual activity with a person with a mental disorder impeding choice);

(kc) s.31 (causing or inciting a person, with a mental disorder impeding choice, to engage in sexual activity);
(kd) s.32 (engaging in sexual activity in the presence of a person with a mental disorder impeding choice);
(ke) s.33 (causing a person, with a mental disorder impeding choice, to watch a sexual act);
(l) s.47 (paying for sexual services of a child);
(m) s.48 (causing or inciting sexual exploitation of a child);
(n) s.49 (controlling a child in relation to sexual exploitation);
(o) s.50 (arranging or facilitating sexual exploitation of a child);
(p) s.52 (causing or inciting prostitution for gain);
(q) s.57 (trafficking into the UK for sexual exploitation);
(r) s.58 (trafficking within the UK for sexual exploitation);
(s) s.59 (trafficking out of the UK for sexual exploitation);
(t) s.61 (administering a substance with intent).

3A

(1) Any case in which sentence is passed on a person for an offence under one of the following—
(a) ss.11 or 12 of the TA 2000 (offences relating to proscribed organisations);
(b) ss.15 to 18 of the TA 2000 (offences relating to terrorist property);
(ba) ss.19 (disclosure of information: duty), 21A (failure to disclose: regulated sector) or 21D (tipping off: regulated sector) of the 2000 Act;
(ca) s.39 of the 2000 Act 9 (disclosure of information);
(c) s.38B of the TA 2000 (failure to disclose information about acts of terrorism);
(d) s.54 of the TA 2000 (weapons training);
(e) ss.57 to 58A of the TA 2000 (possessing things, collecting information and eliciting, publishing or communicating information about members of the armed forces etc. for the purposes of terrorism);
(f) s.113 of the ATCSA 2001 (use of noxious substances or things to cause harm or intimidate);
(g) s.1 or 2 of the TA 2006 (encouragement of terrorism);
(h) s.6 or 8 of the TA 2006 (training for terrorism);
(i) s.54 of the Counter-Terrorism Act 2008 (offences relating to notification);
(j) s.23 of the Terrorism Prevention and Investigation Measures Act 2011 14 (offence of contravening a TPIM notice);
(k) s.10 of the Counter-Terrorism and Security Act 2015 (offences of contravening a Temporary Exclusion Order or not complying with a restriction after return).

2 Any case in which sentence is passed on a person for one of the following—
(a) an offence under s.20 of the OAPA 1861(inflicting bodily harm);
(b) an offence under the following provisions of the CDA 1971;
(i) s.1(1) (destroying or damaging property);
(ii) s.1(1) and (3) (arson);

(iii) s.2 (threats to destroy or damage property);

(c) an offence under ss.1 to 5 of the FCA 1981; where there is jurisdiction in England and Wales by virtue of any of ss.63B to 63D of the TA 2000 (extra-territorial jurisdiction in respect of certain offences committed outside the United Kingdom for the purposes of terrorism etc).

3 Any case in which sentence is passed on a person for an offence under one of the following—

(a) s.4 of the Aviation Security Act 1982 (offences in relation to certain dangerous articles);

(b) s.114 of the Anti-Terrorism, Crime and Security Act 2001 (hoaxes involving noxious substances or things) where the court has determined that the offence has a terrorist connection under s.30 of the Counter-Terrorism Act 2008 (sentences for offences with a terrorist connection: England and Wales).

4 Any case in which sentence is passed on a person for—

(a) attempting to commit a relevant offence;

(b) inciting the commission of a relevant offence; or

(c) an offence under ss.44 or 45 of the SCA 2007 (encouraging or assisting an offence) in relation to a relevant offence.

(2) In this paragraph, *"a relevant offence"* means an offence set out in paragraph 2(a) to (hb), (j), (k), (ka) or (l) or paragraphs 3 or 3A.

*Note: The SI was last amended on 19 November 2019 by The Criminal Justice Act 1988 (Reviews of Sentencing) (Amendment) Order 2019 (SI 2019/1397) and on 1 December 2020 by the Sentencing Act 2020.*

**123-005 Deferred sentences** A deferred sentence may be referred by the Attorney General under the unduly lenient sentence scheme: *Attorney General's Reference (No.22 of 1992)* [1994] 1 All E.R. 105; (1993) 14 Cr. App. R.(S.) 435; [1993] Crim. L.R. 227.

**123-006 Time limits** Notice of an application for leave to refer a case to the Court of Appeal under s.36 above shall be given within 28 days from the day on which the sentence, or the last of the sentences, in the case was passed: CJA 1988 Sch.3 para.1.

The day on which the sentence was passed does not count for this purpose: *Attorney General's Reference No.112 of 2002* [2003] EWCA Crim 676.

An application to the Court of Appeal for leave to refer a case to the Supreme Court under s.36(5) above shall be made within the period of 14 days beginning with the date on which the Court of Appeal conclude their review of the case; and an application to the Supreme Court for leave shall be made within the period of 14 days beginning with the date on which the Court of Appeal conclude their review or refuse leave to refer the case to the Supreme Court: CJA 1988 Sch.3 para.4.

**Pre-hearing matters**

**123-007 Goodyear indications** The advocate is personally responsible for ensuring that their client fully appreciates that any sentence indication given by the judge remains subject to the entitlement of the Attorney General (where it arises) to refer an unduly lenient sentence to the Court of Appeal: *Goodyear* [2005] EWCA Crim 888; [2005] 1 W.L.R. 2532; [2006] 1 Cr. App. R.(S.) 6.

**Registrar writes to sentencing judge** The standard letter makes plain that it is not for the judge to comment generally on the Attorney General's application. It invites the sentencing judge to provide any information which will not be apparent from the papers and the transcript. One example might be where a "text" has been placed before the judge. The Registrar will then consider whether any further such information needs to be placed before the court and counsel. The letter makes clear that it is not permissible for a judge to add to their sentencing remarks. Assistance sought is limited to information of which the judge was aware but which is not before the court: *Attorney General's Reference (Bailey)* [2018] EWCA Crim 1640; [2018] 4 W.L.R. 159; [2018] 2 Cr. App. R.(S.) 50. **123-008**

### The hearing

**Electronic service** Service of the notification may be conducted via electronic means: *Attorney General's Reference (Lindley)* [2016] EWCA Crim 1980; [2017] 1 Cr. App. R.(S.) 39. **123-009**

**Reference does not preclude an appeal** Where a sentence is referred under the unduly sentence scheme, the offender has not yet exercised the statutory right to apply for leave to appeal: *Hughes* [2010] EWCA Crim 1026; [2010] M.H.L.R. 188. **123-010**

**Powers of the court** On a reference the Court of Appeal may: **123-011**

- (i) quash any sentence passed on the offender in the proceeding; and
- (ii) in place of it pass such sentence as they think appropriate for the case and as the court below had power to pass when dealing with them, CJA 1988 s.36.1. At the hearing of the Attorney General's Reference the court has, at least in theory, the power not only to uphold or increase the original sentence, but also to reduce it or to impose a different form of sentence: *Hughes* [2010] EWCA Crim 1026; [2010] M.H.L.R. 188.

If one of the offences for which an offender has been sentenced falls within the scheme, then the Attorney General may, with leave, refer the case to the Court of Appeal and that court may sentence the offender differently in respect of any conviction obtained in those proceedings: *Attorney General's Reference (Clews)* [2019] EWCA Crim 769, [2019] 2 Cr. App. R.(S.) 40.

**Test to apply** The court may only increase sentences which it concludes were unduly lenient. It cannot have been the intention of Parliament to subject defendants to the risk of having their sentences increased — with all the anxiety that that naturally gives rise to — merely because in the opinion of this court the sentence was less than this court would have imposed. A sentence is unduly lenient where it falls outside the range of sentences which the judge, applying their mind to all the relevant factors, could reasonably consider appropriate: *Attorney General's Reference (No. 4 of 1989)* [1990] 1 W.L.R. 41; (1989) 11 Cr. App. R.(S.) 517; [1990] Crim. L.R. 438. **123-012**

**CACD is a court of review** It is clear that the power of this court to declare a sentence unduly lenient depends entirely on what was put before the original **123-013**

sentencing court. It is not open to the Attorney General to rely upon further evidence not placed before the sentencing court to justify the Reference: *Attorney General's Reference (No.79 of 2015) (Nguyen)* [2016] EWCA Crim 448; [2016] 4 W.L.R. 99; [2016] 2 Cr. App. R.(S.) 18.

**Attorney General conducting hearing on different basis to that at Crown**

123-014 **Court** It is permissible for the Attorney General to conduct a reference on a different basis to that advanced in the Crown Court. Very often it is that departure which results in the view that the sentence was unduly lenient. The court's function was to decide whether or not the sentence imposed was unduly lenient: *Attorney General's Reference (Stewart)* [2016] EWCA Crim 2238; [2017] 1 Cr. App. R.(S.) 48; [2017] Crim. L.R. 490.

In such circumstances, however, the court should be cognisant of the potential unfairness to the defendant and a reduction in sentence may be appropriate: *Attorney General's Reference (Susorovs)* [2016] EWCA Crim 1856; [2017] 1 Cr. App. R.(S.) 15; [2017] Crim. L.R. 337.

Additionally, where the Attorney General sought to depart from a concession made by prosecuting counsel in the context of a Goodyear indication, close consideration would be required: *Attorney General's Reference (Powell)* [2017] EWCA Crim 2324; [2018] 1 Cr. App. R.(S.) 40; [2018] Crim. L.R. 494. It is suggested that such a departure at a reference hearing should only be entertained where the court can be sure of no unfairness to the offender.

123-015 **Information not before the sentencing judge** The power to declare a sentence as unduly lenient depended entirely on what was put before the original sentencing court. It is not open to the Attorney General to rely on further evidence not placed before the sentencing court to justify the reference: *Attorney General's Reference (No.19 of 2005) (WB)* [2006] EWCA Crim 785.

Once the court has concluded that a sentence, as passed, was unduly lenient based on the facts as known to the judge, the responsibility of the Court of Appeal is to pass the appropriate sentence for the case. In those circumstances, it is open to the court to take into account whatever new information is available, whether or not it is adverse to the offender: *Attorney General's Reference (No.79 of 2015) (Nguyen)* [2016] EWCA Crim 448; [2016] 2 Cr. App. R.(S.) 18.

123-016 **Double jeopardy: general** The practice of making a reduction for so-called "double jeopardy" (the fact of being sentenced for the same offence twice) has fallen out of favour in recent years and reductions are increasingly difficult to obtain. See *Attorney General's Reference (No.45 of 2014)* [2014] EWCA Crim 1566 for more details.

123-017 However, the practice is not dead. It is submitted that circumstances giving rise to a submission that a reduction is due must extend beyond the usual arguments surrounding finality of sentence, legitimate expectation and the effect of being sentenced twice. For a recent example of where a reduction was obtained, see *Attorney General's Reference (Ferizi)* [2016] EWCA Crim 2022; [2017] 1 Cr. App. R.(S.) 26.

**Double jeopardy: murder** Where a reference relates to the determination of minimum term in relation to the mandatory life sentence, the Court of Appeal shall not, in deciding what order under that section is appropriate for the case, make any allowance for the fact that the person to whom it relates is being sentenced for a second time: CJA 1988 s.36(3A). **123-018**

# DISPARITY OF SENTENCE

*References: Archbold 5A-99*

## General

As a general rule, when two or more offenders are convicted of the same offence, and their individual responsibility is the same, and there is no relevant difference in their personal circumstances, they should receive the same sentence. Where one offender has the benefit of personal mitigation which is not available to other offenders, the other offenders should not be given the benefit of that mitigation. **124-001**

Where there is an unjustified disparity in the sentences passed on two offenders, the Court of Appeal may reduce the more severe sentence if the disparity is so substantial as to create the appearance of injustice: *Fawcett* (1983) 5 Cr. App. R.(S.) 158.

Disparity arguments will not be entertained where the alleged disparity is based on other cases in the Crown Court, separate to that of the defendant: *Large* (1981) 3 Cr. App. R.(S.) 80; [1981] Crim. L.R. 508.

When considering disparity arguments, it is dangerous for a court to draw inferences from the sentences imposed on counts that were not the "*lead*" count: *Planken* [2017] EWCA Crim 1807; [2018] 1 Cr. App. R.(S.) 24; [2018] Crim. L.R. 347. **124-002**

Note: Disparity arguments often proceed on the erroneous assumption that the sentence with which the comparison is drawn is correct (or at least "not wrong"). It is suggested that a lenient sentence imposed on a co-defendant neither provides evidence of the manifest excess of the defendant's sentence, nor does it entitle them to a reduction on the grounds of fairness or equity. The sentencing court's primary task is to impose a sentence which is just and proportionate and considerations of grievance felt by one defendant or another are very much secondary.

## Test

The correct consideration is not whether the appellant feels aggrieved but whether the public, viewing the various sentences, would perceive that the appellant had suffered an injustice: *Lowe*, *The Times,* 14 November 1989. **124-003**

## The proper approach to sentencing multiple defendants

Where an offender has already been sentenced by one judge, another judge who on a later occasion has to deal with their accomplice should pass the sentence on the accomplice which they consider appropriate, without regard to the sentence passed on the other offender: *Broadbridge* (1983) 5 Cr. App. R.(S.) 269. **124-004**

A difference in sex is not in itself a reason for discriminating between offenders: *Okuya* (1984) 6 Cr. App. R.(S.) 253; [1984] Crim. L.R. 766.

### No objectionable disparity

**124-005** There is no disparity if a difference in sentence reflects a difference in the respective:

(a) culpability of the offenders;
(b) ages of the offenders: *Turner* unreported 4 October 1976;
(c) previous convictions: *Walsh* (1980) 2 Cr. App. R.(S.) 224; or
(d) the existence of personal mitigating factors peculiar to one of them: *Attorney General's Reference (Nos. 62, 63 and 64 of 1995) (O'Halloren)* [1996] 2 Cr. App. R.(S.) 223.

There is no disparity where one offender has received an appropriate sentence and their co-defendant has received a lesser sentence as a result of statutory restrictions which apply only to them, or where an accomplice has been sentenced in a foreign jurisdiction where sentencing laws and practices are different from those of England and Wales: *Harper* (1995) 16 Cr. App. R.(S.) 639; [1995] R.T.R. 340 and see *Lillie* (1995) 16 Cr. App. R.(S.) 534.

There is no disparity if one offender who is likely to respond favourably to a community order is dealt with by means of a community order and the other offender is not: *Devaney* [2001] EWCA Crim 1997; [2002] 1 Cr. App. R.(S.) 109.

The fact that one defendant received a lenient sentence is no reason to reduce a proper sentence on another; there is no objectionable disparity where an appropriate sentence has been imposed: *Saliuka* [2014] EWCA Crim 1907.

### Circumstances capable of amounting to objectionable disparity

**124-006** There may be objectionable disparity if one offender receives a more severe sentence than a co-defendant, and there are no relevant differences in their responsibility or personal mitigation: *Church* (1985) 7 Cr. App. R.(S.) 370; [1986] Crim. L.R. 271:

(a) where two offenders receive the same sentence, despite a difference in their responsibility or personal mitigation: *Goodacre* [1996] 1 Cr. App. R.(S.) 424; and
(b) where the difference in their sentences is either too large or too small to reflect the difference in their responsibility or personal mitigation see, for example: *Tilley* (1983) 5 Cr. App. R.(S.) 235.

# M: MAXIMUM SENTENCES

# TABLES OF MAXIMUM SENTENCES

## Assaults on Emergency Workers (Offences) Act 2018

| | | |
|---|---|---|
| Section 1 (common assault and battery) | *2 years* | **125-001** |

## Aviation Security Act 1982

| | | |
|---|---|---|
| Section 1 (hijacking) | *Life* | **125-002** |
| Section 2 (destroying aircraft) | *Life* | |
| Section 3 (endangering safety of aircraft) | *Life* | |
| Section 4 (possessing dangerous article) | *5 years* | |
| Section 6 (inducing offence) | *Life* | |

## Bail Act 1976

| | | |
|---|---|---|
| Section 6 (failing to surrender) | *12 months (on indictment)*<br>*3 months (summarily)** | **125-003** |

*Notes*

*Where an offender is dealt with by the Crown Court for a bail offence, otherwise than on a committal by a magistrates' court under BA 1976 s.6(6) they are to be dealt with as if the bail offence were a contempt of court. In the youth court, an offender under the age of 18 may not be committed to custody for a bail offence.

## Bribery Act 2010

| | | |
|---|---|---|
| Section 1 (bribery of another person) | *10 years* | **125-004** |
| Section 2 (requesting, agreeing to accept or accepting a bribe) | *10 years* | |
| Section 6 (bribery of foreign public official) | *10 years* | |
| Section 7 (failure of commercial organisation to prevent bribery) | *Fine* | |

## Child Abduction Act 1984

| | | |
|---|---|---|
| Section 1 (taking out of UK without consent) | *7 years* | **125-005** |
| Section 2 (taking child out of lawful control) | *7 years* | |

Penalty provision: Section 4

## Children and Young Persons Act 1933

| | | |
|---|---|---|
| 125-006 | Section 1 (ill-treatment or neglect etc.) | *14 years** |
| | Section 25 (procuring child to go abroad by false representation) | *2 years* |

*Notes*

* If the offence is committed on or after 29 September 1988 to 27 June 2022, the maximum sentence is 10 years. For offences committed before 29 September 1988, the maximum sentence is two years.

## Companies Act 2006

| | | |
|---|---|---|
| 125-007 | Section 993 (fraudulent trading) | *10 years** |

*Notes*

* The offence may be charged where a relevant event occurs before that date and another relevant event occurs after that date. If so, the maximum sentence is seven years. See The Companies Act 2006 (Commencement No. 3, Consequential Amendments, Transitional Provisions and Savings) Order 2007 (SI 2007/2194) para.46.

## Computer Misuse Act 1990

| | | |
|---|---|---|
| 125-008 | Section 1 (securing unauthorised access) | *2 years** |
| | Section 2 (unauthorised access with intent) | *5 years* |
| | Section 3 (unauthorised modification) | *10 years*** |
| | Section 3ZA (unauthorised acts with serious damage) | *14 years* |
| | Section 3ZA (unauthorised acts with serious damage to national security or human welfare of types in (3)(a) or (b) | *Life* |
| | Section 3A (providing tools for unauthorised access) | *2 years* |

*Notes*

* (if offence committed on or after 1 October 2008).

** (if offence committed on or after 1 October 2008; otherwise five years).

## Contempt of Court Act 1981

| | | |
|---|---|---|
| 125-009 | Section 14 (contempt of superior court) | *2 years* |

## Copyright Designs and Patents Act 1988

| | | |
|---|---|---|
| 125-010 | Offences under s.107(1)(a), (b), (d)(iv) or (e) | *10 years* |
| | Offences under s.107(2A) | *2 years* |

## CRIME AND DISORDER ACT 1998

| | | |
|---|---|---|
| Section 29(1)(a) (racially or religiously aggravated unlawful wounding) | *7 years* | **125-011** |
| Section 29(1)(b) (racially or religiously aggravated assault occasioning actual bodily harm) | *7 years* | |
| Section 29(1)(c) (racially or religiously aggravated common assault) | *2 years* | |
| Section 30 (racially or religiously aggravated criminal damage) | *14 years* | |
| Section 31(1)(a) (racially or religiously aggravated causing fear of violence) | *2 years* | |
| Section 31(1)(b) (racially or religiously aggravated intentional harassment) | *2 years* | |
| Section 32(1)(a) (racially or religiously aggravated harassment) | *2 years* | |
| Section 32(1)(b) (racially or religiously aggravated causing fear of violence) | *14 years** | |

*Notes*

* If committed on or after 3 April 2017; otherwise seven years.

An offence under s.31(1)(a) or (b) is a specified offence (CJA 2003 Sch.15).

## CRIMINAL ATTEMPTS ACT 1981

| | | |
|---|---|---|
| Section 1 (attempted murder) | *Life* | **125-012** |
| Section 1 (attempting indictable offence) | *As for offence in question* | |

*Notes*

Special provisions apply to attempted incest. See Sexual Offences Act 1956.

An attempt to commit an offence which is a specified offence (CJA 2003 Sch.15), or a scheduled offence (SOA 2003 Schs.3 or 5) is also a specified offence or a scheduled offence.

## CRIMINAL DAMAGE ACT 1971

| | | |
|---|---|---|
| Section 1(1) (criminal damage) | *10 years** | **125-013** |
| Section 1(2) (criminal damage with intent to endanger life) | *Life* | |
| Section 1(3) (arson) | *Life* | |
| Section 2 (threatening to damage property) | *10 years* | |
| Section 3 (possession with intent) | *10 years* | |

Penalty provision: Section 4

*Notes*

* If the value of the damage does not exceed £5,000 and the matter comes before

the Crown Court under CJA 1988 ss.40 or 41, or PCC(S)A 2000 s.6, the maximum sentence is three months.

## CRIMINAL JUSTICE ACT 1925

| | | |
|---|---|---|
| **125-014** | Section 36(1) (making false statement to procure passport) | *2 years* |

## CRIMINAL JUSTICE ACT 1961

| | | |
|---|---|---|
| **125-015** | Section 22 (harbouring escaped prisoner) | *10 years** |

*Notes*

* If committed on or after 16 May 1992; otherwise two years.

## CRIMINAL JUSTICE ACT 1988

| | | |
|---|---|---|
| **125-016** | Section 134 (torture) | *Life* |
| | Section 139 (possessing sharp bladed or pointed instrument) (if offence was committed before 12 February, 2007; two years) | *4 years* |
| | Section 139A (possessing offensive weapon on school premises) | *4 years** |
| | Section 139AA (threatening with article with a blade or point or offensive weapon) | *4 years* |
| | Section 160 (possessing indecent photograph of child) | *5 years*** |

*Notes*

* If an offence under s.(1) was committed before 12 February 2007 the maximum is two years.

** If an offence was committed before 11 January 2001, the offence is summary only with a maximum sentence of six months.

## CRIMINAL JUSTICE ACT 1993

| | | |
|---|---|---|
| **125-017** | Section 52 (insider dealing) | *7 years* |

## CRIMINAL JUSTICE (INTERNATIONAL CO-OPERATION) ACT 1990

| | | |
|---|---|---|
| **125-018** | Section 12 (manufacturing or supplying scheduled substance) | *14 years* |
| | Section 19 (having possession of a Class A controlled drug on a ship) | *Life* |
| | Section 19 (having possession of a Class B or temporary class controlled drug on a ship) | *14 years* |
| | Section 19 (having possession of a Class C controlled drug on a ship) | *14 years** |

*Notes*

* If offence committed on or after 29 January 2004; otherwise five years.

Offences under ss.12 and 19 are drug trafficking offences for the purposes of the Drug Trafficking Act 1994 and the POCA 2002 Sch.2.

## Criminal Justice and Public Order Act 1994

| | | |
|---|---|---|
| Section 51 (intimidating witness) | *5 years* | **125-019** |

## Criminal Law Act 1967

| | | | |
|---|---|---|---|
| Section 4 (assisting offender) | | | **125-020** |
| | Sentence for principal offence fixed by law | *10 years* | |
| | Maximum sentence for principal offence 14 years | *7 years* | |
| | Maximum sentence for principal offence 10 years | *5 years* | |
| | Otherwise (normally five years) | *3 years* | |

## Criminal Law Act 1977

| | | |
|---|---|---|
| Section 1 (conspiracy to commit offence punishable by life imprisonment) | *Life* | **125-021** |
| Section 1 (conspiracy to commit offence for which no maximum is provided) | *Life* | |
| Section 1 (conspiracy to commit offence with specified maximum term) | *Maximum term for offence in question* | |
| Section 51 (bomb hoax) | *7 years** | |

*Notes*

* If committed on or after 31 October 1991; otherwise five years.

## Customs and Excise Management Act 1979

| | | |
|---|---|---|
| Section 50 (importing undutied or prohibited goods) | *7 years* | **125-022** |
| Section 68 (evading prohibition of exportation) | *7 years* | |
| Section 170 (evading duty, or prohibition) | *7 years* | |
| Section 170B (taking preparatory steps) | *7 years* | |

*Notes*

Where an offence under ss.50, 68 or 170 relates to class A drugs, the maximum is life imprisonment; where the offence relates to class B or class C drugs, the maximum is 14 years (if the offence relates to class C drug committed before 29

January 2004, the maximum is five years).

Where an offence under ss.50, 68 or 170 relates to goods prohibited by the FCA 1981 ss.20 or 21, the maximum sentence is 10 years.

Where an offence under s.50, s.69 or s.170 relates to nuclear materials, the maximum is 14 years. Where an offence under ss.50, 68 or 170 relates to certain prohibited weapons within the meaning of the FA 1968 s.5(1) (excluding weapons falling within ss.5(1)(b) or 5(1A)(b) to (g)), the maximum sentence is life (if committed on or after 14 July 2014; otherwise 10 years).

Offences involving the importation or exportation of controlled drugs are drug trafficking offences for the purposes of the Drug Trafficking Act 1994 and the POCA 2002 Sch.2.

## DOMESTIC VIOLENCE, CRIME AND VICTIMS ACT 2004

**125-023**

| | |
|---|---|
| Section 5 (causing or allowing death of child/vulnerable adult) | *Life* |
| Section 5 (causing or allowing serious injury of child/vulnerable adult) | *14 years* |

## EXPLOSIVE SUBSTANCES ACT 1883

**125-024**

| | |
|---|---|
| Section 2 (causing explosion likely to endanger life) | *Life* |
| Section 3 (attempting to cause explosion, or possessing explosive substance with intent) | *Life* |
| Section 4 (making or possessing explosive substance) | *Life** |

*Notes*

* If offence is committed on or after 13 April 2015; otherwise 14 years.

## FIREARMS ACT 1968

**125-025**

| | |
|---|---|
| Section 1 (possessing firearm without certificate) | *5 years* |
| Section 1 (possessing shortened shotgun) | *7 years* |
| Section 2 (possessing shotgun without certificate) | *5 years* |
| Section 3 (selling firearm, etc.) | *5 years* |
| Section 4 (shortening shotgun) | *7 years* |
| Section 5(1) and (1A) (possessing, etc., prohibited weapon) | *10 years* |
| Section 5 (2A) (manufacturing or distributing firearms) | *Life* |
| Section 16 (possessing firearm with intent to endanger life) | *Life* |
| Section 16A (possessing firearm with intent to cause fear of violence) | *10 years* |
| Section 17 (using firearm to prevent arrest, or while committing scheduled offence) | *Life* |
| Section 18 (carrying firearm with intent to commit offence) | *Life* |

| | |
|---|---|
| Section 19 (carrying firearm other than an air weapon in public place) | *7 years* |
| Section 20 (trespassing with firearm) | *7 years* |
| Section 21 (possessing firearm as former prisoner, etc.) | *5 years* |

Penalty provision: Schedule 6.

## FORGERY AND COUNTERFEITING ACT 1981

**125-026**

| | |
|---|---|
| Section 1 (making false instrument with intent) | *10 years* |
| Section 2 (making copy of false instrument with intent) | *10 years* |
| Section 3 (using false instrument with intent) | *10 years* |
| Section 4 (using copy of false instrument) | *10 years* |
| Section 5(1) (custody or control of false instrument with intent) | *10 years* |
| Section 5(2) (custody or control of false instrument, no intent) | *2 years* |
| Section 5(3) (making machine, etc., with intent) | *10 years* |
| Section 5(4) (making machine, etc., no intent) | *2 years* |

Penalty provision: Section 6.

## FRAUD ACT 2006

**125-027**

| | |
|---|---|
| Section 1 (fraud) | *10 years* |
| Section 6 (possession of article for use in fraud) | *5 years* |
| Section 7 (making or supplying article for use in fraud) | *10 years* |

## IDENTITY DOCUMENTS ACT 2010

**125-028**

| | |
|---|---|
| Section 4 (possession of false identity document with improper intent) | *10 years* |
| Section 5 (possession of apparatus etc. with improper intent) | *10 years* |
| Section 6 (possession of false identity document) | *2 years* |

## IMMIGRATION ACT 1971

**125-029**

| | |
|---|---|
| Section 24A (obtaining admission by deception) | *2 years* |
| Section 25 (facilitating illegal entry) | *14 years* |
| Section 25A (assisting asylum seeker) | *14 years* |
| Section 25B (assisting entry in breach of deportation order) | *14 years* |

## Incitement to Disaffection Act 1934

| | | |
|---|---|---|
| 125-030 | Section 1 (seducing member of forces from duty) | *2 years* |
| | Section 2 (possessing document, etc.) | *2 years* |

Penalty provision: Section 3.

## Indecency with Children Act 1960

| | | |
|---|---|---|
| 125-031 | Section 1 (gross indecency with child)<br>(If the offence was committed on or after 1 October 1997; otherwise two years). | *10 years* |

This Act was repealed by the SOA 2003 with effect from 1 May 2004, but its practical effect has been preserved by the Interpretation Act 1978 s.16. See note to Sexual Offences Act 1956.

## Indecent Displays (Control) Act 1981

| | | |
|---|---|---|
| 125-032 | Section 1 (displaying indecent matter) | *2 years* |

Penalty provision: Section 4.

## Infanticide Act 1938

| | | |
|---|---|---|
| 125-033 | Section 1 (infanticide) | *Life* |

## Infant Life (Preservation) Act 1929

| | | |
|---|---|---|
| 125-034 | Section 1 (child destruction) | *Life* |

## Knives Act 1997

| | | |
|---|---|---|
| 125-035 | Section 1 (marketing combat knife) | *2 years* |
| | Section 2 (publishing material) | *2 years* |

## Mental Health Act 1983

| | | |
|---|---|---|
| 125-036 | Section 126 (possession of false document) | *2 years* |
| | Section 127 (ill-treating patient) | *5 years** |
| | Section 128 (assisting absconded patient) | *2 years* |

*Notes*

* If the offence was committed on or after 1 October 2007; otherwise two years.

## MERCHANT SHIPPING ACT 1995

| | | |
|---|---|---|
| Section 58 (endangering ship) | *2 years* | **125-037** |

## MISUSE OF DRUGS ACT 1971

| | | |
|---|---|---|
| Section 4(2) (producing Class A drug) | *Life* | **125-038** |
| Section 4(2) (producing Class B drug) | *14 years* | |
| Section 4(2) (producing Class C drug) | *14 years** | |
| Section 4(3) (supplying Class A drug) | *Life* | |
| Section 4(3) (supplying Class B drug) | *14 years* | |
| Section 4(3) (supplying Class C drug) | *14 years** | |
| Section 5(2) (possessing Class A drug) | *7 years* | |
| Section 5(2) (possessing Class B drug) | *5 years* | |
| Section 5(2) (possessing Class C drug) | *2 years* | |
| Section 5(3) (possessing Class A drug with intent to supply) | *Life* | |
| Section 5(3) (possessing Class B drug with intent to supply) | *14 years* | |
| Section 5(3) (possessing Class C drug with intent to supply) | *14 years** | |
| Section 6(2) (cultivating cannabis plant) | *14 years* | |
| Section 8 (occupier of premises permitting supply, etc. of Class A drugs) | *14 years* | |
| Section 8 (occupier of premises permitting supply, etc. of Class B drugs) | *14 years* | |
| Section 8 (occupier of premises permitting supply, etc. of Class C drugs) | *14 years** | |
| Section 9 (opium) 14 years | *14 years* | |
| Section 11(2) (contravention of directions) | *2 years* | |
| Section 12(6) (contravention of prohibition on prescribing in relation to Class A drug) | *14 years* | |
| Section 12(6) (contravention of prohibition on prescribing in relation to Class B drug) | *14 years* | |
| Section 12(6) (contravention of prohibition on prescribing in relation to Class C drug) | *14 years** | |
| Section 13(3) (contravention of prohibition on supplying in relation to Class A drug) | *14 years* | |
| Section 13(3) (contravention of prohibition on supplying in relation to Class B drug) | *14 years* | |
| Section 13(3) (contravention of prohibition on supplying in relation to Class C drug) | *14 years** | |
| Section 17(4) (giving false information) | *2 years* | |
| Section 18 (contravention of regulations, etc.) | *2 years* | |
| Section 20 (assisting offence outside United Kingdom) | *14 years* | |

| | |
|---|---|
| Section 23 (obstructing search) | *2 years* |
| Penalty provision: Schedule 4 | |

*Notes*

* For all class C drug offences it is 14 years (if committed on or after 29 January 2004; otherwise five years.

## Modern Slavery Act 2015

**125-039**

| | |
|---|---|
| Section 1 (slavery, servitude and forced or compulsory labour) | *Life* |
| Section 2 (human trafficking) | *Life* |
| Section 4 (committing an offence with intent to commit an offence under s.2) | *10 years** |

*Notes*

* Unless the offence is committed by kidnapping/false imprisonment, then the maximum is life.

## Obscene Publications Act 1959

**125-040**

| | |
|---|---|
| Section 2 (publishing obscene article or having article for publication) | *5 years** |

*Notes*

* If the offence was committed on or after 26 January, 2009, otherwise three years.

## Offences Against the Person Act 1861

**125-041**

| | |
|---|---|
| Section 4 (soliciting to murder) | *Life* |
| Section 16 (threatening to kill) | *10 years* |
| Section 18 (wounding with intent to cause grievous bodily harm) | *Life* |
| Section 20 (unlawful wounding) | *5 years* |
| Section 21 (choking, etc., with intent) | *Life* |
| Section 22 (administering drug with intent) | *Life* |
| Section 23 (administering noxious thing to endanger life) | *10 years* |
| Section 24 (administering noxious thing to injure, aggrieve or annoy) | *5 years* |
| Section 27 (abandoning child) | *5 years* |
| Section 28 (causing grievous bodily harm by explosion) | *Life* |
| Section 29 (using explosives with intent, throwing corrosive substance with intent) | *Life* |
| Section 30 (placing explosive substance with intent) | *14 years* |
| Section 31 (setting spring gun, etc.) | *5 years* |
| Section 32 (endangering safety of railway passengers) | *Life* |

| | | |
|---|---|---|
| Section 33 (throwing object with intent to endanger rail passenger) | *Life* | |
| Section 34 (endangering rail passenger by neglect) | *2 years* | |
| Section 35 (causing grievous bodily harm by wanton driving) | *2 years* | |
| Section 36 (obstructing minister of religion) | *2 years* | |
| Section 38 (assault with intent to resist arrest) | *2 years* | |
| Section 47 (assault occasioning actual bodily harm) | *5 years* | |
| Section 58 (procuring miscarriage) | *Life* | |
| Section 59 (supplying instrument, etc.) | *5 years* | |
| Section 60 (concealment of birth) | *2 years* | |

## Offensive Weapons Act 2019

| | | |
|---|---|---|
| Section 6 (possession of corrosive liquid in public) | *4 years* | **125-042** |

## Official Secrets Act 1911

| | | |
|---|---|---|
| Section 1 (act prejudicial to safety of state) | *14 years* | **125-043** |

Penalty provision: Official Secrets Act 1920 s.8(1).

## Official Secrets Act 1920

| | | |
|---|---|---|
| Section 1(1) (gaining admission to prohibited place) | *2 years* | **125-044** |
| Section 1(2) (retaining document, etc.) | *2 years* | |
| Section 3 (interfering with police officer or sentry) | *2 years* | |

Penalty provision: Section 8(2).

## Official Secrets Act 1989

| | | |
|---|---|---|
| Section 1 (disclosing information) | *2 years* | **125-045** |
| Section 3 (Crown servant making disclosure) | *2 years* | |
| Section 4 (unauthorised disclosure) | *2 years* | |
| Section 5 (unauthorised disclosure by recipient) | *2 years* | |
| Section 6 (unauthorised disclosure) | *2 years* | |

Penalty provision: Section 10.

## Perjury Act 1911

| | | |
|---|---|---|
| Section 1 (witness making untrue statement) | *7 years* | **125-046** |

| | |
|---|---|
| Section 1A (false statement for foreign proceedings) | *2 years* |

## PREVENTION OF CRIME ACT 1953

**125-047**

| | |
|---|---|
| Section 1 (possessing offensive weapon) | *4 years** |
| Section 1A (threatening with offensive weapon in public) | *4 years* |

*Notes*

* If committed after 4 July 1996, otherwise two years.

## PRISON ACT 1952

**125-048**

| | |
|---|---|
| Section 39 (assisting escape) | *10 years* |
| Section 40B (bringing etc. list A article into prison) | *10 years* |
| Section 40C (bringing etc. list B article into prison) | *2 years* |
| Section 40CA (possession of knife in prison) | *4 years* |
| Section 40CB (throwing article into prison) | *2 years* |
| Section 40D (transmitting recordings in and out of prison) | *2 years* |

## PRISON SECURITY ACT 1992

**125-049**

| | |
|---|---|
| Section 1 (prison mutiny) | *10 years* |

## PROCEEDS OF CRIME ACT 2002

**125-050**

| | |
|---|---|
| Section 327 (concealing, etc.) | *14 years* |
| Section 328 (arrangements) | *14 years* |
| Section 329 (acquisition, use and possession) | *14 years* |
| Section 330 (failure to disclose: regulated sector) | *5 years* |
| Section 331 (failure to disclose: nominated officers in the regulated sector) | *5 years* |
| Section 332 (failure to disclose: other nominated officers) | *5 years* |

## PROTECTION FROM HARASSMENT ACT 1997

**125-051**

| | |
|---|---|
| Section 3 (breach of injunction) | *5 years* |
| Section 4 (causing fear of violence) | *10 years** |
| Section 4A (stalking involving fear of violence or serious alarm or distress) | *10 years** |

*Notes*

* The maximum sentence is 10 years if the offence is committed on or after 3 April 2017; otherwise five years.

## PROTECTION OF CHILDREN ACT 1978

| | | |
|---|---|---|
| Section 1 (taking, distributing, possessing, publishing indecent photograph of child) | *10 years** | **125-052** |

Penalty provision: Section 6.

## PUBLIC ORDER ACT 1936

| | | |
|---|---|---|
| Section 2 (unlawful organisation) | *2 years* | **125-053** |

Penalty provision: Section 7.

## PUBLIC ORDER ACT 1986

| | | |
|---|---|---|
| Section 1 (riot) | *10 years* | **125-054** |
| Section 2 (violent disorder) | *5 years* | |
| Section 3 (affray) | *3 years* | |
| Section 18 (using words to stir up racial hatred) | *7 years** | |
| Section 19 (distributing material to stir up racial hatred) | *7 years** | |
| Section 20 (performing play to stir up racial hatred) | *7 years** | |
| Section 21 (distributing recording to stir up racial hatred) | *7 years** | |
| Section 22 (broadcasting programme) | *7 years** | |
| Section 23 (possessing material to stir up racial hatred) | *7 years** | |

Penalty provision: Sections 1–3, those sections. Sections 18–23, Section 27(3).

*Notes*

* The maximum penalty is seven years unless the offence was committed before 14 December 2001, in which case it is two years.

## REPRESENTATION OF THE PEOPLE ACT 1983

| | | |
|---|---|---|
| Section 60 (personation) | *2 years* | **125-055** |

## ROAD TRAFFIC ACT 1988

| | | |
|---|---|---|
| Section 1 (causing death by dangerous driving) | *14 years* | **125-056** |
| Section 1A (causing serious injury by dangerous driving) | *5 years* | |
| Section 2 (dangerous driving) | *2 years* | |
| Section 2B (causing death by careless or inconsiderate driving) | *5 years* | |
| Section 3ZB (causing death by driving while unlicenced, disqualified or uninsured) | *2 years* | |
| Section 3ZC (causing death by driving: disqualified drivers) | *10 years* | |

| | |
|---|---|
| Section 3ZD (causing serious injury by driving: disqualified drivers) | *4 years* |
| Section 3A (causing death by careless driving, having consumed alcohol) | *14 years* |

## SEXUAL OFFENCES ACT 2003

125-057

| | |
|---|---|
| Section 1 (rape) | *Life* |
| Section 2 (assault by penetration) | *Life* |
| Section 3 (sexual assault) | *10 years* |
| Section 4 (causing sexual activity with penetration) | *Life* |
| Section 4 (causing sexual activity without penetration) | *10 years* |
| Section 5 (penetration of child under 13) | *Life* |
| Section 6 (assault of person under 13 by penetration) | *Life* |
| Section 7 (sexual assault on person under 13) | *14 years* |
| Section 8 (causing person under 13 to engage in sexual activity involving penetration) | *Life* |
| Section 8 (causing person under 13 to engage in sexual activity without penetration) | *14 years* |
| Section 9 (sexual activity with person under 16) | *14 years* |
| Section 10 (causing person under 16 to engage in sexual activity) | *14 years* |
| Section 11 (sexual activity in presence of person under 16) | *10 years* |
| Section 12 (causing person under 16 to watch sexual act) | *10 years* |
| Section 13 (child sex offence committed by person under 18) | *5 years* |
| Section 14 (arranging child sex offence) | *14 years* |
| Section 15 (meeting person under 16 with intent following grooming) | *10 years* |
| Section 15A (sexual communication with a child) | *2 years* |
| Section 16 (abuse of trust by sexual activity) | *5 years* |
| Section 17 (abuse of trust by causing sexual activity) | *5 years* |
| Section 18 (abuse of trust by sexual activity in presence of child) | *5 years* |
| Section 19 (abuse of trust by causing child to watch sexual act) | *5 years* |
| Section 25 (sexual activity by person over 18 with family member under 18) | *14 years* |
| Section 25 (sexual activity by person under 18 with family member under 18) | *5 years* |
| Section 26 (person over 18 inciting family member under 18 to engage in sexual activity) | *14 years* |
| Section 26 (person under 18 inciting family member under 18 to engage in sexual activity) | *5 years* |
| Section 30 (sexual activity involving penetration with person with mental disorder) | *Life* |

| | |
|---|---|
| Section 30 (sexual activity not involving penetration with person with mental disorder) | *14 years* |
| Section 31 (causing or inciting sexual activity involving penetration by person with mental disorder) | *Life* |
| Section 31 (causing or inciting sexual activity not involving penetration by person with mental disorder) | *14 years* |
| Section 32 (engaging in sexual activity in presence of person with mental disorder) | *10 years* |
| Section 33 (causing person with mental disorder to watch sexual act) | *10 years* |
| Section 34 (offering inducement to person with mental disorder to engage in sexual act involving penetration) | *Life* |
| Section 34 (offering inducement to person with mental disorder to engage in sexual act not involving penetration) | *14 years* |
| Section 35 (inducing person with mental disorder to engage in sexual act involving penetration) | *Life* |
| Section 35 (inducing person with mental disorder to engage in sexual act not involving penetration) | *14 years* |
| Section 36 (causing person with mental disorder to watch sexual act by inducement etc.) | *10 years* |
| Section 37 (causing person with mental disorder to watch third party sexual act by inducement etc.) | *10 years* |
| Section 38 (sexual acts involving penetration by care worker with person with mental disorder) | *14 years* |
| Section 38 (sexual acts not involving penetration by care worker with person with mental disorder) | *10 years* |
| Section 39 (care worker inciting person with mental disorder engage in sexual act involving penetration) | *14 years* |
| Section 39 (care worker inciting person with mental disorder engage in sexual act not involving penetration) | *10 years* |
| Section 40 (care worker engaging in sexual act in presence of person with mental disorder) | *7 years* |
| Section 41 (care worker causing person with mental disorder to watch sexual act) | *7 years* |
| Section 47 (paying for sexual service involving penetration by person under 13) | *Life* |
| Section 47 (paying for sexual service by person under 16) | *14 years* |
| Section 47 (paying for sexual service by person under 18) | *7 years* |
| Section 48 (causing person under 18 to become involved in prostitution or pornography) | *14 years* |
| Section 49 (controlling prostitution by person under 18) | *14 years* |
| Section 50 (facilitating prostitution by person under 18) | *14 years* |
| Section 52 (causing or inciting prostitution) | *7 years* |
| Section 53 (controlling prostitution for gain) | *7 years* |
| Section 57 (arranging arrival for purposes of prostitution) | *14 years** |

| | |
|---|---|
| Section 58 (facilitating travel for purposes of prostitution) | *14 years** |
| Section 59 (facilitating departure for purposes of prostitution) | *14 years** |
| Section 59A (trafficking people for sexual exploitation) | *14 years*** |
| Section 61 (administering substance with intent to enable sexual activity) | *10 years* |
| Section 62 (committing offence with intent to commit sexual offence) | *10 years* |
| Section 63 (trespass with intent to commit sexual offence) | *10 years* |
| Section 64 (sexual penetration of adult relative) | *2 years* |
| Section 65 (consenting to sexual penetration by adult relative) | *2 years* |
| Section 66 (intentional exposure) | *2 years* |
| Section 67 (observing private act) | *2 years* |
| Section 69 (sexual act with animal) | *2 years* |
| Section 70 (sexual penetration of corpse) | *2 years* |

*Notes*

* These offences were repealed on 6 April 2013, see The Protection of Freedoms Act 2012 (Commencement No. 5 and Saving and Transitional Provision) Order 2013 (SI 2013/470) for transitional and saving provision.

** This offence was repealed on 30 July 2015, see The Modern Slavery Act 2015 (Commencement No. 1, Saving and Transitional Provisions) Regulations 2015 (SI 2015/1476) for transitional and saving provision.

## SERIOUS CRIME ACT 2007

**125-058** Section 44 (encouraging or assisting commission of offence, believing it will be committed) ... if the anticipated offence is murder, life imprisonment, otherwise the maximum sentence for the anticipated or reference offence.

Section 45 (encouraging or assisting commission of offence, believing it will be committed) ... if the anticipated offence is murder, life imprisonment, otherwise the maximum sentence for the anticipated or reference offence.

Section 46 (encouraging or assisting commission of one or more offences) ... if the anticipated or reference offence is murder, life imprisonment, otherwise the maximum sentence for the anticipated or reference offence.

## SEXUAL OFFENCES ACT 1956

**125-059** Most sections of the Sexual Offences Act 1956 are repealed with effect from 1 May 2004, by the Sexual Offences Act 2003. References in other statutes (such as the PCC(S)A 2000 s.161) are also for the most part repealed by the Sexual Offences Act 2003. The liability of an offender to be sentenced for a sexual offence committed before 1 May 2004, depends on the Interpretation Act 1978 s.16, which provides:

"Without prejudice to section 15, where an Act repeals an enactment, the repeal does not, unless the contrary intention appears,—

(c) affect any right, privilege, obligation or liability acquired, accrued or incurred under that enactment;

(d) affect any penalty, forfeiture or punishment incurred in respect of any offence committed against that enactment;

(e) affect any investigation, legal proceeding or remedy in respect of any such right, privilege, obligation, liability, penalty, forfeiture or punishment; and any such investigation, legal proceeding or remedy may be instituted, continued or enforced, and any such penalty, forfeiture or punishment may be imposed, as if the repealing Act had not been passed."

This section therefore preserves the effect of the Sexual Offences Act 1956, and preserves the effect of statutory provisions referring to provisions of that Act, in respect of offences committed on or before 1 May 2004.

| | |
|---|---|
| Section 1 (rape) | *Life* |
| Section 2 (procurement of woman by threats) | *2 years* |
| Section 3 (procurement by false pretences) | *2 years* |
| Section 4 (administering drugs) | *2 years* |
| Section 5 (intercourse with girl under 13) | *Life* |
| Section 6 (unlawful sexual intercourse with girl under 16) | *2 years* |
| Section 7 (intercourse with defective) | *2 years* |
| Section 9 (procurement of defective) | *2 years* |
| Section 10 (incest by man with girl under 13) (attempt, seven years) | *Life* |
| Section 10 (incest by man) (attempt, two years) | *7 years* |
| Section 11 (incest by woman) (attempt, two years) | *7 years* |
| Section 12 (buggery with person under 16) | *Life* |
| Section 12 (buggery with animal) | *Life* |
| Section 12 (buggery of person under 18 by person over 21) | *5 years* |
| Section 12 (other forms of buggery) | *2 years* |
| Section 13 (indecency by man over 21 with man under 18) | *5 years* |
| Section 13 (indecency by males) | *2 years* |
| Section 14 (indecent assault on woman) | *10 years* |
| (If the offence was committed on or after 16 September 1985: otherwise two years, unless the victim was under 13 and her age was stated in the indictment, in which case the maximum is five years). | |
| Section 15 (indecent assault on male) | *10 years* |
| Section 16 (assault with intent to bugger) | *10 years* |
| Section 17 (abduction) | *14 years* |
| Section 19 (abduction of girl under 18) | *2 years* |
| Section 20 (abduction of girl under 16) | *2 years* |
| Section 21 (abduction of defective) | *2 years* |
| Section 22 (causing prostitution) | *2 years* |
| Section 23 (procuring girl under 21) | *2 years* |
| Section 24 (detention in brothel) | *2 years* |

| | |
|---|---|
| Section 25 (permitting premises to be used by girl under 13) | *Life* |
| Section 26 (permitting premises to be used) | *2 years* |
| Section 27 (permitting defective to use premises) | *2 years* |
| Section 28 (causing prostitution of girl under 16) | *2 years* |
| Section 29 (causing prostitution of defective) | *2 years* |
| Section 30 (living on earnings of prostitution) | *7 years* |
| Section 31 (controlling prostitute) | *7 years* |
| Section 32 (man soliciting) | *2 years* |
| Section 33A (keeping brothel used for prostitution) | *7 years* |

## SEXUAL OFFENCES (AMENDMENT) ACT 2000

**125-060** Section 3 (abuse of position of trust) *5 years*

*Notes*

This Act was repealed by the SOA 2003; but see the note to the Sexual Offences Act 1956.

## SUICIDE ACT 1961

**125-061** Section 2 (aiding suicide) *14 years*

## THEFT ACT 1968

**125-062**

| | |
|---|---|
| Section 7 (theft) | *7 years* |
| Section 8 (robbery) | *Life* |
| Section 9 (burglary of dwelling) | *14 years* |
| Section 9 (burglary of building other than dwelling) | *10 years* |
| Section 10 (aggravated burglary) | *Life* |
| Section 11 (removing object from public place) | *5 years* |
| Section 12A (aggravated vehicle taking resulting in death) | *14 years* |
| Section 12A (aggravated vehicle taking not resulting in death) | *2 years* |

*Notes*

If the offence is aggravated vehicle taking by reason of causing damage, and the value of the damage does not exceed £5,000, the offence will normally be dealt with as a summary offence and the maximum sentence is six months.

| | |
|---|---|
| Section 13 (abstracting electricity) | *5 years* |
| Section 15 (obtaining by deception) | *10 years* |
| Section 15A (obtaining money transfer by deception) | *10 years* |
| Section 16 (obtaining pecuniary advantage) | *5 years* |
| Section 17 (false accounting) | *7 years* |

| | |
|---|---|
| Section 20 (destroying valuable security etc.) | *7 years* |
| Section 22 (handling) | *14 years* |

*Notes*

If the s.12A offence is aggravated vehicle taking by reason of causing damage, and the value of the damage does not exceed £5,000, the offence will normally be dealt with as a summary offence and the maximum sentence is six months. The definition of burglary is amended by the SOA 2003 to omit references to an intent to rape; offences which would formerly have been charged as burglary with intent to rape will now be charged as trespass with intent, contrary to s.63.

## THEFT ACT 1978

**125-063**

| | |
|---|---|
| Section 1 (obtaining services) | *5 years* |
| Section 2 (evading liability, etc.) | *5 years* |
| Section 3 (making off without payment) | *2 years* |

Penalty provision: Section 4.

## VALUE ADDED TAX ACT 1994

**125-064**

| | |
|---|---|
| Section 72 (fraudulently evading VAT, etc.) | *7 years* |

## VIOLENT CRIME REDUCTION ACT 2006

**125-065**

| | |
|---|---|
| Section 28 (using another to hide weapon etc.) | |
| If weapon is prohibited weapon (with exceptions) and offender is over 16 | *4 years* |
| If weapon is prohibited weapon (with exceptions) and offender is over 16 | *10 years* |
| Other cases | *5 years* |

# INDEX

LEGAL TAXONOMY

FROM SWEET & MAXWELL

This index has been prepared using Sweet & Maxwell's Legal Taxonomy. Main index entries conform to keywords provided by the Legal Taxonomy except where references to specific documents or non-standard terms (denoted by quotation marks) have been included. These keywords provide a means of identifying similar concepts in other Sweet & Maxwell publications and online services to which keywords from the Legal Taxonomy have been applied. Readers may find some minor differences between terms used in the text and those which appear in the index. Suggestions to *sweetandmaxwell.taxonomy@tr.com.*